Gender, Patriarchy and Violence

Gender, Patriarchy and Violence

The Case of Punjab and Haryana

Edited by

Rajesh Gill

RAWAT PUBLICATIONS

Jaipur • New Delhi • Bangalore • Guwahati • Kolkata

ISBN 978-81-316-0866-1

Published by
Prem Rawat for **Rawat Publications**
Satyam Apts, Sector 3, Jawahar Nagar, Jaipur 302 004 (India)
Phone: 0141 265 1748 / 7006 Fax: 0141 265 1748
E-mail: info@rawatbooks.com
Website: www.rawatbooks.com

New Delhi Office
4858/24, Ansari Road, Daryaganj, New Delhi 110 002
Phone: 011 2326 3290

Also at *Bangalore, Guwahati* and *Kolkata*

Printed at Nice Printing Press, New Delhi

Contents

Section II
Emerging Forms of Gender Violence: A Field View

Section III
Handling Gender Violence: Policies and Statutes

Section IV
Conclusions and Inferences

Contributors

Abha Chauhan, Professor and Chairperson, Department of Sociology, University of Jammu, Jammu.

Amandeep Singh, Assistant Professor, Department of Evening Studies, Panjab University, Chandigarh.

Geeta Joshi, Professor, Department of Laws, Panjab University, Chandigarh.

Justice K. Kannan, (Former Judge) Punjab and Haryana High Court, Chandigarh.

Kanwalpreet Kaur, Assistant Professor, D.A.V. College, Chandigarh.

Komal Sharma, Assistant Professor, Post Graduate Government College for Girls, Chandigarh.

Kumool Abbi, Professor and Chairperson, Department of Sociology, Panjab University, Chandigarh.

Laxmi Devi, Research Scholar, Department of Geography, Panjab University, Chandigarh.

Madhurima, Professor and Coordinator, Department of Sociology, University School of Open Learning, Panjab University, Chandigarh.

Nirmala Devi, Research Officer, Centre for Excellence (CPEPA), Panjab University, Chandigarh.

Puneet Kaur Grewal, Research Officer, Centre for Excellence (CPEPA), Panjab University, Chandigarh.

Rajesh Gill, Professor, Department of Sociology and Coordinator, Centre for Excellence, (CPEPA), Panjab University, Chandigarh.

Rajni Bala, Associate Professor, Baring Christian College, Batala, Punjab.

Rakesh Thakur, Associate Professor, Post Graduate Government College, Chandigarh.

Reena Chaudhary, Assistant Professor, Department of Sociology, University School of Open Learning, Panjab University, Chandigarh.

Richa Walia, Research Officer, Centre for Excellence (CPEPA), Panjab University, Chandigarh.

Sarvar Abbi, Research Scholar, Department of Sociology, Panjab University, Chandigarh.

Satinder Kaur, Guest Faculty, University School of Open Learning (Women's Studies), Panjab University, Chandigarh.

Smita Bhutani, Professor, Department of Geography, Panjab University, Chandigarh.

Sukhwant Singh Sidhu, Assistant Professor, Post Graduate Government College, Chandigarh.

1

Introduction

Rajesh Gill

Punjab and Haryana are the two Indian states which have experienced enormous agricultural and economic development in the past, thanks to the Green Revolution. These also happen to be the two states which have demolished the proposition that economic development automatically results in social and human development. After almost 50 years of a successful Green Revolution, these states stand today as the epitome of gender inequality and patriarchy, with a cultural fixation on honour, often culminating into diverse forms of violence against women, both within as well as outside home. Lying at the bottom at the national level, these states had the lowest child sex ratio in 2011 Census, mainly as a result of a strong son preference and persistent killing of the female foetus, popularly called female foeticide. Neither the law nor extensive publicity have been successful in diluting the fixation on the preferred birth of 'sons' over daughters. Cases of eve teasing, molestation, rape, domestic violence, etc. continue to haunt these states, as depicted by the data released by National Crime Record Bureau from time to time. It is important to note that these statistics are based only on the reported cases, while a large number of cases go unreported primarily due to the huge premium placed on reputation, family honour and so on. The intolerant attitude of caste panchayats, popularly known as *khaps* in Haryana, has added fuel to fire, by issuing diktats against the couples and their families who tie marital knots against the norms sanctioned by these panchayats. Marriages within the same *gotra* or within same village are thus banned, and if ever solemnized, invite the wrath of these panchayats, making life hell for the couples as well as their families. Giving a damn to the fundamental right to life and liberty granted by the Constitution of India, these panchayats declare their own norms, which have to be followed by people at all costs. This demonstrates how powerful cultural norms are; how strong the cultural fixation is and how casually the constitutional provisions are taken on ground.

This book is a compilation of articles which were presented at a National Conference organized by the Centre of Excellence on 'Cultural Fixation on Honour: A Gender Audit of Punjab and Haryana' in September 2014 as a part of a UGC funded research project under the Scheme of CPEPA (Centre with Potential for Excellence in Particular Area). The authors took pains to update and revise their articles for publication and I am extremely grateful to them. By and large the articles in this volume are focused on the states of Punjab and Haryana and describe the contemporary situation regarding gender violence in these states with the help of statistics as well as primary data. The book is divided into four sections. The first article, entitled 'Delivering Gender Justice: An Introspection from Legal Perspective' by Justice K. Kannan, provides the backdrop to this volume and demonstrates the subjectivity involved in the judge made law by citing some very interesting and relevant case laws on honour killings and protection homes. The author has very effectively brought out the fact that merely legislative measures are not going to help unless those implementing these laws internalize and bring into practice the constitutional spirit of equality, justice and freedom. He underlines that despite such progressive laws and constitutional provisions, the age old systems of caste hierarchy and patriarchal mindset have persisted all along, not only among the masses, but even among the implementers of these laws. Citing various judgments, he demonstrates how the reasoning given by the judges speaks volumes about their own patriarchal attitude. The author must be commended for bringing out such a critical self appraisal being a part of judiciary himself.

Section I includes articles dealing with the conceptual issues. Madhurima, in her article 'Women in Punjabi Culture: A Glimpse through Punjabi Literature', highlights the persistent age old cultural ethos which has been extremely patriarchal, reflected through common language, proverbs, etc. She brings out the cultural fixation by narrating three famous love tales of *Heer-Ranjha, Sohni-Mahiwal* and *Sassi-Punnu*. While these narrations endorse the subjugated role of women along with a denial of freedom of choice in life, these also bring out the nexus between gender, caste and status; so characteristic of typical Punjabi society. Even after centuries, this region continues to kill young men and women, with the aim to control their sexuality and as a deterrent to the violation of caste and community norms governing marriage alliances.

Nirmala Devi in her article, 'Khaps and Gender in Haryana: An Interface', provides a comprehensive description of caste panchayats, their origin as well as their functioning in the state of Haryana, particularly with a focus on gender issues. Again, the nexus between caste and gender is confirmed, wherein women continue to be considered by their community as carriers of honour and purity. Different yardsticks are used even today in such a progressive state of Haryana for men and women; and women, right from birth, are constantly kept under scanner. Interestingly, this article brings out that with the increase in gender violence as also a spurt in cases of love matches, it is the girls especially in rural areas, who are pushed to the wall, again using the pressure of these communities or caste/*khap* panchayats.

Rakesh Thakur in his article 'From Critical Theorizing to Sociological Appreciation: Locating the "*Ishq*" amidst "*Ijjazat*", "*Izzat*" and "*Lok Biradari*"' makes an attempt to understand the interface between woman's agency and structured patriarchal norms with the help of Giddens' theory of structuration.

Using the intervening variables of '*izzat*', '*ijjazat*' and '*lok biradari*', the author beautifully portrays the constant process of negotiation which a woman undertakes, hanging between her own individuality, desires and the social strictures binding her completely in the name of honour, *izzat, ijjazat*, etc. Giddens' idea of interplay between agency and structure is very aptly used by the author to bring home his viewpoint. The interplay between structure and agency is used as a very apt framework to describe the ground reality.

'Gender, Caste and Politics in *Khaps*' again endorses the cultural fixation especially in the state of Haryana, focusing upon the close nexus between caste and gender. With the political force used by *khaps*, the gender-caste nexus plays havoc with women, holding them responsible for violence against them and for their own violation. It is strange that men are neatly exempted from all this, as if it is their birth right to exhibit their masculinity and sexuality, even at the risk of violating social norms and taboos. Amandeep Singh in this article reveals the political game played by the caste panchayats, despite their illegality, completely sidelining the constitutionally elected village panchayats.

'The "Violence of the Green Revolution": Women, Production, Reproduction and Falling Sex Ratio in Punjab' is an article in which Kumool Abbi very lucidly links the growing irrelevance of women and women's work in Punjab with the aftermath of Green Revolution, technological development and State policies. She makes an argument that instead of enhancing the worth of women and the girl child, these policies, e.g. two child norm as well as dissociating the woman from the process of production, have aggravated the marginalization of women. It is the family of the young woman who is forced to meet the bulgeoning dowry demands of the groom's family and the demands have become much more expensive with the coming of new technology.

Rajesh Gill in her article entitled 'Gendered Spaces and Issues of Safety in Cities' makes use of various academic writings to describe the gendered spaces in the urban centres particularly cities. Most of the public spaces in cities being masculine, physical safety and mobility remain huge issues for women, who keep on identifying 'safe' and 'unsafe' public spaces. She brings out quite interesting arguments on this theme proposed by feminists, presenting a new dimension of gender violence to the fore. Cities, she argues, continue to be exclusive in terms of gender apart from caste and class, amidst the global agenda of inclusive cities. The theme put forth in this article can be used to empirically examine the nature, form and kinds of gender violence in the urban centres, which otherwise are taken as symbols of freedom, democracy and modernity.

Section II of the book entitled *Emerging Forms of Gender Violence: A Field View* brings out the field view particularly in the states of Punjab and Haryana on gender violence. The various articles in this section highlight the forms of gender violence within and outside the home, across life cycle and caste demarcations. The persistence of institutional support to patriarchy is reflected in the political, social, cultural and administrative domains. This section has four articles dealing with different forms of gender violence.

Smita Bhutani and Laxmi Devi in their article on 'Gender and Ageing in Punjab and Haryana: Some Issues' gives a very comprehensive description of the issues relating to elderly from a gender perspective. She makes extensive use of statistical data, quantitative in nature, to indicate the growing problems faced by the elderly, especially the women who continue to be care givers even in their old age. Workforce participation rates tend to significantly vary between men and women. She draws conclusions on the basis of both secondary as well as primary data.

Sarvar Abbi in her paper 'Rape and its Aftermath: Lived Experiences of Victims with Indian Law' talks about the huge gaps between the constitutional spirit of gender equality and the ground reality soaked with patriarchal mindset, which often results into the victimization of the victims especially in case of crimes against women. Citing several judgments on rape cases from the state of Punjab, she brings out the gradual rise of feminist jurisprudence, although at a slow pace, amidst the deep seated structures of patriarchy in the justice delivery system. In a very interesting manner, Abbi underlines the stigma that a woman has to face if she decides to report rape and fight for justice. The whole process of trial further terrorizes and humiliates her, often treating her as the culprit. That legislation alone is not sufficient to deliver justice to women victims of rape is meticulously brought out by the author in this article.

In 'Women and Agency: A Story of Struggle for Empowerment', Kanwalpreet Kaur discusses five case studies with the objective of highlighting the role of women's 'agency' in getting empowered. The article shows how even in most adverse circumstances, a woman with her grit and determination can improve her life chances and ensure an independent dignified survival for herself and her children. Based upon narratives of five women, the article shows how the women by breaking the cultural barriers and boldly swallowing the ridicule by the community, scripted their own destiny. The article makes an interesting point that by waiting for things to change for better may not help. It is the agency within that can realize the project of women empowerment.

'Education and Women Empowerment: A Case of Batala' presents the complexities involved in the project of women's empowerment despite education, mainly due to the persistence of patriarchical mindset among different stakeholders in educational institutions. Rajni Bala, on the basis of an empirical study conducted in Batala town in Punjab, brings out the limited role played by education in empowering women since they themselves continue to reel under the influence of patriarchy, unable to free themselves of its shackles. That mere education and employment cannot make women empowered in real sense of the term, is effectively brought out by the author in this article with illustrations from the field.

The plight of young women who get struck by the charm of NRI men looking for Indian brides, particularly in Punjab, is very aptly described by Komal Sharma in her paper entitled 'Abandoned Wives of NRI Husbands: A Saga of Victimization'. Based upon 20 case studies of such abandoned brides in Punjab, the author presents a qualitative analysis of the factors leading to such marriages apart from the various kinds of abuse these brides have to suffer after entering such matrimonial alliances. The analysis brings out the stark reality that despite so much awareness about fraudulent NRI marriages, parents of the girls often jump to such matrimonial proposals, avoiding all verifications and pushing their daughters into such relationships. The study shows that these girls too get easily infatuated by these NRI men and their flamboyant lifestyle, and suddenly are filled with high aspirations. The paper underlines the significance of social prestige and stigma attached with match-making to which these young girls often become a prey.

Puneet Kaur Grewal focuses upon the fixation of mindset in Punjab and Haryana on 'honour', putting the whole burden on women, young and old. She goes on to corroborate her argument by quoting profusely from the folk culture of Punjab and Haryana, showing a strong patriarchal bent of mind of the total society. Such a belief system is further strengthened by religion, which again prescribes fixed notions for men and women, of course placing men at a higher pedestal. The proverbs and folk songs sufficiently underline the deep seated gendered language and social norms, which continue to remain sacrosanct despite enormous changes in contemporary societies.

In another interesting article, Richa Walia describes an issue which has remained a taboo all through history, i.e. menstruation and its cultural connotations. Based upon an empirical study conducted in the state of Haryana, the author brings out the stigma attached with menstruation, which a girl internalizes at the time of her first experience of it and continues to live with it thereafter. Religion makes a little difference. What is most interesting however is that it is not only 'others' who treat a menstruating woman as 'impure'; but the woman herself feels 'dirty', 'polluted' and 'untouchable' during that period. The study also underlines the fact that due to cultural stereotypes, young girls suffer enormously as students in schools, where they are ridiculed, in addition to going through the hassle of disposing off the 'dirty cloth' without anybody's knowledge. Ironically, menstruation is found by the author to instill a feeling of guilt among the girls.

Section III of this volume focuses upon *Handling Gender Violence: Policies and Statutes*. This part of the book brings out the legal and policy issues associated with gender specifically in the states of Punjab and Haryana. Abha Chauhan, in her article entitled 'Gender Implications of Interface between Personal and Customary Laws: The Meos of Mewat in Haryana', presents a comprehensive description of the interface between gender, caste and religion in the context of its legal connotations for women among Meos in district Mewat in Haryana. Meticulously analysing both the secondary and primary data, the author relates the persistence of patriarchal institutions and practices through the domination of personal and customary laws among Meos, with definite impact upon the Meo women. With very low levels of female literacy and a strong hold of conventional village panchayats, the laws governing property rights, marriage, divorce, etc. continue to be biased against women. This article underlines the complete domination of customary laws over the constitutional laws in this part of the state of Haryana.

In 'Gendercide in the Womb! Law Alone Won't Do' Geeta Joshi addresses the issue of female foeticide, which has in fact increased manifold with the improved technology and an easy access to it. Dwelling upon the socio-cultural factors promoting son preference, the author goes on to talk about the commercialization of sex determination technology leading to an increased incidence of gendercide. While legal provisions have been made to act as a deterrent, the author makes a case for amending the existing law, to give it more teeth. However, it is argued that law alone is not sufficient and the cultural preferences and the mindset need to be radically changed to achieve gender equality. Stressing upon the current practice of gendercide, Joshi cautions against its probable repercussions, which may prove disastrous.

An interesting argument is presented by Sukhwant Sidhu in his article, 'Assessing Land Acquisition Law from Gender Perspective', by highlighting the gender issues involved in the process of land acquisition and its aftermath. The author talks about the Right to Fair Compensation and Transparency in Land Acquisition Rehabilitation and Resettlement Act, 2013 and its implementation in the context of S.A.S. Nagar, a district in Punjab. Developing his arguments on the basis of a Social Impact Assessment analysis by conducting a field study on land acquisition, the author has found that its impact has been differential on men and women. Sudden affluence in the form of monetary compensation for land has resulted in alcoholism and conspicuous consumption among men, affecting women adversely. The author, on the basis of his field survey, has found a spurt in cases of domestic violence against women.

Reena Chaudhary in her article, 'Legal Protection for Women against Sexual Harassment at Workplace in India: An Assessment', brings out the relevance of the recent law enacted by Indian Parliament to counter sexual harassment of women at workplace. Giving a detailed background in which this law has evolved, she discusses some landmark judgments wherein 'sexual harassment' of women came to be recognized as a problem requiring redressal. However, the author highlights the vital issues coming in the way of the effective implementation of the Sexual Harassment of Women at Workplace (Prevention, Prohibition and Redressal) Act, 2013 and calls for an aggressive campaign at grassroots level, to instill confidence among women to report cases of sexual harassment against them.

'Women in Short Stay Homes: A Study at Amritsar, Punjab', authored by Satinder Kaur, depicts how destitute women land up in Short Stay Homes, which despite providing them shelter and vocational skills, fail in rehabilitating them mainly due to the social hiccups emanating out of the patriarchal structures within and outside homes. These women carry with them the social stigma and are discarded by their families, with no intention whatsoever to own them.

The last part, i.e. Section-IV, presents *Conclusions and Inferences* drawn out of various chapters of the book. An analysis of Punjab and Haryana on the question of gender indicates the persistence and resilience of patriarchy in the context of caste and politics, especially in rural and agrarian context. This has been conceptualized as a case of 'Cultural Fixation', signifying the predominance of conventional patriarchal mindsets, nullifying the impact of constitutional spirit of equality and liberty, especially gender equality, education, migration and modernization. The gender division of labour and subjugation of femininity to the masculine power continues to be legitimized through religion, language, tradition, customs and caste norms. That is why any number of social legislations would fail to change the situation for the better so long as religion, caste and communities continue to justify patriarchy.

2

Delivering Gender Justice

An Introspection from Legal Perspective

Justice K. Kannan

From the positivist concept of law as the King's fiat and hence legitimate, even if whimsical, to the present day understanding of law as a tool of social engineering driven through the constitutional principles of equality and guarantees against arbitrariness, we have traversed a long distance. In the context of gender issues particularly of empowering women, to the extent to which we have provided for certain guarantees in the Constitution, they could be protected through law. But social degradation of women and violence against them just do not vanish by legislation. Their causes lie deeply entrenched in our psyche cultivated through centuries of cultural practices adopted in our lifestyles. They are not cloaks that could be easily discarded. They have entered our blood stream and putrefied our flesh and bones. The UNICEF Report 2012 says that 57 per cent of Indian boys and 53 per cent of girls between 15 and 19 years think wife-beating is justified. The UNDP Human Development Report 2011 says India ranks 129 out of 146 countries in the Gender Equality Index, behind Bangladesh (112) and Pakistan (115). We are discussing what the whole of India is concerned about and since we are in Chandigarh, we have taken understandably a regional bias with the topic, 'The Gender Question in Punjab and Haryana: Legal, Political and Cultural Dimensions'. The legal, political and cultural underpinnings require us to examine:

- Gender Justice through Legislation: Success and Failure
- Gender Justice through Public Policy: Success and Failure
- The Politics of Gender: A Stocktaking
- Gender Violence: An Issue or Only Story for Media
- The Stubborn Culture: Any Remedies?

Whatever subjects that we identify as seriously skewed against women, we will find that there already exist laws to address them. You name violence against women; one can point out to Protection of Women against Domestic Violence Act. Violence is not just at home, it is at the work place, we had *Vishaka Guidelines* till recently and now we have legislation in place, The Sexual Harassment of Women at Workplace (Prevention, Prohibition and Redressal)

Act, 2013. Molestation, rape, stalking, lewd comments and outraging modesty of women, female foeticide, child marriage, trafficking and prostitution, dowry, acid-throwing, witch branding are all serious issues. We have criminalized all these actions and perpetrators of these offences could be severely dealt with through law by court machinery. Increased representation in legislative bodies by reservation of exclusive constituencies for women; improvement of literacy for women by providing for horizontal reservation for women; equal work, equal pay for women, all of them have statutory recognition in place. Textual reading of any of these enactments will satisfy you about the insights of the legislators and the drafting skills that would leave no scope for anyone to complain that there is anything amiss. If it is a math class, the teacher will dismiss any further discussion and will clap his hands with a satisfactory abandon, 'Q.E.D.!' Unfortunately, we are not solving a mathematical problem nor are women mere numbers or formulae to deal with!

We must remember that an orderly change in the society cannot take place through the instrument of law alone. Law has limitations of what it could do. In India, over the ages, caste system is well structured and every person that is born, even for parents without religious affiliation, is born into a particular caste. You could wish away religion, if you like, but you cannot discard caste. Another major issue is the patriarchal mindset that objectifies woman only as a reproductive machine who begets male children and helps the continuance of family tree through male progeny down the ages. Neither caste nor patriarchy could be effaced only through law. If you have the law, the resistance to the enforcement will come from the very source which has perpetrated this system. Social reform through law ought to be complemented by collective will of the people that is prepared to make an objective appraisal of some of our despicable ways of life, some of our archaic customs, the structure within the family and some of our questionable convictions about the gender stereotypes.

It is possible to identify some of the gender issues, the judicial approaches, their failures and the need to find answers, also outside the realm of law. Honour killings of women, runaway couple cases and addressing property rights of women suggest themselves as test cases of how these laws are understood by judges, lawyers and the people at large.

Inter-caste marriages cause tension to the marrying couples as well as to the families in many a situation. If the bride or groom or both are murdered, it is referred to as honour killing since it is purported to be done to preserve the honour of the family; the accusing finger is invariably at the woman, who, it is perceived as having brought down the honour of the family by marrying a person outside caste or religion or within the same *gotra*. The *gotra* opposition to marriages is a slightly different genre. Here is the assertion that customs and traditions shall be respected. Customs are important sources of law but their legitimacy or primacy to obtain statutory approbation cannot always be presumed. There are more customs abrogated by law than approved by it. Social reformation would not have been possible if statutory laws were always to have been suborned to customary practices. The approvals for *sagotra* marriage came through judicial pronouncements of Madras High Court in

1888 and 1895, by the Bombay High Court in 1908 and Lahore High Court in 1933. The Hindu Marriage Removal of Caste Disabilities Act of 1946 was enacted subsequently declaring *sagotra* marriage to be valid. The Supreme Court said famously in *Lata Singh v. State of UP and another* that there is nothing honourable about these honour killings. Look at the problems that courts face. There is no special law to deal with these cases. The same principle relating to burden of proof exists – proof beyond reasonable doubt; presumption of innocence otherwise proved guilty; the prosecution to succeed on the strength of its case and not weakness of defence. In a typical case of honour killing, witnesses do not show up. They are either relatives who share the same sense of outrage against inter-caste union and hence are unwilling to testify against the perpetrators of offence or they are scared to depose against the community heads who may actively support the crime for fear of ostracization; Witnesses are mostly relatives and blood being thicker than water, would not help the law enforcers to track the guilty and bring them to book. If they are brought to court, they are hostile and do not support the versions made earlier to the police when they give evidence in courts. The Supreme Court lamented in *Jita Ram v. State of Haryana:*

> So far, there is no specific law to deal with honor killings. The murders come under the general categories of homicide or manslaughter. Generally in such type of killings eye-witnesses are not forthcoming to support the case of the prosecution. This is a biggest problem before the investigation agency and the Court while dealing with such type of cases. In such cases where the witnesses of honour killing become hostile, a heavy duty is cast on the Court to closely scrutinize the evidence in order to reach to the truth.

Investigation itself is tardy because the investigation agency is seldom convinced that there is anything serious to be investigated. A Division Bench of Panjab and Haryana High Court said in *Gurdev Singh v. State of Haryana:*

> Material on record showed that Investigating agency in such a sensational case has bungled at each and every stage. Investigating officials had just investigated the matter for the purpose of giving disposal to the investigation. They have not evinced any interest as warranted in this case, to collect materials as against the accused in a crime which was virtually thrown a challenge to the society itself.

Punishment is never consistent. In some cases, five-year imprisonment for causing murder is seen to be sufficient. The delay in disposal of the case itself is seen as a circumstance to justify a lenient sentence. In *State of Punjab v. Jagtar Singh and others,* look at how the SC justified its reasoning for a lenient sentence:

> Mr Kuldip Singh, then strenuously urged that the accused persons have been awarded only five years of rigorous imprisonment and it is ridiculously less. He pointed out that even according to the High Court, this would amount to honour killing which cannot be taken lightly. The argument is undoubtedly correct. However, considering that the incident in question took place in the

> year 1993 and thus 18 years have passed. Further, considering the fact that the accused persons had not even crossed the age of 25 years at the time when the incident took place and further considering the fact that they have already undergone rigorous imprisonment for five years and have come out of jail, we are not inclined to interfere with the quantum of sentence and would choose to dismiss this appeal. We order accordingly.

Perhaps, every issue of what the court was taking for sustaining a lenient sentence is open to serious challenge. What if the case has taken a long number of years? Why should it go to reduce sentence? So what if the accused is young? If he had been old, would it have been different and justified a sterner sentence? Sentence undergone for five years – how could it be a mitigating circumstance? If he had been on bail, would it have mattered? Some judgments have called for very stiff punishment. In *Bhagwan Dass v. State (NCT) of Delhi*, the accused killed his married daughter by strangulating her with electric wire for being in an incestuous relationship with her uncle. The court said:

> Honour killings for whatever reasons come within the category of rarest of rare cases deserving death punishment. It is time to stamp out these barbaric and feudal practices.

See the climb down in the following case to justify commutation to life sentence from capital punishment. *Dilip Premnarayan Tiwari and Anr. v. State of Maharashtra* was a case of a Brahmin girl of UP marrying a Malayali boy of lower caste, with whom she was in love, against the wishes of her parents and family members. Two brothers of the girl wreaked vengeance and killed husband, his father and sister and injured other family members. Death sentence awarded by trial court was commuted to life sentence by High Court, when it said, 'Triple murder was not a diabolic murder nor had the murderers acted in depravity of their minds by disfiguring the bodies'. Death sentence had been awarded by the trial court on the following grounds:

1. Helpless victims
2. Unarmed victims
3. Victims woken from sleep at midnight
4. Manner of inflicting injuries, 20–30 serious injuries on death of the deceased, whereas even a single injury would have been sufficient to kill, shows the barbarous attitude.
5. Attacking ruthlessly six persons, two were let off presumed to be dead, seeking to wipe off the entire family.
6. Attack on every vital organ
7. Young boy was brutally assaulted
8. The time chosen was past midnight, hence clearly premeditated
9. Assault on lower caste based on caste hatred
10. Murders committed after seven months of marriage – the attack was highly premeditated and not in the heat of moment.

Death sentence commuted life imprisonment on following considerations:

1. The age of the accused person being between 20–25 years.

2. Their clean past, in the sense they were not involved in any offence previously.
3. It was a family defeat – sometimes family members of the girl have to suffer taunts and snide remarks even from the persons who really have no business to poke their nose into the affairs of the family.
4. The psyche of the offender in the background of a social issue like an inter-caste community marriage, though wholly unjustified would have to be considered in the peculiar circumstances of this case.
5. No doubt the murders were brutal, but triple murder was not a diabolic murder nor had the murderers acted in depravity of their minds by disfiguring the bodies.
6. Mere number of persons killed is not by itself a circumstance justifying the death sentence.

Read the Court's reasoning:

> Sushma was the younger sister of this accused. It is a common experience that when the younger sister commits something unusual and in this case it was an inter-caste, inter-community marriage out of the secret love affair, then in the society, it is the elder brother who justifiably or otherwise is held responsible for not stopping such affair. It is held as the family defeat. At times, he has to suffer taunts and snide remarks even from the persons who really have no business to poke their nose into the affairs of the family. Dilip, therefore, must have been a prey of the so-called insult which his younger sister had imposed upon his family and that must have been in his mind for seven long months … . The sister had become pregnant. Till such time as she became pregnant, there might have been some hopes in the family to win her back but once she became pregnant, even that distant hope faded away and, in our opinion, that is the reason why this ghastly episode took place … . This was further aggravated because of the so-called higher status of a Brahmin family on the part of Dilip (girl's brother) and so-called non-Brahmin status of Prabhu. Dilip undoubtedly was a young person not even having crossed his 25 years of life and not having any criminal antecedent. If he became the victim of his wrong but genuine caste considerations, it would not justify the death sentence. The murders were the outcome of social issue like a marriage with a person of so-called lower caste. However, a time has come when we have to consider these social issues as relevant, while considering the death sentence in the circumstances as these. The caste is a concept which grips a person before his birth and does not leave him even after his death. The vicious grip of the caste, community, religion, though totally unjustified, is a stark reality. The psyche of the offender in the background of a social issue like an inter-caste-community marriage, though wholly unjustified, would have to be considered in the peculiar circumstances of this case.

A different sentiment was expressed in *Mayakaur Baldevsingh Sardar and anr. v. The State of Maharashtra* which was a case of a Sikh woman contracting love marriage with a boy who though also a Sikh, but belonged to an inferior caste and also was economically weak. Mother of the girl and her four others committed murder of husband and three others of his family on this account. Sentence of life imprisonment had been awarded to the accused. Trial Court awarded death sentence, but High Court converted it into life imprisonment. Supreme Court concluded that accused deserved death sentence as that offence was diabolical in nature and victims were helpless individuals. Head of one of the victims was separated and both arms of another victim were chopped off. Accused had, at the time of delivering judgment by the SC, already served more than eight year sentence. The court had interesting observations about judges' attitudes in dealing with punishments:

> We have something to say on this aspect. The efficacy or otherwise of the death penalty is a matter of much debate in legal circles – with two diametrically opposite views on the subject. However, as the penal code visualizes the imposition of this penalty, the circumstances under which it should be imposed are also a matter of discussion, the broad principle being its award in the rarest of rare cases. Undoubtedly also while categorizing a case the facts would predominate but the predilection of a Judge, is a human factor (and a factor whose importance cannot be minimized) but as Judges applying the law we must also be alive to the needs of society and the damage which can result if a ghastly crime is not dealt with in an effective and proper manner. We also notice that while Judges tend to be extremely harsh in dealing with murders committed on account of religious factors they tend to become more conservative and almost apologetic in the case of murders arising out of caste on the premise (as in this very case) that society should be given time so that the necessary change comes about in the normal course. Has this hands off approach led to the creation of the casteless utopia or even, a perceptible movement in that direction? The answer is an emphatic no as would be clear from mushrooming caste based organizations controlled and manipulated by self appointed Commissioners who have arrogated to themselves the right to be the sole arbiters and defenders of their castes with the license to kill and maim to enforce their diktats and bring, in line those who dare to deviate. Resultantly the idyllic situation that we perceive is as distant as ever. In this background is it appropriate that we throw up our hands in despair waiting ad infinitum or optimistically a millennium or two for the day when good sense would prevail by a normal evolutionary process or is it our duty to help out by a push and a prod through the criminal justice system?

The present case is a classic example of what we mean. Both parties are Sikhs, a religion which had its genesis in a revolt against casteism with the belief that there was only one caste – humanity – imbued with one spirit, humanism and thus promoted the brotherhood of men with the ethos that no one was good or bad as all had emanated from the same *Noor* (light). And the ironic realism; the accused are Jat Sikhs a proud and aggressive community which has produced some of India's most valorous soldiers and helped fill India's granaries – unwilling to accept the victims as equals – they being Matharu Ramgariah Sikhs, artisans by profession – and in their garbled perception inferior in every way and unsuitable for their daughter. It has case in Rajvinder's statement that she had been the favourite child of her parents but the events show that notwithstanding this deep filial attachment they were of the opinion that she was better dead than alive.

Look how helpless is the court's response to all these situations. In *Arumugam Servai v. State of Tamil Nadu* (2011) 6 SCC 405, the Court's directions were as under:

> (i) All the state governments are directed to immediately suspend the District Magistrates/Collectors and SSPs/SPs or other concerned officials if they fail to apprehend those responsible for honour killing or prevent such incidents despite having advance knowledge and also to charge-sheet them and proceed against them departmentally (ii) feudal minded persons deserve harsh punishment. Only in this way can we stamp out such acts of barbarism and feudal mentality.

In *Lata Singh,* the court said:

> We, therefore, direct that the administration/police authorities throughout the country will see to it that if any boy or girl who is a major undergoes inter-caste or inter-religious marriage with a woman or man who is a major, the couple are not harassed by any one nor subjected to threats or acts of violence, and anyone who gives such threats or harasses or commits acts of violence either himself or at his instigation, is taken to task by instituting criminal proceedings by the police against such persons and further stern action is taken against such persons as provided by law.

Has anything stopped? There are reports of more and more honour killings. Absence of law, would you say has contributed to this menace? How does anyone dream that by tougher sentences, these crimes will be stopped?

There is another type of litigation that has caste as the genesis for the travails of young couples – 'Runaway couple cases'. The cases of youngsters on the run, with parents on hot pursuit to drive the union asunder and to ensure that the two does not culminate their relationship in matrimony, are ever on the rise. In *Pardeep Kumar Singh v. State of Haryana*, the Punjab and Haryana High Court gave several meaningful directions, like:

> (i) Whenever any intimation is received by the SSP/SP of concerned District regarding the marriage of a young couple with a threat and an apprehension of infringement of the right of life and liberty by the police at the instance of the family members of one of the spouses, the SSP/SP concerned will consider the representation and will himself/herself look into the matter and issue necessary directions to maintain a record of the said intimation under Chapter 21 of the Punjab Police Rules.
>
> (ii) On receipt of above said intimation of marriage by any police officer, necessary directions will be issued to the concerned Police Station to take necessary steps in accordance with law to enquire into the matter by contacting the parents of both boy and girl – The matter regarding age,

consent of the girl and grievance of her family will be determined – In the eventuality of any complaint of kidnapping or abduction having been received from any of the family members of the girl generally the boy (husband) will not be arrested unless and until the prejudicial statement is given by the girl (wife) – Arrest should generally be deferred or avoided on the immediate receipt of a complaint by the parents or family members of the girl taking into consideration the law laid down by Hon'ble Supreme Court in Joginder Kumar's case.

(iii) If the girl is major (above 18 years), she should not forcibly be taken away by police to be handed over to her parents against her consent – criminal force against the boy should also be avoided.

(iv) So far as the threat to the young couple of the criminal force and assault at the hands of the private persons is concerned, it would always be open to the police to initiate action if any substantive offence is found to have been committed against the couple.

(v) In case of any threat to the breach of peace at the hands of the family members of the couple it will always be open to the State authorities to take up the security proceedings in accordance with law.

(vi) It will not be open to the 'runaway couple' to take law in their hands pursuant to the indulgence shown by the police on the basis of their representation sent to the SSP/SP of the concerned District (What does this mean?).

(vii) If despite the intimation having been sent to the SSP/SP there is an apprehension or threat of violation of right of personal life and liberty or free movement, the remedy of approaching the High Court should be the last resort.

(viii) In case there is an authority constituted for issuance of marriage certificate as per the law laid down by Supreme Court in Seema's case (supra) in the concerned districts, the couple of so called 'run away marriage' should get the marriage registered in compliance with the directions of the Supreme Court and a copy of the same should also be forwarded to the police alongwith the representations or any time subsequent thereto.

(ix) Nothing said hereinabove will prevent the immediate arrest of a person who fraudulently entices a girl with false promises and exploits her sexually as per the statement of the girl.

Here again, nothing has changed. The police do not rush assistance to protect the couple. If ever a girl arrives with the husband for protection or when the couple is caught, the parents of the girl are informed to receive 'reward' from the parents, register a rape and abduction case against the husband and mute the wailing girl to 'safely return' to the parents. If they show up in registrar's office for marriage registration, the registrar would refuse registration and would insist on the presence of parents.

Some of the court's pronouncements are even shocking. In *Amnider Kaur and Another v. State of Punjab*, the court said that a girl aged 16 who is in a runaway situation is not entitled to protection from police since the marriage of a (Brahmin) girl with a (Jat Sikh) boy was stated to be violative of the provisions of the Child Marriage Restraint Act. What has the invalidity of the marriage to do with protecting a young girl fleeing for life? In *Kirti Goyal and another v. State of Punjab and others*, the court counselled the runaway couples:

> Though the petitioners are entitled for protection to their life and liberty in the given facts and circumstances of the present case but at the same time, it is also expected from them and other young citizens like them that before running away from their homes for performing this type of rebellion marriage, they must think twice, besides, listening carefully to their respective parents who are not their enemies but real well wishers. Let us welcome the dynamic social change and evolution by only subject to the social control and moral values with are centuries old and have not lost their shine even today.

What social values do we welcome, the idea that a girl cannot romance with a boy of her choice? Where is dynamic social change possible if girl shall not pick a boy from another caste? Is it in defiance that we secure the social change or by mutely submitting to century old value system of marriages within the bounds of caste, religion and the patriarchy?

See a new trend in *Sandeep Kaur and another v. State of Punjab*. A runaway couple arriving in court to seek protection against blood thirsty parents faced a situation of court direction that the boy shall deposit ₹ 5 lakh in the name of wife to show his bonafides and financial stability. When he failed to do, the police was directed 'to enquire into the character and antecedents of boy and thereafter appropriate action in accordance with law and submit a report within a period of 3 months'.

In every one of the three cases, you can see the concern of a judge who may be a parent of an adult daughter, who is worried about the changing social mores; scared for the virginity that maybe lost to the woman in a relationship; concerned that the girl maybe cheated. Haven't you heard of a case of a daughter of a judge of a High Court sending a letter to the Supreme Court complaining that she was held as a captive in the house against her consent to prevent her from marrying the boy of her choice? The SC liberated the girl but does the scenario worry you about the persons in whose hands we have placed our trust in protecting constitutional rights of every citizen to life and liberty?

What is the appropriate age for a woman to have a relationship with a man? Should there be love in the air or suspicion and fear of amoral relationship of unmarried man and woman? There is a certain hypocrisy in assuming that every intimate relationship between unmarried man and woman should culminate only in marriage; that pre-marital sex does not exist in India and if it exists, effort must be made to get the couple married; if the male that had sex with a woman is guilty of sexual violence and rape, the rapist shall marry the girl, *a la* Hindi movie villain who will get duly reformed into the hero. What would you call a society that hounds a woman with notices for appearance in several criminal cases in various parts of Tamil Nadu for her views on pre-marital sex? She had not a reprieve till the SC interceded to protect her freedom of expression and quashed all criminal cases (*S. Khushboo v. Kanniammal*). Caste is sacred and a girl that picks a boy of her own choice outside her caste has no right to live. Untouchable caste woman is, however, touchable in dark alleys and behind bushes.

Make a personal audit of how a woman is treated at home; the language that we employ, the works that we assign if we have a boy and girl in the house; the educational plans. A boy is an asset and the daughter is a liability. The son stays on with the parents and the daughter must be dispatched through matrimony immediately. It is expected that the son takes care of the parents in the old age, while the daughter will have no such care responsibility. Presence of a girl in the family itself is seen as giving rise to dangerous situations. Abort before she arrives. If she had arrived, snuff the life out. Have you heard of this Punjabi couplet?

Gur khaen, puni katten; apnaen bhaiya ghallen, which if translated means, *Eat your sugar, spin your thread; send a brother in your stead.*

These incantations were recited two or three times at the time of dispatch of an unwanted female child, who was killed, a piece of *gur* placed in the mouth of the child, a skein of cotton laid on her breast and put into *gharas* or water pots and buried in the ground. Coldstream's Census Report of 1881 as recorded in the *Punjab District Gazetteer*, records: 'The parents have hundreds of ways at their command to put a female child to death, and can defy all the efforts of the Police to detect them. The plan which the parents adopt is to report sickness, and then death, which is sure to follow. Their hakims refuse to give medicines, because they know it will never be given and that the application to them was nothing more or less than a blind to be used if occasion should arise. They are heartlessly careless of their daughters' health; they expose them to all the inclemencies of the weather. And sometimes buy strong medicines to bring on sickness; the mother even sometimes causes her infant daughter to refuse natural nourishment by rubbing the nipple with bitter aloes and other specifics.' The situation may not be as bad now but do you have any doubt that if she had grown up and married of her own choice without parent's consent, murder would have been the result. If she married with parental consent, denied her property rights. If she had demanded a share, she would have practised deceit by pleading oral release of her rights. Substantial marriage expenses and dowry at the time of marriage of daughter are themselves disincentives to provide for share in property as well. There is no end to her travails. Even the matrilineal system prevalent in Kerala allowed the line of succession through female but the person that managed the property was only a male, who was the *karnavan*. Hindu Succession Act Sec. 14 recognizes rights of women to hold property as full owners have brought the maximum number of litigations in the civil courts. The recent changes in Hindu Succession Act, giving the right to a female property by birth in ancestral property has hardly brought about a big change in the pattern of holding property in the family. Joint family system is fine but it is doubtful if the joint holding of the property for a daughter will be possible even after her marriage, when she moves over to her husband's house. Kerala perhaps is not any less better with the abolition of the Joint Family Holding in 1974 through legislation.

Sometimes it is suggested that it is illiteracy that is the cause for pall of gloom that has brought about the pathetic state of women. Literacy is good in itself for a variety of reasons, but it has nothing specific to do away with the problem of discriminatory practices or violence against women. By increasing the levels of literacy, how do we shed the patriarchal mindset? One cannot take an argument that women suffer because they do not know their legal rights. We are talking about social practices that cut across the economic and literacy divide. A seminar of this type has a meaning only if it yields to not merely identifying ills afflicting the society that give this cultural fixation on honour; that which drives a woman's existence to the precipice of doom. We have to usher a new era of cultural shift; obtain reformatory approaches to annihilate caste and reach the goal of banishment of high caste conceit and redefine new cultural mores. If we don't see caste system going, it is not because caste has still relevance for reservation for jobs and education. Reservations for backward classes and scheduled castes are constitutional norms; they ensure social justice; don't despise it. It is the upper caste mentality that is the cause of present state of malady. It is never the dalit parents in a hot pursuit of the so-called higher caste boy or girl to murder. Let Sharmas and Joshis reform; let Goels and Gargs relent; let Malhotras and Aroras shed their superiority complex. Ask if Jat Sikh does not think that all other castes are inferior to that of his/her. Carry a campaign against matrimonial ads specifying higher caste names. There is a need for establishing new practices of the groom's family sharing all the marriage expenses. None of these changes could be brought through law. One Guru Nanak, one Raja Ram Mohan Roy, one Narayana Guru is not sufficient. Every one of us must carry the reformative spirit of all those social reformers in our hearts and deeds.

Legislative changes protecting women's rights cannot change social practices that degrade women. Violence against women is actually a social crime. It is not an occurrence in isolation: but is the result of many, many factors that include everything from patriarchy and cultural mindsets, to economic issues and illiteracy. The law as it stands addresses the crime – and in that, is only being a band-aid. It is neither looking at, nor even attempting at addressing the undercurrents that cause the crime to thrive. Legislation should be combined with effective policy and awareness drives that effect a shift in mindsets. Banish upper caste identity in all its forms. Challenge the patriarchal mindset in your personal lifestyle and social interactions. Influence others in bringing about the change. It is a long road ahead. You need to start the journey somewhere. We are late. Run, don't walk. Arise and awake, don't tolerate injustice; confront and annihilate, don't allow archaic value systems to get the better of you. Don't just preach; practice. Begin at your home, today, now!

References

Amnider Kaur and another v. State of Punjab, 2010(1) PLR 790.
Arumugam Servai v. State of Tamil Nadu, (2011) 6 SCC 405.
Bhagwan Dass v. State (NCT) of Delhi, (2011) 6 SCC 396.
Dilip Premnarayan Tiwari and another v. State of Maharashtra, (2010) 1 SCC 775.
Gurdev Singh v. State of Haryana, 2011(2) RCR (Criminal) 950: 2012(1) CCR 135.
Jita Ram v. State of Haryana, 2011(4) RCR (Criminal) 57.
Kirti Goyal and another v. State of Punjab and others, 2012(3) RCR (Criminal) 172.
Lata Singh v. State of UP and another, (2006) 5 SCC 475.
Mayakaur Baldevsingh Sardar and another v. State of Maharashtra, (2007) 12 SCC 654.
Pardeep Kumar Singh v. State of Haryana, 2008(3) RCR (Criminal) 376.
S. Khushboo v. Kanniammal, (2010) 5 SCC 600.
Sandeep Kaur and another v. State of Punjab, 2014(1) RCR (Civil) 1015.
State of Punjab v. Jagtar Singh and others, (2011) 14 SCC 678.

Section I

Gender and Patriarchy in Punjab and Haryana: Some Conceptual Issues

3

Women in Punjabi Culture

A Glimpse through Punjabi Literature

Madhurima

Punjab, being the gateway into northern India, was fated to be a perpetual field of battle and the first home of almost all the conquerors who came by land route. Only a few invaders, if any, brought their wives along, and most of those who settled in their conquered domains acquired local women. Thus, the blood of many conquering races came to mingle, and many alien languages – Arabic, Persian, Pushto, and Turkish – came to be spoken in Punjab. Further, the religion of the aboriginals was subjected to the Vedantic, Jain, and Buddhist religions of the Aryans, and to the Islamic faith of the Arabs, Turks, Mongols, Persians, and Afghans. Out of this mixture of blood and speech were born the Punjabi people and their language (Singh 1999). Grewal (1999) refers to an earlier period in Punjabi history to suggest the emergence of a distinctive Punjabi culture out of interaction between a diverse range of racial, linguistic and religious groups.

It is reasonable to argue that the emergence of a distinct Punjabi culture, Punjabi language and religion are different milestones in the evolution of a distinct Punjabi identity. Sikhism subsequently introduced Gurmukhi as a script of the Punjabi language during the period of Guru Angad Dev, the immediate successor of Sri Guru Nanak Dev ji (1469–1539), the founder of the Sikh faith. This raised the status of Punjabi language written in Gurmukhi script to a sacred language. Geographical location, economic way of life, cultural characteristics, the development of Punjabi language and its own script and the emergence of Sikhism, all contributed in diverse ways to the formation of a Punjabi identity.

This paper highlights how patriarchy got enshrined into the Punjabi identity as a result of the historical background of the state and its people. Women got pushed into the private domain and clear cut demarcations appeared between the two genders, i.e. men and women, who had been socialized peculiarly into their masculine and feminine roles, through generations. This became the genesis of a Punjabi society, which was patriarchal to the core, with a much glorified male culture, with a subdued and subordinated role of the woman through her life cycle. Patriarchy got strengthened in the economy, polity and other dimensions of life in Punjab, cutting across caste and religion. Interestingly, despite the ideology of Sikhism propagating gender equality, the lust for a male child and superiority of men became the hallmark of Punjabi culture and society. The patriarchal spirit of Punjabi culture is best reflected in the popular culture, comprising its folk songs, *qissa-kavya* and fiction.

I

Punjabi folk songs are an extremely important untapped source for gaining an insight into the Punjabi history and culture. These songs, supposed to be performed in different contexts and on different occasions, contain layers of meanings. The Punjabi folk songs serve as a repository of local culture, beliefs, social structure and response to historical change. Most of these folk songs are sung by women, through which women have kept the Punjabi oral tradition alive. It is also believed that since women were not educated they used to express their feelings through these songs. A strand of continuity of cultural life is reflected in the folk songs. These folk songs bring together the intensity of relationships, the pithy, suggestive quality and harmless irony of languages, and lit the raw and unsophisticated experience of emotions. It is also argued that women express their deep desires, frustrations and grudges through songs which they would not be able to express otherwise in the restrictive and patriarchal environment (Nilsson 1984; Raheja and Gold 1994).

There is ample evidence available in the Punjabi folk literature showing that the birth of a son was regarded more fortunate than that of a daughter:

- *Hoote mate, khand kheer khate*
  (Back and forth, eating the rice porridge.)
- *Sone di gad ghara de ..., Roopepeengpawa de, Ute kake nu Bithade*
  (Get me a golden jewel, Honey, get me a swing, let my son sit on it.)
- *Alar balarbawe da, Bawakanakliavega*
  (Oh my innocent son, the son will bring the wheat)
- *Bawibehkechattegi, Bawakanakpihevega*
  (The daughter will sit and winnow it, the son will get it grinded)
- *Bawimannpakavegi, Bawabehkekhavega*
  (The daughter will bake the chappatis, the son will sit and eat)
- *Ek veer deinverabba, Saun khan nu bada chit karda*
  (Oh God give me a brother, my heart feels to pledge for him)
- *DhianHondiya ne daultanbaiganiya, Has has tor babla*
  (Daughters are treasurers that belong to someone else, Oh Father, marry them off with a smile)
- *Sadachiriyan da chambavei, bablassaudjana*
  (Ours is a flock of sparrows, Oh dear Father, we'll fly away)
- *Sadilambiudaarivei, babalkehre des jana*
  (On a long, long flight, we know not to which land we shall go)
- *Teremehala de wichwichvei, Babalkhedankonkhede*
  (Who shall play games in your mansion, Oh dear Father?)
- *Meriyankhedanpotriyan, dheigharjaapne*

(My granddaughters will play here; you must depart, for that is your home)

- *Terejumeidhiveibabla, thoridarupeveibabla*
  (A daughter is born to you, Oh, Father, drink less)
- *Bahroayajat*
  (A peasant back from work)
- *Aunde de gharkuri ho giye*
  (Found a girl is born to him, the moment he came home)
- *Zamindaraterenalburi ho giye*
  (Oh, landlord such bad thing occurred to you)
- *Ambe ne ambe*
  (Mother o mother)
- *Mere sattbharajamme*
  (You bore me seven brothers)
- *Jis din se meinjanamdharya, Mamihumaki hoi*
  (The day I was born, the aunt went mad)
- *Babal de gal tukpholgiya, Peer nalokye koi*
  (The Father felt like a noose around his neck, no Lord has helped)
- *Saregharmatamchhagya, Khushinadisse koi*
  (The whole house is mourning, there's no joy)
- *Gurhkhain, puunikatin, app nah aayin, bhaiyaghali.*
  (Eat jaggery and spin thread, don't come, send brother instead).

These folk songs depict how the birth of a daughter was conceived as a misfortune for the father, who got loaded with immense responsibilities. Brother was to be treated as a valuable treasure by a sister, who was a temporary member of her parental family, was supposed to move out after her marriage. The birth of a son was followed by celebrations, since he was treated as a permanent economic asset and protector of the family, while a daughter brought sorrow and morose. While grandmothers prayed for grandsons, sisters prayed for brothers and so on. Not one but at least seven sons were prayed for, as they were believed to bring fortune to the parents.

The Punjabi folk songs continuously hummed by the women at home go a long way in gender socialization. Right from the childhood, male and female children internalize the socially accepted gender roles, apart from acquiring self-esteem commensurate with their social value as depicted through these songs. Gender images portrayed by folk songs therefore reveal a great deal about the societal attitudes toward gender. These pass on the values and behaviour patterns associated with masculinity and femininity to young boys and girls, who are trained to fit into these roles. A sister for instance grows up into a woman valuing her brother as a precious gift that has to be preserved at all cost, and she goes on longing for a son after her marriage, carrying forward the tradition of patriarchy. Actually giving birth to son(s) is the only source through which she could raise her social status and prestige.

II

Another strong literary tradition in Punjab has been the *qissa-kavya*, a lyrical epic poem which emerged in Punjabi literature through the assimilation of the folklore by the people of Punjab between the 14th and 16th centuries, and which has played a major role in valorizing romantic love. In this section an effort has been made to present legendary romantic tales of Punjab, carrying the representation of women in various love legends. *Heer-Ranjha, Sohni–Mahiwal, Sassi-Pannu*and *Mirza-Sahiban* are briefly discussed. These are tragic love stories, scripted in medieval times. Believed to be partly historical and partly sociological, these are etched on a typical Punjabi psyche. The protagonists in all these stories are punished with death for flouting social norms. All these epics reveal a social structure of medieval Punjab with arranged marriage as a social norm, regulated by caste endogamy and village exogamy as the prevailing rules of mate selection. It is necessary to see these legendary love stories within the general perspective of our cultural patterns, linked both with the past popular tradition as well as with the Punjabi literature depicting the popular culture of Punjab.

Heer-Ranjha

The present paper has reference to Waris Shah's *Heer-Ranjha*. It is one of the tales narrated in unison by the waters of the Chenab. The celebrated legend of *Heer-Ranjha* remains a part of the glorious oral literature of Punjab. Deedu Ranjha was the son of a big landlord belonging to a caste called Ranjha Jat from a place called Takt Hazara near river Chenab. Moju Chaudhary had great love for his son Ranjha, partly because of him being a late child, and mainly because of his attractive personality and innocence. Ranjha was brought up with great love and care. Unlike his brothers, Ranjha neither showed any interest in farming nor did he learn to plough or sow and reap. He just knew how to play flute. With practice he obtained a mastery over it and whosoever heard it would get hypnotized. He would go from place to place, people of his town with his sweet melodies. After the death of his father Ranjha was given the unproductive land by his brothers and was ill-treated by their wives. Ranjha subsequently left his village and went away.

Heer was an extremely beautiful young woman born into a wealthy Jat family of Syal clan in Jhang, Punjab. Ranjha accidentally met her on a river bank. It happened to be love at first sight. Heer took him to her parents as a new cowherd. Ranjha would play flute and Heer would fall for his tunes. Rumours of their love affair spread fast. Her parents (her father being a village chief) too came to know about it and refused to give their daughter to a cowherd. Undeterred, Heer and Ranjha continued meeting secretly, but eventually, they were detected by Kaido, Heer's uncle. Under social pressure, Heer was married off to a man named Saida Khera and thus separated from Ranjha.

Heartbroken, Ranjha became a loner and started roaming across the countryside. This was when he met Jogi Baba Gorakhnath, became his follower and went on to become a Jogi. He started reciting the name of Alakh Niranjan and wandered throughout the state of Punjab and finally happened to reach the village where Heer was residing after her marriage. They both again met and decided to elope but were caught. Heer was sent back to her parents' house. Heer's parents believed that she had brought dishonour to the whole family and therefore, they decided that Heer be killed. They also befooled Ranjha by showing consent to his marriage with Heer and asking him to get his wedding party (*baraat*) from Takht Hazara. On the wedding day, Kaido poisoned the food which was to be consumed by Heer. When Ranjha learnt that Heer had consumed poisoned food and died, Ranjha was so heartbroken that he also consumed the same food and died with her.

Sohni-Mahiwal

Fazal Shah Sayyad, a Punjabi poet, wrote the very popular *qissa Sohni-Mahiwal*. As per this tragic love story, in the 18th century, there was a porter named Tulla in a village along the Chenab river in Punjab and he belonged to Kumhar caste. He used to create the most lovely earthenware pots in the region. As his daughter Sohni grew up, she began helping her father and would draw floral designs on pots. His pottery was famous.

One day, a very wealthy young man called Shahzaada Izzat Baig from the city of Bukhara (in Uzbekistan) came to Tulla's home to buy some pottery. While he was examining the pottery, he saw Sohni and was enchanted by her beauty and fell in love with her. Just to get a glimpse of Sohni he would come up every day to buy pottery. Sohni also fell in love with him.

When he had spent all his money, instead of returning to his hometown, he took up the job of a servant in Tulla's house. He would take their buffalos for grazing. Soon he came to be known as *Mahiwal,* a buffalo herder. When people started spreading rumours about their love, the Kumhar community showed resentment since they had the tradition of marriage within their own community. Sohni was forcefully married into another potter family in the same village. Extremely dejected, Mahiwal renounced the world and started living like a *faqir* in a hut opposite Sohni's house across the river. The lovers continued to meet secretly. At night, Sohni, who was unhappily married, would come by the riverside and Mahiwal would swim across the river to meet her. Since Sohni could not swim she would use a baked earthenware pot to cross the river. The rumours of their romantic rendezvous spread. One day Sohni's sister-in-law decided to kill Sohni. She followed Sohni and saw the place where she kept the hard baked pitcher. She replaced her baked pitcher with an unbaked one. The next night, Sohni took the pot and began her journey to meet Mahiwal. When she was a quarter of the way across, she realized that something was wrong. The sturdy piece of pottery that served as her lifesaver was melting into the water. She called for Mahiwal. When Mahiwal saw Sohni drowning, he swam as far as he could but he could not hold himself up against the current. While holding on to each other, they both got drowned in the Chenab River, meeting a tragic end.

Sassi-Punnu

Sufi poet Hashim Shah is famous for his *qissa-kavya* of *Sassi-Punnu*. The legend of Sassi Punnu is the story of love between a prince and a princess. At the time of her birth astrologers predicted that she would bring misfortune to the family. The King ordered that the child be put in a wooden box and thrown in the river Sindhu. A washer man found the wooden box and the child inside. He believed that the child was a blessing from God and took her home. As he had no child of his own, he decided to adopt her and named her Sassi. She grew up into a beautiful maiden and her beauty became the talk of the town. The King came to know about her and asked her to come to his palace but she refused. Punnu, the Prince of Baluchistan, also heard about Sassi and got desperate to meet her. He travelled to Bhambore. He sent his clothes to Sassi's father (a washerman) so that he could catch a glimpse of Sassi. When he visited the washer man's house, Sassi and Punnu fell in love at first sight. Sassi's father was dispirited hoping that Sassi would marry a washer man and no one else. He asked Punnu to prove that he was worthy of Sassi by passing the test as a washer man. Punnu agreed to prove his love by washing clothes. However, while washing, he tore all the clothes as being a prince he had never washed any clothes. He, thus, failed the test. However, before returning the clothes he hid gold coins in the pockets hoping that it would keep the washer man quiet. The trick worked, and Sassi's father agreed to the marriage.

Punnu's father and brothers were against his marriage to Sassi (Punnu being a prince and she being a washer man's daughter). For their father's sake, Punnu's brothers travelled to Bhambore. First they threatened Punnu but when he did not relent, they tried more devious methods. They agreed for marriage of Punnu and Sassi. Punnu was surprised to see his brothers supporting his marriage. On the first night the brothers pretended to enjoy and participate in the marriage celebrations and forced Punnu to drink different types of wines. When he was intoxicated they carried him on a camel's back and returned to their hometown.

The next morning, when Sassi got up, she realized that she had been cheated. With grief, she ran barefoot towards the town of Kech Makran. She had to cross miles of desert, but alone she continued her journey. The journey was full of hazards. Throughout the journey Sassi continued calling Punnu. She was thirsty and saw a shepherd coming out of a hut. He gave her some water to drink. Seeing her incredible beauty, he tried to force himself on Sassi. She ran and got buried in quicksand. When Punnu woke up in Makran he could not stop himself from running back to Bhambore. On the way he called out for Sassi to which the shepherd told Punnu about demise of Sassi. Punnu died in grief and was also buried in the same mountain valley as Sassi.

Mirza-Sahiban

This *qissa* was reportedly written by a 17th century Punjabi poet, Piloo, in an oral or ballad form. Ever since, many writers have reproduced this love story in various versions. Mirza and Sahiban were cousins, were of the same age group and studied together till they grew up as adolescents and got immensely attracted towards each other. Sahiban, the beautiful daughter of the chief of Syals fell in love with Mirza. Mirza was Wanjhal Khan's son, who had the status of a Chaudhary in the tribe of Kharal Jat. Mirza lived in the house of his maternal uncle (Sahiban's father) in Syal. Soon their friendship changed into love. This relation was not liked by Sahiban's family. Mirza was the nephew of that family and cousins could marry among Muslims. Syals considered Mirza's clan inferior. Mirza was sent back to his village when their love had become public. Sahiban's father betrothed her to a man from the Chadhar clan.

Sahiban sent a message to Mirza to save her as she never wanted to get married. On the other hand, Mirza's sister requested him not to go to Sahiban and be with her since it was also her wedding day and she wanted her brother to be by her side. Besides, his entire family warned that the Syal community was very violent and one shouldn't interfere in their matters, but they failed to convince Mirza. Mirza arrived at the wedding venue riding his mare, where the mehndi ceremony of Sahiban was going on and took her away. On learning that their sister Sahiban had been abducted by Mirza, her brothers followed them. Mirza was confident about his abilities as an archer as well as the speed of his mare Bakki. He decided to take rest despite Sahiban's consistent warnings of danger. When Mirza was resting with his head on Sahiban's lap, her brothers caught them. They overpowered and killed Mirza with arrows. Sahiban threw herself over Mirza's body to cover him from any further hits. A shower of arrows rained on Sahiban and both of them died.

Discussion

These portrayals presented above through the *qissa-kavya* provide a peep into the plight of women in Punjabi society in medieval times. It is important to note here that the killing of all these lovers depicts different forms of honour killing, which have assumed a different shape in the modern times. Honour killings were generally executed when a woman rebelled to her family's diktat to obey the traditional norms established by the community to which she belonged, or when her 'dissolute behaviour' brought dishonour to the whole family. If other tactics to make the woman abide by the verdicts of her family failed, the ultimate solution was to kill her. These murders were culturally sanctioned and designed to uphold a specific moral order. The family members were not ready to accept the decisions of the young women to marry men of their own choice. In these legends, the women are shown as being bold and pro-active, and through their initiatives each of them attempted to define the contours of man-woman relationship based on love in a refreshingly new manner. The crucial theme in all these legends is that marriage was not considered to be an individual choice. More importance was given to caste and family background. Girls who eloped with their lovers were believed to have brought disgrace not only to their family but also to the whole society, thus inviting severe punishment.

Another very significant similarity among these stories relates to the societal modes to tame and control the sexuality of young women, within the context of religion and caste. In all these tragic love stories, the women once caught on the wrong foot, flirting around with men of different castes or communities would be immediately married off by their families, with the objective of sabotaging their love affairs. When Sohni even after her marriage continues to meet her lover Mahiwal, it is taken to bring dishonour to her matrimonial family and her sister in law causes her death. All these stories revolve around the notions of masculinity and femininity, focusing upon the premium the society laid on the need to control the sexuality of the young women, for the sake of family honour, purity of caste and so on. What is interesting is that although through centuries, these love stories have been eulogized and celebrated, no body, at least in Punjabi society and culture, ever likes to have a Sassi or Heer or Sohni in his/her own family. If Sassi was extraordinarily beautiful or if Sahiba's beauty was irresistible, it became a liability for their parents. The beautiful nexus between gender, caste and class portrayed in these stories still continues to prevail till date.

The legends reinforced an ideology that every girl who tried to disobey the established social codes would meet a similar fate. These also created an image of a good daughter being obedient and submissive to social norms. She was supposed to give priority to family honour over her personal desires and priorities. Any relationship violating caste and religious boundaries was forbidden and any violation, especially by a daughter was not to be tolerated even if it meant her death. Further in almost all the folk tales, there is a direct involvement of fathers and/or brothers of the girls and in a few cases, first-hand involvement of the paternal or maternal uncles and family friends has been observed. Noted folklorist Alan Dundes (1980) noted that there is a clear cut gender differentiation in a patriarchal society where women are associated primarily with homemaking and domestic servitude and are expected to marry, while men are associated with activeness and independence; women are told what they should do, which is act like women, and what they should not do, which is act like men; thus, the negative reactions to 'tomboys' and 'whistling girls'. All the decisions with regard to their lives are taken by men.

III

This section of the paper focuses on modern Punjabi literature focusing upon Bhai Vir Singh and Amrita Pritam, two very prominent writers. One story by each of these two writers has been chosen and discussed with a view to bring home the immensely patriarchal society in Punjab.

Sundari by Bhai Vir Singh

Bhai Vir Singh is also called the father of modern Punjabi literature. His story entitled 'Sundari' is based on a folk song, narrating the tale of a young beautiful Hindu girl Sursti who later embraced Sikhism and was renamed Sundari.

The story begins with Sursti in the courtyard of her house, where she is singing, dancing and laughing with her friends. Sursti outshines all the other maidens in terms of physical beauty. Soon thereafter, she is abducted from the jocund crowd by the Mughal chief who was out hunting with his accomplices and who happened to see her.

Sursti's father, her brother, the would-be bridegroom, and two members of her village Panchayat go to the chief to plead for her return. The father with folded hands respectfully begs the Mughal to return his daughter. The son follows him requesting that the Nawab return his sister as an act of 'charity'. The fiancé falls at the chief's feet, offering all his wealth in exchange for Sursti, but Nawab refuses. Sursti's brother falls unconscious. Her father begins to cry. Her fiancé, in fear lest the chief ask him to surrender his property, runs away.

Disillusioned by the weak and frightened fiancé, Sursti boldly unveils her face and authoritatively asks the members of her family and members of the village Panchayat to return. She then decides to immolate herself. Another brother of Sursti, Balvant Singh, who had become a Sikh receiving the rites of Khalsa initiation, lived in the jungle with his companions and carried on a desperate, though unequal, battle with their persecutors. On the evening of Sursti's wedding, he happens to visit his home. Hearing of the tragedy that had befallen upon his sister, he immediately turns his horse in pursuit of her. As he reaches near the Nawab's camp, he observes a pile of logs, a corner of it alight. He rushes to the spot and pulls Sursti away from atop the pyre. Once rescued, Sursti faces the choice of returning home or accompanying her brother to the Sikh camp and lead a hazardous life in the jungle. She decides to accompany her brother. However, en route to rejoin the Khalsa, they are captured by the Nawab. Sursti is forced to be converted and become the Nawab's wife and Balvant is to convert as well. However, Khalsa army storms in and rescues both of them upon which they all return to Khalsa camp. Sursti then requests that she stays and serve the Khalsa as their sister. Soon thereafter she takes *amrit* and becomes Sunder Kaur alias Sundari. Most of the text subsequently involves Sundari eluding the lustful Nawab and exhibiting behaviour that Veer Singh believes is the model for contemporary Sikh women.

The story depicts women as weak and a source of lust. It is only men who can save them as happened in this narration. After she is saved, she is given the job of cooking and a caretaking. She is portrayed as an object to be grabbed or taken back by men through might, with no regard for what the woman wants. Since, Sundari is a beautiful woman, so the Nawab wants to take her along. Physically vulnerable, a woman so easily gets polluted by the vicious acts of a man, rendering her stigmatized for rest of her life.

'Pinjar' by Amrita Pritam

Amrita Pritam's 'Pinjar' is a revenge story set in the wake of Partition. Pritam has shown how women become the prime victim of violence and prone to unimaginable torture and humiliation at the hands of the people belonging to the other community.

'Pinjar' is the story of Puro, a young Hindu girl, who gets separated from her family at the time of Partition. Puro is betrothed to a wealthy young man Ram Chand from a promising family. Meanwhile, even before she gets married, Puro is kidnapped by a Muslim man Rashid who had ancestral dispute with Puro's family. One night Puro manages to escape back to her parents. Her parents turn her away on the pretext that if Puro came to stay with them they all would be killed. Left with no support Puro goes back to Rashid. After a few months Puro's parents marry off Puro's brother and sister. Puro is not invited on these occasions. Puro also gets pregnant with Rashid's child. She gets depressed and has a miscarriage.

During the Partition, Puro comes to know that her brother's wife who also happened to be her fiancé's sister is caught in riots. She helps her to escape. She meets her fiancé who shows inclination to accept her but Puro refuses. But she challenges the obsession with borders and boundaries. She reaches the climax of acceptance and challenge. She declares her choice and comes back to Rashid. Ram Chand responds with tremendous empathy to Puro and bids tearful farewell to her.

The novel focuses on the convincing choices the writer accords to a female character despite her conservative cultural situation. Pinjar is the women's cry against her fate and abuse. Puro embodies the injustice since she is bound to old values and cannot discard the ties that failed her in times of need. Puro, thus, makes the non-normative choice to refuse the offer of inclusion and interpolation into family, community and nation that was once denied to her. In doing so she recreates her own identity, 'Hamida' which had been once thrust upon her.

Amrita Pritam's Pinjar tells the story of love and hate. It also tells of the feelings, reconciliation, recovery and reaccepting of women abducted in different circumstances during pre-Partition and Partition periods. Pinjar reiterates the societal belief that a woman very easily loses her chastity and purity and once polluted, she becomes a curse for her own family. Already victimized, her own parents would reject her, lest her siblings may lose their life opportunities. For no fault of hers, she gets stigmatized, victimized and abandoned by her own relatives, for the fear of society.

Discussion

The study of language and gender is an interdisciplinary endeavour. Although many researchers have been concerned primarily with documenting gender-related patterns of language use, yet the present paper has made use of language as a lens through which the social and political aspects of gender relations are viewed. The power a society grants to its males affects and is reflected in day-to-day interactions, which does not occur in a vacuum.

The word honour depicts very comprehensive connotations in Punjab and is considered as a very significant constituent of socio-cultural values. Traditionally, *zarr* (wealth), *zoroo* (women), and *zameen* (land) have been considered as three integral constituents of honour in this region and there have been historical traditions of pursuing violence and executing killings for reinstating the honour in case of an assault on any of the three. Even during the present era, there are reports of frequent incidents of killings revolving around these three elements. Moreover, the connotation of honour and honour killings related to women is multidimensional. In the first kind of instance, if a woman of the family is disrespected, teased, sexually harassed or exploited by a man, it is considered as an attack on the honour of male family members, often causing violence against the accused which may result into his killing as well. Then there are instances where in case a married woman establishes extra-marital relations with a man, it is considered as assassination of his honour by her husband.

Another form of honour-related violence, often resulting into honour killings, consists of a girl establishing romantic or sexual relationship with a boy and/or willing to marry with the boy of her own choice. The romantic or sexual relationship of the girl is considered as an infringement of honour by the male members of the girl's family and hence is not tolerated.

Even if the girl is willing to marry the boy of her own choice, it is acknowledged as hurting the honour of the family. The situation gets more aggravated when the boy with whom the girl has established relationship and/or is willing to marry belongs to an inferior caste, or a different religion. There are obvious probabilities of honour-based violence against the girl which usually results in the killing of the girl, the boy or of both.

Kurkiala (2003) revealed that murders in the name of honour killing are generally culturally sanctioned, designed to uphold a specific moral order. Majority of the honour killings are committed because the family members disapprove pre-marital relationships of their daughters. Moreover, in the male dominated and patriarchal society of the region, cultural norms, traditions, and misinterpretation of religion tend to offer justifications for the prevailing gender inequalities that deny women their rights in the private and public spheres. In these systems, patriarchal ideology helps explain beliefs that a woman is the property of men. This perception prevails among different classes, rich and poor, where daughters are forced into marriages of convenience or battered for the greater good of the family. More importantly, the patriarchal systems give power to men. Men enjoy benefits from patriarchal systems that reinforce their sense of masculinity. Men are expected to dominate, to control, and to be the authority figures and decision-makers within their families and community.

In conclusion it can be stated that women in Punjabi culture have always been treated as the property of men. The normative culture serves as a control mechanism. It stipulates what ought to be the pattern of life and behaviour in the society. It is more effective than the formal control system especially if the cultural elements are properly internalized through effective socialization, which in turn tends to reinforce this ideology. The use of honour refers to control over female behaviour and loss of such control brings woman's family within the context of larger community enforcement. The traditional concept of honour killing is rooted in the perception that women are the property of the male members of the family in as much as it is the honour of these men that is affected if a woman violates cultural codes or social norms. In short, this paper has analysed folk songs, *qissa-kavya* and novels to highlight the gendered world of Punjabi society. The paper provided evidence of how folk songs are mostly sexist and their continued use in everyday life contributes to the social construction and reproduction of patriarchal gendered ideology as a means of social control, mostly used by men and elders to shape and maintain the existing gender relations.

References

Dundes, Alan. 1980. *Interpreting Folklore*. Berkeley: University of California Press.

Gill, Harjeet Singh. 2003. *Heer Ranjha and Other Legends of Punjab*. New Delhi: Harnam Publishing House.

Grewal, J.S. 1999. 'Punjabi Identity: A Historical Perspective', in P. Singh and S.S. Thandi (eds), *Punjabi Identity in a Global Context*. New Delhi: Oxford University Press, pp. 41–54.

Gumtala, Charanjit Singh. 1997. *Peelu Qissa Mirza Sahiban*. Ludhiana: Punjabi Writers' Cooperative.

Kurkiala, Mikael. 2003. 'Interpreting Honour Killings: The Story of Fadime Shindal (1975–2002)'. *Anthropology Today*, 19(1), 6–7.

Linton, R. 1945. *The Science of Man in the World Crisis*. New York: Columbia University Press.

Nilsson, Usha. 1984. 'A Selection of Women's Folk Songs'. *Journal of South Asian Folklore*, 19(1), 117–123.

Pritam, Amrita. 2003. *Pinjar*. New Delhi: Hind Pocket Books (original work published in 1950).

Raheja, G.G. and Gold, A.G. 1994. *Listen to the Hero's Words: Reimagining Gender and Kinship in North India*. Berkeley: University of California Press.

Shah, Hashim. 1985. *Sassi Punnu* (translated by Chritopher Shackle in English). Lahore: Vanguard Books Ltd.

Singh, Bhai Vir. 1985. *Sundari*. New Delhi: Bhai Vir Singh Sahitya Sadan.

Singh, Gurdev (ed.) 1974. *Sohni Fazal Shah*. Ludhiana: Lahore Book Shop.

Singh, Khushwant. 1999. *A History of the Sikhs, Vol. 1: 1469–1839*. Reprint with corrections (first edition 1963). New Delhi: Oxford University Press.

Singh, Nahar. 1983. *Punjabi Lokgeet: Kavi di Sirjan Parkirya*. Chandigarh: Lokayat Prakashan.

Sital, J.S. 1961. *Heer Waris, Bhumika*. Patiala: Punjab Sahit Sammelan.

4

Khaps and Gender in Haryana

An Interface

Nirmala Devi

In the past, due to an age-old ideology of village brotherhood and systematic working of *khap* panchayats (wherever these were in force), harmonious relations existed within and across the neighbouring villages. The members of *khap* panchayats held enormous economic, social and political power in the local area. These consisted of rich elderly people who forced their customary views that were repressive in nature, against the statutory provisions. This traditional form of authority existed as an accepted norm to settle day-to-day issues and problems. Though these were suppressive or repressive in nature yet were widely accepted by people irrespective of caste and income. However, as the country progressed due to modernization, urbanization and globalization, the elected bodies have come into existence as legally recognized local bodies. Hence all the day-to-day issues and problems are now referred to these constitutionally elected bodies, which give ruling as per the legal provisions contained in the constitution of India. At the village level, quite often these legal rulings tend to be contrary to the existing age-old norms of the *khap* panchayats and are mostly resisted by members of village community who are powerful and hold traditional khap authority. Such a conflicting situation frequently leads to serious kinds of feuds within the agrarian societies, challenging the constitutional provisions granting freedom and equality to all citizens irrespective of caste, creed, religion and gender. This situation needs to be addressed and handled more intensively, cautiously and firmly. Hence, a comprehensive study needs to be undertaken at the grassroot level where progressive and modernized ideologies are resisted by the age-old customary norms.

The present research paper has been divided into three parts. First part of the paper deals with brief background of khaps including its origin, functions and structure. The second part of the paper deals with the interface between *khaps* and gender in which discriminatory and derogatory practices which are prevalent in *khap*-dominated areas will be discussed. The focus will be on social issues where *khaps* have played an important role and given dictates like honour killings (due to Sagotra marriages, inter-caste marriages, inter-religion or inter-community marriages, declaring husband-wife as brother and sister), rape, female foeticide, dress code, use of modern technology like mobile phones, etc. Finally, the third and last section gives the conclusions and inferences.

A Brief Background of *Khaps*

'Khap' is an age old body of an ancient concept which has written references found back in the Rig Vedic times. The exact origin of *khap* panchayat till date is not known but is commonly believed that they came into existence around 600 AD. Some believe that *khaps* have apparently been in existence since the 7th century or may be even earlier in some parts of India. *Khaps* are said to have coronated the 12-year-old Harshvardhan, who gave them a saffron flag with a bright red sun in the middle. Historically, it has been a decentralized system of social administration in the north-western states like Haryana, Madhya Pradesh and Punjab. *Khap* panchayat is sort of tribal organization.

The word 'khap' has its roots in Sanskrit. It is derivative of *kashtrap* meaning 'domain'. According to *Encyclopedia of Haryana* (Sharma 2011: 33), it is derived from the word *khep*. It is an institution, wielding control over a particular area where it has supremacy or sovereignty. It is believed to have been created by the upper caste 'jaats' to consolidate their power and position in the community. It is titled either in the name of clan/*gotra*, which dominates that region, or by the name of particular geographical area. It regulates not only the social customs of the dominant clan of the Jaats of the khap but also of the Jaats of other clans living in its jurisdiction.

The first type of khap panchayat comprises single caste and single *gotras*; the Dahiya Khap, the Hooda Khap, the Malik Khap also known as Gathwala Khap. The second type of *khap* comprises single caste with *multi-gotra*, i.e. Meham Chaubasi in Rohtak district and the third type of *khap* comprises of multi-caste with *multi-gotra*, i.e. Bawal Khap of Bense Chaurasi which includes 84 villages in Rewari District. A *khap* panchayat has been described as a clan council by an anthropologist on the basis of his doctoral study in the school of Oriental African Studies, London (Pradhan 1966). It has been defined as a multi village panchayat (Sanghwan 1986). Prem Chowdhry, a social historian from Delhi University, denotes it as a caste council or caste panchayat (Chowdhry 2004). All of them agree that these are forms of traditional panchayats.

Khap panchayat termed by Chowdhry (2006) as a 'caste panchayat' that emerged as a collective body is wholly patriarchal in nature. These panchayats are unelected, illegal and unconstitutional bodies. For making their authority legitimate, the *khap* panchayat are interfering and thrust their influence on social issues specially pertaining to marriages, eloping couples and female foeticides. Caste, class, status gender and patriarchy are usually dominant and play an important role in the action of *khap* panchayats.

According to Pradhan, the *khap* could be defined as 'a unit of a number of villages organized into a political council for the purpose of social control' (1966: 336). Participation in the Sarv Khap Panchayat is open to all members of *khaps* that come together on a particular issue. However, it is the *pradhan* of a *khap* who calls the meeting of the Sarv Khap. A meeting is called when an issue is of a serious nature or difference between two *khaps* crops. Women and people from low castes were not allowed to participate in the meetings of Sarv Khap Panchayat (Sanghwan 2008).

Structure of *Khap* Panchayats

A *khap* panchayat may range from one to eight villages; or from 12 to 24 presently 32 villages and larger panchayat may cover as many as 84 villages. The members of the dominant caste have always controlled the meetings of *khap* panchayats. In case of differences between members of the dominant and low caste groups, the former are able to control the latter and enforce decision upon them. This is normally achieved through threat of economic sanctions and fear of physical violence. According to Pradhan (1966), there may be five categories of panchayats.

Figure 1

Categories of Khap Panchayats

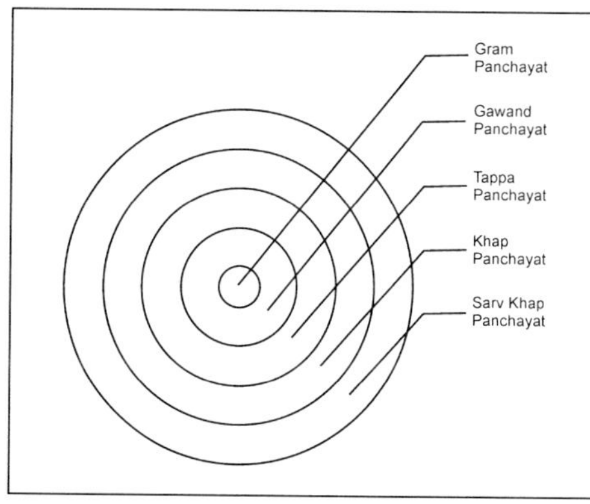

Functions of *Khap* Panchayats

Khap panchayats are reported to have come into existence as a maintenance system in ancient societies. The *khap* panchayats were administrative, adjudicative and executive bodies with police and military powers. They functioned on the same pattern as village and *thamba* councils but, nevertheless, they were more powerful as these *khaps* could exert social and traditional authority, which was more acceptable to the society. The *khap* panchayats are believed to have been multi-caste bodies. It has also been claimed that *khap* panchayats had fought against repression and forcible conversion of Hindus to Islam by Aurangzeb. These have also been reported to play an active role in the Revolt of 1857. There are instances of their role in the movement for prohibition, resistance to emerging regime and state repression on various occasions (Pradhan 1966). The settlement of inter-caste disputes or breach of peace and order, such as thefts are settled by the *khap* panchayats (Pradhan 1966). Issues such as breaking of social taboos, customs, rituals and hierarchy are used as mobilizing strategies (Chowdhry 2006). Out-casting is the final weapon in the hands of the traditional *khap* panchayat. Any offence for which a person who is likely to be thrown out of his caste requires an inter-village panchayat of the caste members so that punishment is widely known and supported. At times the offender is even expelled from the village. The recent cases in Haryana show the frequent intervention of the *khap* panchayat, enjoying no legitimacy in law, which has attempted to change relationships and impose its own preferences, subsuming the individual/family will to that of the village/collective, and prioritizing the village and *biradari's izzat* over that of individual/family (Chowdhry 2004). The weakness of the elected constitutional panchayat institutions is also responsible for the continued strength of the *khap* panchayats (Singh 2010).

Source of Strength of *Khap* Panchayats

In the Jat dominated areas of Haryana and western Uttar Pradesh, the *khap* panchayats derive their strength mainly from the following:

(a) The strength of the traditional *khap* panchayats lies in the persistence of strong kinship feeling among various *gotras* of Jaats. This is based on their belief that being the progeny of a common ancestor they have ties of blood.

(b) Another source of their strength flows from the prevalence of the concept of '*bhaichara*' (brotherhood) commonly seen among the clans living in villages having common boundaries.

(c) A third source of their strength comes from the traditional institution of '*gawand*' panchayats (neighbourhood panchayats) for resolving the inter-village disputes in adjoining villages (Pradhan 1966).

Due to the above factors these panchayats remain motivated to strengthen their traditional authority. The members of *khap* panchayats have a vested interest to hold on to the power and this also keeps them motivated.

Khap Panchayats: Unconstitutional in Spirit

Venkatesan (2011) explained caste as one of the main problems of being conservative and not changing with times. He stated that Supreme Court of India had declared *khap* panchayat as an illegal institution and was an unconstitutional body. The *khap* panchayats, directly or indirectly, often encourage honour killings or other institutionalized atrocities against young boys and girls of different castes and religions who get married or wish to get married. A Bench of Justice Markandey Katju and Gyan Sudha Misra declared that *khap* panchayats in today's scenario are totally illegal and have to be stamped out (Venkatesan 2011).

Social Issues: *Khaps* Taken Stand in Recent Times

- Honour killings
- Eloping couple or runaway couple
- Rape
- Female foeticide
- Dress code
- Use of information technology
- Lowering the age of girls for marriage to 16 years in October 2012.

Khap Panchayat – Their Barbaric and Unconstitutional Dictates

- Declaring a married couple as brother and sister, (Satish and Kavita, village Meham Khedi, district Rohtak)

- Ostracizing families and murder of young couples in the name of honour, (Vedapal and Sonia, district Jind; Ravinder and Shilpa, district Jhajjar)
- Stripping a woman,
- Mass rape of a woman to take revenge,
- Stuffing shoe into the mouth of a man and parading him in the streets of a village,
- Blackening the face of somebody and putting him on a donkey and taking him round in the village and such other inhuman acts (Chaudhry 2014)
- Khaps to enforce dress code in Haryana.

Supreme Court's Stand on *Khap* Panchayats

In the past, *khaps* issued diktats on dress code making it mandatory for women to cover their body from head to toes. Unmarried girls have been forbidden to use cell phones or to go for shopping, asking them to stay at home. The reason for issuing such diktats is the belief that use of mobile phones by young girls will encourage their intermixing with the opposite sex while western dresses like jeans attract the males. The bench of Honourable Justices Aftab Alam and Ranjana P. Desai, of Supreme Court of India, while hearing a PIL which sought protection of young couples marrying inter-caste or within the same *gotra* remarked that *khaps* dictate on women's dress and use of cell phone is unlawful and said that *khaps* can't decide on women's dress code and carrying of mobile phones (cited by Mahapatra 2013).

Review of Literature

Khap panchayats are in limelight because of their interference in social issues like marriages, elopement, female foeticide, rape, etc. This part of review will bring out some facts on the recent resurgence of the *khap* panchayats in matters related to honour killing.

Role of Upper Caste Men in Decision-Making

Studies by Singh (1961), Pradhan (1966), Aggarwal (1971), Miller (1975), Sanghwan (1986), Hayden (1999), Chaudhry (2010), Singh (2010), Kumar (2012) and Saini (2012) have revealed that decision-making was always in the hands of upper castes and these panchayats used to dominate over members of weaker sections, lower castes and women. These institutions used to play the functions of providing justice to the people with fairness; resolving the disputes, providing security to its people, and protecting them from foreign attacks and social control. Issues of wider and conflicted interests were resolved by these self-styled panchayats and included broader range of issues. *khap* panchayats played the function of social control in the local region. The settlement of dowry and divorce cases, property disputes between brothers and inter-caste disputes or breach of peace and order, such as thefts were settled by the *khap* panchayats. Upper caste men played the major role in all these decisions, though fair decisions were expected from *khap* panchayats yet at times the interest of the upper castes influenced the decision-making.

Derogatory and Discriminatory Practices Faced by Women in *Khap* Dominated Areas

Studies by Chowdhry (2006), Singh (2010), Chaudhry (2010), Kaur (2010), Sanghwan (2010), Gill (2012), Deswal (2012), Chowdhary (2011), Garg (2011), Venkatesan (2011), Welchman and Hossain (2006), Jafri (2008) and Dogra (2015) are indicative that class, status, gender and patriarchy play important roles in the action or inaction by *khap* panchayats. *Khaps* are patriarchal bodies where women are often victims of derogatory and discriminatory practices. Rules are relaxed for boys but never for girls. Young couples violating the norms of caste endogamy and clan exogamy, inter-caste, inter-religion or inter-community marriages face extreme forms of violence by families as well as *khap* panchayats. Breaching the order of *khap* panchayat is likely to be accompanied by getting killed, ex-communicated, blackening of faces, shaving of head and atrocities like beating, declaring the violators as out-caste, etc. The rights of the poor, Dalits, women and young boys and girls are snatched away in the name of tradition, brotherhood and honour. Dogra (2015) in an article entitled 'What a Man's Gotta Do' elaborates what does it means to be a man in India? What shapes the masculinity of India's son? What is the single biggest challenge that girls growing up in a *khap* land encounter nowadays? She has highlighted the traditionally laid down rules that restrict the movements of girls and women. The unwritten code of conduct for girls is to cover their heads, walk shyly, not to laugh aloud or even talk on their cell phones in public. Only a girl or a woman who abides by all these unwritten codes is respected by one and all.

Primacy of Social Norms over the Statutes

Gill (2012) has explained that social norms and values wield much greater power in life of an individual as compared to law. She highlighted that this kind of situation is prevailing in rural part of north India, especially Rajasthan and Haryana, where both men and women are in a dilemma over whether to follow the social diktats of *khap* panchayats or to abide by law. In regions dominated by *khap* panchayats, social norms have greater weight than any statute. For this reason, there has been the resurgence of *khap* panchayats even after the establishment of constitutional bodies. Sarpanch of Bibipur village said, *'Khaps are more powerful than any government body, and prove it in this endeavour'* (cited by Shukla 2012).

Theoretical Perspective

The concept of repressive laws given by Emile Durkhiem can be compared to decision-making or diktats by the *khap* panchayat in Haryana. These can be interpreted as social sanctions imposed by members of *khap* panchayat enjoying traditional authority on the members who try to break the norms of the group. Repressive laws are accepted by the society as routine decisions and these rulings gradually establish traditional authority. Weber's 'traditional authority' is based on a claim by the leader, and a belief on the part of followers, that there is a virtue in the sanctity of age-old rules and powers. The question, which perplexes one, is that as the country has progressed due to modernization, globalization, etc. and elected bodies have come into existence in the form of legal authority then why *khap* panchayats are still enjoying traditional authority and imposing repressive laws on people who are in a subordinate position? Robert K. Merton's concept of 'dysfunction' would help to understand the functions of *khap* panchayats in past and in present times. This perspective will also throw light on positive and negative functions in society. It would help in exploring the grey areas of *khap* panchayats. The feminist theory, emphasizing upon the role of patriarchy in creating gender discrimination, can give a hint about how existing division of labour and patriarchy driven decision-making process in Haryana society are creating inequalities between men and women.

Objectives of the Study

1. To explain the interface between *khap* panchayats and gender;
2. To find out why women/girls still face discriminatory and derogatory practices which are prevalent in the *khap* dominated areas.

Research Methodology

The research was conducted in the state of Haryana, including the districts of Sonepat (Dahiya Khap), Rohtak (Meham Chaubasi Khap) and Rewari (Bawal Khap). Three of the *khaps* were representing the *khaps* of Haryana. Dahiya Khap based on single caste and single *gotra*, Meham Chaubasi Khap based on single caste and multiple *gotra*, and Bawal Khap based on multi-caste and multi-*gotras* respectively.

The research paper is based on both primary and secondary data. Primary data were obtained from different categories of respondents, i.e. members of *khap* panchayats (Pradhans of Khaps, Tappa, Gawand and Gram Panchayat), sarpanch of the selected villages (Meham Khedi, Sisana and village Bibipur from Jind district) and local villagers, including both men and women of different age group. Apart from this interviews with social activist and members of NGOs were conducted in state of Haryana.

Data were obtained by using methods such as personal interviews, observation, narratives, group discussion and persons who were directly dealing with such cases of honour killing.

Khaps and Gender: The Interface

The practices of the *khap* panchayats have often been seen in the context of maintaining the caste endogamy and *gotra* (clan) exogamy, the two fundamental norms of establishing marital relations in north Indian society. This also involves the issue of women and gender relations, as more often women considered as the sole custodians of honour and prestige of caste, *gotra* and family are often subjected to violence and punishment. This necessitates an examination of gender relations in a society where such institutions are still able to command social obedience.

Marginal Representation of Women

The structure of *khap* panchayat in the past was always a male-dominated institution. The literature too highlights the domination of men in this age old institution. Women were totally invisible in the structure and working of *khap* panchayats till 2010. Strong criticism for being male dominated institutions compelled these bodies to give birth to 'Women Wing of Sarv Khap Panchayats' in 2010. Dr Santosh Dahiya, a women educationist in Haryana was made President of this Women Wing and, hence, the inclusion of this wing into the structure of *khap* panchayat took place. Though the women wing was incorporated in *khap* panchayat yet till date it exists without any meaningful role or authority. This women wing is only a cover-up while practically it plays a puppet's role in the hands of male members of *khap* panchayat. During fieldwork in village Bibipur in Jind, the researcher observed that one of the women members was very authoritatively snubbed by the leader of the *khap* panchayat during a meeting of Sarv *Khap* Panchayat in Haryana. *Khap* panchayat is an exclusively male dominated institution and the women have no place or any say in it. Women have largely remained excluded from it.

Gender Bias in *Khap* Panchayats

The very mention of *khap* panchayat is a traumatic experience and brings horrifying images to mind of those murdered couples who married or dared to get married after falling in love. Couples are murdered and gang raped if they dared to fall in love. They issue diktats to ostracize families, declare marriages as null and void, declare husband-wife as brother-sister and give discriminative and derogatory orders. In their system a girl falling in love with a boy from the same *gotra* is the worst crime possible on earth. Harsh and stricter punishments are announced, such as the guilty can be expelled from the village, publically made to drink urine, paraded naked, beaten up or even killed (Chaudhry 2014). Their families are also boycotted and sometimes made to pay heavy fines.

According to Chowdhry, both men and women embody notion of honour, but differently. The woman is repository and man is regulator of honour. Therefore, the greatest danger to the ideology of honour comes from the woman. One often repeated phrase is: *Ladki ke sath uski kutumb ki izzat judi hai* (the honour of every family is connected to its daughter). A woman dishonours her family by what is considered her shameful physical behaviour. This stretches from observing *sharam* (modesty) to *lihaaz* (deference) to her sexuality. Honour is overarching concept which regulates and puts into affect the practice of *purdaah* and its attendant ideology of seclusion as controlling device (Chowdhry 2006).

Honour Killing as *Khaps'* Diktat

Honour killings are a major reason why *khaps* have attracted all the negative media coverage. In recent times, there have been numerous cases of honour killings in various forms attributed to *khap* diktats. Welchman and Hossain (2006) explored honour killing to be an extreme kind of violence against women committed by male members of the girl's family due to women's extra-marital relationship, suspected adultery and pregnancy outside marriage. It is believed that female family members perceived to have brought dishonour and shame upon the family must be eliminated.

Notions of honour serve as an indicator of familial worth. During the fieldwork in rural Haryana the researcher came across cases in which girls were killed by male relatives, by making them eat pesticide tablets and then their bodies were disposed of by burning secretively at night. The family members often cover it up saying that she committed suicide or just pass it off as natural death. Most of the times at village level the traditional panchayats are held when issues related to marriage erupt and are decided at the village level only. This can be seen as a reflection of *khap* ideology in rural Haryana. In the case of Satish and Kavita of Khedi Meham in district Rohtak, though both left the village, but it was Kavita who was told to leave the house while Satish was allowed to stay in the village by traditional panchayat. There are many cases in which girls are being killed in the name of honour. Teachers in some government schools shared that they came to know about these cases only on checking the attendance register. They are then told by the villagers and students that the girl had been poisoned and cremated at night. *Khap* panchayats are directly and indirectly found to be involved in all such cases. Parents of the girls fear the diktats issued by *khaps* in case they violated their diktats.

Caste Endogamy and Gotra Exogamy (Khaps Look Down towards Choice Marriages)

In rural Haryana, especially in *khap* belt one has to strictly follow the rules of caste endogamy and *gotra* exogamy. There is a concept of *bhaichara* and it is very strong in *khap* belt. A boy or a girl from the same *khap* is considered brother and sister. Marriages within the same village or even neighbouring villages are prohibited. Couples who defy these get killed by intolerant families and *khap* panchayats. During fieldwork in July 2012, Khazan Singh Sanghwan, Professor of Sociology at the Maharshi Dayananad University, Rohtak, observed that the principle of *khap* exogamy and caste endogamy ensured that even different *gotras* falling in a particular *khap* could not inter-marry. Similar notion was told by a *khap* member during fieldwork in Haryana in the village 'Sisana' in district Sonepat:

> *Gaon mien bhi na ho, gotra mien bhi na ho, inter-caste mien bhi na ho.*
>
> Marriages should not be solemnized in the same village or in the same Gotra nor take place in a different caste.
> (Male respondent, 50 years, Jat, Pradhan of Dahiya Khap, village Sisana, district Sonepat)

Love Marriages

Love marriages are not heard of; these are considered as a taboo to the family and people indulging in these are looked down upon. When villagers (respondents) were asked how they perceived love marriages and whether it was a good thing, most of the respondents said:

> *Apni marzi se shaadi karna galat hai, maa baap ki narazagi se shaadi karna galat hai ismien ladki ki jyada galti hoti hai.*
> It was wrong to get married without the consent of the parents. The girl is largely to be blamed and held responsible.
> (Male respondent, 45 years, Jat, member of Dahiya Khap, village Sisana, district Sonepat)

Other respondents said:

> *Love marriage agar biradari me ho to sahi hai, aur maa baap ki marzi se ho to theek hai.*
> If love marriage takes place in the same caste, it is still considered as acceptable and if it is with the knowledge of parents it is still okay.
> (Male respondent, 45 years, Jat Caste, Meham Khedi, Rohtak)

It was observed during fieldwork that a love marriage is still acceptable if the families of the girl and boy are powerful and influential. Hence it is the economic and social status of the families which determined the acceptance or rejection of a choice marriage.

Inter-Caste Marriages

In *khap* belt of Haryana when the villagers and members of *khap* panchayats (respondents) were asked as to how they perceived inter-caste marriages in villages. What should be done to the couple who had solemnized inter-caste marriages? Most of the respondents said,

> *Goli Maar Deni Chahiye Chhokri Ko, Rishta Nata Khatam Kar Denge*
> Girls should be shot dead. All relations with the girls must be ceased by her family and community members.
> (Woman respondent, 40 years, Jat Caste, Meham Khedi Rohtak)

In most of such cases the girl bears the punishment. The mindset of the villagers and *khap* members is quite rigid and conservative when the issue of the women is there. If anyone indulges in such kind of marriage alliance, either the couple gets eliminated or the family expelled from the village. It was observed that the same village, same gotra, love marriages, choice marriages and inter-caste marriages are considered a curse to the family and such kind of marriage alliance is considered a serious crime committed by the couple in the rural belt of India, especially Haryana. It is not acceptable to the villagers, community and girl's family has to bear the humiliation at the hands of community, often leading to bloodshed.

Here is a very famous case of honour killing in Haryana reported widely in media;

Manoj and Babli Case (2007) in which both were killed by girl's family and their bodies were thrown into a *nalla*. In this case both girl and boy were brutally murdered but Manoj's family's sufferings did not end there. His mother and sister had to face humiliation by *khap* members. They were traumatized, threatened and social boycott was announced. One of the *khap* members came to their house and offered money to stop the case and when Manoj's sister resisted *khap* member told her mother:

> *Teri bhi do ladkiya inka bhi wo haal kar dunga*
> You too have two daughters who will meet the same fate.
> (Manoj's sister, 25 years, Jat Caste, village Karora)

Being women, it was very difficult for them to fight against the system. It was in this case that Additional Session Judge passed the sentence of Capital Punishment to five and life term to two *khap* members. Such kind of killings were rampant in Haryana and raised ire in the society as well as in Government that former Union Home Minister, P. Chidambaram was compelled to react, 'Who are Khap Panchayats? Who gave them the right to kill in the name of honour?' (Singh 2010). Even Supreme Court of India declared them as an unconstitutional body.

During the fieldwork member of *khap* panchayat said:

> A legal ban on such marriages would also help curb the menace of honour killings and female foeticide which has brought a bad name to Haryanvi society.
> (Om Prakash Dhankar, a *khap* leader, Jat caste)

He further stated, 'People kill their daughters out of the fear that one day they might elope with men of the same *gotra*'. Question arises why kill the daughter for fear of her eloping or getting married. Why there is no fear that boy too might elope with a girl?

During the discussion on asking about female foeticide from pradhan of Dahiya Khap, he said:

> *Kanya bhroon hatya us din khatam ho jayegi, jis din ladkiya safe ho jayegi.*
> The day girls are safe in this environment, female foeticide will stop.
> (Pradhan of *khap*, Rohtak, Jat Caste)

The Pradhan too believes that girls and their families have to feel secure in order to stop foeticide. During a discussion, local villagers said:

> Women are unsafe in Jind as police does not take crime against women seriously.
> (Pradhan of *khap*, Rohtak, Jat Caste)

They further said that it was better to kill their girls in the womb than loose them to kidnappers.

Pradhan of Dahiya Khap further said:

> *Ladki pedda karte hai, paalte poste hai; 18 saal tak, fir bhag jati hai.*
> We give birth to a girl and then bring her up for 18 years and then she elopes away with a boy.
> (Pradhan of *khap*, Rohtak, Jat Caste)

Interpretation: During the fieldwork it was observed that in rural Haryana love marriages are not acceptable to the community especially due to the several restrictions based on *gotra* and village exogamy apart from caste endogamy. In all these complexities, if a boy or a girl decide to have a choice marriage, their decision becomes unacceptable to the community and then it becomes an issue of 'honour' for the family as well as of the village. Notion of honour is triggered if the girl is from the same village because she is seen as a daughter of the village. Boys and girls from the same village are considered brother and sister. In villages it is the girl who is held responsible for elopement not the boy. A fear of *khap* panchayat was clearly visible among villagers, thus discouraging them from adopting any change in the existing social norms governing marriage. Due to the fear of *khap* sanctions, girls are not allowed to use mobile phones or wear western dresses, lest they go astray.

Elopement and safety of girls are two main reasons why girls are not preferred in Khap Land of Haryana. The villagers expressed their views as '*mahol khraab hai ji*' meaning that social environment has deteriorated because of the influence of TV, mobile phones and social networking sites. Villagers stated that crime against girls/women had increased and girls were not safe.

In the end, therefore, it is the girl who is at the receiving end. If the girl retaliates to a boy's proposal and does not give in to his advances she is beaten up, forcibly picked and raped or acid is thrown on her to disfigure her face. If she gets married and gives her consent then again the society, community, the *khaps*, and the villagers hold her responsible. There is also a threat to girls who refuse to submit to the advances made by boys and for which they have to pay a price. Any girl who chooses to denounce does so at the risk of being demonized for offending the boy's sentiments.

Cases of Gender Violence: Fallout on Girls

In 2011, 733 cases of rape were reported in Haryana as per NCRB data. Apart from this, many such assaults go unreported. Before Delhi Gang Rape in 2012, there were many incidents of gang rape in which Dalit girls were raped by the Jaat boys in Haryana and many others never get reported. In one such case in October 2012, a 16-year-old girl was abducted by a group of seven men from Jaat community. One girl versus seven boys and yet the girl was held responsible for being gang raped for which she and her family were penalized by the village community. The suffering of the victim and her family did not end there. The assault was filmed by the men on their mobile phones. Later the MMS was circulated in this immensely obstinate society. Father of the victim, despite enormous efforts, failed to get an FIR registered in this case and faced so much humiliation that he poisoned himself. As per a newspaper reporting the victim said:

> They dragged me inside the car and blindfolded me, and then they took me by the side of the river and took turns to rape me while the others kept watch.
>
> The young rape victim added:
>
> The girls in my neighbourhood have stopped going to school and I am frightened too.

What is the end result? Family of the girl suffered humiliation at the hands of community and society. The barbaric experience of this girl and many others amounts to social shame and getting stigmatized. In yet another case on 29 July 2014, a Dalit couple was stripped for pursuing a rape case in village

Kahnaur, district, Rohtak. The couple was stripped naked and beaten up by upper-castes residents of their village. In this case, the woman was gang raped by upper-caste men and then was 'pressurized' to withdraw her complaint. The *khap* panchayats, as an effort to resolve the problem of frequent gang rapes, passed the diktat *marry them young* to avoid rape cases. Subey Singh Nain, Pradhan of Binain Khap, said:

> Marrying the girls off early would prevent rapes.
>
> (Subey Singh Nain 70 years, Binain Khap Jaat Caste)

Marrying the girls off at the age of 16 will be good for them as they will have their husbands to take care of their sexual needs and hence they will not venture out of their home, according to the members of *khap* panchayat.

Another *khap* representative from Haryana said:

> Boys and girls should be married by the time they turn 16; so that they do not stray ... this will decrease the incidents of rape.
> (Subey Singh Nain 70 years, Binain Khap, Jaat Caste)

Another prominent *khap* member said:

> As soon as the children attain puberty, it is natural for them to have sexual desires but when these are not fulfilled, they stray ... so there should not be any minimum age limit for marriage.
> (Member of Binain Khap, 50 years, Jaat Caste)

As per the Constitution of India, legal age of marriage is 18 years for girls and 21 years for boys. In *khap land* of Haryana and Uttar Pradesh members of *khap* panchayats advocate an early marriage, even if that means defying law, especially for girls, as a strategy to prevent rapes. Hence, it is proposed that girls should be married off the age of 16 years. The Pradhan of Meham Chaubasi, when interviewed, opined that 'right age for a girl to get married is 14 years'. In rural Haryana, the parents of girl/s as well as the people at large forming a community, are always apprehensive about girls eloping with low caste boys. To avoid such incidents, they believe that girls should get married at a young age irrespective of the legal age of marriage. The whole burden of honour of the family, the caste and the village is placed on young girls, while boys are free to enjoy relationships, without any risk of losing honour. Such is the premium placed on honour that even gang rapes are justified in case a girl violates the *khap* diktats.

Common Justifications Offered for Gang Rapes

1. Girl getting into a relationship with a boy against the norms.
2. Gang rape of the sister as a revenge.

In January 2015, head of one village council in West Bengal sentenced a 22-year-old woman to be gang-raped for having a relationship with a man outside of her community. The 'punishment' was carried out by 13 neighbours whom the victim had known all her life. The community's strict policing of honour codes was pushed to an extreme. Notions of revenge and honour have always been intertwined. This reasoning of honour stands no logic.

In another case, a village head presiding over a kangaroo court ordered the rape of a 14-year-old girl in Jharkhand to punish her brother, who had sexually assaulted another woman of the village. Outdated views on family honour which see women as its repository are often responsible for such obnoxious acts committed in the name of honour. When women are seen as a source of honour, they risk being doubly victimized. Once by their families and communities, who zealously restrict their freedom, and a second time if they become target of those seeking revenge.

Girls' Education in *Khap* Belt: Fear of Sending Girls to Schools

In Haryana, educational institutions, especially after the basic education, are located at a distance from the village. Members of *khap* panchayats and local villagers in districts of Rohtak and Sonepat during interviews expressed their fear over sending their daughters to schools at a distant place. Community members were particularly anxious and concerned about the safety of their daughters. The fear of sexual violence, abuse/harassment, eve-teasing was commonly shared views by them. Notion of family, community honour and prestige also results in the girls' drop-out from the school. Similar findings were found in a study by Chander Suta Dogra in which she highlights that the girls were not sent to schools as villagers were of the firm belief that to educate girls was to invite disgrace on the family for they were '*sure to get involved with someone outside*' and bring disgrace to the family (Dogra 2015).

Dress Code Diktats by *Khaps*: Haryana and Uttar Pradesh Women to be Covered from Head to Toes

The decision of a self-styled *khap* panchayat to ban girls from wearing jeans has been endorsed by the heads of village councils, who too believe that the ban is necessary for preventing young couples in their villages from eloping. The *khap* panchayat led by Battisa Khap Council head Baba Suraj in Bhenswal village had on January 16 passed the diktat claiming that wearing jeans had a 'bad effect' on young women and incidents of eve-teasing had increased due to their 'objectionable clothes'.

> We believe that a woman should be covered from head to toe in loose fitting clothes that do not attract the male eye. Our idea of beauty is a woman whose hands alone are visible. Even her eyes should preferably be under a veil.
>
> (Rajinder Singh, vice-president of Barah Birohar Khap, 18 January 2011)

A member of a *khap* panchayat was even found to be advocating burqua for girls. Another diktat was passed in Uttar Pradesh banning girls from wearing jeans and keeping mobile phones claiming that these had a 'bad' effect on them and were responsible for eve-teasing incidents. Another panchayat of Gujjar community in Jadwad village has too passed a diktat banning wearing of jeans and use of mobile phones by unmarried girls.

During fieldwork it was found that majority of respondents, both men and women said:

> Wearing jeans is not good as boys get attracted to it and it gives rise to crimes.
>
> (Group discussions with men and women in Meham Khedi, district Rohtak)

One of the girls from *khap* belt said:

> I am ok with not wearing jeans and not using mobiles. We should keep control on ourselves.

The women folk especially the girls, since childhood, are taught to be submissive, to be quite, not to speak in front of elders, to wear a veil in front of elders, etc. They (women) too start believing that such diktats and acts are acceptable norms. Following this fatwa, a principal of a Model School in Rohtak has issued a dress code for girl students. Since the inception of the school, as back as in early 1950s, skirt down to the knees has been the dress for girl students. But now due to dress code by *khap* panchayat 'salwar kameez' has been introduced. What is disturbing about this fatwa is the ideology of Hindu Mahasabha and *khap* panchayats which have been demanding ban on jeans and mobile for girls on the ground that this attracts men and leads to molestation and rape.

Ban on use of Social Media, i.e. Whatsapp, Facebook and Mobile Phones

In November 2014, *khap* panchayat in Shoram village in Uttar Pradesh's Muzaffarnagar district passed a bizarre diktat, banning girls from wearing jeans, using mobile phones and the internet. The members of the *khap* panchayat also asked the residents of the villages not to use social networking websites such as WhatsApp and Facebook. *Khap's* diktat did not end with banning love marriages or mobile phones. It also advocated restrictions on wearing jeans for girls. It was believed that these 'objectionable clothes' had a bad effect on the villagers, provoking eve-teasing and encouraging young couples to elope.

Measures to Curb Female Foeticide

Khaps of Haryana, lately in news for issuing diktats like declaring a married couple as siblings, ostracizing families and killing in the name of honour, etc. can now be seen reforming their image by taking up serious social issues like female foeticide. Chaudhry (2014) stated that *khaps* have faced criticism relating to their structure. Traditionally women were not allowed to participate in the *khap* panchayats proceedings, though vital decisions concerning women's lives are taken. To overcome this criticism, a women wing of the Sarv *khap* Panchayats was made on 13 April 2010 but only for show and for documentation they were shown as existed. On one of the visits to a joint meeting held by Kandela *khap* of district Jind in the village Bibipur in July 2010, it was noticed that more than 200 *khaps* from all over India had came on a common platform. But there was hardly any representation of non-Jaats in that *khap* meeting, though that *khap* was labelled as 'Sarv Jaatiya Khap'. Even the representation of women, on the issue concerning women in general, was missing. No discussion on issues like female foeticide, increasing number of dowry cases and insecurity of the girls took place. There was no clear understanding of the problems and no effective organization structure existed during the 'Sarv Khap Meeting' on female foeticide. *Khaps* were trying to build their positive image using social issues like female foeticide. On the account of highly skewed sex ratio (877) and child sex ratio (830) and with the dismantling of the traditional *bhaichara* bondage in rural hinterland, girls in the villages feel highly insecure and even the problem of eve-teasing, molestation, sexual assault and gang rape, etc. are assuming alarming proportions in rural society. *Khaps* so far have not displayed any appropriate strategy that will curb this menace. Rather, the patriarchal mindset of locals and the *khaps* often tends to blame girls, their education, clothes, hair style, etc. For this phenomenon mindset of society at large results sometimes in penalizing the victims and letting of the wrong doers. *Khaps* often blame the media for highlighting them in negative but, on the other hand, media is the only cause where such atrocities can be brought to book and the nation gets involved in curbing such institutions wrong doing which ultimately affects the overall raising the progress of the country.

Khap Panchayats allow Inter-Caste Marriages (April 2014)

Marriage outside one's caste and within one's *gotra* is not allowed. It is against the principle of *khap bhaichara*. Recently in April 2014, Satrol Khap of Haryana allowed inter-caste marriages within 42 villages amending an age-old norm. The historic decision was taken by a five-member committee of the Satrol *khap* panchayat in village Narnaud. The panchayat also allowed marriages within 42 villages under its jurisdiction, which, till now, was banned. The *khap*, however, continued to ban inter-caste marriages in the same and bordering villages and the ban on same-*gotra* marriages also continues.

> The decision was taken in the wake of the declining male-female sex ratio in the State and the changing social fabric.

The current norms of marriage have existed for quite some time now and are believed to be some 600–700 years old. Now times have changed and one of the members of *khap* panchayat said:

> Nowadays, interaction between men and women has increased and it is not possible to keep them away from each other. Love affairs are very common.

During the fieldwork, members of a *khap* did say that changes were required in these age old norms yet overall changes seem a difficult task that needs to be handled tactfully, strategically and also while keeping the prestige of *khap* panchayats. Without involving *khap* panchayats, such revolutionary changes seem to be impossible to be put into effect. Hence *khaps* panchayats will have to be involved for bringing about structural changes in the agrarian patriarchal communities.

Conclusion

The age old institution of '*khap* panchayat' has now been brought to the limelight by media for their regressive dictates, their interferences in the personal lives of the villagers and their control of day-to-day affairs of the people. The ground realities as observed by the researcher were clearly visible that the harmonious relation that existed in the past was due to an age old orthodox ideology and the supremacy (numerical and economical) enjoyed by the *khap* members and is accepted by the villagers. This gender-biased, male-dominated and caste-based ideology is no more tenable in the developing states where government machinery has become active after 1959. The domination of *khap* panchayat as seen now is gradually eroding. *Khap* panchayats do not constitute legally elected bodies. The member of *khap* panchayat are predominantly 'Jaats' drawing their strength from their numbers (numerical strength) and landholdings. The concept of 'kinship', 'bhaichara' and 'gawand' also add to their power. *Khap* panchayat's orthodox ideology violates the basic fundamental human rights especially of the women and girls living in the *khap* belt of Haryana.

The Supreme Court too has openly acknowledged the existence of *khap* panchayat as an illegal, gender biased, orthodox and criminal minded body that needs to be plugged and rooted out of the system. These *khap* panchayats issues illegal fatwas on eloping couples. Dress codes for girls are issued and then they support illegal punishments such as rape of the women for violating the existing norms of 'khap bhaichara'. Orders are given in the village for lowering the marriage age of girls from 18–16 years. The punishment and fatwas are different for weaker sections of the society and those influential and powerful. The rules are different for men and women. Sometimes rules are relaxed for the boys but when it comes to girls the rules become very rigid and hard.

Justice Verma Committee has slammed *khap* panchayats for their influence on honour killings and called *khap* panchayats as an extra-constitutional body that restrains the right of men and women to select a partner of their choice and it has no sanction of law in India. The role of *khaps* is not only restricted to limiting a woman's right to choose her partner for matrimonial purpose but extends to putting restraints on her personal freedom and liberty. Be it the way she should be dressed and also lays restrictions on her movements and mobility. The Supreme Court of India has called *khap* panchayat's diktat on women dress code and putting restriction on women for carrying of mobile as unlawful. Such diktats are against basic human rights, i.e. the right to life and liberty and the right to freedom. 'Political leaders' takes no stand against their barbaric diktat. They remain silent because they draw vote banks from *khap* panchayat members. They equate *khap* panchayats with NGOs working for the social reforms of the society.

Khap panchayat system lacks transparency, accountability and objectivity. Hence the social, gender and other ground realities for the State development are being overlooked. This has called for a deep introspection as to whether this Khap Institution has kept up to the expectation of the villagers and the society as whole or as a hindrance in social structure. The society needs to be saved from its own erratic *khap* panchayats, since the functioning of this unconstitutional institution has disillusioned all. It is illustrative of the incredible debasement of our national character. Female foeticide, non-inclusive of female members in *khaps*, illegal dictates, issuing illegal fatwas, illogical and unaccountable suggestions and decisions have brought all legal agencies together to smoke them out of this system.

References

Aggarwal, P.C. 1971. *Caste, Religion and Power: An Indian Caste Study*. Delhi: Shri Ram Centre for Industrial Relations.

Census of India. 2011. New Delhi: Office of the Registrar General of India.

Chaudhry, D.R. 2014. *Khap Panchayat and Modern Age*. New Delhi: National Book Trust of India.

Chowdhry, P. 2004. 'Caste Panchayats and Policing of Marriages in Haryana: Enforcing Kinship and Territorial Exogamy'. *Contributions to Indian Sociology*, 38(1), 1–42.

—. 2006. *Contentious Marriages and Eloping Couples: Gender, Caste and Patriarchy in Northern India*. New Delhi: Oxford University Press.

Haralambos, M. and Heald, R.M. 1980. *Sociology: Themes and Perspectives*. New Delhi: Oxford University Press.

Hayden, R.M. 1999. *Disputes and Arguments Among Nomads: A Caste Council in India*. New Delhi: Oxford University Press.

Hughes, J.A., Sharrock, W.W. and Martin, P.J. 2003. *Understanding Classical Sociology*. New Delhi: Sage Publications (original work published in 1995).

Human Rights Watch. 2004. 'Honoring the Killers'. 16(1E), Human Rights Watch Publication.

Jafri, A.H. 2008. *Honour Killing: Dilemma, Rituals and Understanding*. New Delhi: Oxford University Press.

Kannabiran, K. and Singh, R. 2008. *Challenging the Rule(s) of Law: Colonialism, Criminology and Human Rights in India*. New Delhi: Sage Publications.

Kaur, Ravinder. 2010. 'Khap Panchayats, Sex Ratio and Female Agency'. *Economic and Political Weekly*, XLV(23), 14–16.

Khan, T.S. 2006. *Beyond Honour: A Historical Materialist Explanation of Honour Related Issues*. New Delhi: Oxford University Press.

Kumar, A. 2012. 'Khap Panchayats: A Socio-Historical Overview'. *Economic and Political Weekly*, XLVII(4), 59–64.

Miller, D.B. 1975. *From Hierarchy to Stratification: Changing Pattern of Social Inequality in a North Indian Village*. New Delhi: Oxford University Press.

Pradhan, M.C. 1966. *The Political System of Jats of Northern India*. New Delhi: Oxford University Press.

Ritzer, G. 1988. *Sociological Theory*. New Delhi: McGraw Hill (original work published in 1983).

Sanghwan, Jagmati. 2010. *In the Name of Honour: Let Us Love and Live*. Rohtak: All India Democratic Women's Association.

Sanghwan, K.S. 1986. *The Rural Elite and Multi-Village Panchayats in Haryana: The Case of Chaubisi in District Rohtak*. An unpublished Ph.D. thesis submitted to the Department of Sociology, Panjab University, Chandigarh.

—. 2008. 'Khap Panchayats in Haryana: Sites of Legal Pluralism', in Kalpana Kannabiran and Ranbir Singh (eds), *Challenging the Rule(s) of Law: Colonialism, Criminology and Human Rights in India*. New Delhi: Sage Publications, pp. 331–354.

Sharma, S. 2011. 'Haryana Mein Khap Panchayat Parampra', in *Encyclopedia of Haryana, Vol. 2: Itihaas Khand Bhaag 2*. New Delhi: Arun Maheshwari, pp. 198–210.

Singh, B. 1961. *Next Step in Village India: A Study of Land Reforms and Dynamics*. New Delhi: Asian Publishing House.

Singh, R. 2010. 'The Need to Tame the Khap Panchayats'. *Economic and Political Weekly*. 17–18. Vol. 45, No. 21.

Strauss, Anselm and Corbin, Juliet. 1990. *Basics of Qualitative Research: Grounded Theory Procedures and Techniques*. New Delhi: Sage Publications.

Welchman, Lynn and Hossain, S. 2005. *Honour: Crimes, Paradigms and Violence Against Women*. London: Zed Books.

Yadav, Bhupendra. 2009. 'Khap Panchayats: Stealing Freedom'. *Economic and Political Weekly*, XLIV(52), December, 16–18.

Newspaper Articles

Chaudhry, D.R. 11 April 2010. 'Bringing Khaps to Justice'. *The Tribune*, Chandigarh, p. 12.

——. 1 August 2010(a). 'Feudal Mindset in the Heart of Darkness'. *Sunday Herald*, p. 1.

——. 26 September 2010(b). 'Killings in the Khap Belt'. *The Tribune*, Chandigarh, p. 13.

Deswal, Deepender. 12 April 2012. 'Khaps Warn Against Film on Honour Killing in Festival'. *The Times of India*, Chandigarh.

Dogra, C.S. 2015 (April 12) 'India's Sons: What does it mean to be a Man in India?'. *Indian Express*.

Garg, Lajpat Rai. 1 August 2011. 'Govt Must Act to Stop Honour Killings'. *The Tribune*, Chandigarh.

Gayatri, Geetanjali. 26 April 2009. 'In the Name of Justice'. *The Sunday Tribune*, Chandigarh, p. 8.

Gill, Rajesh. 20 April 2012. 'Substance of a Woman'. *The Tribune*, Chandigarh.

Kumar, Ajay. 18 December 2011. 'Don't Let Khap Come in the Way of Love'. *Sunday Daily Post*, Chandigarh.

Mahapatra, Dhananjay. 15 January 2013. 'Khaps Diktats Retrograde, Illegal'. *The Times of India*.

Saini, Ravinder. 29 January 2012. 'Khap Panchayat Bans Cultivation of Paddy in Jhajjar Region'. *The Tribune*, Chandigarh.

Shukla, Vandana. 16 July 2012. 'Bibipur Women Stuck to Their Brief: An Analysis'. *The Tribune*, Chandigarh.

Venkatesan, J. 20 April 2011. 'Stamp Out Khap Panchayats: Court'. *The Hindu*.

Internet Sources

http://archive.asianage.com/columnists/not-justice-436

http://barandbench.com/content/212/khaps-history-now-becoming-burden#.u1t2r1x6nig

http://indiatvlb-1131326834.ap-southeast-1.elb.amazonaws.com/news/india/sc-says-khaps-diktat-on-women-s-dress-cellphone-ban-illegal-19661.html

http://timesofindia.indiatimes.com/india/khap-diktats-retrograde-illegal-sc/articleshow/18025504.cms

http://www.hindu.com/2011/04/20/stories/2011042065891300.htm

http://www.thehindu.com/news/national/other-states/khaps-say-early-marriage-can-curb-rape-cases/article3975235.ece

5

From Critical Theorizing to Sociological Appreciation

Locating the *'Ishq'* amidst *'Ijjazat'*, *'Izzat'* and *'Lok Biradari'*

Rakesh Thakur

The central concern of this paper is to understand the dynamics of the processes that goes into the creation of an extremely fecund masculine category of *'mardaangi'* (manhood/masculinity). It is imperative to understand this at a conceptual level so as to delve deep into the process underlying the creation of 'lok biradari' (local community). At another level, this commonality of masculine affiliation, often kin based, in turn is the bedrock on which the patriarchy perpetuates itself. The paper would argue that this understanding is rooted in patriarchal structure which cuts across different regions of north India. The patriarchal structure is extremely fecund when it comes to reproducing the ideals of family, marriage and the submissive *'adarsh nari'* (the ideal woman), primarily a male social construction. This scheme of things has continued since ages only to be punctuated by instances of brutal violence, whenever a woman, whether it be, *'beti'* (daughter), *'behan'* (sister), *'bahu'* (daughter-in-law), *'bhabhi'* (sister-in-law) or any female kin, has expressed her desire to take decisions contrary to the patriarchal values. In this paper the term *'ishq'* is suffused with multi-layer connotations. Primarily it is used as a symbol to denote a capacity within a woman about making choices over one's own body (sexual and reproductive) and adhering to these choices according to her own free will. Likewise, the paper argues that the idea of 'ishq', amidst difficult terrain, is not entirely new. Whenever the individual feminine behaviour becomes a threat to patriarchy, it elicits varied responses and honour killing is one of the extreme reactions by the collective manifested in this ghastly and violent act. Honour-based violence is a common occurrence cutting across a variety of cultures and communities. It has been widely reported in countries like Iran, Afghanistan, Turkey, India, Pakistan, France, Canada, Germany and many other nation-states. Honour killing is the most extreme form of honour-based violence in which an accused person, mostly a girl or a woman, is brutally murdered by the members of her own family or community. Thus, what is happening in India is not an isolated phenomenon but the patterns cut across the patriarchal globe. Undoubtedly the expression of individuality (agency) as a pronounced expression has evoked profound and dangerous diatribe from the collective.

With the churning of time, change is inevitable which is reflected in the subtle storm brewing across these patriarchal bastions. There is a hint of resistance and change where individual feminine agency is subverting the established patriarchal order. The feminine is decisively deciding the trajectory that her life would undertake, even at times at the cost of *'zindagi'* (life) itself. Thus, women's free will, i.e. *'marzi'* comprises the agency contesting and resisting the patriarchal structure comprising of *'ijjazat'* (permission), *'izzat'* (honour), and *'lok biradari'* (community).

In this essay, which is a sociological chronicling of social change, the sociological imagination would locate the discourse amidst the thematic concerns of 'domination', 'collaboration' and 'resistance'. The paper would interpolate these with the socio-historical constructs like 'jaat' (caste) and 'biradari' (community) as the pillars of patriarchal and feudal society. To understand the patriarchal construct, the term Lok Biradari (a conglomeration of 'jaati' based collectives cutting across region) would be used as a nom de plume to encompass the varied patriarchal connotations which it carries. Moreover, it would be argued that the troika of *'ijjazat'* (permission), *'izzat'* (honour) and *'lok biradari'* (Community) conspires to create a grand narrative of the 'righteousness' which not only belittles the *'Marzi'* (individual wish) of 'her being' but sets the mood underlying the acute gender inequality across Haryana, Punjab, Rajasthan, Uttar Pradesh in particular and the Hindi heartland in general.

At the theoretical level the paper borrows from Anthony Giddens the structure-agency debate, in an attempt to provide theoretical underpinnings to the understanding of honour killings in the Indian society. For Giddens, structure and action/agency are two sides of the same coin. Neither structure nor action can exist independently; both are intimately related and complimentary. To understand this process, it is important to analyse the inherent dynamics underlying 'social order' and 'social reproduction'. The question which Giddens raises is that if individuals find it difficult to act in any way that they fancy, what is the nature of those invisible social forces which provide resistance? Giddens provides an answer by drawing an analogy with language: although language only exists in those instances where we speak or write, people react strongly against others who disregard its rules and conventions. In a similar way, the 'rules' of social order may only be 'in our heads'; they are not usually written down, and often have no formal force to back them up, but nevertheless, people can be shocked when seemingly minor social expectations are not adhered to.

So people's everyday actions reinforce and reproduce a set of expectations and it is this set of other people's expectations which make up the 'social forces' and 'social structures' that sociologists talk about. As Giddens puts it, 'Society only has form, and that form only has effects on people, in so far as structure is produced and reproduced in what people do' (Giddens and Pierson 1998: 77).

In this backdrop, this paper argues that though in contemporary India 'ishq' is primordially understood as a romantic conception, it is imperative to locate the feminine 'ishq' amidst the patriarchal maze; it has to be understood, at least in part, in relation to its particular socio-cultural and politico-historical contexts. This is important because the conceptualization of the term and its socio-cultural and political implications help us position the question as to how does the empowerment conundrum falters at the door step of '*beti–vyvahar*' (daughter's code of conduct) which is a cardinal 'rites of passage' in an individual's life and then for her family and finally the '*jaati*' centric *biradari*, to which her family belongs.

Honour is the most cherished value in the Indian sub-continental patriarchal families. Families gain and lose honour through money, power and improper behaviour of women. Actions appropriate to the normative codes (structure) maintain the purity and honour of the family, lineage and caste while non-adherence to these normative codes defiles it. The ideology of honour is a gendered notion where both men and women embody it in totally different ways. The women as sisters and daughters are the repositories of 'family honour'/*izzat* of their own families. Further, after a woman gets married, she becomes the repository of *izzat* of her husband's family as '*lugai*',' '*biwi*' (wife), and '*bahu*' (daughter-in-law). On the other hand, men in case of the family in which she is born, i.e. father, brothers, and after marriage, the in-laws (father/brother) and husband are regulators of this '*izzat*'. The greatest threat to this honour lies in the woman; her body and conduct, due to her reproducing and procreating capacity. Thus, by imposing controls over a woman's sexuality and her choices and by evoking the notions of 'honour' and 'dishonour', families condition women into distinguishing between appropriate (righteous) and inappropriate (shameful) behaviour. Any inappropriate behaviour like refusing to enter an arranged marriage, being in a relationship disapproved by family, having sex outside marriage, dressing in certain ways, etc. is seen as an attack on family honour. The honour thus lost is then sought to be restored through honour-based violence and in most cases by honour killing of the wayward women. The '*marzi*' of women is seen as a threat to the normative in-practice pattern which is the bedrock on which the age old patriarchal structure survives.

Traditionally, the boundaries of a caste had been maintained by prohibition of food and marital transactions (called '*roti vyavahar*' and '*beti vyavahar*' in north India) with members of other castes. It is the prohibition of inter-caste, inter-religion, intra-*gotra*, inter- and intra-regional marriages which are an indication of forcible imposition of the male dominated hierarchical patriarchy, rigidly segmenting the whole region into various mutually rival groups. Violation of traditional marriage norms and inter-caste marriages account for most cases of killings in the name of preserving honour. The traditional norms of marriage include caste endogamy, *gotra* exogamy, hypergamy and village or territorial exogamy. The principles of caste endogamy and hypergamy are seen as central to the rules of marriage as these help in the social reproduction of caste and its purity as a system. The concepts of 'honour' and 'shame' operate to restore the male dominance which is presumed to have been compromised and endangered by the post-colonial legal empowerment of women in India. As defined by Abu Odeh, honour crime is the killing of a woman by her father or brother for engaging in or being suspected of engaging in sexual practices before or outside marriage (Welchman and Hossain 2005) and includes different types of manifest violent behaviour against her like assault, confinement, imprisonment, interference with choice in marriage, declaring her to be minor and insane including her brutal murder (Welchman and Hossain 2005). Gender-based violence against women is defined as violence directed against a woman because she is a woman and affects her disproportionately (Welchman and Hossain 2005: 24). By invoking the twin notions of honour and dishonour, the families try to regulate the inappropriate behaviour of a woman. What is sacred and inviolable is *izzat* or *gairat*, i.e. honour and it is always presumed to be justified to kill and die for honour (Omvedt 1990: 5–6). An action to uphold honour or *izzat* is always a male prerogative while women may only incite action. Different types of contentious and mixed marriages like those violating the rule of caste endogamy, territorial exogamy, religious exogamy, widow remarriage and *gotra* exogamy are treated as an attack upon *izzat* (Welchman and Hossain 2005) and have invariably led to honour crimes, confrontations and violence in India. The agricultural caste groups in northern India follow caste endogamy in addition to village, clan and territorial exogamy while settling marriages. Within the same caste, Hindus follow the rule of *gotra* exogamy. The concept of caste honour is usually appropriated by the upper castes in India who do not recognize any honour being possessed by the lower caste groups (Chowdhary 2007: 19). While inter-caste marriages are believed to weaken the differences existing among the different caste groups and disturb the caste hierarchies, it is particularly a marriage or a love affair between a high caste girl and a low caste boy, which is severely contested and criminalized. Even the police and the judiciary at times act as mute spectators and passive supporters of the honour protectors. The punishment for violating the rule of endogamy and exogamy is expulsion and excommunication of both families from the caste and village apart from the killing of the mother and child and even sometimes ritual death (Chakravarti 2003: 68). The rules of ex-communication are horrendous since no one would dine, drink, socialize or transact economically with the outcaste, the barber would not offer his services, the Brahman would refuse to perform religious functions, no man would marry his children and the attendants of the dead would refuse to perform the funeral rites (Banerjee-Dube 2008: 71). In northern India, particularly in the Haryana region, young persons are challenging the caste and kinship ideologies upheld by the senior male members of the castes by breaching the sexual codes and taboos, by defying demands of caste status, hypergamy and village exogamy and are thereby, discarding the notions of traditional honour. Elopement of the young couples in love in defiance of their family, caste and village customs and sentiments result in direct violence perpetrated by the male family members on them and more particularly on the girl. Breach of the caste and community moral norms as also the family and kinship codes by a woman leads to greater social resistance and protest since it is treated as a direct attack on the patriarchal power and is deemed fit to be crushed, controlled and channelled. Women's respectability determines that of the men, family and the whole caste. This kind of social ethos leads to either killing the woman or forcing her to commit suicide by the family members. Many times, she is forced to enter into a greatly compromised marriage where the bridegroom is either a widower, an old man, a man with children, a handicapped or a drunkard, not matching her educational qualifications or a fit for nothing person. Thereafter, the family severs all connections with her (Chowdhary 2007: 10–11). Whenever, a young couple elopes after marriage or for marrying, usually the girl's family tries to criminalize their action and contest the validity of the marriage. It is alleged that the girl is a minor and charges of kidnapping, abduction, wrongful confinement or rape are slapped against her husband and his family members for harassing them. For the loss of their family's honour, the honour of the offending family is attacked. This strategy is adopted to force the married couple to surface or to withdraw from the much disputed marriage. After surfacing, in majority of the cases, the couple runs the risk of humiliation, physical injury, death and decisions of caste panchayat. Death penalty is regarded as a valid method of retrieving the lost honour. At times, the woman is pressurized by her own family to endorse the allegation of her kidnapping or is sometimes solitarily confined by the family members or is sent to the state run protective homes (Welchman and Hossain 2005: 308–330). For re-establishing the family honour, presumed guilty girl or woman must be retrieved and punished and cannot be disowned. Usually absorbing her back into the traditional *biradari* network being a difficult task, her physical elimination appears to be a better honourable option open to her family. She is made to take the stigma which can be removed only by extinguishing her, i.e. the object of dishonour. On the contrary, no stigma is attached to the perpetrators of the honour crimes who are absolved of their guilt on the premise that sacrificing the natural bonds of love and kinship for preserving and restoring honour purifies the family. Rampant in north India, honour crimes are slowly showing their ugly head even in other parts of the country. Failing to resist effectively due to their filial values and familiarity with the perpetrator, Indian women have been the victims of humiliation, torture and exploitation and face the risk of the worst forms of violence, terror, deprivation, discrimination and devaluation. Moreover, violence and such crimes being behind 'closed doors' hardly leave any remedy for them. Preservation of family honour at all costs results into her safety, choices and rights being compromised.

Khap panchayats are at centre of terrorizing the social scene with their ominous presence. *Jaat-Biradari Panchayat* (*khap* panchayat), the governing body of each caste in India, enforces conduct appropriate to the caste. The caste and village councils exercise complete control on an individual's conduct (Devi 1998: 48). Being part of the socio-political life of village communities, they are informal decision-making caste-based bodies consisting of the elderly and wise men drawn from their respective castes. They are mostly dominated by the land-owning classes and the upper caste members who are not elected or self-appointed but are the members by consensus of the community and sometimes hold the post by heredity (Chowdhary 2007: 33–35, 96). Since caste perpetuates through the institution of marriage (Rajshekar 2007), the dominant caste in the region arrogates to itself the power of regulating the marriage behaviour of the endogamous groups (Chakravarti 2003: 33–34). The size and composition of the panchayat vary with the gravity of the problem (Chowdhary 2007: 97–98). *khap* panchayat, an endogamous, clannish institution, usually a Jat body exists around Delhi, some parts of Haryana, western Uttar Pradesh and the adjoining areas. It is a *gotra* centric panchayat covering a cluster of villages dominated by a particular *gotra* of Jats. All *khap* members are supposedly linked through blood and a common genealogy leading to the evolution of many marital taboos and the ban on same village and same *gotra* marriages. Marriages within the neighbouring villages belonging to other *khaps* are also banned. Any marriage in violation of these rules is met with stringent punishments and barbaric edicts by the *khap* panchayats like annulling the marriage, declaring the married couple as siblings and dissolving their marital tie, ostracizing the families and ordering killings, (Chaudhry 2010), temporary or permanent ex-communication, corporal punishment, religious expiation (Kuppuswamy 1989: 185, 192; Gupta 1991: 37) or forcing the girl to divorce her husband. Death executed by the caste panchayats is one of the worst articulations of violence. Usually, violence and death are considered preferable to condoning or accepting a mixed marriage (Chowdhary 2007: 163). The sanctions also include nominal or substantial fining, ritual expiation, public humiliation which means blackening the face or rubbing the nose in dust before the aggrieved party or the entire gathering, touching other's feet, shaving the head or drinking or dipping the nose in the urine of one or more persons, beating, giving feast to the caste members, outcasting, expelling from the village or requiring the offender to repent by seeking forgiveness of the village elderly (Chowdhary 2007: 98–100). Outcasting being a serious punishment requires the approval of an inter-village panchayat of the caste members (Chowdhary 2007: 100). Thus, the much disapproved inter-caste marriages are usually resolved by the family members in a confidential way by forceful elimination of the couple or the girl. But, when the news spreads in the wider community, it is tackled by the community acting through the traditional caste panchayat wielding wide dictatorial power as extra-judicial authorities, with almost no legal knowledge and imposing justice according to its own notions. Applying and enforcing repressive gender and caste codes, these attempt to operate as parallel legal systems in the country. The intervention of these traditional bodies has been at the cost of individual rights, more particularly woman's rights (Chowdhary 2007: 12–14, 139). In many cases, even if a family approves an inter-caste marriage or itself arranges such marriage, the caste panchayats have objected to such marriages and have penalized the families by expelling them from the biradari or by socially boycotting them (Chowdhary 2007: 168–172). *Biradari* refers to not just one concrete structural unit at the village level but rather to patrilineal connection, real, putative or fictional and includes the agnates and cognates. It sometimes refers to the entire village, irrespective of the differences in caste, class or creed. Observing the norms of the *biradari* is must for the *izzat* of the caste, group or village. *Biradari* uses caste panchayats for settling issues of marriage and sexual affairs amongst other matters (Chowdhary 2007: 95–96). Each caste has its own *biradari* to enforce its rules but when the matter cannot be settled by the caste panchayat of a particular caste group due to a few households of that caste in a village, it is usually referred to the dominant caste of the region which then assumes the power of enforcing the internal behaviour of the endogamous group (Chowdhary 2007: 150). For deciding a matter, the traditional panchayat mobilizes a large number of people on the basis of family, kin, got, caste, community and village, even from outside the local area, making the panchayat all the more powerful. The dominant caste leaders settle the dispute of the castes below them only by the unanimous consensus of the presiding leaders. If they do not agree, the panchayat meeting is dissolved without any decision being taken. Later, either a similar panchayat or a larger panchayat involving many more villages is reconvened. Any decision to which the powerful elements in the village strongly oppose cannot be taken. But a powerful person can ignore the wishes of the majority, if he had not participated in the decision or disagrees with it. Once the decision is taken, its enforcement is the responsibility of the leaders of the village in which the penalized party lives (Chowdhary 2007: 98–100). As per the recent diktat issued by the *khap* Maha-Panchayat, killings cannot be avoided in same *gotra* marriages since they are immoral in the Hindu society and should be banned and the guilty should be punished (Pandey 2010). Thus, the Indian social-set up operates as the major catalysing factor behind the increasing rate of the honour crimes committed against women in India.

Today, prohibition of food transactions has ceased to act as a barrier between castes. Marriage remains as the last and strongest bastion for the preservation of caste. Caste endogamy helps in maintaining the purity of caste and ensures the perpetuation of caste exclusivity. Women are considered as the 'gateways' of a caste. It then becomes essential that a woman's sexuality is protected and policed in order to safeguard the purity of a caste. The rule of hypergamy (principle of a woman marrying a man ranking higher than her in caste status) also acts as a tool of maintaining caste purity. Historically, caste is related to control over land and other productive resources. In many areas the status-based hierarchy of caste overlaps with class hierarchies. This helps to explain why dominant caste groups zealously guard their caste boundary which is seen in their violent reaction to marriage which transgresses traditional marriage norms. Thus, caste embodies both social and material power. Marriages which seek to diminish this social and material power are again seen as an attack on honour ultimately leading to honour killing. Earlier, it was only the upper caste members who were conscious of maintaining their caste purity. Of late, control over women's sexuality and endogamy has been considered as a means of caste mobility through the process of sanskritization by imitating the ritual practices of the higher castes. Thus, honour killing is now practiced across all caste groups especially the dominant castes.

Such killings are motivated by the perception that the actions (*marzi*) of an accused person (the woman) have brought dishonour to the family or the collective denomination (family/up-*jati*/village/*khap*) which constitutes the structure on which patriarchy thrives. The immediate family or the concerned up-*Jati* of the girl and the boy or the territorial village or the all-encompassing *khap*; all these are inherently intertwined. Sociologically it can be argued that whether at a personal level, or in familial interaction or amidst community living, people go through a socialization process, being heavily dependent on the existing social structures, yet at the same time social structures are being altered by their activities. Put in different words, this means that social structures are the medium of human activities as well as the result of those activities. Interestingly social structures not only restrict behaviour but also create possibilities for human behaviour. The point is, it is not all about the restrictions people encounter in unrolling their behaviour in space and time, but people also contribute to the creation of a certain time-space structure. The whole socio-cultural churning in north India regarding the rules of mate selection can be understood within the prism of this structure agency debate. The loosening of the old social fabric and creation of new social tapestry is an ongoing process, but sadly afflicted by violence and honour killing.

Structuration theory is based on the premise that the classic actor/structure dualism has to be reconceptualized as a duality, i.e. the duality of structure. The structural properties of social systems exist only in so far as forms of social conduct are reproduced chronically across time and space. The structuration of institutions can be understood in terms of how it comes about that social activities become 'stretched' across wide spans of time-space. In structuration theory, 'structure' is regarded as rules and resources recursively implicated in social reproduction; institutionalized features of social systems have structural properties in the sense that relationships are stabilized across time and space. 'Structure' can be conceptualized abstractly as two aspects of rules, i.e. normative elements and codes of signification. Giddens further elaborates that resources are also of two kinds: authoritative resources, which derive from the co-ordination of the activity of human agents, and allocative resources, which stem from control of material products or of aspects of the material world (Giddens 1984).

Giddens' main claim for his theory is that it draws together the two principal strands of social thinking. In the structuralist tradition, the emphasis is on structure (constraint), whereas in the phenomenological and hermeneutic traditions the human agent is the primary focus. Giddens' theory of structuration explores the question of whether it is individual or social forces that shape our social reality. He eschews extreme positions, arguing that although people are not entirely free to choose their own actions, and their knowledge is limited, they nonetheless form the agency which reproduces the social structure and leads to social change. Giddens writes that the connection between structure and action is a fundamental element of social theory; structure and agency form a duality that cannot be conceived of apart from one another and his main argument is contained in his expression 'duality of structure'. At a basic level, this means that people make society, but are at the same time get constrained by it. Action and structure cannot be analysed separately, as structures are created, maintained and changed through actions, while actions are given a meaningful form only through the background of the structure. The line of causality, therefore, runs in both directions making it impossible to determine what is changing what. In Giddens' own words (from *New Rules of Sociological Method: A Positive Critique of Interpretative Sociologies* 1976: 104): 'The production of interaction has three fundamental elements: its constitution as 'meaningful'; its constitution as a moral order; and its constitution as the operations of relations of power.'

In this regard he defines structures as consisting of rules and resources involving human action; the rules constrain the actions, the resources make it possible. He also differentiates between systems and structures: 'The duality of structure'. Giddens is of the view that social actions create structures, and it is through these social actions that structures are produced and reproduced, so that they survive over time. Indeed, Giddens (1984) uses a single word, 'structuration', to describe the way that structures relate to social actions, so that certain sets of social relationships survive over space and time. Giddens talks about the 'duality of structure' to suggest both that structures make social action possible, and at the same time that social action creates those very structures. He says, 'structure has no existence independent to the knowledge that agents have about what they do in their day-to-day activity'. In other words, it is you, I, and, i.e. every other individual, who create structures. Giddens identify two aspects of structure; 'rules' and 'resources', in everyday life. He further elaborates that rules are procedures that individuals may follow in their social life. Sometimes interpretations of these rules are written down: for example, in the form of laws or bureaucratic rules. Such written expressions are not the rules themselves. Thus, a rule might state that shopping involves paying a shop assistant, while the written interpretation of a rule of this sort might be the law of theft. Members of society can reproduce such structural rules, or the rules can be changed through the development of new patterns of interaction. The second aspect of structure, resources, also comes into being through human actions and can be changed or maintained by them. Resources take two forms: allocative resources and authoritative resources. Allocative resources include raw materials, land, technology, instruments of production, and goods. For Giddens, such resources are never just there, given by nature; these only become resources through human actions. Constraints, according to Giddens, do not therefore determine actions, but operate 'by placing limits upon the range of options open to an actor'. In society, humans are constrained by the existence of power relationships. Giddens sees all social action as involving power relationships. He sees power as the ability to make a difference, to change things from what they would otherwise have been, or as he puts it, 'transformative capacity'. For Giddens, the idea of human agency involves the idea of transformative capacity, and this capacity of power may be used to change things, or the actions of other people. It can, therefore, be used to exercise power over other people, and so constrain people and reduce their freedom. At the same time, though, power also increases the freedom of action of the agents who possess it. What restricts one person enables another to do more. Structures are the 'rules and resources' embedded in agents' memory traces. Agents call upon their memory traces of which they are 'knowledgeable' to perform social actions. 'Knowledgeability' refers to 'what agents know about what they do, and why they do it.' Giddens divides memory traces (*structures-within-knowledgeability* into three types:

- Domination (power): Giddens also uses 'resources' to refer to this type. Authoritative resources allow agents to control persons, whereas allocative resources allow agents to control material objects.
- Signification (meaning)
- Legitimation (norms): Giddens sometimes uses 'rules' to refer to either signification or legitimation. An agent draws upon these *stocks of knowledge* via memory to inform him or herself about the external context, conditions, and potential results of an action.)

When an agent uses these structures for social interactions, they are called *modalities* and present themselves in the forms of facility (domination), interpretive scheme/communication (signification) and norms/sanctions (legitimation).

Though honour killings have been historically persistent, it has only recently received wide media attention globally. As a result, honour crimes are being highlighted as a social evil in a modern society where there is conflict between traditional and modern values. Githa Hariharan, in her article in the *Telegraph* (dated Sunday, 10 October 2004) titled 'Bloodthirsty Honour' wrote:

> In India, adults may vote, but they cannot marry who they choose what is this terrible 'honour' that wreaks such pain and terror on people simply because two young people have exercised their right to choose their partner. It is an honour that tends to attach itself to rigid codes, usually caste or religious codes. It also tends to be a code formulated by the male elite so their 'honour' can flourish in the patriarchal framework. This is the sort of honour that celebrates women committing johar or mass sati; I remember an obnoxious sound and light show I took my children to years ago in Gwalior which placed the achievements of Tansen and women committing 'suicide' on an equally glorious footing.

It is a useful thing to perpetuate a tradition of martyrdom, especially when women's bodies are vulnerable to being viewed as the vessels of national honour. It was this unholy honour that provided the motive for otherwise 'normal' men to kill their own sisters and wives and mothers during the Partition 'disappearances' and murders which have been covered by a conspiracy of silence, and by the more acceptable belief that these women were abducted or killed by men from the other side. In her book *The Other Side of Silence,* Urvashi Butalia takes on this myth that the perpetrators of violence were always 'outsiders'. She writes about a man she interviewed in Amritsar, Mangal Singh, whose family killed 17 of its women and children. He refuses to use the word killed; he says they became 'martyrs' in keeping with Sikh pride. The women, he says, were willing to become martyrs: 'The real fear was one of dishonour.' But, asks Butalia, who had the pride and the fear? It is not a question that Mangal Singh was willing to examine. Similarly, in *Borders and Boundaries: Women in India's Partition*, Ritu Menon records the account of a Partition survivor, Durga Rani. In this account, two types of honour killings occur: one in anticipation of dishonour; the other as a way to cope with dishonour. Consider, on the one hand: 'In the villages of Head Junu, Hindus threw their young daughters into wells, dug trenches and buried them alive. Some were burnt to death, some were made to touch electric wires to prevent the Muslims from touching them.' On the other hand, Durga Rani gives us an idea of what happened to many women who had been abandoned after being raped and disfigured. They could not be 'kept' any longer because their 'character' was now spoilt. In some cases, as in that of a girl who was raped by 10 or more men, the only way to deal with the dishonour was murder; the girl, says Durga Rani, was burnt by her father.

All these years after Partition, this dishonourable honour still stalks the land, wreaking its barbaric violence on both men and women, but preferably on women.

Most cases are reported from Punjab, Haryana and parts of western Uttar Pradesh. The statistics are disturbing: 23 such murders were reported during 2002 and 2003 in Muzaffarnagar alone. Thirty-five young couples were declared 'missing'. And in Punjab and Haryana, one out of every 10 murders is an honour killing. In most of the cases, where the girl is from an upper caste, the boy is the target of violence, usually by the girl's family. Often, girls who are murdered for 'destroying the honour of the family' are cremated without any legal formalities and the deaths concealed.

Behind the statistical wall is a collection of stories that tell of violence and fear unleashed on the basis of a shameful rationale. In Hoshiarpur, Punjab, 22-year-old Geeta Rani, a Rajput woman, married Jasvir, the son of the only *Jaat* family in the village. Her parents did not object to the match. But the Rajputs in Jasvir's village, including a suspended police officer, decided to 'teach him a lesson' for marrying one of 'their' women.

Within two months of the marriage, he was killed after which his hands and legs were cut off. One hand was thrown into Jasvir's aunt's house. Now, the widowed Geeta and her widowed mother-in-law live in fear, struggling to pay security guards to keep them safe. 'Not even the nightmare of the 1984 riots was this bad,' says the mother-in-law.

In Jhajjar, a Jaat woman from Talav village married a Dalit. She was forced to return to her father's home, and there both she and her sister were murdered. So were a Dalit woman and a man, who were accused of helping the girl to elope. The villagers who recounted the story were clear about one thing: the administration was careful to protect the upper castes.

Several of these cases illustrate not only the violation of the right to choose a marriage partner, but also the role caste panchayats play in perpetuating illegal and inhuman social codes. Among the other states, Gujarat being a good example, increased communalization has led to more intolerance, and more violence in cases of Hindu-Muslim marriages. In a country that is blessed with all kinds of communities, intermarriage is not only a constitutional right of every adult citizen, but also the inevitable way to celebrate the bonds among us. There is very little point in sending our children to schools or allowing them to vote, in short, in pretending they are adults 'if they cannot marry who they choose.'

In India, the tradition of honour killing was first viewed in its most horrible form during Partition when many women were forcefully killed so that family honour could be preserved. Today even after 69 years of Independence, economic growth and development, honour killings continue to plague our society. Honour killings are widely prevalent and cut across the regional, caste, class, urban, rural and religious identities. Media reporting of killing of innocent couples in love like Manoj and Babli, Bhavana and Abhishek and many others show the society its ugly side.

Honour killings are a blatant violation of the fundamental rights enshrined in the Indian Constitution. The right to equality, right to life and personal liberty, right against exploitation are certain fundamental rights which are compromised during the crime of honour killing. Also, honour killing goes against the human rights and women rights as declared by the United Nations.

The Supreme Court of India has also taken a stern view of honour killings. It has described honour killings as among the 'rarest of rare' cases, thus advocating capital punishment for it. In the view of the Court pronouncements, honour killings are barbaric and feudal practices which need to be stamped out as they are a blot on the nation. It has also observed that there is nothing honourable in such honour killings. Describing honour killings as the 'rarest of rare' cases, the Supreme Court said those behind the crime should get the death sentence.

'This is necessary as a deterrent for such outrageous, uncivilised behaviour. All persons who are planning to perpetrate 'honour' killings should know that the gallows await them,' a bench comprising Justice Markandey Katju and Justice Gyan Sudha Misra said.

'In our opinion honour killings, for whatever reason, come within the category of rarest of rare cases deserving death punishment,' the judges said. The observation assumes significance because life imprisonment is the usual punishment for murder convicts and the death sentence is an exception, awarded only in the rarest of rare cases.

Justifying capital punishment for honour killings, Justice Katju, who wrote the judgment for the bench, said it was time to stamp out these barbaric, feudal practices which are a slur on the nation. "There is nothing honourable in honour killings and they are nothing but barbaric and brutal murders by bigoted persons with feudal minds,' he said.

The strong views expressed by the Supreme Court in its various judgments against honour killing along with the certain provisions of the Indian Constitution should ordinarily be a good deterrent against such practices. However, it is seen that honour killings continue to persist as they are rooted in strong socio-cultural traditions and, therefore, have some sanction of the society.

In northern India, particularly in Haryana, young persons are challenging the caste and kinship ideologies upheld by the senior male members of the caste by breaching sexual codes and taboos, by defying demands of caste status, hypergamy and village exogamy and thereby discarding the notion of honour. Elopement of the young couples who want to live life on their own terms/destiny assertive individual choices in defiance of their family, caste and village customs results in direct violence perpetrated by the male family members on them and more particularly on the girl. A dishonourable act by a woman leads to greater social pressure and protest since it is treated as a direct attack on the patriarchal power. The social thought that woman's respectability determines that of the man, family and the whole caste leads to either killing the woman or forcing her to commit suicide by the family members.

Locating the conditions of rural hinterland in northern India within the structuration theory, the structure-agency narrative can be viewed in the following manner. Whenever a young couple, the primary determinant being the feminine gender (agency), tries to subvert the existing patriarchal norms and listens to its individualistic yearnings in opposition to collective sentiments and takes recourse to the law of the land to elope and to marry, the girl's (agency) family (a unit of structure) tries to criminalize their action and contest the validity of their marriage. The girl and her individuality are seen as an anathema by the structure at large. Out here the structure resists the usurpation of its binding norms and values as a sacrilege. In context of the structuration theory the primordial unit which collectively defines the structure is the family and it is these many families forming a clan, living in a geographical region, belonging to an exogamous unit and thus leading to a formulation of *bhaichara*, (brotherhood). These *bhaichara* (brotherhood) based over a large geographical region would have been formed based on agro-centric primordial clannish ties. This *bhaichara* is a patriarchal umbrella which protects the long cherished established norms of patriarchal discourse existing in the cultural scape of northern India. The reproduction and continuous existence of this cultural scape can be understood as 'structure'. Structure is regarded as rules and resources. Recursively implicated in social reproduction. The institutionalized features of social systems have structural properties in the sense that relationships are stabilized across time and space. In villages these are more pronounced, stabilized and acquire violent overtones. The opposition demonstrated by the *biradari*, the *bhaichara* which constitute the patriarchal structure, is not only emotive but has strong political and cultural overtones as this union also usurps the rules of *betivyvahar* consisting of rules and resources involving human action; the rules constrain the actions, the resources make it possible. The structure to make the matter worse for the agency conspires in the name of *izzat*; cries foul at the union against its *ijjazat* and, thus, portray the Lok Biradari as under threat. It is alleged by the family that the girl is a minor and charges of kidnapping, abduction, rape, etc. are slapped against her husband and his family members. Many a times these charges are fictitious and are couched in falsehood. Usually, the protectors of law too have sympathy with the members of the girl's family as they also come from the same social background, in terms of kinship alliances, and *jaati* solidarity. In this region selection in government jobs and electoral victory of a candidate at political hustings is more based on the *jaati* (caste) to which he belongs to, rather than his qualifications pertaining to job or his qualities as a public servant. As a result, many a times the police too, instead of thwarting the barbaric diktats of *khap* panchayats, facilitate the continuous hounding and harassment of the defiant young couple even if they are legally married in Haryana and Punjab. Such marriages seek to further erode the caste differences and this results into a strong backlash by the dominant Jaat community. The notoriety of *khap* panchayat is a testimony to the ways in which the structure tries to reaffirm itself. The control over authoritative and allocative resources roles played by *khap* panchayats has led to severe form of torture, killing and other types of harassment of the young couples which marry against customary norms and traditions.

Violence against women clubbed with the prohibition on marital choice is a total negation of their rights. The right to choose a life partner at the time of marriage constitutes an integral part of her right to self-preservation. In a modern society, the rule of law along with the rights of individuals needs to be given credence over outdated traditions. The Hindu Marriage Act, 1956 and the Special Marriage Act, 1959 allow for same *gotra* and inter-caste marriages respectively. These laws were made so that social divisions in society can be reduced and all communities can live peacefully with each other. There is a need to control the power of the *khaps* as these are extra-legal bodies encroaching upon the rights and freedom on innocent couples. In changing times, *khaps* need to introspect and adapt to social changes taking place in society; a beginning has been made in this direction by the Satrol *Khap* in Haryana which has allowed inter-caste marriage. Women need to be made more educated and aware of their rights so as to defend themselves against such inhuman practices. Legal reforms are also required along with changes in the justice and criminal system that must support young couples and save their lives and dignity. Thus, the solution to the problem of honour crimes lies in the combination of women empowerment, gender sensitization, social awareness and legal reforms. Love is not a crime and honour killing is no solution. The patriarchal societies need to understand this and reconcile their traditional customs and norms with modern times. The time has come where the chroniclers of contemporary times share the concern of *ishq* (agency) and the righteous rebelliousness is being celebrated as an antidote to the overbearing cultural confines of Hindi heartland (structure).

To conclude the essay, at a time when the line between tradition and modernity blurs and *ishq* straddles the modern tradition divide and looks for its manifestation in the land of Heer-Ranjha, Laila-Majnu, Shireen-Farhad, Manoj-Babli and many other untold tales of love and yearning, I would end with a quote of Plato, 'You should not honour men more than truth.' And … love.

References

Altekar, A.S. 1959. *The Position of Women in Hindu Civilization: From Prehistoric Times to the Present Day.* Delhi: Motilal Banarsidass Publishers.

Banerjee-Dube, I. (ed.) 2008. *Caste in History*. New Delhi: Oxford University Press.

Bowen, P. (ed.) 1998. *Themes and Issues in Hinduism*. London: Cassel.

Buhler, G. 1990. *The Laws of Manu*. New Delhi: Ahuja Book Company.

Butalia, Urvashi. 1998. *The Other Side of Silence: Voices from the Partition of India*. New Delhi: Penguin Books.

Chakravarti, U. 2003. *Gendering Caste: Through a Feminist Lens*. Calcutta: Stree.

Chaudhry, D.R. 2010. 'Feudal Mindset: In the Heart of Darkness'. *Deccan Herald*, 1 August.

Chowdhary, P. 2007. *Contentious Marriages, Eloping Couples: Gender, Caste and Patriarchy in Northern India*. New Delhi: Oxford University Press.

Devi, L. (ed.) 1998. *Social Stratification Setup and New Approaches to Sociology*. Lucknow: Institute for Sustainable Development and New Delhi: Anmol Publications.

Dewan, V.K. 2000. *Law Relating to Offences Against Women*. New Delhi: Orient Law House.

Giddens, Anthony. 1976. *New Rules of Sociological Method: A Positive Critique of Interpretative Sociologies*. London: Hutchinson & Co. Ltd.

——. 1984. *The Constitution of Society*. Cambridge: Polity Press.

Giddens, A. and Pierson, C. 1998. *Conversations with Anthony Giddens: Making Sense of Modernity*. California: Stanford University Press.

Gupta, D. (ed.) 1991. *Social Stratification*. New Delhi: Oxford University Press.

Hariharan, Githa. 2004. 'Bloodthirsty Honour'. *Telegraph*, 10 October. http://www.telegraphindia.com/1041010/asp/opinion/story_3848937.asp

Jois, M.R. 2002. *Ancient Indian Law: Eternal Values in Manu Smriti*. Delhi: Universal Publishing Company.

Kuppuswamy, B. 1989. *Social Change in India*. Delhi: Konark Publications.

Liddle, J. and Joshi, R. 1986. *Daughters of Independence: Gender, Caste and Class in India*. New Delhi: Kali for Women and London: Zed Books.

Malhotra, Anshu and Mir, Farina (eds) 2012. *Punjab Reconsidered: History, Culture and Practice*. New Delhi: Oxford University Press.

Menon, Ritu and Bhasin, Kamala. 1998. *Borders and Boundaries: Women in India's Partition*. Delhi: Kali for Women.

Nabar, V. 1995. *Caste as Woman*. New Delhi: Penguin Books.

Nair, Shalini. Updated: 17 December 2015 11:04 am. http://indianexpress.com/article/explained/gender-inequality-index-in-south-asia-india-leads-in-poor-condition-of-women/#sthash.esmxrppl.dpuf

Omvedt, G. 1990. *Violence Against Women: New Movements and New Theories in India*. New Delhi: Kali for Women.

Pandey, S. 2010. 'Talking Tough: "Khap" Panchayats Refuse to Mend Medieval Ways'. *Deccan Herald*, 15 November.

Rajshekar, V.T. 2007. *Caste: A Nation Within the Nation: A Recipe for a Bloodless Revolution*. Bangalore: Books for Change.

Rao, M. 2008. *Law Relating to Women and Children*. Lucknow: Eastern Book Company.

Roohi, S. and Samaddar, R. 2009. *Key Texts on Social Justice in India*. New Delhi: Sage Publications.

Singh, Gynant. http://indiatoday.intoday.in/story/honour-killings-sc-for-death-sentence/1/137621.html

Welchman, Lynn and Hossain, S. (eds) 2005. *Honour: Crimes, Paradigms and Violence Against Women*. London: Zed Books.

6

Gender, Caste and Politics in *Khaps*

Amandeep Singh

Although various theoretical frameworks have described Indian caste system primarily as a system of social stratification, the institution has enormous political ramifications especially in the agrarian social structure. It is a well documented fact that traditionally, the caste, political and economic hierarchies converged, creating a system of stratification that enfolded the social, economic and political hierarchy. However, different caste groups have been dominating both numerically as well as politically in different parts of the country as also within regions. There are a series of traditional panchayats dealing with different kinds of issues. As highly patriarchal and male dominated, these *khap* panchayats have primarily been the gendered spaces, marginalizing women in rural milieu.

Panchayats of different kinds range from ad hoc gathering of lineage leaders to planned convocations of people from many villages. If a quarrel among brothers cannot be settled at the lineage level, any one of them can take the case before the panchayat at the next higher level, i.e. *gotra* or the caste panchayat of the village. There is no formal or regular mechanism of appeal from a judgment (decision) made at one level to a council of broader scope. A man dissatisfied with a judgment can bring his case to a larger panchayat if he has influence enough to persuade the elders to reconsider the case. Some of the caste groups like the Jaats have various levels of panchayat (Pradhan 1966). The larger organization includes units ranging from five to eight villages the next higher level may have as many as 20 villages. The principal higher unit is that of the clan area which may cover as many as 84 villages (Chowdhry 2007).

Wider problems that may drag on for long periods are decided by the caste panchayat unless there are too few households of a particular caste group in the village. In such a case, either the village panchayat takes over or the dominant caste leaders settle the dispute arising among castes below them. Caste matters that cannot be settled by the caste panchayat of a particular caste group are occasionally referred to the dominant caste. In certain cases involving more than one village, the aggrieved party will call upon his family or village caste leaders to have a meeting with his counterpart in the other village. In case of differences between members of the dominant and the lower caste groups, the former are able to control the latter and enforce decisions upon them. This is normally achieved through threats of economic sanctions as well as using or threatening physical violence. It is natural that the lower caste groups have severe reservations regarding such panchayats. The egalitarian aspect of the traditional panchayat stands dissolved when confronted with the ground reality of social and caste hierarchy.

For arriving at a decision, the traditional panchayat mobilizes a large number of people on the basis of family, kin, *gotra*, caste, community and village, including persons from outside the local area. By bringing in a wider *biradari* from outside the village, links are activated which make the panchayat appear more powerful. Issues such as breaking of social taboos, customs, rituals and hierarchy are used as mobilizing strategies. Being highly emotive strategies, these succeed in uniting people and closing ranks and cleavages in rural society. In this the concept of 'village honour', based upon idealized norms and village *biradari*, produces a powerful plank. Gender in this system is a very important catalyst that places the whole responsibility of saving the honour of the women. It is, therefore, the women who carry the whole burden of maintaining the purity and sanctity of caste and *biradari* (community). Violating community norms has different meaning for men and women, the latter holding much greater accountability in case of any violation.

Once the decision is taken, its enforcement is the responsibility of the leaders of the village in which the penalized party lives. The sanctions applied by the caste or the village panchayat are usually in form of fine, to be deposited in a common fund of the panchayat, ritual expiation, public humiliation, which could be blackening the face or rubbing the nose in dust before the aggrieved party or even the entire gathering, touching other's feet, shaving the head or drinking or dipping the nose in the urine of one or more persons. Sometimes the offender is required to express their repentance by touring the village to seek forgiveness of elders of the village. He must give an assurance that he would never err again. The final weapon in the hands of the traditional panchayat is outcasting. Outcasting is an extreme form of group withdrawal. Any offence for which a person is likely to be thrown out of his caste requires an inter village panchayat of the caste members so that the punishment can be widely known and supported. However, exclusion from one group does not necessarily mean total rejection by society. A family may sever relations with one of its members, but other members of the caste group need not follow suit. Similarly, an offender may be cut off from normal relations with his caste group and village but may still be able to maintain relations with his caste fellows in other villages. When a man is outcast, no other man from his caste will allow its members to smoke with him the *hukka*, a symbol of caste solidarity. In extreme cases, people will not allow an outcast family to draw water from the well. They will also not give them fire from their hearth. Finally, outcasting makes it extremely difficult to marry off children, as no one will give or take a daughter from an outcast household. At times, the offender is expelled from the village. Even the threat of such a sanction has great force. Some recent cases in Haryana show an increase in such punishments.

The exercise of caste politics through *khap* or caste panchayats has been a peculiar phenomenon in the state of Haryana, which has witnessed, in the recent past, strong presence of these *khap* panchayats in an utter violation of the Constitution that has provided for the democratically elected village panchayats under the 73rd Constitutional Amendment Act. While systematic studies are needed to understand the intricacies involved in the co-existence of both statutory panchayats and unconstitutional but customary institutions of khaps, literature is coming up from various sources on the subject.

The *khap* may be defined as a unit of a number of villages organized into a political council for the purpose of social control. The *khap* area may be inhabited either by a predominant caste having most of the agricultural land in its possession, or by more than one clan, each clan having a number of villages to itself and being predominant in them. When a clan had only five or so villages under its jurisdiction, proving to be too few for the purpose of common defense, two or more adjoining clans of similar strength might organize their villages into a common *khap*. When this happened, the headship of the *khap* was given to the most numerous clan, which had the highest number of villages under its jurisdiction. Such a *khap* has the same principles of *khap bhaichara* and exogamy as any other *khap* (Pradhan 1966). Apart from Jaat *khaps*, as the most prominent, there are also *khaps* of other castes and communities. A *khap* is generally named after the dominant clan or caste which first organized it into a political group. Even so, it includes other castes and communities living within the villages and coming under the jurisdiction of the *khap* council. They have their own caste councils modelled after the dominant clan or caste and with the same *khap* villages under their jurisdiction. The internal affairs of a caste are decided by its own caste council, but the inter caste disputes and other matters of common interest are decided by the *khap* council. Thus the *khap* council comprises the members of not only the dominant clan but also of other castes. All the castes use the term '*khap* panchayat' even of a meeting held by their own caste, if it is organized at the level of all the *khap* villages. To distinguish a caste council from a *khap* panchayat of all the castes, the caste names are added. The *khap* as a political unit is based on the principles of local contiguity and *khap bhaichara* or brotherhood. It is supported by *khap* exogamy practiced both by the *Jaats* and by other castes of the *khap* area.

Functions of the *Khap* Councils

The *khap* and *sarv-khap* councils have three kinds of functions: adjudicative, legislative and executive, though this division has no statutory basis or support, except for the traditional basis. Executive and legislative powers tend to be the preserve of the *khap* and *sarv-khap* councils because of their political effectiveness and wide jurisdiction enjoyed by these over the Jaat community and the region due to their historical primacy. The councils of the larger political units are called when the smaller units have failed to settle a dispute. A council with a greater span of social control is in a better position to bring pressure upon the individual or group concerned. The primary function of the *khap* council is to decide disputes between the castes and villages under its jurisdiction and to maintain peace and solidarity within the Jaat community and various castes of the *khap* area. It also acts as a political unit of appeal. Several *khaps* of an area together comprise a *sarv-khap* panchayat. Acceptance of the decisions of a *sarv-khap* council meeting rests upon a sense of community of interests, of unity and solidarity between various *khaps*, which is backed by the centuries old tradition of cooperation and shared responsibilities. Moreover, to negate the ideology of belief in the *sarv-khap* council would automatically mean negating the influence of the *khap* and caste councils themselves.

Sanctions

The sanctions exercised by various *khap* and *sarv-khap* councils can be classified into positive and negative sanctions. Positive sanctions tend to reward the individual while negative sanctions penalize him/her. Most common sanctions exercised by these *khaps* include 'stopping the *hukka*' of the individual or his family. Economic sanctions such as fines and economic restitution are common and can be ordained by any political council. They are not used against kinship groups but only against individuals.

Actually *khaps* or caste panchayats wield much more power than the statutory panchayats in states like Haryana. These panchayats, though devoid of any legality, often have ordered harsh punitive measures against couples marrying within the same *gotra* or village (because boys and girls of the same gotra or village are considered brothers and sisters). Such has been the political clout of these panchayats, which normally are dominated by the upper castes, Jaats in Haryana that no political party has so far dared to openly oppose their dictates. *Khaps* are clans and these correspond to gotra within caste groups. The customary rules regulating marriages in Haryana are directly in contravention of the constitutional provisions on marriage. According to the Hindu Marriage Act, 1955 marriage within certain prohibitory degrees of relationship is not permitted while no other restrictions on the choice of a marriage partner exist. In north India, most caste groups prohibit marriage within three or four *got*. In certain instances the principle of *got* exogamy is enlarged by clustering several other *gots* represented in the same village. Further there is also the rule of village exogamy whereby a boy and a girl of one village are considered to be brother and sister. At times, marriage within the *khap* area (the area controlled by a clan) is also prohibited. The principle of village exogamy means that all men and women of the same clan, the same localized clan and the same village are bound by the morality of brother and sister and therefore both sex and marriage are prohibited between members of any of these units (Hershman 1981: 133–134). This extends to the *khap* area covering more than one village. These prohibitions create *bhaichara*, a very important social group leading to *biradari*.

Any breach of these prohibitions invites the ire of *biradari* which decides the course of punishment through the caste or *khap* panchayats. McKim Marriott (1962) argues that *biradari* refers not just to one concrete structural unit at the village level but rather to patrilineal connection, real or putative or fictional, at any level of segmentation. Caste or *khap* panchayats are normally used by the *biradari* to settle disputes regarding violation of rules of marriage and social intercourse. However, many of these caste panchayats, especially in Haryana, have not only been openly defying the law but have also sanctioned murder and abduction in cases where members have refused to follow their diktats. They continue to do this with no fear that the political class or the civil and police administration will in any way take them to task.

Khap panchayats are a part of the rural social structure and have existed in the past. There are four kinds of traditional panchayats in rural north India, viz., caste panchayat, village multicaste panchayat, the farmer retainer panchayat and any single purpose panchayat (Yadav 2009). The four corner stones of rural life are 'unity', 'honour', 'community' and 'brotherhood.' Chowdhry (2004) argues that the effectiveness of statutory panchayats remained shallow whereas traditional panchayats have made their presence felt on social issues. The main work of traditional panchayats revolves around issues threatening the peace of villages, disputes over property and inheritance and sexual or marital transgressions. These *khap* panchayats are very active in Haryana and Uttar Pradesh while these have little influence in Punjab (Chowdhry 1996). Traditionally panchayats always have been male institutions. Powerful elements of the dominant castes usually participate in their deliberations and support their decisions. The punishments declared by these panchayats are mostly archaic ranging from payment of fine, ritual expiation, public humiliation by blackening of the face, rubbing the victim's nose into dust, shaving of the head and dipping the victim's nose and face in human urine.

Outcasting an accused has been the harshest punishment. Chowdhry (1996) argues '... The open exhibition of its power is evidenced in the attempt of the panchayat to change relationships and impose those of its liking, subsume the individual/family will to that of the village and prioritise the village and biradari's izzat over that of individuals ... .

Khap panchayats not only are dominated by upper castes, these also are patriarchal in character. In her report on a caste panchayat in Bhiwani district in 2002, Dhagamwar (2009) stated that this panchayat found it easier to decide cohabitation issues rather than property claims. Chowdhry narrates the caste of Darshana Gehlot who married Ashish Dagar in village Jondhi in 2004. The Gehlot *gotra* panchayat declared the couple, despite their two-year-old son, to be brother and sister. In order to demonstrate to the villagers that Darshana was a sister and not a daughter in law of the village, she was brought to the *gotra* panchayat by removing her veil. She was ordered to be remarried and the husband's family was ordered to meet the expenses by selling off its land and was given a week's time to leave the village forever. In case of their failure to do so, violence against them could be allowed. Dagar's family approached the Maha-Panchayat for review of the case. Bowing before the

Maha-Panchayat, the family apologized and asked for mercy in the name of the son of the couple. The Maha-Panchayat formed a committee which though did not condone the marriage, yet did not dissolve it too. Darshana was expelled out of the Gehlot *gotra* and her husband's family was outcaste for two years. The couple was debarred from entering the village for life but their son could visit his grandparents in Jondhi (Yadav 2009).

The *khap* panchayats consist of the powerful elements of dominant caste. They are the self-proclaimed custodians of village norms, rural culture and public morality. Given their huge influence at the village and regional levels, no political party opposes their parochial, patriarchal and biased stand against the so-called violators of public morality defined by them. The intervention by *khap* panchayats indicates an assertion of the united power and domination of upper caste, particularly the older male members over younger men and women. It often works as a resistant force to the eroding dominance of upper caste in the agrarian social structure. This becomes especially relevant in view of the constitutional panchayats that have been established in villages as a consequence of 74th Amendment. This diminishing power is sought to be resurrected through the traditional panchayat which uses social problems, especially issues relating to contentious marriages. Instead of democratic and fair decisions taken by these khap panchayats, as visualized, on many occasions one of the concerned parties is not even present or is too thinly represented (Chowdhry 2004). For arriving at a decision, the traditional panchayat known as *khap* mobilizes a large number of people on the basis of kinship, caste, got, community and village. Such a process has worked just the opposite to what has been envisioned in the Constitution of India in the name of equality, democracy and secularism. Strangely however, the multiple divisions within the village in terms of caste, kinship and *gotra* join together through *khap* panchayats, calling for a unanimous decision. The dominant caste groups, though severely divided into factions and interest groups, throw their might behind the traditional panchayats. This is the reason that even the State does not dare to challenge the decisions of these *khaps* for the fear of antagonizing their electorate.

Recent Challenges to *Khap* Panchayats

Of late, however, there has been a strong protest against these *khap* panchayats coming from civil society groups, urban middle class educated people who condemn the highly feudal and barbaric decisions taken by these panchayats against young men and women flouting the customary rules set by the *khaps*. The protests against increasing 'honour killings' and diktats of the *khap* leaders have questioned their legitimacy and challenged their decisions. Marriages under police protection defying death threats from *khap* panchayats have challenged the authority of such panchayats. The recent landmark judgment in the case of honour killing of a couple named Manoj and Babli, in Haryana, that awarded capital punishment to five and life sentence to two, is a strong warning against the role of *khap* panchayats in such killings. These panchayats, on the other hand, are opposed to this judgment and are demanding an amendment of the Hindu Marriage Act, 1955. Since this judgment, the panchayats are struggling to reinforce their legitimacy as they fear of similar verdicts in other cases of honour killings.

By mobilizing large numbers in support of customs and rituals based on family, kinship, *gotra*, caste, community and village, the *khap* panchayats also enjoy wider and higher political support from the gram panchayats for the fear of loss in elections. Therefore, the sarpanches do not oppose the diktats of the *khap* panchayats. By redefining their image as catalysts of social change, they have been successful in generating support from certain politically powerful sections of society (Ray 2010).

Resentment evoked by the extreme actions taken by *khap* panchayats has also resulted in affected parties taking recourse to law. This introduces an external element into an essentially private and internal matter of a caste/community. Courts are being increasingly used to settle questions of material interests, although internal disputes relating to marriage, etc. continue to be handled by caste men. Personalizing inter-caste disputes effectively delinks them from the State and its law and order apparatus. Recourse to the courts over personal issues internal to the caste is generally not approved. In case recourse to law is taken, it is done only against grave social pressure and incurs a great deal of community displeasure. Moreover, in cases of contentious marriages, state agencies like the police and the local administration want the matter to be settled by recognized wielders of traditional authority. The court can, however, be moved only after the community has taken an unconstitutional or illegal decision. Not many people exercise this option.

The growing breach of the panchayat's decision has emerged as a serious concern. In this connection, a *sarv-khap* panchayat of 84 *khaps* met in village Charkhi Dadri on 19 August 2001. It commented upon the weakening hold of the traditional panchayats and deplored the factionalism and its politicization which had crept in especially in recent years, pitting one *khap* against the other. The panches agreed that matters that could earlier be solved easily by a village or *khap* panchayat could no longer be solved satisfactorily without being challenged. There was a growing tendency to take such cases to court. All these acts of defiance were not only posing threats to the existence of the traditional panchayat but were also attacks on its honour. In cases where the court steps in, caste panchayats have been compelled to ignore the actual marriage which had been the focal point of dispute and confrontation and have carried on with other sanctions over which they have control. This shift from the core issue of marriage highlights the use of marriage issues to settle or establish relative claims of status and hierarchy within a caste group. This may also help explain why the panchayats take up certain cases and not others. It is a well established fact that for each case taken up by the caste panchayat there are several similar cases of breach of kinship and territorial exogamy which go without raising any controversy.

It has been observed that the attempt to reverse a traditional panchayat's decision may well lead to permanent antagonism, revenge and violence to severe retribution. Approaching the court of law or police as an alternative structure for conflict resolution certainly leads to a dramatic loss of prestige of the panchayat as well as its delegitimation. It is a public way of refusing to obey its dictates. On the other hand, going to court means further transgression of the norms of community, compounding the earlier transgression. It is construed as an even greater challenge to the panchayat's decision, leading to a further hardening of its posture. The traditional leadership considers the judiciary, run by people who have no knowledge of rural culture and customary practices. Any one taking recourse to it is similarly condemned and stereotyped as westernized and alien to rural life values. The State and its laws are blamed for all marriages that go against traditional norms and customary practices.

References

Chowdhry, Prem. 2002. *Contentious Marriages, Eloping Couples: Gender Caste and Patriarchy in Northern India.* New Delhi: Oxford University Press.

——. 1996. 'Contours of Communalism: Religion, Caste and Identity in South-East Panjab'. *Social Scientist*. Social Scientist via JSTOR.24(4/6):130:163.doi:10.23713517797.

——. 2007. *Contentious Marriages, Eloping Couples*. New Delhi: Oxford University Press.

——. 2004. 'Caste Panchayats and the Policing of Marriage in Haryana: Enforcing Kinship and Territorial Exogamy'. *Contributions to Indian Sociology*, 38(1 and 2), 1–41.

Dhagamwar, Vasudha. 2009. Panch Parmeshwar. *Economic and Political Weekly*. 1 August, Vol. XLIV (31): 13–16.

Pradhan, M.C. 1966. *The Political System of the Jats of Northern India*. Bombay: Oxford University Press.

Ray, Suranjita. 2010. 'Khap Panchayats: Reinforcing Caste Hierarchies'. *Mainstream*, XLVIII(30), 17 July, 1–14.

Yadav, Bhupendra. 2009. 'Khap Panchayats: Stealing Freedom'. *Economic and Political Weekly*, XLIV(52), December, 16–18.

7

The 'Violence of Green Revolution'

Women, Production, Reproduction and Falling Sex Ratio in Punjab

Kumool Abbi

The paper seeks to explicate the dynamic inter-linkages between the productive, reproductive and social roles of Punjabi women in the context of the present socio-economic development scenario, and in doing so declining juvenile sex ratios in Punjab (Census 2001, 2011) which has been a subject of much concern and recent debate in scholarly, journalistic and public-political circles.

In particular, the paper seeks to point out certain crucial inter linkages between (i) techno-economic change centring on patterns of production and earning a living; (ii) social transformation relevant to women's day-to-day maintenance and change of lifestyle, social positions and identities; (iii) reproductive behaviour including desired family size, sex-preference, contraception, abortion and other family regulative or fertility reductive practices. The paper draws a crucial connection between the policies of State, their violent impact on women and shows how they have contributed to the declining relevance of women in the cultural landscape of the Punjab. The two policies which would be critically looked at are the Green Revolution in Punjab and its link to the government population policies explicating the two child norm. In a reactive combination of both Punjab represents the crucial confluence of modern technology and its interaction with an agrarian ethos and feudal values.

The paper attempts to take away the analysis of falling sex ratios from numbers and statistics and stereotypical notions to women's own lives in their everyday experience particularly in their relationship to production and reproduction. This paper examines the general work preferences of women, a study based on field work conducted in a village in Punjab, to look at the way that the relationship of women to the production process has undergone a change. In understanding this change it also examines the crucial link with the reproductive cycle that in the agricultural community renders women irrelevant.

The paper, thus, takes up together economic, socio-cultural and demographic issues which are most often treated separately and so their mutual implications either gets ignored or fails to get requisite space or attention. The main contention of the paper is that for an adequate understanding of the present juvenile sex ratio or for that matter sex-ratio in general, there is a need to supplement an in-depth analysis of demographic data with a gender sensitive understanding of the nuances of socio-economic and cultural change.

The analysis is partly based on fieldwork interviews with the village women carried out by the author in the village Shahpur of Patiala district of Punjab, while carrying out a larger research project (Abbi 2003: 270–291, and recent fieldwork conducted in 2008) and partly on the relevant published material, anthropological, sociological, demographic, historical, etc. including secondary analysis specifically devoted to the discussion of sex ratios. The analysis presented here departs from the prevailing mode of analysis, which is predominately demographic. It, instead, specifically focuses on the interconnection between the skewed sex ratio and certain important changes in the productive and reproductive roles of women as well as in their consumption oriented role which is becoming particularly important for promoting and sustaining emerging consumerist lifestyle.

Further, while the paper takes into account the relevant demographic information and analysis pertaining to sex ratio in Punjab, its emphasis is less on the presentation of a detailed quantitative profile of demographic dynamics, and more on identifying sociological inter-linkages.

Women's Productive Behaviour: Changing Roles, Relationships, Lifestyles

It would be appropriate to start with changes in women's productive behaviour. A number of studies have drawn attention to certain characteristic features of the female labour force in Punjab, some concerning cultural norms relating to women, others pointing to empirical observations of actual behaviour. These include (i) *purdah* ideology (partially receding) as well as values of honour or *izzat* rooted in patriarchal relations and imposing certain personal, social and sexual constraints, especially on women's movement outside the home; (ii) the practice of village exogamy; (iii) percentage of female workers being twice as high in urban rural areas than in rural areas and (iv) other female workers being the highest in Punjab as compared to other states of India (unfavourable attitude towards sending females to work, especially married girls, and a higher representation of widows separated or divorced women in the work force) (Abbi 2003: 181). Those concerned with women's work participation emphasize that the capital intensive technology, associated with higher agricultural productively and resulting prosperity has led to the withdrawal of women from the agricultural process in the green revolution areas of Punjab and Haryana. This has not only affected more prosperous large landowners and others but also not so well off landless labourers, artisans and small and marginal farmers, though the nature of women's actual response with regard to the extent and nature of withdrawal varies considerably. The studies of Sandhu (1976), Singh (1986), Sethi (1982), Das Gupta (1987), Shiva (1988), Aggarwal (1989), Bhalla (1989), Chowdhary (1994), Abbi and Singh (1997), Kaur (1998), Rastogi (2000), Raju (2010), Patel (2007), Purewal (2010), Kaur (2010), Kaur and Kaur (2012), Padhi (2014) have highlighted withdrawal of women from agricultural production activities and marginalization of women, as workers or earners, discriminatory wage differentials, undervaluation of specific tasks associated with women, lower proportion of female workers in specified populations (FLP rates), higher incidence of dowry, domestic violence, greater intra-household discrimination, low female survival rates, etc.

Our own study of Shahpur (Abbi 2003) followed by a revisit in 2008 categorized the village women in five categories mainly on the basis of the operational holdings of the agricultural based household, and occupational and other sources of income where the household lacked land and depended on some other sources of income. The categories, thus, arrived at were three categories of farmers, upper, middle and lower and two categories of landless, upper (skilled workers, professionals, businessmen) and lower (agricultural workers, sweepers, casual labour, etc). While clearly recognizing the limitation of such categorization, the paper highlights the growing complexity of the roles of women, the changes in their paid work as well as the work related to non-wage duties of looking after the household, children, guests, maintaining social contracts and generally upholding the social status of the family by projecting a status and an appropriate pattern of living, and also the increasing withdrawal of women from agricultural work being complexly related to the family status, both as a consequence and sustaining factor. This relationship, however, was found to be differentially true of women of different categories and varied with the family resources, status requirements and other relevant existential conditions.

Among the lower landless, agricultural labour, particularly seasonal harvesting on contract basis, continued to be important for both women as well as men. Even those in regular household employment often took leave to take part in it. But as the family resource positions improved women tended to be withdrawn from such work. For some this was just a symbolic marker of family status aspirations, for yet others it was a real step up the status ladder. The upper landless, on the other hand, showed a near total withdrawal from agriculture and growing involvement in tertiary occupations. They also showed a greater interest in children's education and in buying consumer durables, such as televisions, modern furniture, etc.

At each of the upper, middle and lower farmer category levels, the study took note of the family's upward mobility process and its manifestation in values, behaviour and lifestyle. It highlights that women's withdrawal from agriculture involvement with tertiary and other occupations and intense preoccupation with consumption and lifestyle not only had a personal and familial import, but also a wider social significance. On the one hand, it was crucially linked to the individual woman or her family's status maintenance and social mobility strivings and on the other, it had a wider social import in signifying and promoting Punjab's characteristic modernization process.

Notwithstanding the fact, as the study pointed out, the whole household benefitted in various ways from the household gadgets, furnishings and other items of general household consumption, the women get blamed for making excessive consumption demands and being a burden on hard working male breadwinners. In this way, both the women and their contribution to their households get minimized if not rendered totally negative.

Another related aspect of the women's consumption-centred role is related to dowry which, as is well known, is becoming increasingly more expensive and an onerous burden on the bride's parents and so are entertainment expenses and various types of virtually one-sided gifts which the bride's parents are customarily or under covert or overt pressure, required to offer. The point which the study took note of and which needs to be specifically highlighted in the present context is that consumer durables like cars, scooters, refrigerators and other type of luxury items are becoming a regular part of dowry. It has virtually become legitimate to shift the major burden of satisfying the family's consumerist demands upon the women and her natal family. This attitude finds an indirect support from a conception of dowry which is increasingly finding social acceptance, that is, treatment of dowry as the daughters' share of inheritance of parental of ancestral property (Kishwar 1998). Daughters and their husbands or in-laws in their own way, think they should get all they can for the rest will go to the brothers. Even parents and brothers often find this view as a convenient excuse to deny their daughters or sisters their legitimate right to inherit family property. Chakravorty, while discussing the agrarian crisis, highlights how in contemporary Punjab, adding to the debt trap, was the private economy of dowry, not directly attributed to the State in any way but certainly promoted by the market, and terrifyingly held up in a vicious grip by a community based patriarchy, that made marriage contingent upon economic transactions ... (c.f. Padhi 2014: VIII).

Change in Reproductive Behaviour and Sex Ratio

Ever since the publication of the 2001 Census and the provisional figures of the 2011 Census, the consistent decline in India's juvenile female to male sex ratio (girls of the age group 0–6 per thousand boys of the group) has become a subject of serious public concern, scholarly, journalistic as well as political (Bhat 2002; Patel 2004; John et al. 2008; John 2011; Purewal 2010). Though the 1961 Census figures of the juvenile girl population (1976 girls to 1000 boys) were hardly satisfactory, (female to male ratio declined from 941 in 1961, to 930 in 1971, to 934 in 1981 and to as low as 927 in 1991, 933 in 2001 and marginally increased to 940 in 2011), with even the southern states showing the decline since the early 1980s (Patel 2004; John 2011; Kaur 2008). The relevant data from Punjab (1961–2011) created a great concern as along with keeping in tune with the traditional trend of low sex ratios it dipped drastically to 876 in 2001, to a marginal increase of 893 in 2011. The main focus of the continuing anxiety has been the fluctuating juvenile female to male ratio which in the last two decades has suffered a massive decline, about 962 in 1981 to 875 in 1991, dipping to 798 in 2001 (a difference of –77 points) and rising to 846 in 2011, an increase of 48 points. John explains that these 'small improvements' from very low levels only emphasize that in 'Punjab the severity of the practice has only ceased slightly' (John 2011: 10–12). She also elaborates that though the north western states have not fallen further, they have not come back to the 1991 levels. In the 'manipulation game of balancing numbers' factors like strict implementation of monitoring the conduct of sex determination tests in Punjab and their complex interplay with the 'local and micro level contexts' (John 2011: 10–12) have to be studied at length before coming to any conclusions about the 'improvements' and 'real change' in Punjab (John 2011: 10–12). To mention briefly while the 2001 Census, indicated clearly that seven of the 10 districts with minimum decline, including the top-most Fatehgarh Sahib, Patiala, Mansa, Bhatinda, Kapurthala, Sangrur, Gurdaspur, etc. were in Punjab, and the remaining three in the adjoining Haryana, indicating a compact belt of son preference or female dispreference. The provisional data for 2011 Census seems to indicate a more heterogeneous pattern, with the four top-most districts in the range of sex ratio less than 800 in Haryana and Jammu and Kashmir: Jhajjar, Mahendergarh, Rewari, Sambha and Sonipat. Thirty districts in the range of 800–849 (9 in Haryana, 8 in Punjab, 4 in Jammu and Kashmir, 2 in Rajasthan) and 127 districts in the range of 850–899 (21 in U.P., 19 in Rajasthan, 16 in Maharashtra, 10 in Punjab and 10 in Gujarat) (Kumar and Sathyanarayana 2012) indicate the structural embeddedness of the issue of son preference at a very deeper level in Punjab.

Indeed extensive historical and other source materials exist to show that in Punjab (which included Haryana before 1965) son preference and female dispreference along with female infanticide existed among certain elite castes, Rajputs, Khatris and others as far back as the medieval period if not earlier (Browne 1857; Ibbetson 1883; Panigrahi 1972; Malhotra 2002). The last two are, however, particularly relevant to this paper, for they shed light on how, in the British colonial period, despite the colonial governments, professions to the contrary, certain policies and practices of the colonial government led to a deterioration of the Indian women's economic and social position and have since continued to pose problems for them even in the post-Independence India.

For Oldenberg, the British policies resulted in creating a male-centred environment within which patriarchy together with son preference flourished, and the female infanticide, despite the legal ban, continued and even spread to new groups. Prominent among these policies were the agrarian policy designed to augment land revenue which ushered a new regime of commercialization and privatization of land, codification of land and property inheritance laws, including the introduction of the male-centric Ryotwari system which made men the exclusive owners of land, deprived women of their customary rights in land and increased their economic dependence upon and subjugation to men, and new employment policy which recognized certain castes as martial races and favoured their males for recruitment in the army and associated land grants, pensions and other privileges, which favoured the rise of a gender targeted family achievable through selective female infanticide.

Malhotra describes how the emulation of an upper class oriented middle class culture by upwardly mobile Jats and other peasant castes led to values and practices such as *kanyadan* and dowry marriage, stricter norms of women's general conduct and sexual expression, and son preference as well as a tacit acceptance of female infanticide (Malhotra 2002: 48, 55–60, 64; See also Sukkoo and Chakraborty 2010). Thus, the historical sources leave little doubt that Punjab and Haryana's medieval traditions of son preference came to be accentuated further by the male-centric polices of British administration, resulting into gender bias that has since continued to affect people's preferences and practices relating to the family's sex composition.

Though several factors may be invoked to account for the above sharp decline in Punjab's sex ratios, the demographic evidence and analysis mainly point to the skewed sex ratio at birth and higher female mortality in early childhood (Bhat 2002-I, II; Agnihotri 2000, 2003; Retherford and Roy 2002; Nanda and Veron 2005; John et al. 2008, 2009). Such other factors as decline due to difference in migration, under enumeration of females because of reporting errors and decrease in foetal wastage (due to improvement in nutrition, medical facilities, etc.) which favours males are considered of negligible importance (see also Mitra 2011). Bhat, who mainly focuses on all India sex-ratios, in his analysis of 2001 data, cautions against over reliance on 0–6 age group figures as some of the decline may be accounted for by the age group data. He, nevertheless, concedes that as a result of sex-selective abortions, the FMR at birth may have declined by 56 points in Punjab, 51 points in Haryana, 39 points in Himachal Pradesh and about 18 point in Tamil Nadu[1] and 18 points in urban India generally. Nanda and Veron (2005), whose analysis is specifically devoted to Punjab and Haryana, are even more emphatic in highlighting the role of sex-selective abortions and early childhood neglect as a major factor affecting sex-ratio. They argue that in Punjab and Haryana, despite 'impressive economic development', there has been a 'paradoxical' rise in gender bias which is being increasingly expressed in the form of foeticide as against older form of infanticide. Further, they contend that the present population trends 'can be explained by the desire among couples to limit their family size in an environment of continuing son preference, with technology enabling couples to choose a family of desired size and sex (2005: 92–93). See also (Patel 2007; John et al. 2008, 2009). As per SRS data (2001–2008) sex-ratio at birth for Punjab for 2001–2003, 2006–2008, 2007–2009 was 776,836 and 836, respectively and it was 807, 847,849 for Haryana in the same period (UNFPA 2011). The SRS data also elucidated that in terms of 2001–2008, almost 34,465 female births which approximates 15.7 per cent did not occur in Punjab and 32,613 approximating 12.5 per cent did not occur in Haryana (UNFPA 2011). Kulkarni, in his estimates, pegged the sex selective abortions of expected female births during 2001 in Punjab at approximately 19 per cent (c.f. Mitra 2011). Jha et al. (2006) have drawn their estimation of sex ratios for second order births in

India in a study conducted in 1997. In terms of all India figures, the adjusted sex ratio for second birth when the preceding child was a girl was 759 per thousand males and for the third child if the precious two were girls was 719 per thousand males. In contrast, the adjusted sex ratio for second or third order births if the precious children were boys was 1102 and 1176 respectively. In the case of Punjab if the first birth was female, the 'adjusted sex ratio' was 614 for female and 1003 for male and in Haryana, 667 for female and 968 for males respectively (Jha 2006; see also John et al. 2008, 2009; Jha et al. 2011).

To put this paradox in perspective, scholars have highlighted certain economic, social and cultural aspects of development and change in Punjab. These include: change from a traditional agrarian and highly fecund community to one with growth of individuation, consumerist outlook, global orientation, higher aspirations for social mobility, acceptance of contraception, wider availability and use of reproductive technology, exposure to communication, spread of lavish and elaborate marriage ceremonies, difficulty of finding a suitable match for daughters, rapid decline of profitability of agriculture, rise in cost of health care, rising female literacy and other social economics, rising aspirations of a higher standard of living.

Recent studies have emphasized the 'need to examine the mirror image of son preference namely 'daughter discrimination' (Hatti and Sekher 2010: 113–114; Kaur 2008: 109–114). Both have based their work on the study of agrarian communities in south and north India. As Kaur explains, 'even among the seemingly well to do Jats in north India, it is the real and perceived precariousness of agricultural livelihoods that explains the desire of the family for sons' (2008: 110). She explains that daughters are the only 'dispensable' members of the family. Not only are they structurally dispensable (looked at from the point of view of a single family or household) but they represent 'outgoings' so far as household resources are concerned in contrast to sons (Kaur 2008: 112, See also John et al. 2008, 2009; Mitra 2011). Similarly, Hatti et al. have also highlighted how at the 'centre of factors of daughter discrimination stands the family' which is showcased by a 'gender hierarchy as well as generational hierarchy and in both of them daughters come last. This means that intergenerational interests are gendered by nature'. It is these 'intergenerational transfer of resources' (Hatti et al. 2010) which are 'critical in expressing and defining the relative value of sons and daughters' (John et al. 2009). Arokiasamy and Goli in a recent study (2012: 85–94) have attempted to explain this phenomena by 'revisiting the Landholding-Patriarchy Hypothesis' following Banisters (2004) work on China, the hypothesis and its link with skewed sex ratios was empirically tested in India by using data from NFHS-3, 2006, they concluded that 'family-building strategies might arise from societal and familial pressure to opt for male descendents' (Arokiasamy and Goli 2012: 92).

We have no quarrel with these identified changes and their recognized importance. They, including son preference, male female disparities, etc. are very significant features of modern Punjab and of contemporary social life. However, it is our contention that in quantitative demographic accounts, the social inter-linkages of these changes with each other and the social context of childbearing behaviour of the women concerned, rarely if ever received adequate treatment. So, to undo this neglect in respect of Punjabi women we propose to identity certain significant aspects of the reproductive context of the childbearing behaviour of the Punjabi women and to identify and spell out inter-linkages between these and their consumption behaviour, lifestyles, devaluation of women and their work, dispreference for female children and imbalances in sex ratio.

Changes in Reproductive Behaviour and the Childbearing Contexts

There has been a considerable decline in women's fertility, the total fertility having been reduced from 5.9 during 1970 to 2.6 in 1998, by a little over half, 50.9 per cent (SRS statistical report, c.f. Nanda and Veron 2005 Table 5: 131). In 2010 it was below replacement level at 1.8, the figures being 1.8 in the rural and 1.7 in the urban areas (NFHS 3: 49). As compared to the national average of 83.9, the general fertility rate by residence for Punjab is 61.3, being 64.1 in rural areas and 56.8 in urban areas. While the percentage decline in total fertility rate by residence between 1998–2000 and 2008–10 was almost –28 per cent in Punjab, the figures being –26.9 in rural and –19.0 in the urban areas (NFHS 3: 50–51). The percentage change in average crude birth rate by residence between 1998–2000 and 2008–10 is almost 22 per cent, for this period the decline is almost –23 per cent in rural areas and –14.5 per cent in the urban areas (NFHS 3: 32) The mean children ever born (CEB) to ever married women between 15–49 have been pegged at 2.4, a differentiation of 3.1 for non-literate and 1.8 for women with at least 10 years of education (IIPS 2010: 8).

Another significant aspect of the changes in reproductive behaviour relates to the span of reproductive life. It was nine years in 1992, it has come down to 7.4 years (NFHS 1992–93, 1998–99). The AFSR rate by residence 2010 indicates that the fertility is 10.8, between the age group of 15–19, it is 159.9 in the age group of 20–24, and 123.7 in the age group 25–29, while it dips down to 46.7 in the 30–35 age group and it is 11.3 in the 35–39 age group, indicating that the highest level of fertility has been attained in the age group 20–24 years. The mean age of fertility which has been calculated from age specific marital fertility rates (being 345.0 for age group 20–24 and 154.3 for the 25–29 age group) is 26.1, with a slight variation of 25.8 in rural and 26.8 in the urban areas (NFHS 3: 44, 47, 54). While at the national level, 1.6 per cent of live births occur within one year of previous live births, in Punjab the interval in terms of months is 2.7 for 10–12 months, 30.3 for 12–24 months, 23.6 for 24–36 months and 43.5 for 36 and above (NFHS 3: 64). The attitude of the women towards reproduction is shown in terms of fertility intentions of currently married women in Punjab. Among those with no living children, 50 per cent want a child within the next two years, while 32 per cent want a child two or more years later. Among the currently married women with one living child the proportion wanting an additional child soon within two years are 14 per cent and after two years are 37 per cent respectively (IIPS 2010: 8). A detailed micro study of Ropar district (Abbi et al. 2000: 188) showed that more than 80 per cent of women complete their childbearing before they reach 30 years of age and childbearing beyond 34 years has shrunk to negligible proportions. All these strands lead to the vital issue indicating a 'steady shrinking' of women's lives 'devoted to bearing children' due to factors like rising age at marriage, declining age specific fertility rates at younger and older age and declining maternal mortality rates (Malhotra et al. 2012). Thus, while saving women from possible pregnancy and delivery related risks, has also freed them from continual preoccupation with child rearing tasks. The vital social as distinct from demographic significance of this change became particularly manifest when viewed in the context of their greatly increased status appropriate lifestyle maintenance and caring functions referred to earlier.

Moreover, an increasing number of women of younger age between 20–25 years are opting for sterilization after completing their desired family size, their proportion in Ropar district study being 32.6 per cent (Abbi et al. 2000: 188). The data from Punjab emphasizes that female sterilization is the predominant limiting method used by 35.3 per cent of the currently married women between 15–49 years (IIPS 2010: 16), while 45.3 per cent of husbands of currently married women use temporary spacing methods, 18.6 use oral pills, and 16.9 per cent the IUD device. The use of female sterilization, 38 per cent, and oral pills, 19 per cent, are higher in rural areas, as compared to 28.5 in urban areas respectively. The mean age of women at sterilization is 28 years (IIPS 2010: 16). Though female sterilization is more common among women with one or more living sons than those with no living sons, in terms of data, merely 5 per cent of the women between 20–24, 20 per cent between 25–29, 37.2 per cent between 30–34 and 50 per cent between 35–49 years had opted for sterilization (IIPS 2010: 16). It is the 'the potential and unintended consequences of female sterilization' which have been largely 'unrecognized by policy makers and social scientists' (Anukriti and Persson 2012; see also Bhardwaj 2008 and Pervez et al. 2012).

To fully appreciate the profound significance of this change for the women's social lives and marital or sexual relations, we need to see it in the context of the increased longevity of men and women, 66 and 68 years respectively, almost 7.5 per cent of the population is above the age of 65 (Parvin and Visaria 2004: 68; Statistical abstract of Punjab 2004; Table 3.9; PFHS survey 2010: 50) and the consequent increase in average marital duration. The marital duration is approximately 18 per cent, for those married less than five years; 5–9 years; 10–14 years and it is 45.4 per cent for those married more than 15 years or more (NFHS 3: 51). The mean age at marriage for boys is 24.2 and for girls it is 21.3 years. Only 17.2 per cent consummated their marriage before completion of 18 years, while 82.8 per cent consummated their marriage after 18 years (IIPS 2010: 7 and Table 2.2). As per the currently favoured pattern of child bearing, the Punjabi women appear to start childbearing immediately after marriage and continue to produce children at short intervals till desired size and sex combination of the family size is reached. Having completed their desired size, most Punjabi women, as those in many other parts of the country, resort to female sterilization as a conveniently available permanent method of contraception.

This means that while they remain sexually active after about the age of 30 years, as evidenced by the resort to contraception, their sexuality becomes almost totally delinked from reproduction. Thus, for the rest of their lives of active sexuality, another 30 years or thereabout, the pleasure giving/pleasure taking aspect displaces its reproductive function. In a patriarchal and male centred society like Punjab, to the extent a wife is considered a kind of possession of the husband, she too becomes an item of pleasurable consumption. We have no intention to denigrate her humanity, or to equate her with a thing. She continues of course to remain a human being and have the human attributes of agency and choice. But these she exercises while being hedged in by certain oppressive patriarchal and gendered development structures. But besides being oppressive, both the patriarchy and development structures are also hegemonic (in the Gramscian sense of being based on manipulated legitimacy rather than simple coercion). They make these women complicit in their own oppression. Punjabi women's role in foeticide and other forms of cruelty and neglect of their female children attests to this complicity, many of the better educated or otherwise socially or materially privileged among them being no less complicit than the illiterates and poor.

Women's Lived Experiences: *Mukaata* (It is Over and Done with)

The households of village Shahpur, too, follow this general trend, the average family again comprising two sons and one daughter. However, this idyllic pattern at times varies in terms of three daughters and one son, or one son preceded by two daughters or at times two sons and two daughters or even just one son. However, the lower landless households were to some extent excluded from this categorization where the number of children ranged from two to six.

Discussions with the women respondents clearly indicated a general acceptance of small family norm and reconciliation to a quick cessation of childbearing. While for some it was a sense of relief at being 'free' of producing more, as they used the word *mukata* (a task undertaken) for the reproduction of children. But a majority of them accepted a sense of emptiness they felt at such a short span, since the children grew up fast. Jagrup Kaur's insightful comments, perhaps, threw light on this largely unexplored area, 'women have been put on the shelf, with all this family planning, even the myth of fertility associated with us almost every year is over, our productivity is shortlived'. Ram Parmeshwari laughed when she said, 'In our times it was a race with the mother-in-law, when I delivered my son, three months back my mother-in-law delivered a baby girl. She did not survive. My friends would always tease me '*teri sas ne tilli jami* (your mother-in-law produced a matchstick)' Her daughter-in-law feels aghast at such a thought, *'How could I produce a child when my son marries, I would be too embarrassed'*. Ram Parmeshwari replied to this comment with a sarcastic laugh, 'Even you can't, your ovaries would have rusted by then; *massan massan* (barely) you manage with two. Your husband can easily go and get another. We could display the manhood of our husband till the evening of their life'. Sardool Kaur, an older generation grandmother, too feels that 'these days women have become so demanding, always wanting a TV, a car, a scooter, every time their mouth is open. Our men were more sensible, keeping them pregnant every alternate year kept them so busy, that they had no time to think of anything else'.

Baldev Kaur and Dheero, both in their mid-70, highlight the accessibility of women these days to their own *kamra* (room) and the 'double box bed' being an indispensable part of women's dowry, yet they feel women's lives with their husbands are crouched in secrecy. Education has only made the women feel a sense of shame, in discussing about themselves and their bodily functions, as if children fall from heaven. This way women suffer in silence, '*andar hi kuddhi rehendian ne*' (they keep on getting stifled). Bibi Guran, another women in the same category, recounts the occasions when women stored the harvest, sat together and made *durries, parandas, nalas*, cut *saag*, went to the *khala* to wash clothes, even to the fields to answer the call of nature; all these spontaneous occasions provided women with opportunities to get together, share their problems and seek support from each other. Rajbir Kaur too hits at the crucial point, 'If we do not produce or go to work we lose our value. But can we breed like dogs, after all who would look after the child, they need clothes and education; if it is a girl then huge dowry as well'. For Sharanjit Kaur, too, 'The best attention a woman gets is when she is carrying a child, but who can afford more children. Apart from children, one has now so many new needs which have to be fulfilled – Television, cars, motorcycles, etc. the need for them is worse than wanting kids'. Similarly, Baljit Kaur said, 'If we have more children, we become the object of ridicule and would be singled out. More than anything the children would curse us when they would compare themselves with others. After all now none of the young people want a life on the fields, it is either a white collared job or an attempt to try their luck in 'foreign country'. We must first think of what Balwinder Kaur too endorses as a point, 'Even we do not know what is happening in the fields, earlier bebe (my mother) was so knowledgeable and my father-in-law always took her advice, now we are only concerned with the fruits, how they grow no one tells us nor do we ask'.

The issue of female foeticide and sex determination tests comes up after a lot of prolonged interaction when the women open up. Women of all categories are aware of the miraculous capacity of the machines which can identify boys and girls. For all of them the access to such machines is a lifesaver. Many have recounted their trips to Patiala city or to their parental home town to secretly undergo these tests; which are at times fixed by personal contacts, or through one nurse who lives in the neighbouring village and works in a private nursing home. Most of the respondents felt it was better to get the *safai* (cleansing) done in time. The major factors which they feel pushes them for a sex selective abortion are: the spiraling costs of dowry, the traditional concept of son as an inheritor of family tradition, the enhanced status of the mother and lastly a purely economic choice; when out of the two children who are to be born one has to be a son. As Malkiat Kaur emphasizes,

'Who does not feel bad losing one's child. But better not to be born than to suffer the rest of one's life. The pain and loss of blood in an abortion is no less than when delivering a child, one bears it convinced that we are securing the future'. Similarly for Sardool Kaur, 'The more women are becoming items of '*sajawat*' (decoration) of our homes, the more we pay to beautify them and more we pay to someone who chooses them'. Rajbir Kaur, however, sums it up more bluntly, 'Earlier it was the men's '*lor*' (need) now it is ours'.

Related with this is the issue of women being given the primary responsibility of family planning. As most of the women indicated, it would be a quite *tussi dekh lao* (you look after it) from the husband which handed them over the entire responsibility of birth control. This could include traditional methods of birth control, use of *golis* (pills), hystercomy operations, etc. As most women indicated, abortion became the only way out to cover up for an inadvertent *galti* (mistake) which took place, especially with the reluctance of the men to, 'tamper with nature and its processes'. Thus, 'In today's times, with so much *mehangai* (costs) and demands we are able to rectify our mistakes in time and fulfil the responsibility for the welfare of our family'. Interestingly, the women particularly of the lower landless households point out that it is the female '*doctorni*' in the city who always preferred and propagated 'abortions as the only way out' unlike the local village male doctors (mostly RMP or Ayurvedic degree holders), who being largely 'middle aged' usually advised them and their *gharvalas* to carry on, 'accept God's wishes, and not think too much about the consequences', but as the women clarified 'we have to move with the world, if it is a boy one suffers the difficulties of the present for the future, if it is a girl then why invite trouble and get slouched with another sack'.

The women did not totally deny the issue of neglect of female children at birth. Many of the lower landless women highlighted the recent death of an upper class farmer's new-born daughter. As Pritam Kaur mentioned:

> One receives the daughter with so much of *be-man* (lack of desire). While a girl would be attended to by hardly one or two people, a boy would have so many people running after him. This way *be-dhyani* (neglect) would automatically happen.

For Tarsem Kaur an educated wife, it is very simple, *je kuri jaa rahi hai, taan jaan dio* (If a girl is going, let her go). She is after all a *bhaar*, (burden) who will arrange her wedding? but she is vociferous that, 'a girl's death may be a matter of chance, it is not deliberate.' Similarly, for Bibi Guran, 'a new-born girl's death, is not deliberate but *je ho gaya taan ho gaya* (if it has happened, so be it). After all what does one stand to gain by producing a girl, *saanu ki kehnde ho,* what are you telling us? *Eh padhe likhe taan paida hi nahin hoon dinde*, these educated people don't even allow the girls to be born.

These insightful discussions have only highlighted the break-up of the crucial chain of production and reproduction among the rural women. Factors like emerging lifestyles, consumerism, education spiraled by the green revolution have played an important catalyst in severing this chain in a transforming agrarian society. In this backdrop the success of the family planning programme has played havoc with the agrarian ethos of Punjabi rural society.

Thus, the consequences of the green revolution and the successful dissemination of the ideology of family planning have been a growing irrelevance and a reassertion of women's symbolic presence more linked to status roles in an agrarian set-up. Thus, as she loses her link to production and reproduction apart from the absence of transition to new meaningful roles, she faces the dilemma of not being allowed to be born at all. This paradox is clearly a consequence of policies of development imposed on communities without taking into consideration their diversity and mapping their cultural configuration. Therefore, the crucial issue of falling sex ratio cannot be seen in isolation, it has to address the interface between economy and culture. It is at the confluence of these two that the women's body becomes a site of ideological, symbolic and physical violence.

These implications for women have been put in the context by Shiva who sees, 'the Punjab crisis in large measure the tragic outcome of a resource intensive and politically and economically centralized experiment with food production ... . It illustrates that ecological and ethnic fragmentation and breakdown are intimately connected and are an intrinsic part of a policy of planned destruction of diversity of nature and culture to create the uniformity demanded by centralized management systems ...' (Shiva 1991: 111–112). Leading to what Frankel predicted: an accelerated disruption in traditional societies. More rapidly than in other areas, traditional hierarchical arrangements rooted in norms of mutual interdependence and (asymmetric) obligations give way to adversary relations based on new notions of economic interest (c.f. Shiva 1991: 172), thus shaking the edifice of traditional balance between women in their communities.

The violence against women that arises from the epistemological and economic reductionism of agricultural maldevelopment takes place in two ways. The myth that chemicals and machines can replace the life in food and the life of the soil, has led to dispensing with the productive role of women in conservation and in food production and processing. Work and labour that go into maintaining essential ecological processes on the farm and conserving nutrition in food are not registered on the linear scale of inputs and outputs that come from and feed distant markets. Commodification of food production thus either destroys the basis of women's work or devalues it. With the decline in the perceived or real productivity of women is associated a decline in the status in society and within the household' (Shiva 1988: 112). As discussed, with the commercialization of agricultural economy, women's work increases, but the very process of maldevelopment which *increases women's work* in producing sustenance, decreases the value of women's work because it is linked to sustenance, not profits' (Shiva 1988: 113).

Thus, 'for these women, lived reality is informed by a patriarchal paradigm that holds intact women's subordinate position through son preference, land and property rights' (Padhi 2014: 168) while their 'access to work' is linked to 'the women's position in the family and community's location in the caste-class hierarchy' (Padhi 2014: 168). The 'different phases of development and social positioning affect the manifestation of gender differentiation within the same site to shape the forms of gender violence differently, while some forms (like wife beating) tenaciously persist across time, others (infanticide and foeticide) change, while some (human sacrifice, witch-hunting) may be eclipsed or re-emerge (honour killing) and newer forms (acid attacks, 'teasing' and sexual harassment at the workplace) may erupt. Forms of gender violence are shaped by the specificities of socio-economic placement of development culture, caste, strata and location (rural-urban), endangering some women while bypassing others within the same site' (Dagar 2014: 104).

Conclusion

The above account of inter-linkages of Punjabi women's changing roles, relationship, lifestyles in the present day, social and economic developmental contexts, points to the devaluation of social status and dignity of women in certain important respects and increasing domestic violence. In doing so, it attempts to make a case that such social devaluation of women and the recent decline in the juvenile female to male ratio are a sociologically interconnected phenomena and not a simple historical coincidence. The marginalization of women is a vital factor which has led to an economy of loss that describes Punjab today.

Note

1. Tamil Naidu has its own complex historical specificity. It has already taken major strides in family planning and has already achieved a replacement level of fertility. Though it does not have, like Punjab and Haryana, a tradition of sex-discrimination against females, yet there are reports of rising incidence of female foetcide in this state too (George et al. 1992; Chakarth and Athreya 1997 c.f. Bhat 1992b 52–24). The following quotation from Karin Kapadia, however, does seem to suggest certain significant similarities between our account of Punjab and Kapadia's description of a number of groups of Tamil Naidu. Kapadia writes (1996: 66–67):

   The changing context of rural Non-Brahmin marriage has resulted in a drastic fall in the status of women. This is intimately connected with the simultaneous fall in the status of the matripateral kin. Thus, the dominance of MB (Maman) on the stage of Non-Brahmin kinship is revealed to have been wholly dependent on the high valorization of women in Non-Brahmin culture. This high value was largely due to women's participation in productive work outside the home. When higher education and salaried employment recently became available to young men, these options remained closed to young women. This has meant that at marriage, the traditional bride-price system has been reversed, with the parents of salaried sons now demanding 'dowry' from the parents of prospective brides. After marriage, these young women are withdrawn from agricultural labor and thus transformed from agricultural earners into semi secluded housewives. Consequently, they are viewed as economic burdens by both their natal kin and their marital kin.

   Their natal kin become far less interested in taking them back now that they cannot go out to work and can make no contribution to the household income. Thus, the married Non-Brahmin woman's easy access to her parental home (a right so envied by Brahmin women) is steadily being withdrawn today among the upwardly mobile groups This is largely because these groups are too poor to keep their children in school: A good education and the path to salaried employment if offered is entirely outside their reach. Because the income opportunities of men in these poorest classes have not altered, their demands at marriage are not radically different. Traditional bride-price gifts are still given, and today, both sides share the cost of the marriage. But the values of the upper castes and classes constitute a very powerful social influence, so impoverished young men are increasingly emboldened to demand a small 'dowry' because it is the 'sophisticated' thing to do ... . Class has therefore become a crucial factor in rural Non-Brahmin kinship, creating, within each endogamous caste-group, new primarily economic, divisions between 'marriageable' and unmarriageable' .... Kinship obligations and their moral order are being increasingly viewed as obsolete. It is 'urban' norms and the new non-kin marriage patterns that are viewed as *'nagarikam'* (sophisticated, civilized behavior). Many people see them as merely legitimating greed and economic ambition. But those who protest tend to be those whose daughters have been rejected in favor of brides whose parents could give more 'dowry' and the new perception of daughters as a financial liability is rapidly spreading. The final irony is that it is now only the poorest groups in the middle and lower castes who still share the expenses of marriage between affines and still value women in the traditional way. Every-one else is busily 'marrying money'.

References

Abbi, B.L. and Singh, Kesar. 1997. *Post Green Revolution Rural Punjab: A Profile of Economic and Socio-Cultural Change (1965–95).* Chandigarh: Centre for Research in Rural and Industrial Development.

Abbi, B.L., Nanda, A.K., Malhi, P., Agarwal, R.K., Singh, S. and Khnana, S. 2000. *Operations Research on Spacing Methods: A Study of Operational Efficiency of Family Planning Programme in Rupnagar District, Punjab.* Chandigarh: Centre for Research in Rural and Industrial Development.

Abbi, Kumool. 2003. 'Rural Development and Women: Visibly Changing Lifestyle and Invisible Hands', in M.S. Gill (ed.), *Punjab Society: Perspectives and Challenges.* New Delhi: Concept Publishing House, pp. 270–291.

Aggarwal, Bina. 1989. 'Rural Women, Poverty and Natural Resources: Sustenance, Sustainability and Struggle for Change'. *Economic and Political Weekly*, XXIV(43), WS46-WS65.

Agnihotri, S.B. 2000. *Sex-Ratio Patterns in the Indian Population: A Fresh Exploration.* New Delhi: Sage Publications.

——. 2003. 'Sex Ratios and "Prosperity Effect": What Do NSSO Data Reveal?'. *Economic and Political Weekly*, XXXVII(41), 4381–4404.

Anukriti, S. and Persson, Petra. 2012. *Female Sterilization and Spousal Violence*. Columbia University. www.columbia.ed/as3232/slides. violence.pdf.

Arokiasamy, Perianayagam and Goli, Srinivas. 2012. 'Explaining the Skewed Child Sex-Ratio in Rural India: Revisiting the Land Holding-Patriarchy Land Hypothesis'. *Economic and Political Weekly*, XLVII(42), 20 October.

Balakrishna, Radhika. 2005. *The Social Context of Sex Selective Abortions in India.* http://www.hsph.larnard.edu/it21/medicalization/balakrisnansocial-context.

Bhalla, Sheila. 1989. 'Technological Change and Women Workers: Evidence from the Expansionary Phase in Haryana Agriculture'. *Economic and Political Weekly*, XXIV(43), 28 October, W567-W587.

Bhat, P.N. Mari and Zavier, Francis. 1999. 'Findings of National Family Health Survey'. *Economic and Political Weekly*, 16–23 October.

Bhat, P.N. Mari. 2002a. 'On the Trial of "Missing" Indian Females: Search for Clues'. *Economic and Political Weekly*, 21 December.

——. 2002. 'On the Trial of "Missing" Indian Females II: Illusion and Reality'. *Economic and Political Weekly*, 28 December.

——. 2003. 'Two Child Norm: In Defense of Supreme Court Judgment'. *Economic and Political Weekly*, 1 November.

Browne, John Cave. 1857. *Indian Infanticide: Its Origin, Progress and Suppression*. London: WH Allen and Company.

Bryam, Newman. 2007. *A Bitter Harvest: Farmer Suicide and the Unforeseen Social, Environmental and Economic Impacts of the Green Revolution in Punjab, India.* Food First Development Report, January.

Census of India. 2001 and 2011. Government of India: Office of Register General and Census Commissioner, India.

Chand, R., Sidhu, D.S. and Kaul, J.L. 1985. 'Impact of Agricultural Modernization and Labour Use Pattern in Punjab with Special Reference to Women Labour'. *Indian Journal of Agricultural Economics*, XL(3), 352–359.

Chowdhry, Prem. 1994. *The Veiled Women: Shifting Gender Equations in Rural Haryana, 1880–1990*. New Delhi: Oxford University Press.

Dagar, Renuka. 2014. *Gender, Identity and Violence: Female Deselection in India*. New Delhi: Routledge.

Dak, T.M. and Sharma, M.L. 1988. 'Social Framework of Female Labour Participation in Rural Sector', in T.M. Dak (ed.), *Women and Work in Indian Society*. New Delhi: Manohar.

Das Gupta, Monica, Chung, Woojin and Shuzhuo, L. 2009. 'Is There an Incipient Turnaround in Asia's "Missing Girls" Phenomenon?'. *SSS Research Network*.

Das Gupta, Monica. 1987. 'Selective Discrimination Against Female Children in Rural Punjab, India'. *Population and Development Review*, 13(1), March, 77–100.

——. 2005. 'Explaining Asia's "Missing Women": A New Look at the Data'. *Population and Development Review*, 31(3), 529–535.

Government of India. 2012. *Children in India: A Statistical Appraisal*. Social Status Division, Central Statistics Office, Ministry of Statistics and Programme Implementation. mospi.nic.in/mospi_new/upload/children_india.

Hatti, Neelamber and Sekher, T.V. 2010. *Unwanted Daughters: Gender Discrimination in Modern India*. Jaipur: Rawat Publications.

Ibbetson, D.C.J. 1883. *Report on the Census of the Punjab*. Calcutta. Reprint 1993. New Delhi: Low Price Publishers.

International Institute for Population Sciences (IIPS). 2010. District Level Household and Facility Survey (DLHS-3), 2007–08: India. Punjab: Mumbai: IIPS.

Isabelle, Attane and Guilmoto, Chirstopher. 2007. *Watering the Neighbours' Garden: The Growing Demographic Female Deficit in Asia.* Paris: CIRCED.

Jeffery, Roger and Jeffery, Patricia. 1997. *Population, Gender and Demographic Change in North India*. London: Cambridge University Press.

Jha, Prabhat, Kesler, Maya A., Ram, Faujdar, et al. 2011. 'Trends in Selective Abortion of Female Foetuses in India: Analysis of Nationally Representative Birth Histories from 1990–2005 and Census Data from 1991 and 2011'. Published online on 24 May 2011. DOI: 10.1016/50140–6736(11) 60649–1.

Jha, Prabhat; Kumar, Rajesh; Vasia, Priya; Dhingra, Neeraj; Thiruchalvam, Deva; Moineddin, Rahim. 2006. Low Male to Female Sex Ratio of Children born in India: National Survey of 1.1 Million Households. Thalanct.com. Published online 9 January 2006. DOI:10.1016/50140-6736(06)6793-0.

John, Mary E., Kaur, Ravinder, Palriwala, Rajni, Raju, Saraswati and Saheb, Fatehgarh. 2009. 'Dispensing with Daughters: Technology, Society, Economy in North India'. *Economic and Political Weekly*, XLIV(15), 16–19.

John, Mary E., Kaur, Ravinder, Palriwala, Rajni, Raju, Saraswati and Sagar, Alpana. 2008. 'Planning Families, Planning Gender: The Adverse Child Sex Ratio in Selected Districts of Madhya Pradesh, Rajasthan, Himachal Pradesh, Haryana and Punjab'. *ActionAid*. www.cwds.ac.in/2008.planning.families.planning.gender.pdf.

John, Mary, E. 2011. 'Census 2011: Governing Populations and the Girl Child'. *Economic and Political Weekly*. Vol. 46, No. 16, April.

Kapadia, Karin. 1996. *Siva and Her Sisters*. New Delhi: Oxford University Press.

Kaur, Malika. 2010. 'The Paradox of India's Bread Basket: Farmer Suicides in Punjab'. *Praxis: The Fletcher Journal of Human Security*, XXV, 39–60.

Kaur, Pradeep and Kaur, Gian. 2012. 'Factors Affecting Female Labour Force Participation in Punjab: An Inter-District Analysis'. *Journal of Research in Peace, Gender and Development*, 2(4), April, 81–88. http://www.interesjournalorg/jrpgd.

Kaur, Ravinder. 2008. 'Dispensable Daughters and Bachelor Sons: Sex Discrimination in North India'. *Economic and Political Weekly*. Vol. 43, No. 30, July.

Kaur, Rupinder. 1998. 'Female Work Participation: Caste, Class and Gender Analysis in Rural Indian Punjab'. *International Journal of Punjab Studies*, 5(1).

Kishwar, Madhu. 1989. 'Towards More Just Norms for Marriage'. *Manushi*, 55.

——. 1998. 'Rethinking Dowry Boycott'. *Manushi*, 48.

Kumar, Sanjay and Sathyanarayana, K.M. 2012. 'District-Level Estimates of Fertility and Implied Sex Ratio at Birth in India'. *Economic and Political Weekly*, XLVII(33), 18 August.

Karsen, Mattias, Hatti, Neelambar and Gooch, Pernille. 2006. 'Intergenerational Interests, Uncertainty and Discrimination: Conceptualizing the Process of Declining Child Sex Ratios in India'. Lund Papers in Economic History, 105, Department of Economic History, Lund University. www.unfpa.org/.../indiapublishedpapers/unfpapublication 39849.

Malhotra, Anju, Pande, Rohini Prabha and Wamy, Sophe. 2012. 'Fertility Declines and Shifts in Gender Equality in India: A Comparative Analysis of Punjab and Tamil Nadu'. http://paa2012.princeton.edu/papers121946.

Malhotra, Anshu. 2002. *Gender, Caste and Religious Identities: Restructuring Class in Colonial Punjabs*. New Delhi: Oxford University Press.

Mann, R.S. and Mann, K. 1988. 'Status Versus Work and Role of Jat Women', in T.M. Dak (ed.), *Women and Work in Indian Society*. New Delhi: Manohar.

Miller, Barbara D. 1997. *The Endangered Sex: Neglect of Female Children in Rural North India*. New Delhi: Oxford University Press.

Mitra, Aparna. 2011. *Son Preferences in India: Implications for Gender Development*. Department of Economics, University of Oklahoma. http://www.socialeconomics.org/papers/mitra4apdf.

Mohan, Kamlesh. 2006. *Towards Gender History: Images, Identities and Role of North Indian Women*. New Delhi: Aaakar.

Nanda, A.K. and Veron, Jacques. 2005. 'Child Sex Ratio Imbalance, Fertility Behaviour and Development in India: Recent Evidence from Haryana and Punjab', in Isabelle Attane and Jacques Veron (eds), *Gender Discrimination Among Young Children in Asia*. Pondicherry: French Institute Social Science Collections, pp. 91–131.

National Family Health Survey-3. 2006. Chapter 3: Fertility and Fertility Preference. Mumbai: International Institute for Population Sciences. http://hetv.org/india/nfhs3/nfhs: 3.

Nilsson, Marie. 2004. *The Paradox of Modernity: A Study of Girl Discrimination in Urban Punjab, India*. Lund University, Centre for East and South East Asian Studies, MA Programme in Asian Studies.

Padhi, Ranjana. 2014. *Those Who Did Not Die: Impact of the Agrarian Crisis on Women in Punjab*. New Delhi: Sage Publications.

Panigrahi, Lalita. 1972. *British Social Policy and Female Infanticide in India*. New Delhi: Munshiram Manoharlal.

Patel, Tulsi. 2004. 'Missing Girls in India'. *Economic and Political Weekly*, 28 February.

——. 2007. *Sex Selective Abortion in India: Gender, Society and New Reproductive Technologies*. New Delhi: Sage Publications.

Patel, Vibhuti. 2011. 'Tables on Sex Ratio in India and World'. *India Together*, 18 April.

Pervez, Shahid, Jefferey, Roger and Jefferey, Patricia. 2012. 'Declining Child Sex Ratio and Sex-Selection in India: A Demographic Epiphany?'. *Economic and Political Weekly*, XLVII(33), 73–77.

Punjab Development Report 2002–2007. Planning Commission. nic.in/plans/state/plan.

Punjab Human Development Report. 2004. UNDP.

Purewal, K. Navtej. 2010. *Son Preference: Sex Selection, Gender and Culture in South Asia*. UK: Berg.

Rajani, M.B. and Kuzhiparambil, Asha. 2011. 'Epicenters of Missing Daughters: Geo-Spatial Analysis of the Child Sex Ratio in India'. 12th Esri India User Conference. errlindia.com/events/uc2011_files/nted_ucp0060.pdf.

Raju, Saraswati. 2010. 'Mapping the World of Women's Work: Regional Patterns and Perspectives'. Asia-Pacific Working Paper Series, New Delhi: ILO.

Rastogi, Preet. 2000. 'Identifying Gender Backward Districts Using Selected Indicators'. *Economic and Political Weekly*, 25 November – 1 December.

Retherford, D. Robert and Roy, T.K. 2002. 'Factors Affecting Sex Selective Abortion in Punjab, India'. Revised version of paper presented at the 20th Population Census Conference, Ulaanbaatar, Mongolia, 19–21 June.

Rowbotham, Sheila and Linkogle, Stephanie. 2001. *Women Resist Globalization: Mobilizing for Livelihood and Rights*. London: Zed Books.

Sandhu, H.K. 1976. 'Technological Development Versus Economic Contribution of Women in Rural Punjab'. *Social Change*, 6(3 and 6).

Sethi, Raj Mohini (ed.) 2010. 'Socio-Economic Profile of Rural India', (Series II) in *North and Central India, Haryana Himachal Pradesh and Madhya Pradesh* (Vol. V). New Delhi: Concept.

Sethi, Raj Mohini. 1982. *Female Labour in Agriculture*. Chandigarh: Punjab University Press.

Sharma, Ursula. 1980. *Women, Work and Property in North West India*. London: Tavistock Publishers.

Shekhar, T.V. and Hatti, Neelambar. 2010. 'Disappearing Daughters and Intensification of Gender Bias: Evidence from Two Villages in South India'. *Sociological Bulletin*, 59(1), January–April, 111–113.

Shiva, Vandana. 1988. *Staying Alive*. New Delhi: Kali for Women.

——. 1991. *Violence of the Green Revolution: Third World Agriculture, Ecology and Politics*. London: Zed Books.

Singh, K.P. 1986. 'Female Labour Force, Population Growth and Development: The Case of Punjab', in S.L. Sharma (ed.), *Development: Socio-Cultural Dimensions*. Jaipur: Rawat Publications, pp. 85–103.

Snehi, Yogesh. 2003. 'Female Infanticide and Gender in Punjab'. *Economic and Political Weekly*, 11 October, 4302–4304.

Sukkoo, Kim and Chakraborty, Tanika. 2010. 'Kinship Institutions and Sex-Ratios in India'. *Demography*, 47(4), November, 989–1012. soks.wustl.edu/kenship.pdf

The Economist. 2012. 'India's Skewed Sex Ratio'. 27 August.

Times of India. 2001. 'Female Fertility Continues to Drop'. 27 November.

——. 2011. 'Skewed Sex-Ratio may Lead to Social Chaos in Punjab and Haryana'. 3 April.

UNFPA, India. 2011. 'Trends in Sex Ratio at Birth and Estimates of Girls Missing at Birth in India (2001–2008)'. September. unfpa.org/drive/srbbooklet

Unisa, Sayeed. 2009. 'An Investigation into Masculinization of Sex Ratio in India'. www.iipsindia.org. Paper presented at XXVI IUSSP International Population Conference, Marrakech, Morocco, 27 September – 4 October. http://iussp.princeton.edu/papers/91884.

Visaria, Pravin and Visaria, Leela. 2004. 'India's Population', in Veena Das (ed.), *Handbook of Indian Sociology*. New Delhi: Oxford University Press, pp. 61–87.

8

Gendered Spaces and Issues of Safety in Cities

Rajesh Gill

The rise of cities has been interpreted in different ways by scholars, depending upon the positive or negative consequences accompanying the process. For instance, cities have been understood as engines of growth and development by some while these have been believed to lead to erosion of social values and community structures by others. The cities conceptualized by earlier scholars such as Max Weber as fortified/walled were altogether of a different character and have no resemblance with the contemporary cities which are open from all sides, with complete fluidity and enormous technological growth, with no actual boundaries. The world on the whole has been moving towards an urban end, with most of the countries of the world gaining urban in comparison to rural population.

Urbanization has been found to have a positive relationship with economic growth and development although it is not known as to which of the two is the causal variable. Yet, this economic growth/development has been found to be a farce once an intra city analysis is attempted. A city in the developing country, particularly India, is inhabited by residents who directly benefit from the economic growth of the city, its infrastructure, etc. while there is a huge population in the same city which survives in deplorable conditions, with no access to proper housing, food, employment, education, health and so on. While some migrants move into the city to improve their professional and economic prospects, a large majority enter the city just to be able to earn a livelihood to sustain themselves and their families. It is for this reason that it is difficult to make a simplistic generalization, that cities imply economic growth. The architecture, town planning and physical layout of a city clearly point out to the heterogeneity that characterises the city in terms of income, class, religion, region and language. The cities, particularly the metropolitan, have the best of facilities, infrastructure, employment opportunities, but are these equally available to all? That is the real question.

As a city grows, it automatically sifts the population so that gradually certain sections of the population, communities in Indian context, get completely excluded from its core areas.

A major challenge confronting contemporary cities all over the world, therefore, is to make cities inclusive, safer, humane and sustainable not only environmentally, but socially and culturally. Cities will have to evolve methods to forge democratization, political participation by all urban residents, gender equality and full participation by all residents, irrespective of ethnicity, class, caste and religion. These objectives were forcefully brought out by the United Nations in the Second HABITAT Conference held in 1996 at Istanbul. However, empirical evidence points at substantially different trends. For instance, the UN Report of 2008 of HABITAT exposes the increasing disparities/divide within cities of developing countries, while this gap has declined in the developed countries. Indian cities for that matter continue to reflect the worst forms of rich-poor divide in terms of its infrastructure, accessibility and housing. It often gets translated into the social and political divide, most of the decision-making processes hijacked by the upper income, educated urbanites, while the poor, less educated continue to reel under conditions of deprivation and inaccessibility. Actually, the spatial profile of crime in cities could provide an extremely interesting picture of such an urban divide.

Physical exclusion of the urban poor has been sufficiently demonstrated in literature on slums, largely occupied by the army of rural migrants, who find it economically viable and socially comfortable to stay in such illegal colonies. This physical separation or segregation often gets translated into cultural and social exclusion whereby the mainstream urban population has a much better entitlement to roads, public utilities, infrastructure, green belts and so on. Further aggravating the problem, physical and social segregation of urban poor is further reinforced by planners who rehabilitate them on urban periphery, reducing their access to urban advantages, unlike the more affluent urbanites.

Report of UN HABITAT underlines some extremely important characteristics of the contemporary cities of the world, especially those in developed and developing countries of the world. This paper has drawn heavily from this Report while developing arguments and discussions.

State of the World's Cities 2010/2011 Report by UN HABITAT (2008) brings out the need to develop 'inclusive city' by which it implies:

> Cities that share a few basic features that can take different forms in various conditions: they provide the opportunities and supportive mechanisms that enable all residents to develop their full potential and gain their fair shares of the 'urban advantage'. In an inclusive city, residents perceive themselves as important contributors to decision making, ranging from political issues to the more mundane routines of daily life … . The concepts of human relations, citizenship and civic rights are all inseparable from urban inclusiveness. (2008: XIX)

An inclusive city, as defined for the purposes of this report, is one that provides all residents – regardless of race, ethnicity, gender or socio-economic status, with adequate housing and decent basic services, and facilitates equal access to social amenities, opportunities and other public goods that are essential to the general and environmental well-being of everyone (2008: 55).

In contrast to the 'inclusive city', this report explains a 'divided city' as one that fails to accommodate its poorer residents, regardless of the social and cultural riches they might contribute. Social divisions can permeate interactions amongst individuals even in the absence of significant ethnic, racial or other factors of segregation. Fresh divisions constantly emerge and become entrenched, patterns of social inclusion and exclusion preserve benefits for specific social segments based on physical location, shared interests, historic inequalities or other criteria (2008: XII).

According to this Report, thus, an inclusive city, thus, could be built by using the following strategies:

1. Assessing the past and measuring progress
2. More effective, stronger institutions
3. Building new linkages and alliances among the various tiers of government;
4. Demonstrating a sustained vision to promote inclusiveness
5. Ensuring the redistribution of opportunities

Further, urban experience so far indicates that fiscal health of an urban settlement greatly contributes to the infrastructural development as well as reduction in the urban/opportunity divide. Numerous studies have shown that the largest metropolitan cities have much better basic services both for the rich as well as poor as compared to the small and medium towns due to which migrants throng these cities. The municipal corporations of these cities are much more comfortable financially, better connected politically with the funding agencies and attractive for the multinational companies, giving them a clear cut edge over the small and medium towns, with local municipal bodies reeling under fund starvation and administrative neglect. Despite 74th Constitutional Amendment Act, providing for a decentralized and people friendly local administration, the smaller towns continue to be ill administered with completely feudal and centralized power structures. The urban divide in these towns is further likely to aggravate with the privatization of housing and urban management.

Recent literature on urban planning, therefore, has placed enormous emphasis on social planning. Advocates of social planning claim that unlike other forms of planning, social planning is primarily concerned with social reality instead of implying merely the physical layout of a city. Social planning has been conceptualized as a kind of planning that has great concern with social issues, aiming at creating an inclusive city, with no urban divide. Such a conceptualization is accompanied by the rejection of the model of physical planning of city whereby city structure is understood as an outcome of natural forces akin to the survival of the fittest, giving a peculiar shape to the city. It is argued by proponents of social planning that urban planning far from being a scientific and rational exercise, is actually a political venture, dominated by the powerful urban elite. The concept of social planning has emerged primarily with the recognition of culture as an extremely important factor in shaping the cities and their internal structures.

The City as a Symbol of Inequalities

Long back Louis Wirth (1951) in his famous essay underlined that city has heterogeneity in its population which distinguishes from a village. Actually this heterogeneity or difference is more than evident in the urban architecture, residential areas, markets, lifestyles, parks and so on. This difference takes on the patterns of inequality in terms of income, access to urban advantages and urban facilities. While city provides many with improved employment, higher incomes, better quality of life, it hardly makes a difference to millions of poor who remain homeless in the same city. Rex and Moore (1967) long ago argued that city was divided into differentially placed classes which were in persistent conflict with one another over the scare resources of the city. Later on, Pahl (1975) used 'urban managers' as a concept to denote the real estate agents, social workers, urban planners and bureaucrats who controlled the scarce resources of the city. He argued that the decisions of these urban managers in fact led to the distribution of resources differentially to urban residents, resulting into inequality. He was conscious that these urban managers did not function independently and that their decisions were often dependent upon the structured systems and institutions serving the interest of private capital.

The urban theory propounded by Wirth and others, underlining the peculiarities of an urban/city life, understood as a consequence of urban residence, was seriously questioned by Castells in his famous book *The Urban Question* (1972). For him, 'collective consumption', whose social organization took place primarily in cities, was a subject of study for urban sociologists.

Spatial Structures as Symbols of Social Inequalities

There is enormous literature that emphasizes upon the spatial structure of cities leading to inequalities, both socio-cultural and economic. Marxian political economy approach was the first to argue that capital is the principal architect of spatial structures leading to social inequalities (Badcock 1984: 53). Scholars such as Pickvance (1976), Harloe (1977), Mingione (1977), Harvey (1973) and Dunleavy (1980) made significant contributions to the understanding of cities and the study of urban sociology. Manual Castells (1972) and David Harvey (1973) described the city as structured by the history of class struggles.

All over the world, cities have experienced a segregation of the rich and the poor in spatial terms. Schneider and Susser in their book *Wounded Cities* (2003) compare the 'flight to the suburbs' undertaken voluntarily by people for a better quality of life with the forced movement of poor and middle class people to suburbs who have no choice in the matter. They describe these 'edge cities' as unplanned and blighted, inhabited by people who abandoned cities against their will. As described by Janice Monk (1992), expressions of class, race, status and ethnicity are more evident in city space. We spontaneously realize that we are in a working class area at just a cursory glance at the kind of shops, houses, open spaces or their absence, and the material used for the buildings. Similarly, the architectural designs, construction material, size of buildings, etc. clearly indicate the class, race and ethnic status of the people using these areas. The UN HABITAT Report (2008: 11), while describing the process of urban sprawl explains that in some developing countries urban sprawl is the consequence of poverty, not affluence, as informal unplanned settlements on the periphery spring up in response to a lack of affordable housing options within the city itself. It further states that urban sprawl contributes to urban divide, with a negative impact not only on the infrastructure and sustainability of cities, but also on social cohesion, often leading to social segregation and segmentation. Sub-urbanization in developing countries happens mainly as an escape away from poor governance, lack of planning and poor access to amenities. Highlighting the negative fallout of urban sprawl, it further observes that sprawl adds to the costs and inefficiencies of transportation, resulting in higher energy consumption than compact cities. Urban sprawl also causes significant loss of prime farmland and leads to degradation of environmental resources, mainly due to poor planning.

UN HABITAT Report (2008) *State of World Cities 2010/2011* describes the differential land use in cities against the urban poor especially in the developing countries. While urban planning has the potential to build equitable cities, on the contrary, it has often been used as an instrument of exclusion. The Report states:

> Indeed, powerful members of society have used 'master planning' to capture land and provide infrastructure, manipulating land use patterns in favour of the gentrification of entire area in cities. In the process, massive development has taken place to make room for highways, skyscrapers, luxury compounds or shopping malls, to the detriment of the habitats and livelihoods of the poor .... On top of displacing the poor, these self-serving planning policies also fail to provide adequate low cost housing alternatives, making them all the more inequitable. (2008: 90–91)

The UN Report further brings out another recent divisive aspect of the cities through a rapid expansion of 'gated communities' and other protected enclaves of wealth. Apart from social segregation, these gated communities also result in social exclusion, distinguishing between those 'inside' and 'outside'.

Criteria of Exclusion in Cities

That cities, particularly in developing countries, exhibit social exclusion is sufficiently demonstrated in literature. After the Marxist critique of theories of urbanism, the Feminist critique of city gained prominence in urban sociology. It was argued that cities are masculine spaces, gendered enough to exclude women from core locales and public spaces. Critics underlined the inability of social theory and research to handle the issues of gender difference and structured gender inequality (Firestone 1970; Millett 1970; Mitchell 1971). Marxist political economy approach was fiercely challenged for its preoccupation with the effects of capitalist mode of production, thereby totally ignoring the relations of reproduction (Markusen 1980). Literature indicates that unlike ethnic, class and racial differences in city spaces, gender specific spaces in a city are not obvious as one finds both men and women in all neighbourhoods. Yet it is true that in spite of this spatial coexistence, men and women not only use city space in different ways but also experience it differently (Stevenson 2003: 37–38). Early feminism emphasized that women had been disadvantaged by the physical layout of a city. The separation between work and home for instance had greatly reflected and reinforced this disadvantage. This dichotomy was associated by Wilson (2001) to the distinction between public and private domains, with the public linked to the city and the private to the home and the suburbs. Thus, it was argued that although both men and women share spaces in same houses and neighbourhoods, yet they occupy different spaces for work and leisure. Traditionally, men have been moving to their workplace every day, while women have stayed back at home, taking care of their role as homemakers. With this background in place, city centre or downtown was looked upon as a place for men and the suburbs were seen as natural spaces for women and children. The city could be, thus, divided into discrete male and female zones (Saegert 1980; McDowell 1983; Matrix 1984).

Sophie Watson (1988) has dealt with the gendered spaces within the cities at length. She argues that housing location and tenure have played a crucial role in creating patriarchal structures of injustice. Home ownership as the dominant form of housing tenure and suburbanization as the premier residential site have gone to the disadvantage of women. Watson argues that the 'suburbanization of home ownership' results into social and spatial relations that limit women's access to urban facilities, resources, labour market and finance capital, simultaneously reinforcing domestic relationships, again to the disadvantage of women.

Cities have also been interpreted by feminists from the standpoint of women's safety. Women often divide the city spaces into places that are 'safe' and those as 'unsafe'. Dora Epstein (1997) writes in this regard:

> There is a story to this fearing, this fearing that maps the cityscapes into places I will go and places I will not. As speaking subjects, sentient members of urban terrains, we can narrate our cartographies of avoidance, our fearing, far better than we can narrate how the fearing came to be. We know, can articulate, what we have deemed 'unsafe' – the strange, the unfamiliar, the supposedly violent 'other' against we have insulated and barricaded ourselves – and what we have deemed as 'safe' – the lit, the populated, the orderly, or seemingly controlled to which we have clung. We felt justified when violence occurred in the realm of our 'unsafe'; felt shock when it occurred in our 'safe'. (Epstein 1997: 134)

It has, therefore, been argued that the women who consistently and in routine have to use the public spaces for work or other purposes, mark the spaces or locales or areas which are safe and others as unsafe. However, all these spaces may not be the same for all women. While some of such spaces such as escalators/lifts, dark and secluded spaces, masculine spaces, may be identified by all women as unsafe, other spaces may be differently defined by women of different classes, races and ethnic groups. Because of this reason, the Marxist Feminism explaining gender inequality in society in general and city in particular through capitalist mode of production and patriarchy has been refuted on the basis of the varied experiences of women within themselves in the same city. There has, thus, been a shift from taking women as a homogeneous group towards that of women as a differentiated group.

Schools in many slum areas, as corroborated by the UN HABITAT Report (2008: 117), are not child friendly and in some cases are even hazardous for girls. During menstruation, girls will not attend school if basic toilet facilities are not available at school. The heightened risk of sexual violence in poor, overcrowded classrooms hinders educational prospects for girls. More or less unwillingly, girls often give in to unwanted sexual advances from boys or even teachers, leaving them exposed to unwanted pregnancies.

Geographers too have underlined the social relevance of spatial structures. They argue that space is essential to social science, spatial relations exist only because social processes exist and that the spatial and social aspects of a phenomenon are inseparable (Massey 1984; Dear and Wolch 1989). According to Spain (2005: 45), initial status differences between women and men create certain types of gendered spaces and that institutionalized spatial segregation then reinforces existing male advantages. McDowell (1983), a Feminist geographer argues that urban structure in capitalist societies reflects the construction of space into masculine centres of production and feminine suburbs of reproduction. According to this perspective, definitions of femininity and masculinity are constructed in particular places, most notably the home, workplace and community. How men and women should behave in the home are negotiated not only there but also at work, school and at social events (Bowlby, Foord and McDowell et al. 1986). Dwellings often reflect ideals and patterns of relationships between men and women within societies and families.

Although pre-industrial societies had a clear spatial segregation between women and men in terms of home and workplace, in industrial societies too, women tend to be segregated in certain workplaces. Studies have shown that women in typically male occupations earned more and had higher status than women in typically women occupations (Aron 1987). Women have continued to be concentrated in certain occupations all over the world, occupying separate workplaces from men (Baron and Bielby 1985). Thus in modern workplaces, there are not only men's and women's jobs but also men's and women's spaces (Scott 1982). Since more and more women are going out to work and since they do not share most of the workplaces with men, contact between the two genders is reduced. Since public status derives significantly from occupational skills, workplace segregation leads to lower status among women in cities too, spatial relations influencing women's status.

Similar ideas are echoed by Schneider and Susser (2003) who argue that globalizing processes tend to be gendered. Quoting studies from Thailand, Brazil and China, the authors state that younger women easily become commodities selling exotica and sexuality as part of the sensuous image of tourism (Zhen 2001). Globalization has also created a strong and sizeable section of consumers among women, particularly in cities. This is especially true in the off shore pink collar industries. Working as telephone receptionists, programmers and print shop workers, these urban women spend a substantial portion of their wages on fashionable clothes, shoes and cosmetics, considered essential for their work status. In a study, it was found that in the islands of the Caribbean, many working women fly to other islands on their free days using air coupons supplied by their corporate employers, to purchase clothes appropriate to their work status (Freeman 1998). These studies indicate that women in the metropolises have been transformed into a compulsive shopper, spending most of their time and money in the shopping malls.

The UN HABITAT Report of 2008 also highlights the most vulnerable condition of women and girls in cities of the developing countries. It states that girls and young women living in poverty in cities consistently face steeper challenges than their male peers when it comes to acquiring the knowledge and skills they need to live healthy, productive lives. It further suggests that continued emphasis on expanded opportunities for girls and young women, therefore, will be an essential requirement if the Millennium Development Goals are to be met in cities. The Report further states that a majority of young female slum dwellers tend to bear children at an earlier age than their non-slum counterparts. Women who do work in developing countries tend to do so in the informal economy, owing to lack of formal job opportunities in many regions. In developing countries, confinement of slum dwelling women to largely informal jobs provides a stark illustration of a wider phenomenon whereby the formal, secure livelihoods that typically accompany the urban advantage elude too many among the urban population.

Cities also exclude groups from urban advantages on the basis of incomes, in that there exists a huge gulf between the rich and the poor within the city, reflected evidently in the spaces, e.g. markets, eating joints, buildings, parks, etc. used by them. The UN HABITAT Report (2008: 54) endorses this urban divide and states that in Greater Mumbai, the slum population in the western suburbs is as high as 43 per cent, whereas in the city proper it is only 17 per cent. A similar pattern exists in New Delhi District, where 3.4 per cent of the population lives below the poverty line, whereas in the North West District, this proportion is more than 30 per cent. A slum area is typically associated with reduced numbers of schools, clinics and other public and private amenities. Social and cultural barriers continue to deny slum dwellers the opportunity to complete basic education. Children from slum communities are less likely to enrol in school, tend to complete fewer years and are less likely to complete primary or attend secondary school. Education inequalities in both learning and earning outcomes persist in cities. The UN HABITAT report makes the following observation which is very pertinent in this context:

> Based on a systematic comparison of slum with non-slum populations within the same city, and groups of slum dwellers suffering various types of shelter deprivations, this Report demonstrates with compelling evidence that hunger, health and poor education outcomes have strong social class gradients, as measured by the intensity of shelter deprivations. (2008: XIV)

Conclusions and Suggestions

The preceding discussion clearly indicates that contemporary cities, especially in developing countries, are far from being inclusive. The early perspectives on city explaining spatial structuring of the city as an independent phenomenon has long been rejected. That cities take a particular physical shape not due to natural factors, following the survival of the fittest, but due to economic, political, social and cultural factors, has long been realized and corroborated by hundreds of studies. The classical approaches to the understanding of the city have by and large been replaced by Marxist, Feminist and Cultural approaches, whereby a city is understood not merely as a physical habitat, an ecological unit, but mainly a social space, which is designed by the larger socio-political reality of which the city itself is only a part.

Communities or individuals may choose a particular habitat due to their priorities and conscious decisions, primarily cultural in nature. In the process, people with low incomes and capabilities to access the urban advantage, mostly end up landing in the locales discarded by the affluent. Therefore, it is not merely the economic disability that pushes them to these slum areas, unfit for human living, but the social structural handicaps, which perpetually hinder them from sharing city spaces with the rich and influential. Such physical sifting is further reinforced by planners by rehabilitating the poor on the outskirts/periphery of the city, thereby reducing their chances of appropriating urban facilities and infrastructure. They are forced to spend more on transportation, apart from getting deprived of regular employment opportunities. It is certain, therefore, that urban planning so far has contributed to promoting the urban divide instead of reducing it. In recent years, with the coming in of privatization and corporate sector, the prime locales in the cities are occupied with the shopping complexes, malls and restaurants, catering to middle and upper classes of urban dwellers, with absolutely no service for the low income groups, without whom no city can sustain itself. Of late, at least in India as elsewhere, cities have turned out to be the most unsafe locales for women and young girls. Our cities indicate the fact that despite the increase in workforce participation by women, still they are not safe in public spaces. It tends to endorse the feminist approach to urban sociology that cities are primarily masculine spaces.

The commodification of women demonstrates itself most pronouncedly in cities, where marketing strategies use/abuse them to the full. Using their body in commercials, for marketing the products and trafficking has been institutionalized in the urban economies. While the public spaces within the cities, terribly unsafe for women and young girls have multiplied, women find themselves compelled to continue visiting these places, out of financial, social or family compulsions. There have been absolutely no policy initiatives to build safe cities. Women get molested and even raped on public transport, on busy roads and markets, schools and colleges, lifts and so on. This has become a common phenomenon at least in countries like India. While there are stringent laws as deterrents to such crimes, there have hardly been any tangible policy or administrative measures taken by the city administration. Actually city planning has always implied town planning, focused on land use and physical planning, with an utter disregard to the social and cultural dimensions. Having realized now the immense significance of these dimensions, still, no inputs have gone into city planning in terms of social planning.

Advocates of social planning claim that unlike other forms of planning social planning is exclusively concerned with the socio-cultural components of the population. An urban settlement is no longer believed to be an outcome of the principle of the survival of the fittest as opined by classical ecological theorists, but it is conceptualized today as a product of deliberate actions of individuals who matter, while others just happen to be where they are, almost nonexistent in the process of sifting of population as well as services (Gill 2009). It has now been realized that the physical structure of cities is the product of conscious decision-making and social relations, and therefore can never be neutral. What gets built, where, how and for whom – reflects relations of power and the often stereotyped assumptions of planners, architects, and bureaucrats. This puts to serious question the earlier assumption that planning is a rational and scientific exercise aimed at optimizing the resource allocations with greatest returns. The normative aspect of planning is now being prioritized though only in literature so far.

In an interesting disposition, Jo Beall (1997) presented extensive empirical data, both from developed as well as developing countries, to make a case for social planning. With the differential impact of globalization and corporatization, it is obligatory on the part of urban planners to identify the city populations which are most vulnerable, viz., women, young girls, children, differently abled, aged and poor. These differences can no longer be brushed aside as non-consequential. Women and men, elderly, children, adolescents, disabled, racial, linguistic and regional minorities, refugees, newcomers, migrant workers, the affluent and the extremely poor – all have contrasting needs and lifestyles. Any system of governance therefore must accommodate these differences. Experience has shown that while it is easier for policy makers to recognize diversity in theory, it is enormously challenging to work with diversity. It involves the issues of identities and ethnicities. Working with diversities, is a very sensitive and even dangerous exercise, because of the possible political overtures involved.

Experience so far has shown that physical planning is insensitive and inhuman, it must therefore be made more humane and sensitive. Further, whether intentionally or not, physical planning has offered greater benefits to those already in position of economic or political power. Finally, physical planning cannot be separated from social planning because each involves people. As already discussed, contemporary cities have become symbols of insecurity for women. Despite a steep rise in sexual terrorism, these issues have hardly been addressed in any discussion on urban planning. Institutional violence experienced by women through policies such as slum clearance and removal increases their vulnerability to police and land mafia. Though state-run shelters exist in some cities, these have been severely criticized for the high level of corruption and forced prostitution that women inhabitants are coerced into. Women rarely have property ownership and there is absence of alternative support networks and places of refuge in cities. Women often get termed as victims instead of survivors and any support extended to them is seen as welfare rather than empowerment oriented help.

Almost all public spaces are experienced as gendered spaces by women, viz., parks, streets, public transport, market places, cinemas, etc. need to be perceived from the viewpoint of women's safety and convenience. The involvement of women's representatives is crucial and they should work alongside city planners and architects in planning city services and zones. It is vital to bring violence in the cities on the agenda of urban planners and policy makers. A violent environment within and outside the home threatens the lives of one half of the population and prevents women from participating actively in developmental processes, depriving women of security and denying cities the benefit of their creative energy and different insights (Vadera 1997). Functionally, fragmented cities often make it difficult for people, especially women, to manage the tasks of daily life. Women often need to travel outside of rush hours, and destinations different from those of men, e.g. to shops, schools, clinics. As mothers and caregivers, women have to escort others, as working women engaged in informal sector activities, they often have to carry heavy loads. Yet public sector vehicles are invariably designed without women's requirements. This results in women having to struggle with inconvenient public transport system or to walk (Levy 1992).

It is not only women whose special and different needs demand attention of city planners. Our cities, especially their public transport system, traffic, buildings, etc. are highly inconvenient and disastrous for the poor, the disabled, the aged and children. Healey (1995) suggested 'we need to integrate the concept of social diversity into public policy, to make the built environment less like an assault course or a danger zone and to make it more user friendly, safe and secure for everybody-women and men, healthy and the disabled. What we have at present is the 'gendered city', which implies 'a city historically designed by men and for men – but inhabited both by men and women, who have diverse interests and needs at different stages of their lives and in different family and community contexts.' Women and men use and experience cities in different ways and not always in ways anticipated by planners. Wilson (1991) opined that historically, gender stereotyping has profoundly affected urban planning and urban institutions. Women have never been recognized as having an agency due to which their needs and convenience have never been under consideration for urban planners.

To sum up, modern cities must be viewed for the purposes of planning as centres of collective consumption, where it is no longer easy to separate the economic process of production from the cultural. Cities operate amidst the culture industry, a concept evolved at Frankfurt School in Critical Theory, where the spatial connotations of manufacturing and industry have totally been transformed. Cities are inhabited by consumers of this culture industry, who are no longer involved in the production of their own culture. Cities are inhabited by shoppers, going in for branded products and those who cannot afford these, are excluded from the city. This is another kind of exclusion which is yet to be addressed by urban planners. The project of inclusive cities is, therefore, getting more challenging than before.

References

Aron, Cindy. 1987. *Ladies and Gentlemen of the Civil Service*. New York: Oxford University Press.

Badcock, B. 1984. *Unfairly Structure Cities*. UK: Blackwell.

Baron, James N. and Bielby, William T. 1985. 'Organizational Barriers to Gender Equality: Sex Segregation of Jobs and Opportunities', in Alice Rossi (ed.), *Gender and the Life Course*. New York: Aldine.

Beall, Jo (ed.) 1997. *A City for All: Valuing Difference and Working with Diversity*. London: Zed Books Ltd.

Bowlby, S.R., Foord, J. and McDowell, L. 1986. 'The Place of Gender in Locality Studies'. *Area*, 18(4), 327–331.

Castells, Manual. 1972. *The Urban Question*. London: Edward Arnold.

Dear, Michael and Wolch, Jennifer. 1989. 'How Territory Shapes Social Life', in Jennifer Wolch and Michael Dear (eds), *The Power of Geography*. Boston: Unwin Hyman.

Dunleavy, P. 1980. *Urban Political Analysis: The Politics of Collective Consumption*. London: Macmillan.

Epstein, Dora. 1997. 'Abject Terror: A Story of Fear, Sex and Architecture', in N. Ellin (ed.), *Architecture of Fear*. New York: Princeton Architectural Press.

Firestone, S. 1970. *The Dialectic of Sex: The Case for Feminist Revolution*. New York: Bantam.

Freeman, C. 1998. 'Femininity and Flexible Labor'. *Critique of Anthropology*, 18(3), 245–263.

Gill, Rajesh. 2009. 'Planning Urban Settlements for People: A Social Agenda', in Rajesh Gill (ed.), *Contemporary Indian Urban Society: Ethnicity, Gender and Governance*. New Delhi: Bookwell.

Halligan, J. and Paris, C. 1984. 'The Politics of Local Government', in J. Halligan and C. Paris (eds), *Australian Urban Politics*. Melbourne: Longman Cheshire.

Harloe, M. (ed.) 1977. *Captive Cities*. London: Wiley.

Harvey, David. 1973. *Social Justice and the City*. Baltimore, MD: Johns Hopkins Press.

Healey, Joseph F. 1995. *Race, Ethnicity, Gender and Class: The Sociology of Group Conflict and Change*. London: Pine Forge Press.

Levy, C. 1992. 'Transport', in L. Ostergaard (ed.), *Gender and Development: A Practical Guide*. London: Routledge.

Markusen, A. 1980. 'City Spatial Structure, Women's Household Work and National Urban Policy'. *Signs: Journal of Women in Culture and Society*, 5, S23-S45.

Massey, Doreen. 1984. 'Introduction: Geography Matters', in Doreen Massey and John Allen (eds), *Geography Matters!* Cambridge: Cambridge University Press.

Matrix. 1984. *Making Space: Women and the Man Made Environment*. London: Pluto Press.

McDowell, Linda. 1983. 'City and Home: Urban Housing and the Sexual Division of Space', in Mary Evans and Clare Ungerson (eds), *Sexual Divisions: Patterns and Processes*. London: Tavistock.

Miles, Malcolm. 2007. *Cities and Cultures*. London: Routledge.

Millett, K. 1970. *Sexual Politics*. New York: Avon.

Mingione, E. 1977. 'Theoretical Elements for a Marxist Analysis of Urban Development', in M. Harloe (ed.), *Captive Cities*. London: Wiley.

Mitchell, J. 1971. *Women's Estate*. Harmondsworth: Penguin.

Monk, J. 1992. 'Gender in the Landscape: Expressions of Power and Meaning', in K. Anderson and F. Gale (eds), *Inventing Places: Studies in Cultural Geography*. Melbourne: Longman.

Pahl, R. 1975. *Whose City?* Harmondsworth: Penguin.

Pickvance, C. (ed.) 1976. *Urban Sociology: Critical Essays.* London: Methuen.

Rex, J. and Moore, R. 1967. *Race, Community and Conflict: A Study of Sparkbrook*. Oxford: Oxford University Press.

Saegert, S. 1980. 'Masculine Cities and Feminine Suburbs: Polarised Ideas, Contradictory Realities'. *Signs*, 5(3), S93-S108.

Schneider, Jane and Susser, Ida (eds) 2003. *Wounded Cities.* Oxford: Berg.

Scott, J.W. 1982. 'The Mechanization of Women at Work'. *Scientific American*. 247: 3, September. pp. 166–87.

Stevenson, Deborah. 2003. *Cities and Urban Cultures.* Jaipur: Rawat Publications.

UN HABITAT. 2008. *State of the World's Cities 2010/2011: Bridging the Urban Divide.* London: Sterling.

Vadera, Meenu. 1997. 'Violent Homes in Violent Cities: Experience from India', in Jo Beall (ed.), *A City for All.* London: Zed Books Ltd.

Watson, S. 1988. *Accommodating Inequality*. Sydney: Allen and Unwin.

Wilson, E. 1991. *The Sphinx in the City: Urban Life, the Control of Disorder and Women.* London: Virago.

Wilson, E. 2001. *The Contradictions of Culture: Cities, Culture, Women*. London: Sage.

Wirth, Louis. 1951. 'Urbanism as a Way of Life', in P.K. Hatt and A.J. Reiss (eds), *Cities and Society*. Illinois: The Free Press of Glencoe, pp. 46–63.

Zhang, Z. 2001. 'Mediating Time: The "Rice Bowl of Youth" in Fin de Siecle Urban China', in A. Appadurai (ed.), *Globalization.* Durham, NC: Duke University Press, pp. 131–155.

Zukin, S. 1995. *The Culture of Cities.* Oxford: Blackwell.

Section II

Emerging Forms of Gender Violence: A Field View

9

Gender and Ageing in Punjab and Haryana

Some Issues

Smita Bhutani and Laxmi Devi

Gender perspective into all policies, programmes and legislation dealing with ageing was recommended by Madrid International Plan of Action which was a product of the Second World Assembly on Ageing in 2002. It emphasized particularly that a 'gender sensitive' approach is essential in dealing with women, because women, especially elder women, are at a disadvantage in various ways as compared to men. The Plan of Action called upon all member states to eliminate discrimination on the basis of age and gender. For every 100 women aged 60 or above, there were 84 men; but for every 100 women aged 80, there were only 61 men (UNFPA, New York & Help Age International, London).

Gender and Ageing: Theoretical Perspectives

Studies concerning relationship between gender and ageing have been scarce. The most commonly studied theoretical perspectives of gender and ageing related issues are the following:

(i) Life Course Perspective
(ii) Double Jeopardy Perspective
(iii) Age as Leveller Perspective

1. *Life Course Perspective:* Life course perspective is undertaken for understanding connections generally existing between various stages in the course of lifetime (Hatch 2000). Madrid International Plan of Action on various occasions highlights gender differences particularly about older women and older men between earlier and subsequent stages of life. Changes come in the status and role of both men and women as they grow older. They experience events like matrimony and employment bringing about significant changes in the course of life. As the men and women pass to older years, striking differences are to be observed between them. Most women suffer oppression and discrimination all

along and consequently become victims of illness and poverty in later life (Pratt 1997). An alternative possibility is also there. The self-sacrifice undertaken by women in earlier years in bringing up children earns for them the children's emotional loyalty. Women develop stronger emotional bonds with them than their husbands. This pays dividends and old mothers as members of large families are regarded with greater respect and regard. On the contrary, some men in older years are no longer able to earn a living. They experience feeling of rejection and loss of self respect (WHO 2001). The possibility of a different situation is also there. In earlier years, if these men had been in their working years, helpful to others and had rendered voluntary service for others' well-being, they have earned the beneficiaries' good will. Out of gratitude for the goodness shown by them in the past they may be looked upon with concern and respect, even if they are no longer able to earn a living in older years (WHO 2001).

2. *Double Jeopardy Perspective:* This approach is not similar to life course perspective. In this perspective it is considered that some women may have the stigma of old age added to the result of persecution and discrimination that most women have generally had to experience at the hands of men. Already a disadvantaged group as a result of lifelong victimization thus they have to suffer double jeopardy (Chappell and Havens 1980). The *World Population Report* (UNFPA 1998) states that older women 'bear the burden of age old negative perceptions, which are added to the customary social and economic discrimination against women'.
3. *Age as Leveller Perspective:* In this approach it is considered that inequality between men and women begins to decline as they grow older, negative forces act regardless of gender (Markides 1995). Inequality is reduced still further in some cases where women gain authority as mother-in-law over their daughter-in-law who marry into the family. With advancing age, therefore, they come to the same level of well-being as their men counter parts.

In the present study, all the three approaches, discussed above, have been considered and primary data based exercise is conducted to understand ageing process in various stages in the course of a life time; stigmatized status of women and declining gender inequality with ageing.

Results and Discussion

Punjab and Haryana with the state averages of sex ratios of 895 and 879 females per 1000 males, respectively, have the lowest sex ratios in India (Table 1 and Figure 1). As far as sex ratio of aged population (60 plus population) is concerned, there is a significantly larger number of old, particularly oldest old (80 plus) females than the number of females in all ages (Figure 2 and Figure 3) The sex ratio of 80-plus age group was noticeably in favour of females (Table 1) (Figure 3). In this context, it may, however, be noted that United Nations defines 60-plus population as aged population.

In India, the proportion of elderly population was 8.6 per cent in 2011. Kerala was on the top (12.6%) followed by Goa (12.6%), Tamil Nadu (11.2%)

Figure 1
Punjab-Haryana: Sex Ratio of All Ages, 2011

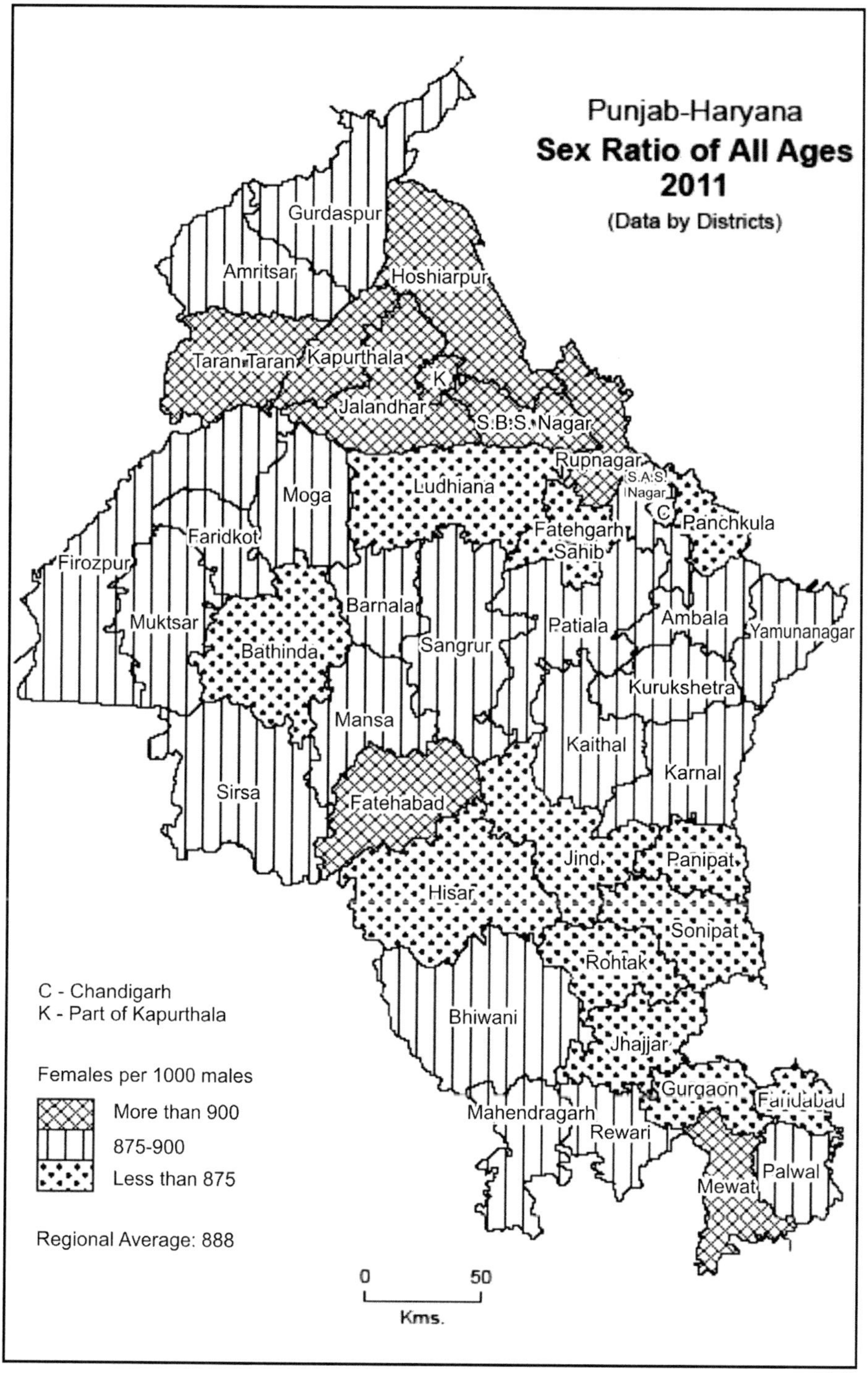

Figure 2
Panjab-Haryana: Sex Ratio of 60+ Age Group, 2011

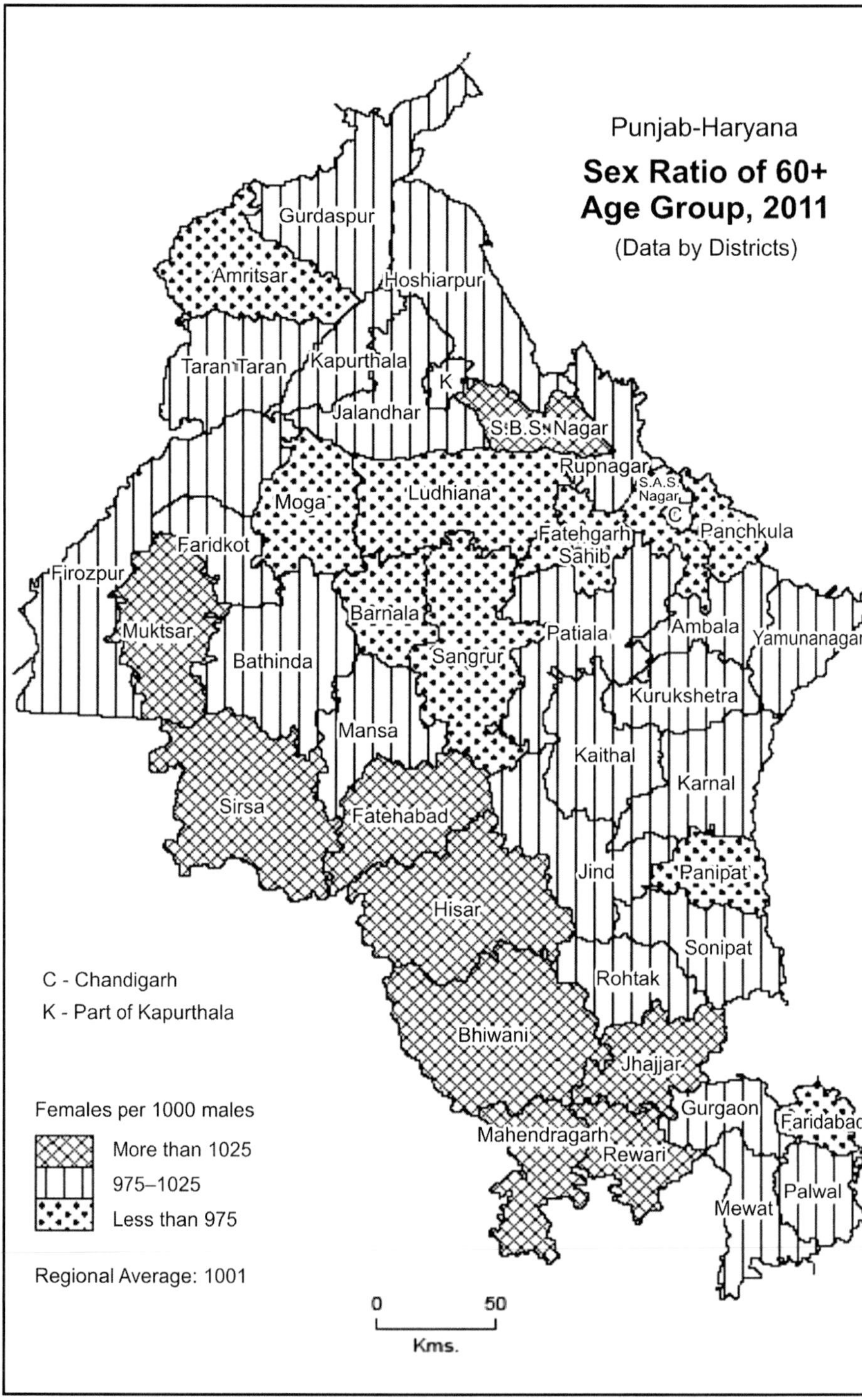

Figure 3
Sex Ratio of 80+ Age Group, 2011

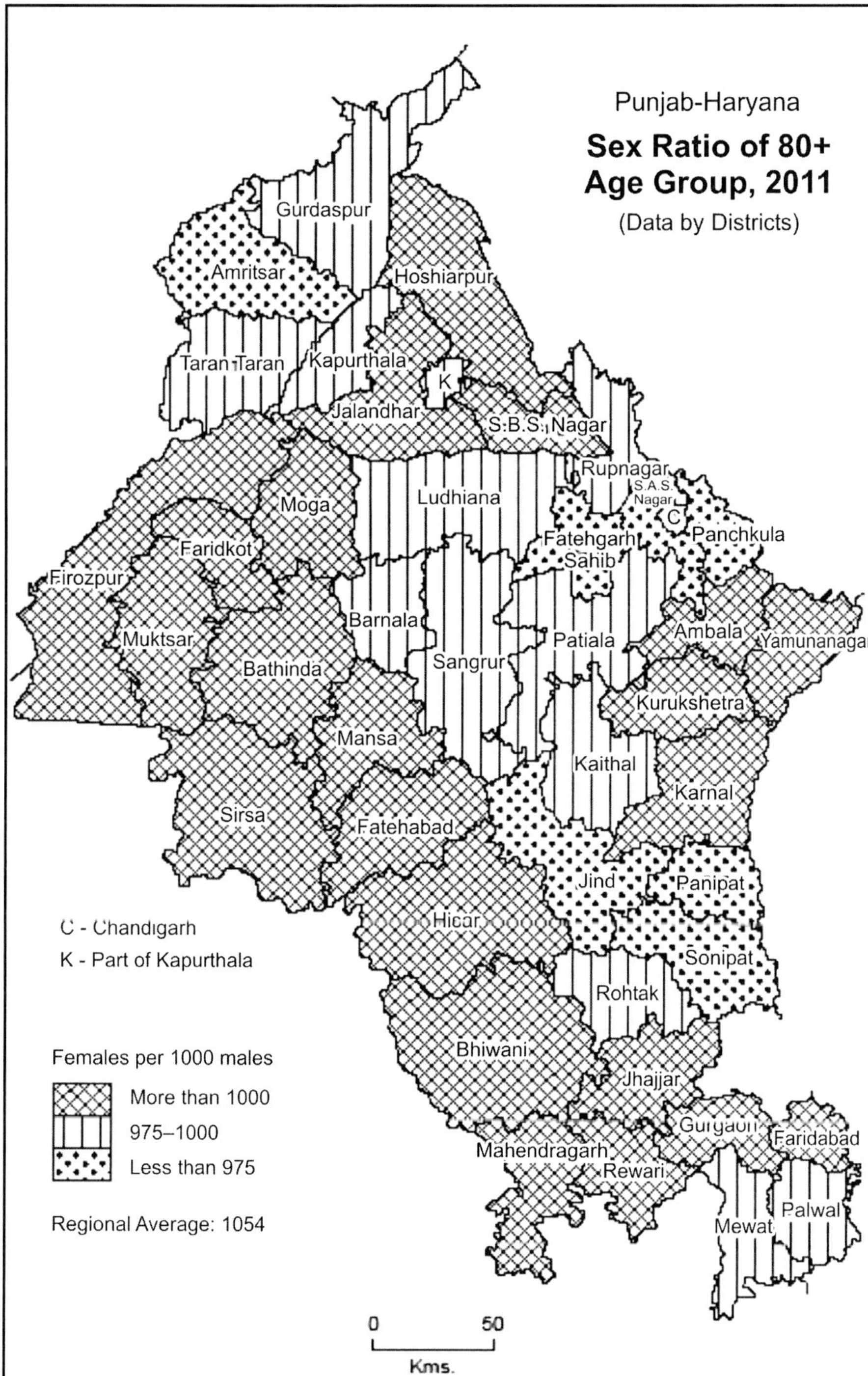

and Punjab (10.4%). In Punjab, Shahid Bhagat Singh Nagar district was on the top with the highest proportion (12.1%) of the elderly population (Table 2). Within this district, out of 462 villages, Herian village was selected by simple random sampling method to understand the relationship between gender and ageing. In this context, it may also be noted that in India nearly 75 per cent of aged population lived in rural areas, according to 2011 Census.

Table 1

Punjab and Haryana: Sex Ratio of all Ages, 60-Plus and 80-Plus Population, 2011

Sr. No.	State/District	All Ages Sex Ratio	60 Plus Sex Ratio	80 Plus Sex Ratio	State/District	All Ages Sex Ratio	60 Plus Sex Ratio	80 Plus Sex Ratio
0	Punjab	895	985	1,040	Haryana	879	1,015	1,058
1	Gurdaspur	895	997	1,012	Panchkula	873	939	970
2	Kapurthala	912	988	1,006	Ambala	885	998	1,067
3	Jalandhar	915	1,017	1,092	Yamunanagar	877	976	1,045
4	Hoshiarpur	961	1,016	1,112	Kurukshetra	888	1,008	1,079
5	Shahid Bhagat Singh Nagar	954	1,049	1,086	Kaithal	881	1,014	1,000
6	Fatehgarh Sahib	871	955	913	Karnal	887	1,007	1,031
7	Ludhiana	873	945	1,007	Panipat	864	9,53	904
8	Moga	893	972	1,100	Sonipat	856	989	932
9	Firozpur	893	1,019	1,111	Jind	871	996	884
10	Muktsar	896	1,047	1,208	Fatehabad	902	1,076	1,269
11	Faridkot	890	995	1,148	Sirsa	897	1,037	1,174
12	Bathinda	868	985	1,090	Hisar	872	1,054	1,071
13	Mansa	883	1,000	1,101	Bhiwani	886	1,072	1,170
14	Patiala	891	988	1,014	Rohtak	867	1,016	1,025
15	Amritsar	889	966	960	Jhajjar	862	1,066	1,080
16	Tarn Taran	900	1,014	1,014	Mahendragarh	895	1,100	1,272
17	Rupnagar	915	1,003	1,008	Rewari	898	1,089	1,205
18	Sahibzada Ajit Singh Nagar	879	903	906	Gurgaon	854	1,011	1,084
19	Sangrur	885	951	990	Mewat	907	977	1,018
20	Barnala	876	926	1,025	Faridabad	873	911	1,026
21	—	—	—	—	Palwal	880	1,003	992

Source: Census of India, 2011.

The selected village, i.e. village Herian, had a total population of about 1000 persons, including 150 aged persons showing a sex ratio of more than 1275 old females per 1000 old males. Data was collected from 125 aged persons (55 males and 70 females) who were available and ready to supply information. The required data pertaining to demographic, social, economic and health aspects of aged population was collected with the help of a well-administered pre-tested interview schedule. The following pages are devoted to the description of not only social and economic characteristics but also the health of aged population in Herian village so as to examine gender and ageing specific issues.

Table 2

Punjab: Elderly Population, 2011

Sr. No.	*State/District*	*Percentage of Elderly Population to Total Population*
0	Punjab	10.3
1	Shahid Bhagat Singh Nagar	12.1
2	Mansa	11.9
3	Hoshiarpur	11.7
4	Moga	11.6
5	Sangrur	11.0
6	Barnala	11.0
7	Rupnagar	10.8
8	Kapurthala	10.7
9	Muktsar	10.5
10	Faridkot	10.5
11	Fatehgarh Sahib	10.5
12	Bathinda	10.4
13	Jalandhar	10.2
14	Tarn Taran	10.1
15	Patiala	10.0
16	Amritsar	9.7
17	Firozpur	9.4
18	Sahibzada Ajit Singh Nagar	9.4
19	Ludhiana	9.3

Source: Census of India, 2011.

Social Characteristics of the Aged

Socio-economic status is often measured as a combination of education, income, and occupation. It is commonly conceptualized as the social standing or class of an individual or group. Socio-economic status is relevant to all realms of behavioural and social science, including research practice, education and advocacy. The social world of the elderly is different from that of the younger people because in every society age plays an important role in defining social status. As the people grow in age, their sets of social obligations and expectations change.

Age and Sex Composition

Age stratification and generational separation have been considered as determinants of the status of older people in society (Phillipson and Baars 2007). In the present study, the age of the aged persons has been categorized as young old; old-old and oldest-old in the age groups of 60–70, 71–80 and above 80 years respectively (Table 3). The corresponding figures of young old, old-old and oldest-old in the sample was 62, 34 and 29, respectively. The number of elderly females was higher than their male counterparts in all age groups (Table 3).

Table 3
Age and Sex Composition of Respondents

Age group (in years)	*Total (%)*	*Male (%)*	*Females (%)*
60–70 (young-old)	62 (49.6)	28 (50.9)	34 (48.6)
71–80 (old-old)	34 (27.2)	16 (29.1)	18 (25.7)
80 yrs plus (oldest old)	29 (23.2)	11 (20)	18 (25.7)

Source: Computed from primary data.

Marital Status and Literacy

Marital status of the elderly is important because it influences the care and support the elderly receive from their life partners.

Table 4
Marital Status and Level of Education of Respondents

Marital Status	*Total (%)*	*Male (%)*	*Female (%)*
Married	74 (59.2)	41 (74.5)	33 (47.2)
Unmarried	2 (1.6)	2 (3.6)	—
Widowed	44 (35.2)	8 (14.5)	37 (51.4)
Divorced/Separated	5 (4)	4 (7.3)	1 (1.4)
Education			
Illiterate	80 (64)	23 (41.8)	57 (81.4)
Literate	33 (26.4)	21 (38.2)	12 (17.2)
High School and above	12 (9.6)	11 (20)	1 (1.4)

Source: Computed from primary data.

The present study reveals that among the total respondents, about 60 per cent were married. It was found that about three-fourths of the elderly males were living with their spouses while the proportion of their female counterparts was less than 50 per cent. Only two elderly males were unmarried and four were divorced or separated (Table 4). There was only one elderly female who was separated. More than 50 per cent of elderly females were widows as against 14.5 per cent widowers. Among the old-old and oldest old, 78 per cent were widows as compared to 22 per cent widowers. This is to be attributed to longer life span of females as compared to males and the general tendency among females to marry males older than themselves (Gulati and Rajan 1999).

Education

Education plays an important role in determining living conditions. Educational standard of an individual substantially affects older adults' expectations of continuing to work beyond an age as compared with another with lower standard of education. Adults with higher education levels are more likely to participate in formal work related to education (Kleiner et al. 2005)

In Herian village, the majority (64%) of the elderly were illiterate. Literacy rate of elderly males was more than double the females' literacy rate. Twenty per cent of elderly males and only 1.4 per cent of elderly females had attained high school or higher education (Table 4).

Family Structure and Family Set-up

Strong family bonds emanating from family structure and family set-up are essential for social support and security particularly of old persons. It was found that about one-third of the elderly were living in small/nuclear families. In this respect again the number of elderly males was higher than their female counterparts (Table 5). It also revealed that majority (57.6%) of the elderly persons belonged to joint families where, in some cases, it was found that 12 to 14 members were living together in one such joint family. Most of them lived with their sons. Only four per cent of the elderly, who had no sons, were living with their daughters. Sixty per cent of elderly males and 55.7 per cent of elderly females in the village belonged to families. The elderly, living in such large families, are expected to be better looked after and might receive better care from younger members in the family.

Table 5

Family Structure and Number of Children of Respondents

Type of Family	*Total (%)*	*Male (%)*	*Female (%)*
Single (all alone)	14 (11.2)	4 (7.3)	10 (14.3)
Nuclear	39 (31.2)	18 (32.7)	21 (30)
Joint	72 (57.6)	33 (60)	39 (55.7)
Number of Children			
With 4 or less than four children	70 (56)	30 (54.5)	40 (57.2)
With 5–6 children	30 (24)	16 (29.1)	14 (20)
With more than 6 children	12 (9.6)	4 (7.3)	8 (11.4)
No child	13 (10.4)	5 (9.1)	8 (11.4)
Number of Son(s)			
With 2 or less than 2 sons	62 (49.6)	30 (54.5)	32 (45.7)
With 3–4 sons	24 (19.2)	9 (16.4)	15 (21.4)
With more than 4 sons	14 (11.20	4 (7.3)	10 (14.3)
No son	15 (12)	4 (7.3)	11 (15.7)
Number of Daughter(s)			
With 2 or less than 2 daughters	64 (51.2)	30 (54.6)	34 (48.6)
With 3–4 daughters	21 (16.8)	7 (12.7)	14 (20)
With more than 4 daughters	10 (8)	5 (9.1)	5 (7.1)
No daughter	30 (24)	13 (23.6)	17 (24.3)

Source: Computed from primary data.

It is interesting to note that 56 per cent of the elderly had less than 4 children and only 9.6 per cent had more than six children (Table 5). During the survey it was also reported that 48.6 per cent of the elderly people were living alone as their children were settled abroad or far away from them in some distant places in India. In such cases the old parents were left behind all alone in the native village. These emigrated/out-migrated children of such elderly generally visit their old parents after a year or so and in some cases, the elderly were visited by their children even after 8 to 10 years. In such a situation elderly felt a sense of social insecurity especially when their son(s) were away from them in far-flung foreign lands.

Role/Responsibility of Elders and their Time Management

Head of the household is one of the indicators which reflect the status, role and responsibility of older persons in their respective family. An elderly person, being considered as the head of the household, means, to a large extent, guarantee of availability of better care and support from the family members. In the present study, less than half (48%) of the elderly reported that they were the heads of their families, due to which they were generally respected in their families. Majority (72.7%) of the elderly males were the heads of their families. There were less than one-third of the elderly females who were heads of their families (Table 6). Most of them were living in single-member families. They could not head the family as they lacked financial intelligence and independence. Most of the elderly widows stated that as long as their husbands were alive, their son(s) especially daughter(s)-in-law dared not question their superiority in the family. But with the death of their spouses such widows had to face humiliation and torture by their own children. Almost one-third of elderly persons said that their children like son, daughter-in-law and close relatives were the heads of the family. In both these cases there was a significant difference between males and females (Table 6).

Table 6

Role/Responsibilities and Free Time of Respondents

Head of the Household/Family	*Total (%)*	*Male (%)*	*Female (%)*
Self	60 (48)	40 (72.7)	20 (28.6)
Spouse	25 (20)	3 (5.5)	22 (31.4)
Children and close relatives	40 (32)	12 (21.8)	28 (40)
Role and Responsibilities			
Decision-maker	50 (40)	32 (58.2)	18 (25.7)
Advisor	40 (32)	16 (29.1)	24 (34.3)
With no important role in decision-making	35 (28)	7 (12.7)	28 (40)
Leisure of the Elderly			
More than 2 hour	90 (72)	38 (69.1)	52 (74.3)
1–2 hour	20 (16)	10 (18.2)	10 (14.3)
Nil	15 (12)	7 (12.7)	8 (11.4)

Source: Computed from primary data.

Moreover, less than half of the elderly people stated that they were the decision-makers in the family-matters, such as children's education and marriage, buying and selling property and arranging social events. There was a difference by age and gender in the elderly persons' role in the household affairs. It was noted that a large proportion (58.2%) of the elderly males irrespective of age within elderly age-groups were decision-makers in the family. On the other hand, there were only about one-fourth of elderly females who had the privilege of being associated with decision-making process.

A large number of the elderly who were decision-makers were living in single and nuclear or small families. Less than one-third (32%) of the elderly particularly males said that they were consulted before taking any important decision in the family. More than one-fifth (28%) of the elderly complained that their role in decision-making process was negligible (Table 6). Most of the elderly females especially widows complained that they were considered as care takers of the house and children. Such elderly women had ill-health and could not participate in household chores and were not given care and respect by the family.

There is no doubt that old people face innumerable difficulties yet there are some lively old persons with strong will power who are not depressed and remain jovial. They cheerfully face the troubles peculiar to ageing and pursue their leisure, domestic and outdoor activities with zeal, enjoyment and stoic endurance. The elderly benefit a great deal from some exercises, social contact and pleasurable activities of skill or fun (Singh 2011).

In Herian village, majority of the elderly had plenty of (more than 2 hours) free time. It is very interesting that in this respect, the number of elderly females was reported to be higher (74.3%) as compared to their male counterparts (Table 6). Obviously, it was the old women's perspective that despite their intense involvement in household chores, they admitted that they were free for more than two hours daily. Sixteen per cent of the elderly reported about 1–2 hours of free time and all of them were in 60–70 age group (Table 6). Fifty per cent of the elderly people said that they utilized their free time by relaxing and getting engaged in household chores. Less than half of the elderly people utilized their free time by participating in spiritual activities; watching TV; meeting friends; doing meditation, reading newspaper, etc. Rest of the elderly (almost all of them were females) in the age group of 71–80 years were taking care of young children. The elderly females reported that to look after young children even for the whole day was one of the most important activities with which they could keep themselves busy. It was also mentioned that when the younger women of the family remained busy in work at home and at work place, the grandparents took care of their children.

Care Takers of the Elderly

The elderly persons, less able of being independent, need the care and support of others in several respects. This may be due to their declining capacity for self-care as they grow older (Palloni 2001).

The present study reveals that about half of the elderly have been cared by their spouse and less than half by their children (Table 7). Among these, some were totally dependent upon their children in sunset years of their life for daily activities like movement, bathing, eating, etc. Most of such old people were above 80 years of age and were bed-ridden. More elderly males than females were found to be dependent on their spouse for care and help.

Table 7

Care Takers of Respondents and Opinions about their Care

Care Takers of the Elderly	*Total (%)*	*Male (%)*	*Female (%)*
Self/Spouse	60 (48)	32 (58.2)	28 (40)
Children	55 (44)	20 (36.4)	35 (50)
Others/Relatives	10 (8)	3 (5.4)	7 (10)

Source: Computed from primary data.

Relations with Family Members and Neighbours

At all ages and in all circumstances, it is the family which provides emotional, social, and economic support to the individual. The ability of the elderly to cope with the changes in health, income, social activities, etc. at the older age depends, to a great extent, on the support the person gets from his/her family members (Soldo and Agree 1998). In the present study, 91.9 per cent of the married elderly said that they had cordial relationship with their spouse. Majority (80%) of the elderly living with their son/s or away from them enjoyed good relationship with them. They reported that their children considered them to be an asset for the family because they could take care of their grandchildren, besides keeping a watch on their house and guiding and advising them from time to time on important household matters. A distinct difference, however, could not be established between elderly males and females in terms of maintaining cordial relations with their children and grandchildren.

Table 8

Relations of Respondents with Family and Neighbours

Type of Relation	*Nature of Relationship*	
	Good	*Poor*
Spouse	68 (91.9)	6 (8.1)
Son(s)	80 (80)	20 (20)
Daughter	92 (96.8)	3 (3.2)
Daughter(s)-in-law	70 (73.7)	25 (26.6)
Grandchildren	90 (94.7)	15 (15.8)
Neighbours	110 (88)	15 (12)

Source: Computed from primary data.

Moreover, about 90 per cent of the elderly were happy with their relationship with their neighbours (Table 8). They indicated that their neighbours are helpful. Most of the aged people got relief from their anxieties, sorrows and grievances, especially when they shared and discussed these with their neighbourhood friends. The proportion of females sharing their experiences with their neighbours was higher as compared to their male counterparts.

Economic Characteristics of the Elderly

Among the socio-economic and health conditions of the elderly in our society, economic status occupies an important position. Ageing diminishes the capacity to work and earn. A reduced capacity for income generation and a growing risk of serious illness are likely to increase the vulnerability of elders to fall into poverty, regardless of their original economic status (Lloyd-Sherlock 2000).

Work Participation and Possessions

In India, the elderly in rural areas, both males and females, have historically been more likely to participate in economic activities than those in urban areas. Rural elderly continue to work but they reduce the number of hours worked, especially with increasing age (Singh et al. 1987). In the present study, more than 50 per cent of the elderly who were surveyed were not engaged in any economic activity (Table 9).

Table 9

Work Participation and Occupation of Respondents

Work Participation	*Total (%)*	*Male (%)*	*Female (%)*
Working	55 (44)	40 (72.7)	15 (21.4)
Non-Working	70 (56)	15 (27.3)	55 (78.6)
Occupation			
Agriculture	40(72.7)	34(85)	6(40)
Business	2(3.6)	2(5)	—
Others	13(23.7)	4(10)	9(60)
Caste-wise			
General	28 (50.9)	25 (62.5)	3 (20)
Backward Class/Other Backward Class	4 (7.3)	3 (7.5)	1 (6.7)
Scheduled Caste	23 (41.8)	12 (30)	11 (73.3)

Source: Computed from primary data.

There was a remarkable difference in male-female work participation. It was relatively higher (72.7%) for elderly males than their female counterparts (21.4%). The difference between the elderly males and females was mainly due to male dominating agriculture and females were not allowed to participate in outdoor economic activities like agriculture in economically prosperous families. Caste norms also often discourage females and widows in particular, from working (Jensen 2005). Among the working elderly male population, majority (72.7%) of them were engaged in agriculture. As agriculture is a male dominating activity in Punjab, the proportion of elderly males was higher as compared to their female counterparts in this activity (Table 9). Among the elderly female workers, majority (60%) of them were earning their livelihood by working as servants in upper caste houses. Only 40 per cent were involved in agricultural activities. Most of them belonged to lower castes, working as agricultural labourers on others' land.

Income of the Elderly and its Sources

In old age, because of physical disabilities, deterioration in work capacities is common; therefore, the source of income is also a big question. Elderly in India do not have adequate income to meet basic needs (UNDP 2000). In the present study an attempt was made to ascertain the income of elderly persons and its sources. The income of the respondents' households was classified into two categories, i.e. (i) elderly persons' earned income by old age and service pension and from other sources of income and (ii) elderly persons' family income. The average income of respondents below 65 years was higher than those aged 70 years and above. The majority (44%) of the rural elderly had a personal monthly income of below ₹ 1,000; 39.2 per cent of them had old age pension as their only source of income. It was an extremely meagre amount of ₹ 250 per month. In general castes, there were only one-third elderly who were receiving a pension of ₹ 1,000 per month (Table 10). Less than one-fifth of the elderly did not have an independent source of income. During the survey it was reported that more than 50 per cent of the elderly females had a family monthly income of below ₹ 5,000 and monthly personal income of below ₹ 1,000.

Only 15.2 per cent of the elderly reported their family monthly income of between ₹ 5,000 and ₹ 10,000. The proportion of elderly males enjoying this income was high as compared to elderly females (Table 9). One–third of the elderly reported their monthly family income of more than ₹ 10,000. Most of such elderly males and females belonged to general caste and had enough agriculture land and foreign-settled children. As far as family income is concerned, there was an insignificant male-female difference (Table 10).

Table 10

Income of Respondents and its Source/s

Monthly Personal Income (In Rupees)	*Total (%)*	*Male (%)*	*Female (%)*
Below 1000	55 (44)	20 (36.4)	36 (55.3)
1000–3000	32 (25.6)	20 (36.4)	12 (17.1)
Above 3000	15 (12)	7 (12.7)	8 (11.4)
Nil	23 (18.4)	8 (14.5)	15 (21.4)
Source of Income	*Total (%)*	*Male (%)*	*Female (%)*
Property	6 (4.8)	5 (9.1)	1 (1.4)
Agriculture	33 (26.4)	21 (38.2)	12 (17.2)
Service Pension	11 (8.8)	3 (5.5)	8 (11.4)
Old Age Pension	49 (39.2)	13 (23.6)	36 (51.4)
Others	26 (20.8)	13 (23.6)	13 (18.6)
Family Monthly Income (In Rupees)			
Below 5000	56 (44.8)	20 (36.4)	36 (51.4)
5000–10000	19 (15.2)	11 (20)	8 (11.4)
Above 10000	42 (33.6)	20 (36.4)	22 (31.4)
Nil	8 (6.4)	4 (7.3)	4 (5.7)

Source: Computed from primary data.

Monthly Expenditure

Expenditure of the elderly persons to meet their daily basic needs and medical requirements reflects their well-being and standard of living. In the present study, a majority of the elderly reported that their monthly expenditure was below ₹ 2,000. The percentage of such females was higher than such males. There was a difference on the basis of caste also. Only 30.4 per cent of the elderly had an expenditure of above ₹ 4,000 p.m. (Table 11).

Table 11

Monthly Expenditure of Respondents

Rupees	*Total (%)*	*Males (%)*	*Females (%)*
Below 2000	52 (41.6)	20 (36.3)	32 (45.7)
2000–4000	35 (28)	19 (34.5)	16 (22.9)
Above 4000	38 (30.4)	16 (29.1)	22 (31.4)
Financial Dependency	*Total (%)*	*Male (%)*	*Female (%)*
Independent	27 (21.6)	22 (40)	5 (7.1)
Dependent on Spouse	18 (14.4)	2 (3.6)	16 (22.9)
Dependent on Children	73 (58.4)	30 (54.6)	43 (61.4)
Dependent on Relative/others	7 (5.6)	1 (1.8)	6 (8.6)

Source: Computed from primary data.

Only 7 per cent of elderly females reported to be financially independent while this percentage was 40 per cent in case of elderly males (Table 11).

Possessions and Economic Dependency

Economic assets of elderly persons reveal their status in respective family and community. In the present study, agricultural land was revealed as the main asset of the elderly. More than two-third of the elderly had their own agricultural land. An overwhelming majority (81.8%) of the elderly males reported agricultural land in their name as compared to their female counterparts (55.7%).

Table 12

Possessions and Economic Dependency of Respondents

Possessions (Agriculture Land/Assets)	*Total (%)*	*Male (%)*	*Female (%)*
Total	84 (67.2)	45 (81.8)	39 (55.7)
General	65 (90.3)	23 (93.6)	35 (87.5)
Backward Class	3 (33.3)	3 (50)	—
Scheduled Caste	16 (36.4)	12 (70.6)	4 (14.8)
Elderly with no Agricultural Land	41 (32.8)	10 (18.2)	31 (44.3)
Financial Dependency			
Independent	27 (21.6)	22 (40)	5 (7.1)
Dependent on Spouse	18 (14.4)	2 (3.6)	16 (22.9)
Dependent on Children	73 (58.4)	30 (54.6)	43 (61.4)
Dependent on Relative/others	7 (5.6)	1 (1.8)	6 (8.6)

Source: Computed from primary data.

In the elderly population of lower castes such as Scheduled Caste and Backward Class and Other Backward Class, there was a striking difference between males and females on the basis of possession of agricultural land or property. It was interesting to note that 70 per cent of the elderly males of Scheduled Caste category had their own land, although in terms of acres it was meagre and the figure for their female counterparts was extremely low. In the category of Backward Class, half of the elderly males owned land while figure for their female counterparts was zero (Table 12).

Only about one-fifth of the elderly were economically independent. The number of males was higher than females (Table 12). Elderly females were more dependent because of their lower work participation, low literacy level, higher life expectancy and widowhood. The elderly females are more likely to be dependent on others, because they have limited control over family income as well as their own earnings (Rajan et al. 2003). More than 58 per cent of the elderly, who were economically dependent on others, received support from their children or grandchildren. Elderly females, as compared to their male counterparts, were more dependent on their children. For finances, 14.4 per cent of elderly were depending on their spouse. There were 16 such old females and only two males. A higher number of old males than old females had possessed agricultural land and enjoyed financial independence (Table 12).

Health Status of the Elderly and Provision of Medical Facilities

Health of the elderly is best measured in terms of functioning of the body. Due to biological ageing, the level of resistance to illness is reduced and recovery takes longer time and the gradual decline in physical strength is common. Health is one of the crucial factors that determine the quality of life among the elderly (Blane et al. 2004). It was found that castes, widowhood and public health measures were major determinants of health status among rural elderly.

Table 13

Health Status of the Elderly and Provision of Medical Facilities

Health Status	*Total (%)*	*Male (%)*	*Females (%)*
Good	30 (24)	16 (29.1)	14 (20)
Poor	95 (76)	39 (70.9)	56 (80)
Provision of medical facilities			
Availability	105 (84)	45 (81.8)	60 (85.7)
Accessibility	60 (48)	35 (63.6)	25 (35.7)
Affordability	72 (57.6)	40 (72.7)	32 (45.7)
Health institution visited by elderly			
Primary Health Center and govt. hospital	75 (60)	30 (54.5)	45 (64.3)
Private and govt. hospital	42 (33.6)	20 (36.4)	22 (31.4)
Never visited any health institution	8 (6.4)	5 (9.1)	3 (4.3)

Source: Computed from primary data.

In Herian village, it was observed that less than one-fourth of the elderly reported themselves to be in good health. Most of them were in the younger old age group of 60 to 70 years. More males (29.1%) were found in good health as compared to their female counterparts (Table 13). Similarly, it was also observed that literate elderly, being aware, enjoyed good health status as compared to illiterate elderly. A very large number (76%) of the elderly people complained about poor health (Table 13). A large number of married, unmarried and divorced respondents were found in good health as compared to widows and widowers.

Provision of medical facilities for the elderly can be measured in terms of availability, accessibility and affordability (Iecovich and Carmel 2009). In the present study, more than three-fourth of the elderly reported about adequate and satisfactory availability of medical facilities within the easy proximity of the study village; while less than half (48%) of the elderly appreciated the easy accessibility of these facilities.

Majority (60%) of the elderly reported that they visited Government Institutions (Primary Health Centre and Government Hospital) for medical assistance. The number of elderly females, in this regard, was higher as compared to their male counterparts (Table 13). More than one-third of the elderly visited both private and government hospitals. Only 6 per cent of the elderly claimed that they never visited any hospital or health centre for medical care.

A loving care and respect of the elderly by their children and grandchildren was no doubt the most earnest desire of the elderly, both males and females.

Emerging Issues

1. Being numerically larger in number than their male counterparts, it is essential that in the matter of care and support the challenges faced by the elderly today and tomorrow are in essence, challenges and problems faced by older women (Kinsella and Velkoff 2001).
2. The fact that old females substantially outnumber their male counterparts, particularly, in the oldest old age group and the difference between the number of elderly males and females in the last category (oldest-old) is so large and continues to grow so fast that many of the challenges faced by the elderly may well be looked upon primarily as challenges faced by older/oldest old women.
3. In addition to the fact that the oldest old women are more numerous than their male counterparts, there is a vast gender gap in the marital status of the oldest old group of males and females. The old females are more likely to be widowed than their male counterparts. First, because they live longer than men and second because they marry men who are older than themselves. Still another factor is that widows are less likely to remarry than widowers.
4. Widows living without any partners are economically vulnerable. They are exposed also to the risk of being socially isolated. The Second World Assembly on Ageing also stressed the need to provide social protection to widows living alone.
5. Older women in most developing countries are at a disadvantage compared to men in the matter of formal education. The Second World Assembly on Ageing stated lack of education among women as the cause of their poverty and exploitability in financial and legal matters. Steps

have, no doubt, been taken to fill the gender gap in respect of level of education, as well as, the number of women going in for formal education but efforts need to be strengthened further.

6. Lower level of women's education has been identified as a factor responsible for failure to access employment opportunity especially in government sector reflecting poor retirement emoluments. This leads to general economic backwardness of women compared to men. Poor income in working years results in poor pensionary benefits and poverty. Older men are better off than older women in securing attractive pension on retirement.
7. Men and women have different health problems in old age. Old women have more health problems than men. Women, however, suffer from illnesses that do not threaten life. This is true in all parts of life. In some social and cultural settings, women more readily report their illnesses than men. Women belonging to lower social status have poor health. It is important, therefore, that due attention be paid to necessary corrective measures with focus on gender in various programmes. Health needs must be duly addressed and special female vulnerability kept in view.
8. Life expectancy among males vis-à-vis females differs at birth and at later ages, but there are other influences too – environmental, social and cultural – that vary over time and setting. Habits of smoking and drinking, for example, are generally linked with higher male deaths than female deaths.
9. On an average, women above 60 expect to live 2–7 years longer than men. The United Nations project that women's life expectancy would increase in the developing countries by almost a year over the next half a century. Lower male life expectancy is disadvantageous to women as it would imply long periods of widowhood of older women. To reduce widowhood among older women, men have to be assured of improvement in life expectancy.

Conclusion

Considering different aspects of social and economic well-being of old men and women, it was discovered that older women may be more disadvantaged than older men. In the context of developing countries, like India, where the sex ratio of old population is noticeably in favour of females and growing rapidly, empirical studies should be conducted and clear-cut distinct policies need to be formulated. For attaining the ideals of gender, not only the disadvantaged old women need to be helped and cared for but also the older men who are disadvantaged. For constructing a gender-just society and for caring and serving the future old generations in an appropriate manner, the need of the hour is to foster a balanced mindset so that both male and female oriented adverse circumstances and deficiencies may first be identified and then worked out in the context of particular background, locale and time.

References

Blane, D., Higgs, P., Hyde, M. and Wiggins, R.D. 2004. 'Life Course Influences on Quality of Life in Early Old Age'. *Social Science and Medicine*, 58, 2171–2179.

Census of India. 2011. New Delhi: Registrar General of India. Retrieved from http://censusindia.gov.in/

Chappell, Neena L. and Havens, Betty. 1980. 'Old and Female: Testing the Double Jeopardy Hypothesis'. *The Sociological Quarterly*, 21(2), 157–171.

Gulati, L. and Rajan, S. Irudaya. 1999. 'The Added Years: Elderly in India and Kerala'. *Economic and Political Weekly*, 34(44), 46–51.

Hatch, L.R. 2000. *Beyond Gender Differences: Adaptation to Aging in Life Course Perspective.* Amityville, NY: Baywood Publishing.

Help Age International. 1999. *The Ageing and Development Report: Poverty, Independence and the World's Older People*. Retrieved from http://www.helpage.org/

Iecovich, E. and Carmel, S. 2009. 'Differences in Accessibility, Affordability, and Availability (AAA) of Medical Specialists Among Three Age-Groups of Elderly People in Israel'. *Journal of Aging and Health*, 21(5), 776–797.

Jensen, T.R. 2005. 'Caste, Culture and the Status and Well-Being of Widows in India', in D.A. Wise (ed.), *Analyses in the Economics of Aging*. Cambridge, MA: National Bureau of Economic Research, pp. 357–375.

Kinsella, K. and Velkoff, Victoria. 2001. *An Aging World.* Washington, D.C.: U.S. Government Printing Office.

Kleiner, B., Carver, P., Hagedorn, M. and Chapman, C. 2005. *Participation in Adult Education for Work-Related Reasons (NCES 2006–040)*. Washington, D.C.: U.S. Department of Education, National Centre for Education Statistics, November, pp. 1–42.

Lloyd-Sherlock, P. 2000. 'Old Age and Poverty in Developing Countries: New Policy Challenges'. Great Britain: World Development, 28(12), 2157–2168.

Markides, K.A. and Black, S.A. 1995. 'Race, Ethnicity and Aging: The Impact of Inequality', in R.B. George (ed.), *Handbook of Aging and the Social Sciences* (4th ed.). New York: Academic Press.

Palloni, A. 2001. 'Living Arrangements of Older Persons'. *United Nations Population Bulletin*, 42/43, Department of Economics and Social Affairs, Population Division, New York.

Palloni, A., Pinto-Aguirre, G. and Palez, M. 2002. 'Demographic and Health Conditions of Ageing in Latin America and the Caribbean'. *International Journal of Epidemiology*, 31, 762–771.

Phillipson, C. and Baars, J. 2007. 'Social Theory and Social Ageing', in J. Bond, S. Peace, F. Dittmann-Kohli and G. Westerhof (eds), *Ageing in Society*. New Delhi: Sage Publications, pp. 68–84.

Pratt, Clara C. 1997. 'Aging: A Multigenerational Gender Perspective'. *Bulletin on Aging*, 2(3), 1–9.

Rajan, I.S., Sankara Sarma, P. and Mishra, U.S. 2003. 'Demography of Indian Aging 2001–2051'. *Journal of Aging and Social Policy*, 15(2–3), 11–30.

Singh, B. 2011. 'Ageing Gracefully'. *The Tribune*, 1 October, 13.

Singh, S.P., Dak, M.L. and Sharma, M.L. 1987. 'Health Needs of Senior Citizens', in M.L. Sharma and T.M. Dak (eds), *Ageing in India: Challenge for the Society*. Delhi: Ajanta, pp. 207–213.

Soldo, B.J. and Agree, E.M. 1998. 'America's Elderly', *Population Bulletin*, 43(3), 1–53.

United Nations Development Programme (UNDP). 2000. New York: Oxford University Press, pp. 1–130.

United Nations Population Division. 1999. *Population Ageing 1999* (Wall Chart). ST/ESA/SER.A/179. New York: United Nations.

United Nations Population Fund (UNFPA). 1998. *The State of the World Population 1998: The New Generations*. New York: UNFPA.

——. 2012. *Ageing in the Twenty-First Century: A Celebration and a Challenge*. New York: Help Age International and UNFPA.

World Health Organization (WHO). 2001. Men, Ageing and Health. Retrieved from http://whqlibdoc.who.int/hq/2001/who

10

Rape and its Aftermath

Lived Experiences of Victims with Indian Law

Sarvar Abbi

This paper documents the social discourse on the offence of rape in India and the resultant violence experienced by women in their lived experience with law. Rape trials in India have been seen to be a Kafkaesque horror which as seen below often reduces a woman in Foucaultian terms 'as a spectacle of degradation'. It also states the changing perception of rape in both law and society revealed through progressive judicial judgements, media and social media activism and also examines whether empowerment and emancipation have truly taken place in society or not which despite the outward semblance of modernity and progressiveness remains paradoxically entrenched in 'multiple patriarchies' (Sangari 2012). The irony, vulnerability and impact of gender violence in India is not just a subject of layered academic scholarship but it moves us all from a 10-year-old child being asked why she did not scream when she was violated for the second time in a trial court in Mirzapur; a 16-year-old committing suicide in Patiala after being harassed by the police repeatedly, the anguish of Suzette Jordan being denied entry in an upmarket restaurant in Parkstreet Kolkatta, to the Uber rape victim admonishing the defence lawyer saying that she could be his daughter after being asked degrading questions to get the brazen reply from the defence lawyer 'do not insult my daughter'.

Woman's Body and the Public Sphere

In a patriarchal society gendering is in favour of men. The social and sexual relations of both men and women are gendered and the gendering process in a patriarchal society is maintained by public opinion. Process of public opinion is not just in the air, in the rural or urban context within which people live: public opinion is a part of that context and does not exist in vacuum. Public opinion is harsher on women as it is created as a mixture of tradition, religion, taboos and sanctions which shape the public opinion, favouring male hegemony.

As put by the *Stanford Encyclopaedia of Philosophy*, 'The humiliation and shame often experienced by rape victims are predictable results and intimate loss of control of one's body. These reactions, not to mention victim's feelings of contamination of having been defiled or desecrated, are often exacerbated by cultural judgements of raped women as dirty and impure or as damaged goods.' In some cultures these ideas are so powerful that a woman who is raped is thought to bring shame on her entire family and such women sometimes become the victims of so-called honour killings at the hands of male relatives, often the entire family commits suicide. In most cases, the victim's father commits suicide, as put by Mckinnon, 'the rape of a female is often a humiliation rite for the men and the other side who cannot in masculinity terms protect their women' (*Encyclopedia of Philosophy*). One cannot imagine the horror, trauma and anguish the victims and their families go through. An adolescent who a day ago was a girl with aspirations, dreams, living casually now has to bear other than the entire trauma of violation, intense scrutiny, disbelief, shame, guilt, etc. She becomes a subject of village group, insensitive questioning and harassment by the police. Often she gives up on life itself or her entire family kill themselves.

The threat of rape, with its false promise that by being good we can avoid disaster, plays an important role in training women in the requirements of femininity describing a feminine bodily compartment that is marked by fear. Cahill observes that the female body well trained in femininity is that of a pre-victim. The feminine body is marked by hesitancy, relative weakness, delicacy and restraint; qualities that in fact render women more vulnerable to violence. The woman or girl is taught to view her body as dangerously provocative and inherently 'rapeable', hence her duty to control, conceal and monitor her body so as not to bring disaster on herself (*Encyclopedia of Philosophy*). It has been observed that from the 17th century, rights began to be seen as inhering in individuals, rather than in groups or communities. This individual, detached from social context and conceived of as constituted by the limits of the body, was clearly male, as feminist critiques have pointed out. Male bodies, being clearly bounded and solid, were considered perfect. Female bodies, on the other hand, were seen as disorderly and penetratable and subject to cyclical changes; their bodily processes were messy and challenged the idea of the closed and controlled body surface; and through reproduction, were divisible, suggesting the unlimitability of their boundaries. Thus, they could never be the rational, indivisible, unambiguous individuals (Menon 1999: 283). Studying the feminist engagement with law, as emphasised by Derrida, 'in understanding of justice the very condition of justice is that one must address oneself to the other in the language of the other. There is violence involved in judging people in an idiom they do not share perhaps even understand ...' (c.f. Menon 1999: 283). In studying sexual violence from the point of view of feminism, Menon says, 'certain experiences ... need to be authenticated by law to have social value and to be recognised as 'real' ... to this extent then these are to be constituted as real and legitimised by legal discourse' (1999: 283). Here as Mackinnon points out 'recourse to the law is seen as necessary and inevitable because it is believed that designing a law around an experience proves it matters; law is the concrete delivery of rights through the legal system' (c.f. Menon 1999: 283). For the victims of rape and their families the legal system is the only recourse to justice.

Gender Violence in North India: Some Insights

A pertinent question to ask is that even after a whole two years of the shocking Delhi gang rape, why have things not changed? If even such a horrific act could not change the situation, what will it take for India to adjust its attitude towards its women? Why do patriarchal outlooks, which led to the girls in Haryana being asked to get out of the bus and then withdraw their complaint, continue to persist even as women in India make enormous strides in education, business, arts, sports and politics (Chaterjee, *Huffington Post*, 17 December 2014).

As it is obvious 'no quick solutions are at hand. Even after promising fast track courts for crimes against women, legal progress for women seeking justice has been slow to be delivered. Families of women that approach law enforcement officers to file complaints are harassed, threatened and hounded, especially in rural areas. While incidences of women reporting complaints have gone up, such crimes remain significantly under-reported (Chaterjee, *Huffington Post*, 17 December 2014).

It can be seen that 'in India's modernizing but still deeply traditional society, social and women's rights activists argue that rapes occur with virtual impunity, and women who betray flickers of independent thought and challenge the male-dominated status quo are especially vulnerable. The problem is particularly acute in impoverished rural India, where women's families face social pressure not to report rapes, police are apathetic about such crimes, and deep caste inequalities provide cover to men who sexually abuse women of lower standing' (Chaterjee, *Huffington Post,* 17 December 2014).

It was observed that in Haryana 'gangs of young Jat boys roam around the villages on motorcycles, stalking Dalit girls. Sometimes, the girls are drawn into romantic relationships and sexual liaisons, which end in gang rapes by the lover and his friends' (WSS 2014: 5). Moreover, as AIDWA (All India Democratic Women's Association) activists from Haryana have explained in detail that 'young women whose dress and demeanour are read to reflect their aspirations of upward mobility, have been singled out for sexual attacks as a way of showing them their place' (WSS 2014: 5). Similarly, the immediate cause of the Muzzafarnagar riots of 2013 as well as the immediate suspicion for the killing of the Badaun sisters is linked to these factors.

Life after Rape

For 'her', the morning has no promise. I say 'her' for in India the identity of the rape victim is not revealed. As if she and not the perpetrators of the crime against her are the 'accused'. Indeed although she is the victim yet there is little succour or solace for a rural rape victim in a patriarchal society. No matter how fierce and righteous her fight, she gets little compassion from the police who are indifferent or worse indulging in her harassment, who believe that she has in some way brought the crime on herself and made herself rapeable. She has to give her statement to the Munshi or the SHO who patronised by the accused, sometimes in reported incidents of indignity tell her to strip and narrate her ordeal or even harass her family members. The village panchayat too treats her as someone who has no sense of shame and honour.

Figure 1
Haryana: 30 Days in a Rape State

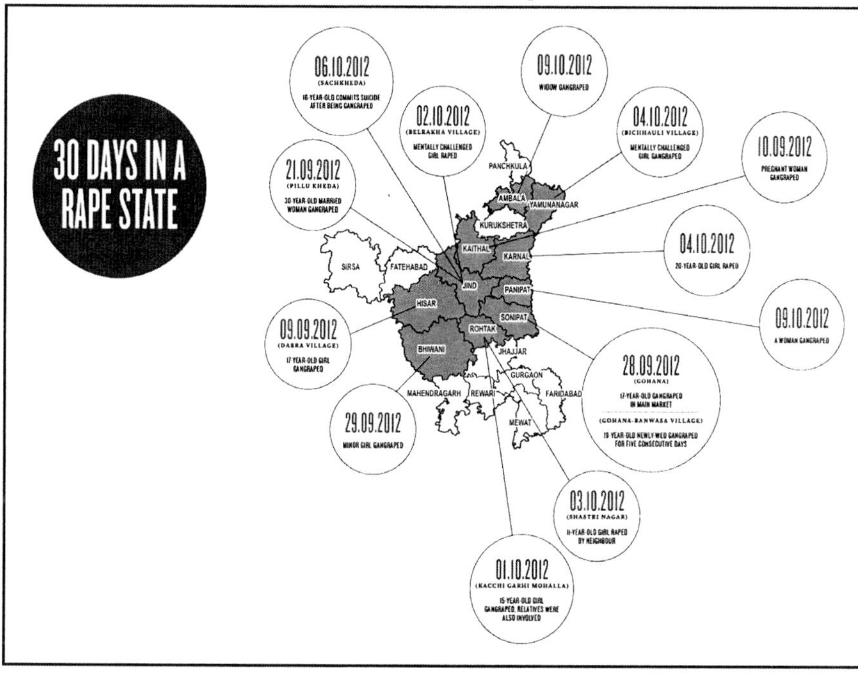

Source: 'Haryana: 30 days in a Rape State', *Tehelka* 22 October, Issue 43 vol. 9, 2012.

A few important examples from Punjab and Haryana elucidate this process experienced by the women who are raped.

I am presenting here some examples of the projection of incidents of rape in a fact finding report of the WSS, as well as in the newspapers. These examples far away from the urban centres highlight the suffering, poignancy and ostracization faced by rape victims in a patriarchal society. They also bring into focus the role of NGOs and media in slowing down in giving a voice to the faceless and attempting to share the plight of the victim despite functioning in traditional stereotypes and power structures.

Sexual Assault of a Schoolgirl in Dabra Village, Hisar District, September 2012

This I5-year-old girl was on her way to visit her grandmother when she was abducted and raped by a gang of eight Jaat boys. The rapes were filmed on a mobile phone and she was told that the clip would be circulated if she spoke about what had happened. She was effectively silenced, but the clip was soon widely circulated. On 18 September, her father, a gardener in a private house, was shown the clip by one of his co-workers. The traumatized father hanged himself. Local activists who came to know of the story mobilized the Dalit community from across the district for a dharna in Dabra on 19 September. The angry crowd refused to allow the body to be cremated until a case was filed. It was only after the DC and SSP gave an assurance that the case would be pursued and the perpetrators brought to book that the dharna was lifted. By the time a complaint of rape and abetment to suicide was filed, the accused had disappeared from the village. Despite the continuous pressure from Dalit groups, the police did everything they could to delay the arrests, intimidate the family and harass the girl. They would pick up young men at random and ask the girl to come to the police station to identify them. When she refused to make identification, she would be taunted with remarks. The police also tried to intimidate her into saying that she had willingly gone with the boys, as claimed in the statement prepared by the police. The police tried to avoid filing charges under the POA Act (Scheduled Castes and Schedule Tribes Prevention of Atrocities Act 1989) by removing every mention of the caste of the accused in the recorded complaint. They also tried several times to implicate Dalit boys, including the girl's brother, in the crime. It took a dharna and four days of protests by Dalit activists to get the police to destroy the so-called 'charge sheet' against her brother. The Jaat-dominated panchayat and some local politicians from the Indian National Lok Dal (INLD) also intimidated and threatened the family, trying to make them withdraw the case and agree to a 'compromise' (WSS 2014: 6). More than a fortnight after the incident, following sustained media coverage and public pressure, the police finally arrested eight of the accused from Uttarakhand and Rajasthan, and charged them under Sections 376 (rape) and Section 306 (abetment to suicide). Following an intervention from the National Commission for Scheduled Castes, the case of rape was tried in a fast track court which completed its proceedings in May 2013. Four of the accused were convicted, while the other four (who had connections with the INLD) were acquitted on grounds of shoddy investigation. The four convicted men have appealed in the High Court and soon they were out on bail.

Following their release, the accused and their families stepped up their campaign of threat and intimidation. The girl was approached and threatened by the wives of two of the accused men and by the local INLD leader. She and her family were given police protection and shifted to a tiny government flat in Hissar town in Haryana. Her mother was given a temporary job as an office assistant in the local Red Cross, but her salary was insufficient to meet the needs of the family. The girl was awarded a compensation of ₹ 2.6 lakh by the Central Government, but the money is yet to be transferred to her account. The girl is now almost 18 and has enrolled in a local girls' college in Hissar town. Her identity has been made public by the sister of one of the accused who is also studying in the same college. In a letter addressed to the National Commission for Scheduled Castes recently, she described the taunts and harassment she has been subjected to in college by her classmates and teachers, most of whom are Jaats.

Her situation took a turn for the worse after she was interviewed by reporters from an Australian TV channel. Some local newspapers carried the interview in which she spoke out about being harassed in college and by the doctors in the hospital. The district collector, the college principal and the chief medical officer came to her house to persuade her to sign a statement disowning the interview. They wanted her to say that she gave the interview while she was in a mentally disturbed state. When she refused, she was told that the CMO was going to declare her mentally ill.

The author of this paper met her in late 2013 and the girl revealed that she had been feeling unwell and running fever for the last several months. She had spells of depression and was often withdrawn and silent. Although she had been assured of free treatment in the Hissar government hospital, she was always asked to pay, and whenever she visited the hospital, she was ignored and humiliated. She had also not been offered any counselling. The accused and their families know where she lives, and have even turned up in town to threaten her and the family, undeterred by the presence of an armed guard. Her brother's life has also changed course after these events, leaving him bitter and depressed. He was doing a computer course from the local ITI but dropped out, unable to cope with the taunts and harassment he faced in the aftermath of the rape and his father's death. He has been promised a government job, but is not sure if that would ever materialize. He lives in the constant fear of the video clip of his sister's rape being uploaded on the internet, bringing more grief to the family. He feels that rapid urbanization and increased access to new technology like mobiles and the internet have made the Jaats even more powerful and oppressive than they were.

With constant support and encouragement from her lawyer and other Dalit activists, the girl, who told us when we first met her of her determination to complete her education and become a lawyer, has made extraordinary progress in recent months. She is volunteering as an activist with an NGO and is helping and supporting other rape survivors (WSS 2014: 5).

The manner in which people around the Dabra rape victim in Haryana reacted gives deep insight into the turmoil faced by the girl and her family (*The Tribune*, 14 October 2012). More than a month after a minor Dalit girl was gang raped in Dabra village near here, a pall of gloom envelopes the victim's home. The victim has not moved out of her house since. She spends her day sulking in a corner of a room, her face covered with a dupatta. The gang rape came as a double blow to the family. Nine days after she was raped, her father committed suicide in desperation. 'Life has changed. The only breadwinner in the family has died. My daughter has been scarred for life. We live in fear and shame. The world has tuned upside down,' rues the victim's mother. The ramshackle house is guarded by the police round the clock. The number of officials of various commissions and leaders of political parties that came calling after the incident hit the headlines has come down substantially. The villagers, who remained in attendance till the victim's father's last rites, are no longer to be seen there. 'Yes, we have received financial help from government agencies. But that is hardly any compensation. My son was promised a government job, but so far they are offering only a temporary job. He needs to be employed so we can at least two square meals a day,' said the mother.

She said she would prefer to move the family out of the village because her daughter is not prepared to come out of the house for both fear and shame. 'And she is not wrong. Who will stop street urchins and unruly youth of the village from taunting her? But who listens?' she added. The fellow villagers have all the sympathy for the victim and the family. But only outwardly.

Visiting news persons are offered appropriate sound bites describing the incident variously as a shame on the village and how it had failed to spoil the *bhaichara* (brotherhood) in the village.

But you move away from the vicinity of the victim's house and you hear altogether different comments, at times sarcastic. Sample this: 'This lowly girl has brought shame to the village. Or, she was caught in the act, so she termed it a rape'. So much for sympathies for the family whose daughter was raped resulting in the death of her father! Hearing this, one tends to agree with the victim's mother that the family needs to be moved out of this village.

A Month *'After Gang Rape, Patiala Teenager Ends Life'* was an important news in *The Tribune* (28 December 2012). The victim left behind an anguished note detailing her ordeal. The police would summon the girl to the police station and ask her uncomfortable questions. The victim was not only harassed but was also called continuously to the police station at the instance of the powerful accused and repeatedly asked to narrate her ordeal (*The Tribune,* 28 December 2012). The sources said that the teenage girl was kidnapped by Balwinder Singh and Gurpreet Singh of Baras village in Patiala district on 13 November. They took her to a tubewell belonging to Sandeep Singh at Brahamanmajra village. The girl was drugged and she was repeatedly raped. The accused persons abandoned her at night. The family said that the victim had approached the police at Badshahpur village. The policemen summoned her alone to the post several times. 'On some occasions, the policemen would take her to the police station in late evening hours. They would seek her to narrate the incident. They also tried to force her to withdraw her complaint. The policemen finally registered the FIR for rape on 27 November when she did not budge', said Gulshan Kaur, the victim's elder sister. She alleged that Balwinder, Gurpreet, Sandip and Shinderpal Kaur kept on threatening the victim despite the registration of the FIR. Shinderpal had helped the accused. The accused threatened the family too and all shifted to the victim's aunt's house at Samana, a town near Patiala. However, the accused intimidated them there too. 'Fed up with the indifferent attitude of the police and continuous intimidation by the accused, she consumed poison on Wednesday around 5 p.m. She was rushed to Rajindra Hospital at Patiala but she died late at night', stated the girl's relative. Her mother Surjit Kaur said that the victim also named the accused in the suicide note. It was shocking that cops arrested the accused only after she died, she added ('Patiala Girl Commits Suicide After Gang Rape, Blames Cops for Humiliating Her', *Mail Today,* 27 December 2012). The deceased's cousin Charanjit Kaur told *The Tribune* that they had approached Ghagga SHO Gurcharan Singh and Patran DSP Harpreet Singh in the matter, but got no help from them. 'Instead, the SHO would send his uniformed men and ASI Naseeb Singh (Badshahpur police post in-charge) to our house at odd hours. 'After we lodged an FIR on 27 November, the accused and the police openly began pressuring us to strike a compromise. They would enter our village at will and ensured that we lived in fear,' said Charanjit, tears rolling down her face (*The Tribune,* 28 December 2012). The Punjab Police dismissed Ghagga SHO Gurcharan Singh and Badshahpur police post in-charge ASI Naseeb Singh on the basis of a preliminary probe and suspended

Patran DSP Harpreet Singh. The three accused have been arrested. Terming the police action hollow, villagers who had gathered at the cremation ground said the action came too late. 'The police should have acted when the girl was alive. What purpose do the arrests and dismissals serve now? Our village has lost a young girl who was first brutally raped and then let down by the system'. said Mukhtiar Singh of Badshahpur village. 'She ran from pillar to post for justice, but in vain'.

Similarly, a 'rape victim' was allegedly set ablaze by six persons in Dhandari Khurd area in Ludhiana on Thursday (*Indian Express*, 4 December 2014). The 17-year-old girl was rushed to a hospital where she was stated to be critical, police said. Ludhiana Police Commissioner Pramod Ban said two persons had been arrested in connection with the incident while others were still absconding. The girl had lodged a complaint of rape against three of them two months ago. The three were arrested and just last week released on bail, Ban said. On Thursday, six persons, including the three rape accused, reached the girl's residence and allegedly set her ablaze after sprinkling kerosene on her, he added. 'The accused, all from Bihar, have been identified. Two of them, identified as Sahjad and Anwar, have been arrested while the search for the rest is on', a police official said (*Indian Express,* 4 December 2014).

In another graphic incident highlighting the brutality of violence, a nurse at Landeke village in Moga district, Punjab (www.sikhphilosophy.net 21 January 2013), was thrown out by the rapists from a car on Bathinda Dabawali road, two days after her abduction. The girl, who had completed her nursing course from Mata Sahib Kaur College in Gidderbaha in 2007, was battling for life at Bathinda civil hospital. According to a statement given to Bathinda's Rama Mandi police station SHO Paramjeet Singh, the girl, who had been looking for a job, was informed by one of her friends that there was a vacancy at a Sector 34 hospital in Chandigarh. She took a bus to Chandigarh on Friday morning and got down at Sector 43 bus terminal when an unknown person came to her asking for an address. Before she could utter a word, the girl was dragged into a car in which another woman and a man were seated. They gagged her and the trio injected her with some drug after which she fell unconscious. When she woke up, she saw four men in a room and one of them was filming her in the nude. When she screamed, he injected her with another dose of some drug. The girl alleged that she was gang raped by the men. On Sunday morning, she was dragged into a car in a semi-conscious condition by the gang. Later, the girl was thrown out of the vehicle at around 5.30 p.m. on Sunday near Rama Mandi area on Bathinda Dabawali road. A car driver, Rohitas Kumar of Kular village in Abohar district, spotted the girl in a serious condition and admitted her to the civil hospital in Bathinda. 'The police have registered a case and a hunt is on for the culprits,' said Gurmeet Singh Kingra, DSP, Bathinda. Poonam Dhillon a doctor of the civil hospital conducted a medical examination of the girl and confirmed that the girl was gang raped.

In terms of 2012 NCRB data, 'A total of 1,07,82,638 verbal, written or suo-moto complaints were recorded by the police across the country in 2012. But 15 states and three Union Territories did not provide separate records for complaints and FIR, and only recorded only FIRs as complaints. The remaining

Figure 2

Reported Cases of Rape in India: 2011

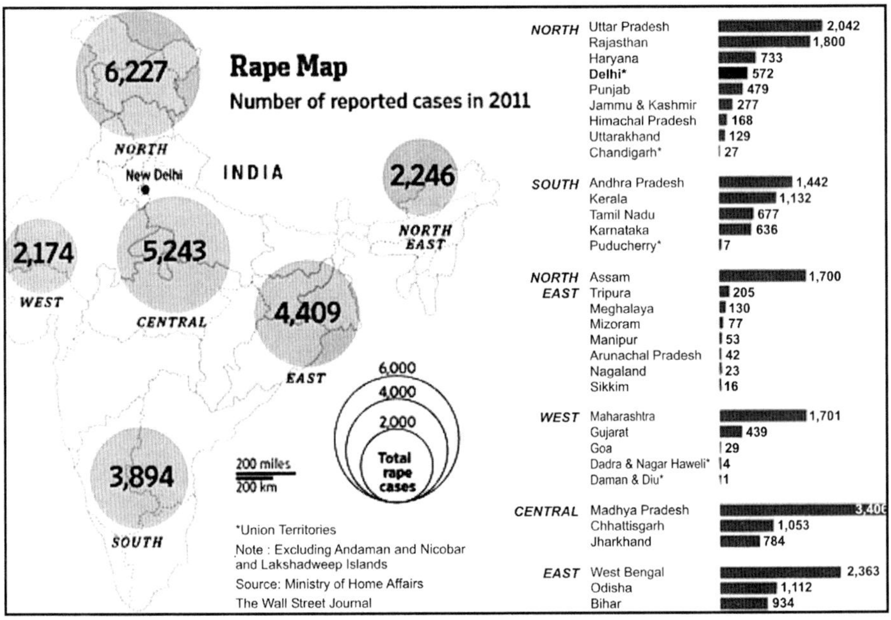

Source: Wall Street Journal, 3 January 2013.

states provided disaggregated data for the total number of complaints received as well as those converted into FIRs. Thirteen states and four UTs received a total of 71,47,332 complaints in 2012. Out of these, only 24,06,253, that is 33.66 per cent, were converted into FIRs. Delhi had the worst record of converting only 2.4 per cent complaints into FIRs. Of the total 38,144 rape cases pending investigation in 2012, charge sheets were submitted only in 21,565 cases (56.5%).

Investigations were still pending in 14,695 (35.95%) rape cases at the end of the year. The charge sheeting rate calculated by the NCRB does not take pending cases into account, hence the provided is as high as 95.6 per cent. This manner of calculation is highly questionable and conceals more than it reveals. Of the total 1,01,041 rape cases pending trial in the courts, trials were completed merely in 14,717 (14.6%) cases. Of these, convictions happened in 3,563 cases, 292 were compounded and withdrawn, and the accused were acquitted or discharged in 11,154 cases. The conviction rate for rape, therefore, was as low as 24.2 per cent in 2012, down from 26.4 per cent in 2011 and 26.6 per cent in 2010. The average number of IPC cases per police personnel was 2.5 in 2012, the same as 2011, contrary to constant refrains of overburdening by the police (Shakeel 2012).

A close reading of the data shows in the context of rape that that the rate of conversion of complaints into FIRs was 33.66 per cent. Of these, charge sheets were submitted in 59.5 per cent cases, trials converted only in 14.6 per cent of cases of which convictions happened in a meagre 24.2 per cent cases. So if a total of 1000 women approached the police with their complaints, FIRs were registered only in 337 cases. Of these, in cases of rape, charge sheets were submitted only in 190. Trials were completed in 27.7 per cent cases and convictions happened only in a total of 6.7 cases, that is, less than 1 per cent cases. Thus, on an average, the criminal justice managed conviction in only 7 out of 1000 complaints for rape. Even if one assumes that FIRs were registered in all complaints of rape, our system managed conviction in only 20 out of 1000 FIRs, i.e. less than 2 per cent cases. This calculation does not take into account the cases which are not reported to law (Shakeel 2012). What is imperative that actions, incremental or monumental, take place continuously at all levels. The government, parliament, courts and police must continue to increase and expand their efforts to deliver justice to these women and make it easier for them to report crimes' (Chatterjee 2014).

Judicial Horror: The Discourse of The Rape Survivors

However, as put by Baxi (2014: 343), 'it is a public secret that while rape survivors are forced to bear the burden of courage against the widespread tolerance of intolerable sexual harm, the law extracts a cost from the survivor who speaks out against rape. The construction of rape as an offence against society in law books and appellate judgements hides the processes by which law's injury to rape survivors is manifested ... the production of such injury is conceived as the cost of administration of criminal justice which remains unproblematised at least from the perspectives of violated women and children. Law assumes that once the female subject is constituted as the desiring subject, a different order of evidence is required to prove injury against society. Hence, courtroom talk demonstrates that to materialise injury the injured witness must mimetically reproduce the act of rape. Such injury inflicted by law is necessary for a crime against society to be proven, in the process eliding the injury caused to an individual testifying against such a crime ... the medico legal certificate occupies a central place in the trail for it imparts structure to the cross examination by recording whether or not two or more fingers could be inserted in the vagina ... this technique supposedly allows actual verification by substituting the penis with two fingers ... the hymen can signify only after this technique is deployed on the body of the violated or the proof of injury is localised to what the vagina reveals to the medical expert. The body of the law thus wounds when it is named as the wounded. Phallocentric law must mimetically do to a woman what the particularised aggressor did to her in order to KNOW that she was raped and to declare that society has been injured by the act. The tremendous psychic costs inflicted on survivors by these violent techniques of gathering evidence are fully ignored. Bearing the brunt of curious and lewd eyes both at the police station and the hospital, the rape survivor is made to experience humiliation over and over again. Rape victims are never made to feel that they are in control of what is happening to them in the aftermath of a police complaint. It is truly appalling that rape survivors are not even given spare clothes to change when their own clothes are confiscated as evidence' (ibid. 2014: 343).

Terming the experience of rape trail as judicial horror, Baxi states, 'defence deliberately feigns ignorance and asks questions which are unanswerable within given normative framework. The defence line of questioning actively shames and restigmatisies the legal subject by deploying customary forms of lawyering … cross examination is perceived as a method of dettering women from testifying in courts of law. The way records are written and questions are framed during the trail convert it into a pornographic spectacle. Documents such as clothes, panchnamma, etc. which serve as a record of seized evidence sexualises woman's body. The production of judicial horror rests on repeated sexualisation of the raped body and demands the exited performance of the rapists' intent in the court of law. Judicial horror is just not given it is achieved within the law. It is not a state of mind, mentality or mere function of judicial, sensitivity or insensitivity rather it stands produced through legal discourse (Baxi 2014: 344).

The transcripts of the following rape trials held in camera substantiate my argument. Twelve year-old Noor Nisa was raped by her stepfather Shakil. Here is her testimony in the court of the public prosecutor in the Mirzapur trail court:

B	Then what did he do? he made you lie down … .
N	He made me lie down and he climbed on top of me.
B	Then he put his place of urination *(peshab karne ki jagah)* into my place of urination. You will say this na?
N	Silent
B	What did his place of urination look like?
N	Silent
B	For how much time did he keep doing like this?
N	Silent
B	A lot
N	A lot …
APP	Do you know why you are in court today? For what have you come here?
N	For rape *(balatkar)*, to testify to rape
APP	Who was raped?
N	I was (her voice drops …)
APP	Then what happened?
N	He took off my salwar. Then he took me near the bushes, Shakil *bhai* took my salwar and threw it off. He pulled my salwar …
APP	Then?
N	Abba
APP	Whose trousers, *(patloon)* … who took off father's trousers?
N	Inaudible
APP	
J	Took off his trousers and what did he do to you?
N	He climbed on top of me.
APP	Then what happened?
N	Then he inserted his place of urination into my place of urination.
J	What did he do?
N	Inserted …
APP	Where did the blood come out from?
Defence lawyer to APP In English	Do not lead.
APP to Defence lawyer	I wouldn't in such cases
Defence lawyer on the day of the incident	What was the time?
N	Silent, she looks confused. Her anxiety seems to grow as defence lawyer asked about time.

Defence lawyer	When he lay you down then a lot of time passed?
N	Silent
Defence lawyer	Speak up, how much time?
N	A lot
Defence lawyer	How much time?
N	Silent
J	How much time passed five minutes, 10 minutes, 30 minutes?
Defence lawyer	How much time?
N	Silent
J	When he lay you down, climbed on you, moved for how much time?
Defence lawyer	Six hours? Do you know the meaning of this, from morning to evening in school it is six hours when you return home in the evening.
APP to Defence lawyer	Do you think she understands what is the meaning of minutes?
J to APP in Gujarati	A 12-year-old should know, make her understand *yaaar*.

At one point the prosecutor turned to the defence lawyer that he appreciated his cross examination: 'In such type of cases, I must recommend your name, no problem, feel free to carry on without any tension. *Bindaas chaliye*'. (Laughter ...)

The courtroom was marked by animated exchanges between the opposing lawyers, occasionally interspersed with laughter.

Noor, however, remained unsure whether laughter was provoked by her answers:

> Defence lawyer:
> Look here then how do you know how much he do how much he do that you did not know, how much did he put his place of urination – half, full ... how did you see you were lying down ... and blood came out.
>
> Defence lawyer:
> When he inserted you screamed then he lay down upon you after that you kept lying, why didn't you scream for a second time?
>
> APP objects:
> Question should be did you cry at that time?
>
> J:
> When he inserted, climbed on you, lay down, then did you scream? You do not understand (irritated). I have explained four times. The faster you understand the faster it will be over.

After the testimony, her mother Hasina Behan walked out of the courtroom her face set in silent anger, 'Does one ask children questions like these ... would these *haram ke* ask questions like these to their own daughters or wives. 'For Hassena Behan by the end of the trail legal normativity appears illegitimate' (Baxi 2014: 344).

We see here that in failing to narrate the stories of particularized injury the law loses 'control of them on their own terms' (Fergusson 1996: 96). 'Testimony is not possible without citing the injury for which the law is evoked ... rigid designators that name a sexualised body achieve this ... . On the one hand the naming attempts to secure meaning and to guarantee that the child describes what happens on the other hand the linguistic display does not overcome the degrading meaning of the naming process' (Butler 1997: 100). This degrading naming describes legal normativity as a field of force. Courtroom then becomes an object that is animated with the dual capacity to both injure and excite. As put by Butler (1997: 85) speech is constituted as display, confession and evidence but not as a communicative vehicle having been deprived of its capacity to stake truthful claims (1997: 85) (c.f. Baxi 2014: 161).

'Adult women testifying to rape are not only unfamiliar with the conventions of the adversial system but when they adopt these conventions then they are constructed as 'loose' women and unreliable witnesses, e.g. when a rape victim speaks with aggression and confidence on the stands she departs from the expectations of what the demeanour of a rape victim should be if she is able to name sexual parts this is interpreted as a sign of looseness and, hence, she is ascribed the capacity to lie about having being raped. If she is unable to cite the details of injury in forensic detail the testimony casts doubt about the veracity of the complaint' (Baxi 2014: 138). As put by Flavia Agnes 'a woman is raped twice once by the perpetuators and once by the law courts.' She talks about the shame and stigma experienced by the rape victim when she chooses to seek justice in the court of law (*The Hindu,* 18 September 2014).

In an interview with a public prosecutor, Baxi was told:

> In sex offence, to establish that particular thing in court you have to say that thing openly. Even in camera trial she hesitates to answer. The defence lawyer keeps asking that particular question, how do you know this particular part is known as this? Then he argues that her character is loose, how does she know everything. Generally, the advantage goes to the accused. Defence lawyer asks questions which no one can answer, e.g. none can give answer to such questions they get scared, she hesitates, she will not be able to answer in sound mind. (2014: 139)

Baxi argues that 'defence lawyers use linguistic and semiotic strategies to force the witness to adopt their categories, induce distress or hostility and subsequently establish her immoral character through her words and demeanour. The outcome of each case is underwritten by the conventions of courtroom talk which systematically accrues blames humiliates and shames the legal subject testifying to rape whether or not there is a conviction at the end of the trial' (2014: 139). As Sue Lees says,

> rape trials can be seen both as operating as a warning and as a way of restricting the activities of women through inciting the fear of public sphere but also through punishing the victim for breaking the silence enforced by the emphasis on female respectability and chastity. The rape trial retains something of the older notion of spectacle that Foucault saw as being displaced by disciplinary power and scientific reason but a spectacle of degradation visited upon by the victim. (c.f. Baxi 2014: 139)

It is further stated in *Bharwada Boginbhai Hirjibhai v. State of Gujarat*, AIR 1983 SC 753: 'A girl or a woman in the tradition bound non permissive society of India would be extremely reluctant even to admit that any incident which is likely to reflect on her chastity had ever occurred. She would be conscious of the danger of being ostracized by the society or being looked down upon by the society including by her own family members, relatives, friends and neighbours. She would face the risk of losing the love and respect of her own husband and near relatives and her matrimonial home and happiness being shattered. If she is unmarried, she would apprehend that it would be difficult to secure an alliance with a suitable match from a respectable family or an acceptable family. In view of these and similar factors, the victims and their relatives are not too keen to bring culprit to book. And when in the face of these factors the crime is brought to light there is a built-in assurance that the charge is genuine rather than fabricated'. In the context of Indian culture, as stated in the case of *Rajinder v. State of H.P.*, AIR 2009 SC 3022, a woman-victim of sexual aggression would rather suffer silently than to falsely implicate somebody. Any statement of rape is an extremely humiliating experience for a woman and until she is a victim of sex crime, she would not blame anyone but the real culprit. While appreciating the evidence of the prosecutrix, the Courts must always keep in mind that no self respecting woman would put her honour at stake by falsely alleging commission of rape on her (Dhirajlal 2014).

It becomes clear in these cases that 'even when justice appears to be done, that is, when conviction is secured, the very demonstration through legal discourse of the violation of the woman re-enacts and resediments patriarchal and misogynist values. In India, feminists have begun to view with concern judgements which take a progressive position on the issue of corroborative evidence in rape trials, but based on notions of women's 'chastity' and 'traditions of Indian society' (Menon 1999: 284). The implications, however, are more serious than feminist critiques tend to recognize. It is not simply that in such decisions the court passively accepts rather than challenges patriarchal values (see for example, *National Law School Journal* 1993: 170). The seriousness lies in recognizing that if it is assumed that tradition bound Indian society would make 'innocent' women reluctant to level false accusations of rape, the same factor can be expected to motivate 'promiscuous' women to hide their promiscuity precisely through such accusations. In other words, convictions can be secured only at the cost of turning the case once more on the axis of the 'guilt' or 'innocence' of the raped woman' (Menon 1999: 284). The 'recent editions of medical jurisprudence manuals are marked by different temporalities retaining sexist and colonial constructions of the lying colonised female subject alongside more contemporary discussions on the trauma of rape' (Agnes 2005; c.f. Baxi 2014: 62) Agnes asserts that change will be possible only when 'at each juncture of writing newer editions the experts abandon the trends of copying from older texts and archaic sexist presumptions' (Baxi 2014: 62). The medical legal dimension of rape trial tries to use forensic and invasive technique on the anatomy of rape victims to ascertain whether they have been actually raped or not. The woman is violated further through medico legal tests that establish penetration, partial penetration, rupture of hymen and the pervagina (PV Test) normally called the finger test. The other categories being: habituated to sex, questionable character whether injuries are self inflicted or lying or consent due to financial motive or spite or being spurned, gold digger psycho neurosis, fantasizing or imagining a situation where she is desired and chased by males, political vendetta, to gain publicity, etc.

To conclude this discussion one can concur with Baxi that: medicalization of falsity is not a neutral representation but a specific combination of power and knowledge, following Michael Foucault that science can be used to make a female body speak despite or even to spite her testimony (2014: 62). The medico legal gaze is arrested by specific body parts that correspond to the evidentiary for the purported crime. The medico legal case is 'the individual as he may be described judged, measured, compared with others, in his very individuality; and it is also the individual who has to be trained, corrected normalised excluded, etc.'. (Foucault 1977: 191; c.f. Baxi 2014: 255).

The cultural judgement on rape even emphasized by the judiciary using words like 'ravages', 'ravished', *zindalash* seem to suggest that rape leads to permanent stigma and shame where a woman's life cannot be rebuilt because of a mere desecration of her body. As Shiv Vishvanathan says, 'Feminism has tried to show that there is a link between shame and sexual violence. If women feel shame at their body as sexual then the experience of rape gets linked with the experience of shame as a permanent state of body' (1994: 12; c.f. Baxi 2014: 11). As put by Sharon Marcus, 'The dictum that rape is worse than death constructs the female body as a wound, a violable inner space ... feminine fear seems to entail a complete identification of a vulnerable sexualized body with the self ... since fear concentrates the self on the anticipation of pain on the conviction that the self will be destroyed on violence' (1992: 394–395).

A judgment made by the Delhi High Court in the case of rape and murder of an old woman in December 2010 sparked a debate on whether sexual intercourse with a post-menopausal woman can be treated as rape. It has also highlighted the indignity of a woman trapped in such a situation. The judgement, in *Achhey Lal v. State Govt of Delhi*, made by a Bench comprising Justice Pradeep Nandrajog and Justice Mukta Gupta on 30 October 2014 delivered by the Delhi High Court let off the accused, 49 years old Achey Lal, waiving off the punishment meted out to the accused on the grounds that even if the intercourse 'has been forceful, it was not forcible'.

'As regards the offence punishable under Section 376 IPC, the deceased was aged around 65–70 years, thus beyond the age of menopause. We find force in the contention of the learned counsel for the appellant that even if the sexual intercourse was forceful it was not forcible and contrary to the wishes and consent of the deceased,' read the judgement. In December 2010, the victim was found dead inside her house in Majnu ka Tila along with an inebriated Achey Lal by a girl at whose house the victim worked. Achey Lal was arrested and eventually sentenced to 10 years of rigourous imprisonment. The post-mortem of the victim revealed that she had sustained injuries on her vagina, and traces of alcohol were found on her, too.

Lawyer activist Vrinda Grover questioned the use of the word 'menopause' by asking on what grounds the Court had arrived at the judgement that the case was not one of rape and where did menopause factor come in here? Menopause is a medical condition, and the mention of the word is extraneous and erroneous. The injuries on the victim's vagina proved that there was forced penetration, and the inference would lead to the criminal case of rape. Also, the judgement said that there are no other injuries, which was clearly a step back to the pre-Mathura era, where one would look for injuries to prove rape. The Mathura rape case led to two amendments: one, there should not be any requirement about explaining injuries for rape. And secondly, consent should be univocal. This case, to my mind, without the privilege of any evidence to be able to construct the case and thus rely on the judgement, is erroneous and not according to the jurisprudence of the Supreme Court,' said Grover (Madhukalya 2014).

Joining the strands together, the pattern deciphered is that usually a victim numbed and shocked still has hope for justice but the indignity, prejudice and stigma she faces and guilt she goes through eventually make her end her life violently especially since the society robs her of a future and punishes her relentlessly. She must prove to the police, society, and panchayat that she was not having an affair with the accused, she was not wearing revealing clothes, she did not go out with the man and she did not in any way bring the crime on herself. It is as if she must prove that she did her best to protect her chastity and virtue. As Foucault says, it is as an unending trial with no recourse to appeal presumption of bringing about the crime upon herself. The rape apart from any physical and psychic consequences to the woman concerned pollutes her and thus the woman who has been raped is now no longer called a victim but a survivor by a section of media. This goes a long way in eliminating the fear, shame, guilt, abuse from the victim to the one who should be actually penalized; the man who raped her.

A rape victim denotes a sense of pity, helplessness, fate of a life ruined or tainted forever. As a survivor she is hardly left with a sense of dignity, a resolve to stand up and walk again, though bruised and battered, to go back to career and relationships, to move on. Those who are sullied, tainted and deserve shame are not the rape victims but her perpetrators who would be brought to task by a sensitized and alert police force. Women must learn from the SURVIVOR of rape not to dread rape as a violation which would leave them sullied forever but to REPORT THE INCIDENCE OF RAPE so that the shame is centred on those who truly deserve it: the rapists. Let us break the silence and sniggering associated with rape. Let us transcend the fear that makes us all dread rape and make us all pre-victims.

More than the pepper spray and learning self-defence techniques the change is about a mentality a perspective of repositioning the status of men and women in our oppressive patriarchal structure with an attitude boldness empathy and openness. When the apex Court guides that rape victims must be counselled and rehabilitated, we have to keep in mind that social perceptions and discourse on rape have gone a long way from using terminology like 'ravished', *zindalash*, 'desecrated for ever' to the fact she can and must move on with her life, rebuild it and be reabsorbed in society. The outrage that followed the Nirbhaya Case, Shakti Mills case, Tehelka case and The Uber rape case show that now women in the urban society are by and large not blamed and stigmatized for being victims of other men's depravity. Marcus (1992), writing about sexual violence, urges that we 'rewrite the rape script in which a single sexual organ defines the self. We do not need to defend our real bodies from invasion but to rework this elaboration of our bodies altogether and to revise the idea of female sexuality as an object as property and as inner space' (Marcus and Poovy 1992: 396; c.f. Menon 1999: 288). Here Judith Butler's (1923) discussion of Freud's *the ego and the id is* particularly significant in which Freud argues that the body does not precede and give birth to the idea of the body rather it is the idea which makes the body accessible as a body (Butler and Scott 1992: 135–143; c.f. Menon 1999: 289). Following Menon's discussion 'feminist practice would be liberated from the stranglehold of the discourse that designates the body as a site of selfhood'. Thus, a woman's sense of self, sense of being pure and impure need not be restricted to her physicality or her embodied body which can be violated but to her sense of selfhood which remains courageous, bold (capable of bringing her perpetrators to book without feeling a sense of discomfort or humiliation while confronted with embarrassing personal questions herself), instead of viewing her raped body as contaminated and harbouring feelings of guilt and worthlessness. Her sense of self can be emancipative, not restricted to the violation of her sexual body. Her self-esteem, personality, psyche and self-worth are capable of being reclaimed and reintegrated into the mainstream of society.

References

Agnes, Flavia. 2012. *Law and Gender Inequality: The Politics of Women's Rights in India*. New Delhi: Oxford University Press.

——. 2014. 'For a Victim-Centric Approach'. *The Hindu*, 18 September.

Arya, Sandhya. 2007. 'Law Institutions and Women'. Delhi University Course Material.

Barnet, Hiliare. 2012. *Sourcebook of Feminist Jurisprudence*. New York: Routledge.

Basu, Srimati. 1999. *She Comes to Take Her Rights: Indian Women, Property and Propriety*. Albany: State University of New York Press.

Batra, Anurag. 2013. 'Media Activism in Delhi Gang Rape Case'. *Vivid*, 22 July.

Baxi, Pratixa. 2014. *Public Secrets of Law: Rape Trials in India*. New Delhi: Oxford University Press.

Bhagat, Rasheeda. 2012. 'Rape is About Power, Not Lust'. *Business Line*, 24 December.

Bhan, Gautam. 2015. 'My Name is Suzette Jordan'. *Economic and Political Weekly*, 1(13), 26–27.

Butler, Judith. 1997. *The Psychic Life of Power: Theories in Subjection*. Stanford, CA: Stanford University Press.

Butler, Judith and Scott, J.W. 1992. *Feminists Theorise the Political*. London: Routledge.

Chakravarti, Paromita and Punjabi, Kavita (eds) 2012. *Women Contesting Culture: Changing Frames of Gender Politics in India*. Kolkata: Stree.

Chakravorty, Uma. 1982. *Rape, Class and State*. New Delhi: People's Union for Civil Liberties.

Chatterjee, Siddharth. 2014. 'Two Years After the Delhi Gang Rape: Is India Losing its Moral Moorings?'. *Huffington Post*, 17 December.

Chowdhry, Poulami Roy. 2013. 'The Delhi Gang Rape: The Making of International Causes'. *Feminist Studies* 39(1), 282–292. www.academia.edu/389530.

Chowdhry, Prem. 2014. 'Masculine Spaces: Rural Male Culture in North India'. *Economic and Political Weekly*, XLIX(47), 41–50.

Dan, Doherty. 2013. 'Old World India Not Immune from Rape Epidemic'. *Fairfax Media*, 14 January.

'Delhi Gang Rape Case: Social Media Fuels Rally at India Gate'. *Economic Times*, 24 December 2012.

'Delhi Gang Rape: Internet Flooded with Strong Comments'. *DNA News*, 18 December 2012.

'Delhi Gang Rapist Sentencing Divides India'. *The Rural*, 1 September 2013.

'Delhi Rape Verdict: Twitter Abuzz with Reactions of Common Man'. *One India*, 10 September 2013.

Fergurson, Robert A. 1996. 'Untold Stories in Law' in *Law's Stories: Narrative and Rhetoric in Law*. Peter Brooks and Paul Genirtz (eds.). London: Yale University Press.

'Gang Rape Sparks India Media Debate'. *BBC News*, 24 December 2012.

Geeta, V. 2007. *Patriarchy*. Kolkata: Stree.

——. 2012. *Gender*. Kolkata: Stree.

'How Do We Stop Rapes? India Looks for Answers'. 20 December 2012. tehelka.com

'Internet Encyclopedia of Philosophy'. www.iep.utm.edu/jurisfem

India Today. 27 December 2012.

Indian Express. 4 December 2014.

'Irrelevant Questions Traumatising Daughter: Uber Victim's Father'. *The Hindu*, 10 March 2015.

Jaidka, Kokil and Ahmed, Saifuddin. 2013. 'Protests Against Delhi Gang Rape Case on Twitter: Analysing India's Arab Spring'. *Jedem: Journal of Democracy*, 5(1), 28–58. www.jedem.org.

Judgement in the Delhi Gang Rape Case – SC No. 114/2013. n.d. www.andrewbuncombe.com/stories from south.

Kahol, Vikas. 2012. 'Patiala Girl Commits Suicide After Gang Rape, Blames Cops for Humiliating Her'. *Mail Today*, 27 December.

Kannabiran, Kalpana. 2014. *Women and Law: Critical Feminist Perspective*. New Delhi: Sage Publications.

'Land, Caste and Sexual Violence Against Dalit Girls and Women in Haryana'. *Women Against Sexual Violence and State Repression (WSS)*, 18 July 2014.

Mackinnon, Catherine. 1989. *Towards of Feminist Theory of the State*. Cambridge: Harvard University Press.

Madhukalya, Amrit. 2014. 'Delhi High Court Judgement on Rape and Murder of 65-Year-Old Sparks Debate'. 4 November. www.dnaindia.com.

Marcus, Sharon. 1992. 'Fighting Bodies, Fighting Words'. www.thehinducentre.com/multimedia/archive/02677.

Mccarthy, Julie. 2013. 'Outside the Big City: A Harrowing Sexual Assault in Rural India'. 8 February. www.mpr.org

Menon, Nevedita (ed.) 1999. *Gender Politics in India*. New Delhi: Oxford University Press.

Mohan, Raman. 2012. 'Dabra Gang Rape Victim Withdraws into a Shell'. *The Tribune*, 14 October.

National Law School Journal. 1993. 'Rape: Challenging the Pedestals of Patriarchy'. Vol. I.

Nath, Triptha. 2013. 'Rural India's Secrets: Whatever Happened to the Three Sisters of Bhandara'. *Women Post/Features*, 20 April.

Nayak, Venkatesh. 2014. 'Preliminary Analysis of Some Statistics Relating to the Offence of Rape as Reported by the National Crime Records Bureau for the Year 2001–2013'.

Rape Statistics: Punjab's Shame. 21 January 2013. www.sikhphilosophy.net

Ratan Lal and Bhirajlal. 2014. The Indian Penal Code. Gurgoan: Lexis Nexis.

Sangari, Kumkum. 2012. 'Politics of Diversity: Religious Communities and Multiple Patriarchies', in Nirmala Banerjee, Samita Sen and Nandita Dhawan (eds), *Mapping the Field: Gender Relations in Contemporary India*. Vol. 1. Jadavpur: Stree.

Shakeel, Albeena. 2012. 'Rape and Honour Crimes: The NCRB Report'. *Economic and Political Weekly*, XLVIII(31), 2.

Sood, Aman. 2012. 'A Month After Gang Rape, Patiala Teenager Ends Life'. *The Tribune*, 28 December.

'The Unassailable Case Against Mr Tejpal'. *The Hindu*, 25 November 2013.

WSS. 2014. Haryana: Land, Caste and Sexual Violence against Dalit Girls and Women: A Report by Women against Sexual Violence and State Repression.

Rape Maps

'A "Rape Map" of India'. *Wall Street Journal*, 3 January 2013.

Manish, Sai and Dubey, Priyanka. 2012. 'Where a Rapist is Considered a "Real Man"'. *Tehelka*, 43(9), 22 October.

11

Women and Agency

A Story of Struggle for Empowerment

Kanwalpreet Kaur

Women aspire for a bigger role in contemporary societies. Irrespective of the social and economic standing, women are doing phenomenal work, be it as skilled, semi skilled or unskilled workers. In the unorganized sector, women have always played a pivotal role, though it was not recognized for a long time and they remain most vulnerable in this sector. At construction sites or in agricultural sector or in the industry, women's labour has largely gone unnoticed. It is, indeed, unfortunate that although women besides playing the role of nurturers have also stepped into the role of providers, yet they continue to be exploited at home as well at the work place. They have proved their mettle even in times of adversaries. It is usually said that men make war and women endure. Shoma A. Chatterji (2006: 203) quotes from a practical guide launched by the International Committee of the Red Cross for those in humanitarian agencies working with women entitled, 'Addressing the needs of Women affected by Armed Conflict: An ICRC Guidance Document'. She says, 'According to the International Committee of the Red Cross (ICRC) women's experience of armed conflict is multi-faceted. It includes isolation, increased responsibility for dependents, physical and economic insecurity, detention, and a higher risk of sexual violence, injury and death.' Women lose fathers, husbands, sons and brothers in wars and then end up supporting families. Women, who, till then, had led sheltered lives, stepped in to protect themselves and their kith and kin. There have been numerous women who were victims themselves and yet relegated themselves to the background for their first priority was their families. In the 'smart wars' of the last two decades, civilian population has been a victim and among them it is the women who have suffered more and have, in the process, been victimized in ways, more than one.

When women are battered and bruised anywhere in the world, it is a shame for mankind. Though groups of people are working on many fronts, yet violence against women continues unabated. Be it the developing or developed countries, women are subjected to untold hardship and suffering.

In the developed world, there might only be small pockets where such discrimination occurs, but, even in these countries, abuse of women cannot be denied, which might not only be physical but mental and emotional too. Child abuse, trafficking of women, kidnapping, honour killings and female infanticide are just a few evils that can be named in the developing and under developed countries directly affecting women. Girls are sold into the flesh trade so that families can sustain themselves. Poverty is one big enemy because of which young, nubile girls are transferred from the safety of their homes to the brothels that exist in big as well as in small cities and towns. Wherever men are stressed they find comfort in women, even if the latter themselves happen to be victims. After a war, the winning party celebrates its victory by using, exploiting and raping the defeated country's women. The exploitation of women continues, irrespective of countries. Fortunately, we are living in a world where large scale wars are discouraged and avoided. Yet, women continue to be denied their rights even during normalcy. Society denies them a life of dignity in their everyday lives. In India, the situation is grim. Laws are made yet violation of these laws goes on blatantly. Women are an asset to the society yet they have to undergo untold sufferings. But the struggle for justice and equality in all spheres continues. This has helped women rise in protest to a great extent. Yet, a majority of the women have to fight within the four walls of their house. And this battle is not new. Even in the past, women had occupied an inferior position. As Romila Thapar writes, 'The Gita, for example, speaks of shudras, vaishyas and women as one category, all being pap-yoni, born of sinful wombs' (2014: 265). Today also women have to fight war on three fronts, which are:
(i) survive
(ii) earn self-respect
(iii) demand basic rights

A large number of women are denied all the three. Gender equality, at least in developing and under-developed countries, still remains a dream for most of the women irrespective of social or economic status. The problem does not merely relate to implementation but it primarily lies in the mind-set of the people. The thinking, attitude and opinion of the people refuse to change as these are deeply entrenched in a patriarchal culture and ideology. Chatterji believes that 'Patriarchy and capitalism operate effectively together to use women as a profitable source of production and reproduction while keeping control over women's labour and perpetuating their inferior status' (ibid. 2006: 12). Unfortunately, it is not only men but also women who transfer the monstrous set of biased attitude, which is horribly aligned in favour of men, to the next generation. This denying of equality to women persists mainly because women are not viewed as agents of change. It is drilled into them since the beginning that they are objects to be owned and trampled with no identity of their own. 'More often than not, women are seen as objects of change rather than as agents of change, imitators rather than initiators, bystanders rather than full participants', Chatterji says (ibid. 2006: 19). The only choice left for women is to help themselves. They have to pick up the broken threads of their lives and put up a brave but silent fight. Unfortunately, the exploitation is prevalent not only among uneducated and poor women, it extends across the spectrum.

Even educated and professionally trained women fall prey and the number is on the rise as women are stepping into the workplace. We have the example of the Additional District Judge, Gwalior, who was sexually harassed by a sitting High Court Judge. She resigned when she turned for help to the Chief Justice of the High Court and was not able to get a hearing from the latter. Her decision was to tender her resignation and seek justice because while remaining within the system, she felt, she couldn't fight it. Her complaint points to a deep-rooted problem in society. She says, that 'while we talk of gender justice on public platforms, in public employment, there is very little respect for women professionals and there is a glass ceiling, which prevents them from moving higher. In her case, this glass ceiling came in the form of sexual harassment, compelling her to resign' (Jaisingh 2014). She had to turn to the Supreme Court for help. Her case 'reminds us that harassment is about unequal balance of power at workplace' (Jaisingh 2014). The complainant herself feels, 'what use is education, if it does not teach you to be respectful of women? (Jaisingh 2014). One wonders, if this is the case of a woman who is in the upper echelons of the society, what would be the condition of women who are illiterate, ignorant and unaware of their rights? If this was not enough for us to ponder, a woman constable reported of rape by a resident of a village, with another woman colleague of the same rank assisting the molestor (*The Tribune* 2014). It may be concluded that irrespective of the strata of the society a woman belongs to, there remains a high probability of her being raped, violated, beaten and even killed. Even Mahatma Gandhi believed that the care of women is not just a collective responsibility but universal responsibility. He argued, 'How can I indulge in pleasures, be alive and eat and drink while somebody ill treats my daughters?' (Gandhi 1999). He was talking in context of women who were molested when the partition of India took place in 1947. But his words continue to be highly relevant in every age.

This paper is a humble attempt to highlight the case of five women who decided to help themselves. They waited for help from their kith and kin and then, from the society, but were finally forced to take decisions on their own so that they could, at least, survive with self respect. For this, they have been rebuked and ridiculed. They have also been criticized by their own families, and surprisingly, even by people, who were strangers to them. Their character assassination has taken place, but after putting up a brave front and adopting a resilient attitude they walk with their heads held high and even manage a good laugh. Their stories are untold and unheard. But such stories need to be told as a lesson for women elsewhere, who might be going through a similar fate. The methods used for obtaining relevant information include personal Interview and observation. Since the participants were illiterate, a questionnaire could not be handed over to them. So, they were interviewed and a conversational method was used. This made the interviewees very comfortable and honest in their responses. The objective of my paper is to highlight the fact that women on their own can be agents of change. It is they who can initiate and usher in fresh winds of change. When women decide to alter their lives, they use their agency to do so.

Case I

Kranti, the first respondent is a resident of village Maloya, situated in the Union Territory of Chandigarh. She spent her childhood in a village in Uttar Pradesh with five siblings in abject poverty. After her marriage her parents were blessed with three more children. So, while after her marriage, Kranti gave birth to her two children, her mother was also blessed with three children. Though Kranti refuses to have more children, she adds with a laugh that her parents in the village will continue to produce more children, because that is the way it happens in villages. So for Kranti, marriage was an escape from the village, which she described as 'a den of death'. Coming to Chandigarh, the City Beautiful, meant a bonus and a better life. She got married into a large family, where she had parents-in-law and four brothers-in-law. Her husband was a rickshaw puller, while her brothers-in-law worked as waiters and cooks at wedding functions. Her mother-in-law worked as domestic help in Chandigarh. Her father-in-law had studied up to Class VIII and was considered a well-meaning and wise man in the *biradari*, that is the 'community'.

Kranti recalls her journey,

> I got married and was very happy. I came to Chandigarh. I liked wearing bangles and supporting all the symbols of a married woman. In village, marriage is the only opportunity that gives you freedom and choice to lead your own life though there are a lot of restrictions from the in-laws' side. Yet, it is mainly the husband who can help one enjoy life. I had huge expectations from marriage as I had been fed up on Hindi movies. Our only exposure to a good life had either been through films or the lavish lifestyle of the zamindars. So coming to Chandigarh, to a city, made my dream come true. But soon my husband started spending his money on alcohol and became an alcoholic. He started beating me.

Initially, she would laugh away the beatings of her husband. Whenever I asked her about the fresh bruises on her body she would justify her husband's action and say,

> It is not he who beats me, it is his alcohol and tobacco every evening. Next morning, when the hangover wanes, I can say anything, even abuse him. He is quiet. My in-laws, initially, helped me. They would stop him and protect me. My mother-in-law gave me her unstinted support. She wished for a grand-daughter, because she had five sons of her own. She believes that with the birth of a daughter, Goddess 'Lakshmi' enters the home. So, she loves my daughter. But when the beatings became more frequent and harsher and I conceived for the second time, I fled to my parent's home in the village. I used to work in houses in Chandigarh but couldn't continue because I had conceived. They all advised me, for the safety of my child, to go away from my husband. I gave birth to a son in the village and then my mother-in-law brought me back. I stay with my in-laws but in my own '*jhuggi*' (a small pitched tent). I earn about ₹ 5,000 per month and the houses in which I work,

> help me a lot with clothes, toys for my children, etc. I also do a little bit of sewing and repair work that helps me to make both ends meet. My priority is my children. I don't leave them on the roadside, but have put them in the crèche, where they are well-looked after from 9 a.m. to 2 p.m. The crèche is run by the Chandigarh Administration and I pay ₹ 500 per child. I am able to work because they are safe in the crèche. I have opened a ₹ 500 savings account in the name of my daughter'.

'What about your son's future?' I ask her. She replies,

> Boys can earn and take care of themselves, but girls have to be taken care of. So I am saving for my daughter.

Kranti decided to leave her husband the day he ran away with their daughter. She trusted him as a father but knowing his wayward ways she feared for her daughter's safety. He went missing with the daughter and returned home drunk. Thankfully, the daughter was with him. Kranti narrates,

> The day he ran away with my daughter, I feared the worst. Once my husband starts drinking, he loses sense of time and place. He drinks till he falls unconscious and is senseless. After a few days he repeated the incident and that was the day I decided to leave him. It is tough to live alone but better than getting beaten up. My in-laws are helping me in bringing up my children. But at the end of the day, the responsibility of my children rests on my shoulders. Life is tough yet it has to be lived.

Kranti is very positive about life. All she desires is to live respectfully and bring up her children well. Out of her meagre earnings she pays ₹ 500 to the creche so that her children are safe and don't grow on the roads. Their safety is her first concern. The phrase, 'liberation of women,' has taken a new turn with Kranti who, though is completely illiterate and does not know about women rights, has left her husband and married her brother-in-law who was unmarried. She was abused by her relatives but is happy in her new life that she chose for herself. With no idea of rights, she is managing to lead a life on her own terms. Together they earn ₹ 15,000 and are blissfully happy. Kranti is not an escapist. As soon as she got married to her brother-in-law she knew that in addition to her two children she would have to bear a child of her brother-in-law. It might seem a harsh reality but she knows it and is willing to face it. As I read stories of scores of teenagers, farmers, students and women commit suicide, I look at Kranti and am in awe of her. Suicide might have been an easy way out for her but she chose to fight it out. Her situation was grim, a woman in an alien city, beaten by her husband and financially dependent on her family. But she picked up the broom to work not only for herself but also to fend for her children. Hers is a story of grit and determination. We need to learn many things from her.

Case II

Guddi, another migrant labourer, is a mother to five children, three girls and two boys. Her first priority was to educate all her children, when she came to

Chandigarh. Having spent her childhood years in Chandigarh, she was married to a small time farmer in a village of Uttar Pradesh. In the village, her mother-in-law troubled her. After two years she picked up her eldest daughter, who is now grown up and married, and took the train to City Beautiful, where she knew that people of various households, where she had worked since childhood, would help her. She left her husband in the village, giving him a choice to follow her or stay behind. He followed her and they built a life together though her husband turned a drunkard and resorted to wife-beating. She says,

> I have built a pucca house in the village with my earnings. I have worked in houses and they have offered me unstinted support. I am known for my honesty and people trust me blindly. I am proud that I have never broken anybody's trust. My wish was that all my children should be educated so I got them admitted in government-run schools. But unfortunately, they were all dropped from school, because I could not keep tuitions. I had heard about the government schools and was impressed by the buildings, grounds, etc. so I thought that my children would be educated. But the education system has failed me. Being illiterate, I could not help them in studies, with the result they were gradually dropped from school. I have encouraged my daughters to learn sewing, stitching and even do a course in the beauty parlour so that they are financially independent. I know how important money is for I have been able to live only because I earned. But my dream of educating my children remains unfulfilled though my youngest daughter, Durga, is still enrolled in a school. I don't know what is wrong with the schools and what do the teachers teach or why they don't teach though, I believe, they got very good salaries.

She further adds,

> My husband puts up a roadside tea-stall and I help him after finishing my work in various houses. Then I relieve him and he gets some rest. Now, our sons also help us. During the marriage season, our sons go and work in the marriage palaces as waiters or wherever the contractor sends them, it can be washing utensils, chopping vegetables, etc. If one doesn't study, one has to do such menial work to meet one's expenses. For many years, my husband would beat me and take away all my earnings. But after some time, one of the ladies, in whose house I work, took me to the post office and opened an account in my name. She would deposit my money there and today, I have a considerable amount as my husband cannot take the money. He dare not approach the lady, who helped me and the money is safe. My husband is quite supportive except when he is drunk. When my third daughter, who is the youngest of our children, was five months old, a couple came in a car and asked him for permission to adopt her. My husband ran with a brick in his hand to hit them. He said we don't give birth to children to sell them. The earnings from this tea-shop are enough. When we grow old, we will return to the village with our savings.

A simple life yet made complicated by having more children than one's resources and lack of education by the system. Yet, in both the cases, marriage remains important. Beatings and alcoholism are a part of life but is taken with a pinch of salt. Compared to other women in their community, these two women are recognized as women with courage. They are sought for advice and play a vital role in encouraging women to work so that they can be financially independent. They have realized the importance of money and the freedom that it can buy. Thus, they are teaching lessons of financial independence to women at the micro level. Policies are made at the macro level but it is at the grassroots that women continue to suffer. Action has to be taken at the micro level, where caste and patriarchy have a firm grip. Romila Thapar professes, 'Caste and patriarchy are intertwined and patriarchy can survive if it can control caste – that means in effect if it can control the code of marriage connections within or outside a pattern of caste' (ibid. 2014: 261).

Case III

Shikha, a domestic help, hasn't had an easy life either. She lost her husband some time back. He worked as a *safai karamchari* with the Chandigarh Administration. The couple was blessed with a son. The salary along with Shikha's earnings gave them a comfortable living. But her husband started drinking. He started spending his entire salary on alcohol. Beatings soon followed. Shikha appealed for help to her mother-in-law and brothers-in-law, but nobody helped. Her mother-in-law was a widow, while the brothers-in-law had their own families. One day, Shikha came to know that her husband had been thrown out of his job, because of absenteeism. She rued the fact that she was not told of this otherwise she would have asked for the job. At least, her son and she would be secure financially. She says, 'I came back to my parents' house where I was not welcomed. But as I had nowhere to go, they had to accommodate me. I have been given a room set, where I live with my son. My meagre earnings help me to survive. There is no financial help from my parents. I tried to give the best education to my son. He is in Class XII and has taken up Commerce. He has managed to be an average student because I couldn't afford tuitions for him. But his father's death has left him numb and deprived. I can't understand why he grieves so much for a father, who had never cared for him. But I try to understand a son's pain. My income is not fixed. I am insecure about my future. The only saving grace is the roof over our head. Alcohol ruined my life and there are many like me. The slums are full of such people. The government doesn't do anything to curtail this evil.' Alcohol, family neglect, lack of education, the factors are many. But at the end of all, it is the woman who is the victim and she has to act as an agent of change herself.

Case IV

Sunita, a beautician, lives life with dignity. The eldest among five siblings, she has four younger sisters and a brother who was born after all the sisters. A boy was needed to look after the parents in old age. Her father retired from a government job and draws a pension. He has married all his children and Sunita is proud of her father who stood by his daughters at all times. Her husband is a contractor and Sunita is blessed with three children, two daughters and a son. All her children go to school. Her father has helped her built her house. Sunita wanted to improve her lifestyle and provide her children with a better standard of living. When her husband's earnings could not give them a decent living, she decided to work. She was doing a beautician course even before marriage. She would cycle to her place of work but eve-teasing and road Romeos forced her to discontinue her course. But after marriage she decided to pick up from where she had left for one earning hand was not enough. Her husband's earnings were not enough to give them a comfortable life. Of course, she had her parent's support. She would leave her daughter with them and go to learn at a lady's place who trained girls. The lady was very supportive and encouraging. Sunita's father paid for the course. Instead of working at a parlour, Sunita decided to work independently as the long working hours made her neglect her child and her house. It was difficult to break even so somebody offered to help her find employment in a prestigious school in the city. She joined but her heart was in her skill that she had learnt, so she left the job and decided to take the risk. Today, she has a long list of valuable customers to whose houses she is a regular visitor. Her touch is personal. For her, the customers are her support. With the money, she gets, she has gradually added more rooms to her house and rents them out. She invests a lot in gold and keeps making ornaments for her children's marriage. She says, 'My daughters go to school. I have tried to tell them the importance of education. I want them to be graduates and pick up a job. But at the same time, I want them to pick up some skill so that they can be financially independent. The other day when my husband told my daughters that their mother deserved a beating, my daughters stood up on my behalf and dared my husband to do so. This is the positive effect of education. I am proud of them. I have worked hard and am proud of myself. It is only with my determination and the help of my parents, especially my father, that I have managed to stand on my feet with dignity and respect. On 'Karva Chauth' my daughter pitches in by applying 'mehandi' on customers' hands and earns her pocket-money. I let her do so because one should know the value of hard work. I pray to God that they are blessed with husbands who do not fall prey to various vices. I am there for my children as my parents have been there for me. My customers respect me and my art. My work is not a burden for me. Rather, it gives me pleasure and my independence. The bonus is I get to meet wonderful people who only give me strength'. Strong words coming from Sunita, who has converted her hobby into her livelihood. Work does not remain work, rather one sails through life. With her meagre earnings she has managed to carve a decent life for herself.

Case V

Rani is a peon in an institute of higher education. She was blessed with two daughters and a son. Her husband had a government job but expired at a young age, leaving Rani to fend for her children as well as for herself. But Rani's humbleness helped her. The whole institute embraced her. She worked tirelessly, contended that her children were growing in a healthy environment, that too academic, for her living quarters were also in the premises of the institute. As a result, her both daughters are lecturers today. She is proud of them but continues with her job as the latter has helped her raise her children with respect and grace. She has worked under many Principals; all have nothing but praises for her. Her hard work and perseverance have paid for her daughters to stand tall on their feet. Being a part of an institute helped her tide over many personal crises in her life. The place gave her security not only for herself but for her children too.

These are just a few women who have managed to put up a brave fight. They defied odds and were determined to survive. They derived strength as they underwent life's journey. Probably, they were not so focused as they started on this journey with no education or family support to back them. With no knowledge of the various laws that the government has made for them, the fight for survival must have seemed impossible. But they feel they have no choice. India is a vast country and woes of women in various parts of India continue unabated. Oppression and suppression of women in the name of caste and religion continues, with no one ready to defy these. When such norms are attempted to be broken, the people who dare to do so have to face the wrath of the caste and religious leaders. Every religion gives due respect to women. According to Quran, men and women are each others' *zawj* (one of the couple) thus indicating equal dignity and love and respect, not obedience or subordination (Wasey 2014: 185). Some give up while a few continue their fight. It is in the remote areas that women suffer most. They don't even have a whiff of the laws that have been enacted for the welfare of women. How would life improve for such women?

The example of 'around 3 lakh women of a cow herding community in Karnataka who are forced out into dingy outhouses or even the road during their menstrual cycle and after pregnancy' is one that is disheartening for any feminist movement (Gatty 2014). This community has refused any change and efforts by the government and social workers. The community believes that it is inauspicious to keep a menstruating woman in the house. Women who are menstruating or those who give birth are forced to move into single-room outhouses made of hay and shared by several homes. The population of Kandu Gollas number is around 15 lakhs in various districts. The government had set up 'mahila bhavans' in Gollerhattis between 2008 and 2013 to house women who are, thus, segregated. But they lie deserted. The Congress government tried to fight this evil through the Karnataka Prevention of Superstitious Practices Bill, 2013 but the bill is pending. It names, 'forced isolation, prohibiting re-entry into the village or facilitating segregation of menstruating or pregnant women' (Gatty 2014), as one of the beliefs that needed to be curbed. Thus, the government is willing to take a step but the community leaders are not ready to co-operate. R. Krishna, a local community leader and a panchayat member, says, 'Who is the government to decide what is blind faith and what is not? We have practices and beliefs that have brought prosperity to our community and that violating them can invite divine wrath. Why object to our belief' (Gatty 2014).

The Road Ahead

Such women, confined to the remotest corners of India, living in a patriarchal society have no chance of liberating themselves. Caste and religion bind the women to shackles of modern day slavery. They are treated only as child bearing machines and to do household chores. Their life is spent rearing children, drawing water from wells kilometres away and working at home. Beatings are a part of their lives. In extreme cases, rape, gang-rape, *begaar* or exploitation by the upper caste men are occurrences which are brushed under the carpet. It is only when women decide to help themselves can the government and other well-meaning people help. Women give birth and usher in new lives to the world it is time that women get a chance to experience the joys of this world. They need to have their own identity as well, as their own life. They have to be given a freedom of choice, the right to choose what is good for them, a right to decide what their body and souls want. It is time for us to stop forcing our choice on women. Only then can the society prosper. With a few women surging ahead, a little change is possible. We need to include women like these as well as from the *Kadu Gollas* (meaning cow herders) who can change and make an actual difference to the position of women in India. It is then that women's struggle for equality will get an impetus. When positive action will penetrate into the deepest packets of the country can we expect a change. India should be more ready to take this giant leap and give due place to its women, who have contributed equally in India's freedom as well as her progress.

The sheer number of these incidents leaves one numb and shocked. The different Acts, laws and other facilities have failed to improve the status of women. The other harsh fact is that gruesome crime, which is of far bigger magnitude, than all these occur frequently all over the country. The acid attacks on women, the gang rapes, honour killings, female foeticide, flesh trade, etc. are just a few gory crimes committed on women. The day-to-day tribulations and heart aches are suffered by a majority of the women. Yet, these women hold families together, sacrificing themselves at the altar of duty. At the end, it boils down to the fact that women have to stand up for themselves and fight each battle to win. Hiding pain in the closet will not help but exposing the wrong can be the solution. A woman makes a home out of a house, she should learn to make it a safe sanctuary for herself too.

Conclusion

Women have surged ahead but at costs which have been too heavy at times. Yet, women have put up a brave front. There are many organizations and well-meaning individuals who are working tirelessly to improve the status of women. A lot has been accomplished but the journey is still long and difficult. But with the spread of education in the society and awareness among people, the path that is strewn with thorns might be carpeted with leaves. It is women who have to take the first step on this road and then take the path to a life full of freedom, equality and dignity. As Shoma A. Chatterji argues, 'In India, for instance, Hindu religious cults defined the power of the woman through the goddesses they worship. The Brahmin priests dropped some of their own male gods and incorporated matriarchal fertility cults into the worship of Lord Shiva going further on to provide 'Brahmanical' husbands for 'non-Brahmanical' mother goddesses. The same Brahman priests upheld Manu's low opinion of women and his ways of treating women. This shows that the Brahmins tried to resolve the contradiction culturally and politically first by acknowledging that women do have power, and then trying to establish and perpetuate the theory that the same power must be controlled by men in society lest it should become dangerous. This gradually led to the control of women by men till the time when women became totally powerless at filial, social, cultural, political and economic levels' (ibid. 2006: 10–11). If women want to improve their status, they need to express the desire to be equal partners in development. They need to have the will to ask for justice and the courage to shun whatever is negative.

Readings

Butalia, Urvashi. 1997. 'Abducted and Widowed Women: Questions of Sexuality and Citizenship During Partition', in M. Thapan (ed.), *Embodiment: Essays on Gender and Identity*. Delhi: Oxford University Press, pp. 90–196.

——. 1998. *The Other Side of Silence: Voices from the Partition of India*. New Delhi: Penguin.

Chatterji, Shoma A. 2006. *Gender and Conflict*. New Delhi: UBSPD.

Desai, Kishwar. 2013. 'When Will Things Change for the Women in India?'. *The Tribune*, Chandigarh, 28 April.

Desai, Meghnad. 2013. 'The Endurance of Politics'. *The Sunday Express*, Chandigarh, 28 April.

Editorial. 2013. 'Death of a Family, When Society Fails its Own'. *The Tribune*, Chandigarh, 29 April.

Gandhi, M.K. 1999. *The Collected Works of Mahatma Gandhi*. 98 Vols. New Delhi: Publication Division.

Gatty, Harsha Raj. 2014. 'Chained to the Cycle'. *The Sunday Express*, 21 December, p. 12.

Jaisingh, Indira. 2014. 'A Judgement That Takes a Stand for Harassed Women'. *The Sunday Tribune*, Chandigarh, 21 December, p. 10.

Manav, Sushil. 2013. 'Haryana's Harsh Reality: How a Rape Ruined a Family'. *The Tribune*, Chandigarh, 28 April.

'Policewoman Alleges Rape in Rohtak'. 2014. *The Sunday Tribune*, Chandigarh, 21 December, p. 4.

Sedhuraman, R. 2013. 'Time to Reset Nation's Moral Compass: Prez'. *The Sunday Tribune*, Chandigarh, 5 May.

Sengupta, Shombat. 2013a. 'Queen Bee Syndrome'. *The Sunday Express*, Chandigarh, 14 April.

——. 2013b. 'Victims Forever'. *The Sunday Express*, Chandigarh, 28 April.

Singh, D.P. 2007. *Female Foeticide in Punjab: Causes and Consequences*. Delhi: Paragon.

Singh, Jupinderjit. 2013. 'They Float Like a Butterfly, Sting Like a Wasp'. *The Tribune*, Chandigarh, 5 May.

Vora, Rajendra and Palshikar, Suhas (eds) 2004. *Indian Democracy: Meanings and Practices*. New Delhi: Sage Publications.

Thapar, Romila. 2014. *The Past as Present: Forging Contemporary Identities Through History*. New Delhi: Aleph.

Wasey, Akhtarul (ed.) 2014. *Feminism, Modernity and Harmony in Islam: Asghar Ali Engineer and His Writings*. New Delhi: Shipra.

12

Education and Women Empowerment

A Case Study of Batala

Rajni Bala

Half of the world's population reels under the pressure of hegemonic masculine ideology. Dowry deaths, domestic violence and exploitation of women continue unabated especially in countries like India. There is an urgent need to empower women socially, economically and politically so that they can break away from male domination and claim equality with them. To this end, education is perceived as an effective means to improve the quality of life of women and also as a powerful force of liberation. It became an accepted fact that the higher the level of education, the greater would be the level of awareness regarding social issues and, therefore, a greater level of sensibility as well as sensitivity. To assess the relationship of education with women empowerment, a study was conducted in the city of Batala in Punjab State. The objectives were to find out the role of education and economic independence in decision-making of women college teachers of Batala city at professional and domestic level. The study also aimed at investigating the power structure in the college administration and the position enjoyed by women college teachers in this structure.

Role of Education in Women Empowerment

The rise of feminist ideas led to a marginal improvement in women's condition, while majority still suffered oppression. Amartya Sen, in his essay 'Many Faces of Gender Inequality', states: 'The afflicted world in which we live is characterized by deeply unequal sharing of the burden of adversities between women and men. Gender inequality exists in most parts of the world, from Japan to Morocco, from Uzbekistan to the United States of America'. Focusing on South Asia, he discovered in the data thrown up by the Census of India 2001 an interesting phenomena – a split India, 'something of a social and cultural divide across India, splitting the country into two nearly contiguous halves, in the extent of anti-female bias in natality and post-natal mortality'.

He concluded by identifying the principal issues, emphasizing the need to 'take a plural view of gender inequality' and calling for new agenda of action to combat and put an end to gender inequality (2001).

In India, in spite of the various measures taken up by the government after Independence and even during British rule, women are still fighting for a respectable life in the society, we still witness dowry deaths, domestic violence and exploitation of women. Till date female foeticide is not an uncommon phenomenon. The ground reality is deprivation, degradation and exploitation.

When it comes to the issue of violence against women, India is not far behind. Recent incidents of rape, molestation eve-teasing and domestic violence have proved that we still have a long way to go in creating an egalitarian society, where women can enjoy the same rights and privileges as their male counterparts in this free world.

Empowering women and bringing equality between sexes has become the priority for many development plans throughout the world. Empowerment is defined as a means of moving from enforced powerlessness to a position of power. It means empowering women socially, economically and politically so that they can break away from male domination and claim equality with them. Kishor and Subaiya (2008) defines women's empowerment as increased control over their own lives, bodies, and environments. A woman is considered empowered when she is able to make the best of her own life – when she has access to education and access to capital and is in a position of throwing away the habits of female subordination and patriarchal messages which were unconsciously internalized through socialization. Instead of accepting the social world as given, empowerment aims at identifying gender inequalities and discrimination previously accepted as 'natural' or 'normal' and challenging them. It means putting on new 'gender spectacles' to question what was previously held acceptable.

To attain this end, education began to be perceived as an effective means to improve the quality of life of women and as a powerful force of liberation. Many studies pointed towards a strong correlation between several developmental indicators and level of literacy of the population. Amartya Sen, in his empirical work, brought out very clearly how the relative respect and regard for women's well-being was strongly influenced by their literacy and educated participation in decisions within and outside the family (2001).

At the same time, educated women were found to be experiencing less domestic violence, regardless of other social status indicators like employment status (Sen 1999). Increased knowledge, self-confidence and awareness of gender equity thus began to be considered as indicators of empowerment process (Murphy-Graham 2008).

Even the UNESCO's World Conference on Higher Education (1998) and the World Education Forum (2000) made a commitment for the attainment of many goals for women's education and empowerment. It was unanimously felt that higher education would open up better paying jobs for women in a country and break the pattern of gender discrimination. It also became an accepted fact that the higher the level of education, the greater would be the level of awareness regarding social issues, and, therefore a greater level of sensibility as well as sensitivity. Keeping this end in view, a new era was envisioned, where education and economic independence would empower women and depress all forms of gender violence and discriminatory practices.

To see the relationship of education and women empowerment, a study was conducted in the city of Batala in Punjab State on 40 female college teachers. Surprisingly, the researcher's study in this regard revealed some startling facts, which indicated that the emancipation and empowerment of women through education and economic independence is another myth perpetuated by the patriarchal society.

Objectives of the Study

- To study the role of education and economic independence in decision-making of women college teachers of Batala city at professional and domestic level.
- To study the power structure in the college administration and the position enjoyed by women college teachers in this structure.

Methodology

The present study was conducted on 40 lady lecturers of Batala city working in different degree colleges. The methodology used was interview method, group discussions and participant observation method.

Observations

Here are some observations about the respondents, who happen to be highly qualified permanent lecturers in colleges. This implies that the respondents are well paid, and are economically independent. The questions that were put forth dealt with issues relating to decisions regarding spending of earnings, decisions regarding personal and family matters, personal experiences of domestic violence, help rendered to parents, awareness regarding laws and legislations for the protection of women's rights, position at their work place, etc. Some of the responses are cited below:

- Most of the women cannot spend their earning according to their own wish. For every minor item (except the daily kitchen items), they need to take permission from their husbands and for their personal expenditures, they wait for the husband's 'good mood'. The question of spending on their own family members is something they can not even think about. Only two of these women reported that they could spend as much as they wanted, but, this arrangement had come at the cost of serious conflict with the husband.
- Majority of the respondents reported that whenever they wanted to go to their mother's place or they tried to help their sick parents, there were fights, in which the woman had to ultimately surrender. To avoid conflicts, they had decided against going to their parent's home or had decided to pamper their husbands up to the extent that they would get permission. A senior lecturer with an ailing mother waits for teacher's strike to visit her mother without the knowledge of her husband.

- Some of these lecturers are living in conditions, where there is no dignity and respect; they are the perfect victims of gender violence, facing physical and mental torture. They are aware about their legal rights, but going to police or court is not a viable option for them. They feel that this will tarnish their image in society and stigmatize them as 'an independent woman living without a husband'. In other cases, there was parental pressure to adjust under all circumstances.
- In 11 cases, college lecturers secretly went through abortions. Three of them aborted their babies because their husbands were not ready to take responsibility of a baby, while in the other eight cases; the women were carrying female foetuses. In all these cases, it was the woman who had to compromise to suit the whims of her husband.

Inferences Drawn on the Basis of Group Discussions

On the basis of various group discussions held with the male and the female teachers, in which researcher was also a part, the over-all conclusions were as under:

- Girls were held responsible for provoking acts of violence and abuse against them.
- Liberal lifestyle of girl students and their openness with boys was considered responsible for overall moral vitiation of environment and increasing crime against women.
- Education of females was directly quoted as one of the main causes for the breakdown of values and family disorganization. The higher the level of education, the more the breakdown of the family. Submission of a woman to man's authority was upheld to be an ideal family structure.
- In educational institutions, especially co-educational institutions, men were perceived to be better leaders and administrators.

The shocking part of the discussion was the conviction of many women teachers, who tacitly agreed with the patriarchal views of their male counterparts regarding male superiority and dominance at professional as well as personal front.

These are indeed disturbing facts, which came to light during the collection of data. It is ironic that teachers, who are role models and beacons of lights giving directions to the young generation, are not able to assert and speak for their own rights, thereby allowing themselves to become passive victims of abuse.

Inferences Drawn on the Basis of Participant Observation

In the general atmosphere in the college, where the researcher teaches, it seems, male dominance has complete social sanction. Some of the observations showing gender insensitivity in these colleges are listed below:

- In committees, women lecturers are generally given reception duties, decoration, preparing students to perform different items. These are all off-the-stage duties, however, when it comes to running the show and receiving the credit, there are only men hogging the limelight. For the last many years it has been observed during different functions in the college that every female teacher who enters the hall looks for seating space at the back, while all the males are conditioned to occupying the front seats only. Innocuous actions in themselves, they speak volumes about the general behaviour, which demands dominance from men and subjugation from women.

- Though the ratio of the male and female teachers is almost same in Baring College, yet, in the teaching union, men are in the decision-making roles as President and Secretary and women are given the task of collecting money, arranging tea during the meetings and paying the bills. In important union matters, lady lecturers are expected to be quite and reticent. When some of the lady lecturers tried to move up the hierarchy of leadership, they were strongly opposed and pushed aside for being incapable of handling 'tough tasks'.
- Till now, in the history of Baring, not even once has any woman worked as a Principal, a Treasurer, a Bursar or a Registrar or even as an office-bearer in the management committee. Whenever any lady has tried to come forward, she has been severely opposed.
- Every meeting dealing with discipline matters starts with an introduction about the deteriorating moral values among girls, who according to many of the teachers, both male and females, are vitiating the atmosphere by acting as decoy for boys. A few male teachers don't mind commenting nonchalantly that dresses of girls encourage rape and molestation. In most of the discussions, where the researcher was also a part of the group, silently listening to the discussion after Delhi gang-rape, the conclusions were that only girls are responsible because they have become too open with boys.

In situations like this, it is not the male mindset alone that can be held responsible for all the ills plaguing the society, women are equally responsible. In spite of their higher education, qualifications, capabilities of handling responsible positions, they have accepted their marginalized status for fear of criticism and fear of being stigmatized as feminists by the general faculty which includes both male and females. So, on the basis of the present study it was concluded both men and women are equally responsible for this gender discrimination and a barrier in the path of social transformation involving emancipation of women.

There are very few lady lecturers who have come forward and openly resisted the discrimination, which runs in the institutes of higher education. Even here, the results are not very positive, as they are selectively weeded out of all the main committees, ignored by the administration and harassed by the authorities for raising their voice. They are branded as prejudiced women and other 'dignified' ladies are advised to avoid their influence.

In spite of education, economic independence and awareness of rights, women continue to live in the marginalized situation rather than opposing discrimination. On the other hand, highly educated men, who are equally aware that they are violating the human rights, are continuing with their patriarchal behaviour resting secure in the fact that they will face no opposition. There are laws to protect women's rights, there is awareness among educated class, but still courage of using law to handle gender violence, and to live a dignified and peaceful life breaking the clutches of patriarchal mindset, is yet to become a norm. So, the general attitude and rigid mindset of highly qualified college lecturers reveals that though education has enhanced employability of women, it has failed to raise the level of sensitivity towards important social issues. Teachers, who are the role models, are in principle, reinforcing gender inequalities, which are ingrained too deep in the Indian psyche. Our present education system and process of socialization too has failed to inculcate social balance, sensitivity and gender equality. The present study found both men and women equally responsible for this gender discrimination and as barrier in the path of social transformation involving emancipation of women

Conclusion

The present study concludes that education and economic independence do not raise the status of women either at domestic or professional level; neither does it empower them to make decisions on their own. It also highlights that highly educated and economically independent teachers continue to occupy marginalized positions in the power structure of educational institutions.

The fact that education enables women to take advantage of all the opportunities available, and the fact that if women have the necessary knowledge and skills, they can open any door and attain equal footing with men, seems hollow when the present data proves that majority of the highly educated and economically independent women still reel under the pressures and demands of male hegemony. Systematic gender discrimination in patriarchal society is the reason why women are not yet able to attain equal footing with men. Though women can be empowered by giving them education, but it is equally true that no one can give power to another. Education that is empowering has to be taken. Education that is given by powerful to the powerless is education for subordination. The common belief that educated women in positions of power can act as agents of ending discrimination against women, and can contribute to the general improvement of the position of women is unfortunately turning out to be a myth. In the present patriarchal system, educated women obtaining positions of power are being co-opted into the patriarchal establishment as 'honorary males'. Their promotions depend on their defending the patriarchal establishment and the security of their position depends on how well they support the patriarchal establishment and find their place within it.

Considering these factors, it is not wholly justified to say that gender discrimination arises from irrational prejudice, and can be eliminated by increased and improved education, which in turn improves rationality. The reality is that patriarchal ideology has its own rationality, and has to be understood from the inside. Within the patriarchal ideology, gender discrimination is justified as a rational division of labour.

Hence, the roots of discrimination remain deeply entrenched even in the minds of the highly educated, enlightened and economically sound elite of our society. Education and economic independence, therefore, are not the panacea for all problems; rather, in the present system, these have become tools that are being used to inoculate subordination and conformity of females and 'naturalness' of male domination.

References

Government of India. 2001. Census of India. New Delhi: Office of the Registrar General of India.

Kishor, Sunita and Subaiya, Lekha. 2008. *Understanding Women's Empowerment: A Comparative Analysis of Demographic Health Surveys (DHS) Data*. DHS Comparative Report No. 20, Calverton, Maryland, USA: Macro International Inc.

Malik, S. and Courtney, K. 2011. 'Higher Education and Women's Empowerment in Pakistan'. *Gender and Education*, 23(1), 29–45.

Sen, Amartya. 2001. 'Many Faces of Gender Inequality'. *Frontline*, 18(22), 27 October – 9 November.

Sen, Purna. 1999. 'Enhancing Women's Choices in Responding to Domestic Violence in Calcutta: A Comparison of Employment and Education'. *The European Journal of Development Research*, 11(2), 65–86.

UNESCO World Conference on Higher Education. 1998. 'Higher Education in the Twenty-First Century Vision and Action'. UNESCO, Paris, 5–9. http://www.unesco.org/education

World Education Forum. 2000. Final Report. Paris: UNESCO.

13

Abandoned Wives of NRI Husbands

A Saga of Victimization

Komal Sharma

The transnational marriages seem to be largely driven by a strong instrumental rationality with the objective of migrating to the western world (henceforth referred to as NRI marriages). These aspirants are very competitive when it comes to finding the match and such marriages are performed with a sense of urgency. Many of such marriages turn out to be fake ones and split soon, with serious long-term consequences not only for the wife, husband, children and families but also for the society and economy as a whole. In this complex scenario, where matrimonial alliances exist between the two continents which naturally involve two different and sometime contrasting legal systems, it makes the issue of NRI marriages more complicated. Lately, there has been a substantial rise in the cases of fraudulent marriages in which the brides have been the major victims. Many a times, once the marriage is solemnized, the NRI husband rushes back to his country of residence leaving behind his newly-wed wife on the pretext that he would make necessary arrangements and bring her to the adopted country. But very frequently this does not happen, and she waits indefinitely only to discover that she has been sexually, economically and socially exploited and dumped.

In some cases, it has been reported that men had married women while holidaying in their native villages with no intention of living with them. There are stories of women who have been married for over 20 years but have only been with their husbands for not more than a week. The most tragic stories perhaps are of women who keep on waiting year after year for their husbands to return. The problem is more serious in the Doaba and Majha regions of Punjab because a larger number of Punjabis from these two regions are settled abroad. It is estimated that more than 50 per cent cases of abandoned women are from the peasantry in Punjab (Chohka 2006).

The report of Ministry of Overseas Indian Affairs (2006) showed that NRIs came to India for short duration, in order to lure and exploited young girls. Such grooms not only exploited the girls sexually but also demanded handsome amounts as dowry from their families. Once married, the situation changed. The woman was mostly not taken abroad on some pretext or the other. She was asked to wait till the laws of the foreign land enabled her to secure a visa for that country. If she was unlucky, she might become a mother meanwhile and at times treated as a maid at her in-laws' home. According to the Report of National Commission for Women (2011), the problem of NRI marriages was manifold and included dowry and other kinds of harassment of married women in foreign countries, like non-consummation of marriage, marriage of convenience, concealment of earlier existing marriage by the husband before marrying an Indian woman and lack of social security faced by an Indian woman on the foreign soil.

Magnitude of the Problem

The National Commission for Women (NCW) in India has revealed that there are 30,000–35,000 cases where NRI grooms have abandoned their brides in India, out of whom about 15,000 are allegedly from the Doaba region of Punjab (Melwani 2005). The Lok Bhalai Party (LBP) is the political party in Punjab which has taken more than 1,000 cases of abandoned brides to the court and has also strived to ensure justice for them and their families (Robert 2005). According to the Party officials, more than 22,000 abandoned brides had got criminal cases registered against their NRI grooms. According to the Party President, out of a total of 30,000 such cases in India, around 15,000 belong to Punjab, including 10,000 from the Doaba region alone (Chaba 2012). The Ministry of Overseas Indian Affairs (MOIA) informed the Lok Sabha that it received 381 complaints of women abandoned by their NRI husbands out of which most of them were from Punjab (Monteiro 2012). The Ministry also registered a sharp increase in the number of cases registered by Indian women against harassment and desertion by their spouses: from 381 cases reported till 14 March 2012, the figure jumped to 418 by 30 June 2012 (Ghosh 2012). The Regional Passport Office (RPO), Jalandhar, had reportedly taken up a major initiative of impounding passports of fraudster NRI grooms who had abandoned their wives. The Passport Office in Jalandhar, till 2012, had seized passports of at least 94 NRIs who had abandoned their Indian brides (Dheer 2012).

Objective of the Study

To analyse various problems faced by the abandoned wives of NRI husbands.

Method

The study focuses on the state of Punjab in view of the magnitude of the problem related to NRI marriages in state in the recent past. The universe of the study comprised the wives abandoned by NRI husbands in Punjab. Within Punjab, the region Doaba which has witnessed a very large number of cases of NRI marriages, particularly those of abandoned wives. Therefore, the study area was restricted to the districts of Jalandhar and Kapurthala (including rural and urban areas). Since it was not possible to obtain a sampling frame, therefore the cases were selected by using non-random method of sampling. The registered cases of abandoned wives by NRI husbands were obtained from the office of Lok Bhalai Party located at Ludhiana. In the view of the qualitative nature of the research issues, the data was obtained by using methods such as personal interviews and narratives. In the present study, 20 cases were taken into an account and with the help of the respondents' narratives, their problems have been highlighted. To maintain confidentiality, names of the respondents have been changed.

Theoretical Framework

Historically, social scientists have examined women's oppression and their social struggle in a multitude of geographic locations and from a variety of theoretical perspectives. Among those addressed below are theories on the argument that a woman's destiny is determined by psychological, physiological or economic forces. These theoretical perspectives represent the complexity of oppression and subordination of women in India and provide the theoretical basis for the proposed research.

Biological Explanation of Gender Discrimination

This approach maintains that the biological characteristics of men and women are the basis of gender differences and discrimination. Murdock (1949) argues that biological differences between men and women are the basis of the sexual division of labour in society. Thus, because of her biological functions of childbearing and nurturing, a woman is tied to the home and because of her physique she is limited to less strenuous tasks. The first scholar to make the distinction between sex and gender was the American psychoanalyst Robert Stoller (1968). He made the observation that the vast majority of population can clearly be categorized as male and female according to their physical characteristics; external genitalia, internal genetalia, gonads, hormonal states and secondary sex characteristics. Because of these differences, women are capable of bearing and suckling children, whereas men are not. According to him, such differences in physique between men and women usually mean that men are stronger and more muscular.

Psychological Explanation of Gender Discrimination

Psychological theories of gender highlight the role of interpersonal relationships, communication in individual learning and cognitive development as the genesis of gender. Social psychologist Chodorow (1978) argues that the social roles of mother and father are not just due to patterns of socialization but due to the psychodynamics of early childhood. In his object relation theory, as boys and girls develop their identities they must become psychologically separate from their parents. Therefore, girls form a behaviour which is more relational, attached and is oriented towards others.

Another perspective is the social learning theory. Social learning theory was developed by W. Mischel (1966) and others, Bandura and Walters (1963) and Lynn (1969). The theory emphasized the significance of the environment in explaining the gender. There are various types of social learning theories, but all of them share a common argument: Violence and aggression are not inherent properties of an individual, rather they are learned behaviour. The social learning theory that is most often used to explain women abuse in intimate relationships is the intergenerational transmission theory (Levinson 1989). The proponents of this theory maintain that male children are more likely to grow up to assault female intimates if their parents abused them or if they observed their fathers assaulting their spouses (Hines and Malley-Morrison 2005).

Socio-Cultural Explanation of Gender Discrimination

Social cultural theories are focused on interpersonal or interactional processes as sources of gender discrimination. A woman's status in society remains defined by her functions (both actual and supposed) within the family (Oakley 1981). Mead (1934) argues that awareness of personal identity arises out of communication with others who pass on the values and expectations of society. Wood (1994) argued that roles are assigned to individuals by the society therefore women are still regarded as caretakers and are expected to provide care to infants and elderly relatives, etc. On the other side, men are meant to fulfil the masculine role successfully and therefore expected to do work and bring an income while the feminine role does not require this. Wollstonecraft (1792) declared that most differences between the sexes are socially created, not natural. The meaning of gender grows out of a society's values, beliefs, and preferred ways of organizing collective life.

The above mentioned gender perspectives are helpful in providing the differences between men and women. These differences have sometimes been seen as the basis for the subordinate position of women in society. Following feminist perspectives dwell upon various factors responsible for the subjugation and exploitation of women in society.

Feminist theories focus on broader social forces such as patriarchy, subjugation and exploitation of women that contribute to violence against women. Most of the feminist theories of women abuse in intimate relationships are of the view that men abuse woman to maintain power and control over them (Dekeseredy and Macleod 1997). However, of all the variants of feminist thought scattered throughout the literature, we begin with Liberal feminism.

Liberal Feminism

Liberal feminism emphasizes gender socialization as the origin of sex differences. According to the Liberal perspective, the obstacles to equal rights for women lie in traditional laws and practices that deny the same individual rights to women that men already have. Millett (1970) believes that gender differences and social identities are the result of social learning. An early contention for women's rights was presented by Mary Wollstonecraft in 1792. In her book *A Vindication of Women's Rights*, she linked women's unfavourable status to their unequal access to education. Equal rights for women in education were sought to achieve women's equality with men. The major thrust of this perspective is on achieving gender equality. Barriers to gender equality are viewed as any law, institution, or person that discriminates on the basis of gender.

Radical Feminism

The Radical feminists attribute women's unfavourable status to the structures of male domination over women. Applied to violence against women, Radical feminist theory argues that men engage in this behaviour because they need or desire to control women (Daly and Chesney-Lind 1988). Beauvoir (1974) asserts that women are subordinate to men because of their anatomy and physiology. Firestone (1970) proposes that reproduction is fundamental to women subjugation. The different reproductive biologies of men and women, it is argued, produce a differential hierarchy as the female reproductive functions physically handicap women and provide men with a natural leverage to dominate women. She argues that the material base for women's oppression lies not in the economic but in biology. Orther (1974) agrees with Firestone that women are universally oppressed and devalued. She compares men with 'culture' and women with 'nature'. She claims that it is not biology as such that ascribes women to their status in society, but the way in which every culture defines and evaluates female biology.

According to Brownmiller (1976), it is not male violence, rather the fear of male violence that subjugates women. Not all women are raped, but the fear of rape guides women's behaviour. The projection of women's persona as sexual objects encourages rape to occur. Thus, the reduction of women to a sexual object is basic to their subjugation. Millet (1970) argues patriarchy as a reason for women's subjugation. Males and females are taught to behave and think in ways which reinforce the biological differences that exist and further provide men with a high status which in turns leads to them filling social roles in which they can exercise mastery over women.

Marxist and Socialist Feminism

Marxist and socialist feminists do not attribute women's exploitation entirely to men. They see capitalism rather than patriarchy as being the principal source of women's oppression and capitalists as the main beneficiaries. Frederick Engels in *The Origin of Family, Private Property and the State* (1884), stated that with the emergence of private property, women's housework sank into insignificance in comparison to man's productive labour. 'The world historical defeat of the female sex with the establishment of capitalism based on private property ownership by men did away with inheritance of property and social position through female line'. Thus maternal authority gave place to paternal authority and property was to be inherited from father to son and not from woman to her clan. The bourgeois families which owned private property emerged as patriarchal families where women were subjugated. Therefore, bourgeois family and private property as a byproduct of capitalism subordinated and oppressed women.

Although maintaining the importance of class system and the relations of production, socialist feminists view capitalism as intersecting with patriarchy to create women's oppression. Many scholars have analysed contemporary gender inequality as a result of both the structures of capitalism and patriarchy. Hartmann's (1979) analysis of patriarchy and capitalism proposed a dual system theory where the two systems are interactive but analytically distinct. Patriarchal relations predate capitalism and are fundamental to the exploitation of women's labour both in the household and in paid employment. Mitchell (1971) argues that the subordination of women involves the interplay between women's role in reproduction, sexuality and socialization of children, on the one hand and with the economic mode of production on the other. In order to tackle women's unfavoured status, Sylvia Walby in *Patriarchy at Work* (1986) attempts to conceptualize patriarchy not only in terms of the complexity of relationships of gender but also subtleties of interconnections of patriarchy with capitalism, which is a relationship of tension and conflict and not of harmony and mutual accommodation. Domestic labour is a distinct form of labour and core to patriarchal mode of production which is essential to exploitation of women by men and is independent of exploitation of proletariats by the capitalists.

To sum up, it can be concluded that all the perspectives are complimentary to each other and cannot be applied in isolation. So a combination of these perspectives can be used to provide the theoretical base for the present study. Patriarchal structures and values, traditional practices and lack of education and decision-making choice among women are primarily responsible for oppression, violence and subjugation of women in India. This is reflected amply in the way women, despite innumerable failed NRI marriages, are forced to agree to such proposals. Women who have been victims of NRI marriages represent the composite circumstances which conditioned them to conform to patriarchal dictates and value system. Marriage in many of these cases is not fixed with the girl's welfare as a priority; instead these proposals are used as an opportunity for the other members of the family to immigrate. Therefore, these NRI overseas marriages have come up with a unique form of violence against women, i.e. desertion of wives by their NRI husbands. In this process, hundreds of girls are victimized, often traumatized in both cases, i.e. when taken abroad by their husbands and when abandoned in India immediately after few months and years of their marriage. The present study has focused on the phenomenon of NRI marriages keeping women at the centre stage, primarily as victims.

Financial Problems Faced by the Victims

Money has been found to be one important factor contributing to violence against women. Dowry has come out as one of the main issues in all the cases discussed in the present study. Most of the respondents were forced by their in-laws to bring in certain amount of money or they should be ready to forget about their NRI husbands. Respondents were shocked to learn that their husbands had married them just to grab dowry. The moment the families of respondents were no longer able to arrange the amount, harassment started.

Melwani (2005) too reported that many of these women were being tortured by their in-laws for dowry, with no financial support. Pothen (1986) found that women were considerably more likely to experience financial hardships followed by divorce/desertion. Furthermore, women living without husbands are dependent on kin, who act as their material, emotional and physical support (Lamb 2000).

Substantiating the above mentioned observations, the following case indicates how significant dowry continues to be in a Punjabi wedding. Once the day for wedding is fixed after the negotiation on dowry, the bride's family begins working towards meeting the demands while major concern of groom's family is to grab the requisitioned amount from the bride's side.

> Before I was brought near the *mandap*, Rahul and his parents started demanding another ₹ 2 lakh in cash from my father. Rahul's father, refused to let the matrimonial knot be tied and said that the marriage would not take place until my father complied with their demand. (Radhika, Case 6)

> At first, Manpreet had agreed for a simple wedding ... a few days before the ceremony, he began demanding more money. He said he was getting a better offer from another girl whose parents were ready to provide ₹ 9 lakhs to him. (Rupinder, Case 11)

> Ranjeet and his mother came to our home and bluntly expressed their demands and said, 'We have a great charm for Ranjeet's wedding so we want to celebrate his wedding in a grand manner, all the relatives should feel happy. We need to do 40 *milnis*, everyone attending will be offered clothes, blanket and ₹ 500 rest you know well. (Gursimran, Case 20)

Rahul's family left Radhika's family helpless by demanding dowry just before the solemnization of the wedding ceremony. The groom's family had used the situational advantage of the wedding on the bride's family to extract material benefits from them. Similar to the case of Radhika, Rupinder and Gursimran had their own troubles in their respective households into which they were married. Rupinder said that she was not willing to get married as Manpreet was expecting a sum of ₹ 9 lakh from her father. Initially Manpreet had said that he would prefer a simple wedding but later he demanded a lavish wedding ceremony. Similarly, in Gursimran's case, her mother-in-law had demanded a lavish wedding because she wanted her son's wedding ceremony to have a touch of luxury. In both the cases, the grooms' families were demanding money even before the wedding without any consideration about the financial situation of the brides' families.

There were a few cases in which the parents of the respondents kept fulfilling the demands in order to facilitate a life for their daughters with dignity at their in-laws' place. The following cases present the issue more effectively:

> After four months, I conceived. It became impossible to stay with my in-laws then as they kept blaming me and also started demanding a Honda City car and a Bullet motor cycle ... . For my father, it was not possible to fulfil their demands, it was out of his reach and he had already spent a lot on the wedding. (Inderjit, Case 2)

> Though it was very difficult for us, we could only manage to give them a Maruti 800 car ... they also asked for ₹ 2 lakh in cash and my brother had to sell his share of land to meet the wedding expenses and fulfil their demands. (Shweta, Case 12)

The families of Inderjit and Shweta were in no state to provide any monetary gifts to their respective in-laws. Parents of Inderjit had directly expressed their inability to meet the future demands of dowry being made to them. Shweta's brother had to sell his share of land to afford her dowry expenses. All these families had spent beyond their capacity yet demands did not to stop.

The grooms' families were not empathetic while demanding huge sums in the form of dowry from the respondents and their families. Despite the attempts by the respondents to explain their situation to their husbands and in-laws, they turned a deaf ear to their pleadings.

> This time my parents could not fulfil their demands as it was an exorbitant amount ... my parents had been fulfilling their demands, though in installments and had never refused them for anything. (Shruti, Case 8)

> But my husband was not ready to understand anything and said, *Eh matter mere te tere fathers da hai, tere aur mere layi eh wadiya rahega je assi iss mamlaye wich naa pahiye* (This is between our fathers. It is best for us to refrain from interfering in any way). (Radhika, Case 6)

In the above narratives, it can be analysed that the husbands of both Shruti and Radhika were very much interested in fetching money from their wives' families. They never bothered to listen to the words of their wives when they tried to give plausible explanation of their situation. The parents of these girls had to borrow huge sums as loan and that too in their middle age. All this was done to make the lives of daughters bearable and respectable. If the demands of their in-laws were not met promptly, the parents knew that their daughters would be harassed at their husbands' home. It appears that the parents of the respondents did yield to the demands of the grooms' families for maintaining their daughters' respect in their new family.

When the respondents showed resistance to the demands of their in-laws and opted to rebel against them, they were harassed in return. Karam and Gursimran are two among those many respondents who had gone against their in-laws' greed.

> She forced me to bring ₹ 20,000, sometimes even ₹ 40,000 .... My parents ... kept on fulfilling their demand in order to maintain my respect and prestige in the family. Finally she asked me to get ₹ 1 lakh. When my family could not fulfil this demand, I was humiliated and turned out of the house along with my children. (Karam, Case 13)

> I questioned him and asked, *'Tuhaadi khud di pay kini achi hai, tussi apni pay kyu nahin use karde, ehne saala wich tussi koi vi saving nahin kitti hunn tak. Pehle tusi mere toh 7 lakh mange, hun 10 lakh mere maan baap hai ATM*

> *machine nahin'* (You are yourself earning a handsome salary, why do not you use your own money? Have you not been able to save anything in all these years? First, you asked me for ₹ 7 lakh, now you are asking for ₹ 10 lakhs, they are my parents not an ATM machine). (Gursimran, Case 20)

Karam and Gursimran had clearly voiced their parents' inability to meet any future demands of their in-laws. Their husbands' families were intolerant towards such resistance and they physically abused them. Some were also thrown out of their houses for voicing protest against their demands.

However, there were cases where the victims were harassed while giving an ultimatum. They were turned out of the house and were forced to bring money. The extracts given below expound on this:

> I was given an ultimatum that if I did not procure ₹ 1 lakh and one gold set, I would not be allowed to stay in their home. (Neetu, Case 5)

> Whenever he called me, he only said, *'Ya tan mainu divorce de de ya duss lakh rupaye liya. Tere peo kol vaise vi waadu paise ne'* (Either divorce me or get ₹ 10 lakhs. Anyway, your father has surplus money). When I showed my helplessness, he abused me as if I were his slave. He asked me for divorce so that he could marry someone abroad and acquire permanent resident status. (Manju, Case 18)

Neetu and Manju were told by their respective husbands either to bring the demanded money or be ready to forget about their marriage. Husbands of both the girls had already expressed their plan of marrying some other woman if families of the respondents failed to bring what was demanded from them.

Most of the respondents were dependent on their in-laws and husbands for their basic necessities and they were often deprived of them. Following cases of Preeti, Shweta and Baljeet depict their circumstances:

> My husband's family neither paid for the expenses at the time of my delivery nor did they come to see the child for almost a month … . They directly told my mother that they could not meet the expenses of my delivery as they had financial crunch and were running short of cash. They said that they had spent ₹ 7,000 on my first delivery and that they had given gold and clothes to my first child. (Preeti, Case 17)

> He gave all his salary to his mother and refused to give anything to me even when I asked for it. (Shweta, Case 12)

> I know that my parents-in-law receive money from their son through a third party but even they do not help me financially. (Baljeet, Case 7)

Preeti's husband did not even bear the expenditure incurred on the delivery of the child; instead her husband's family told her that they did not have sufficient money. Neither the husband nor his family went to see the newborn baby after the birth. Similar to the case of Preeti, both Shweta and Baljit after their, marriage were dependent upon their respective husbands for financial support, which they never got from the irresponsible partners.

There were a few cases where the victims reported that their husbands never had the intention of taking them abroad and they entered matrimony only for financial gains. They were not provided any financial support by the husbands/in-laws and became dependent on their parents with their children. The following quotes bring out the bitter experiences of the victims.

> Deepika has been staying with her parents for the last three years ... . She is not getting any maintenance from her husband. (Deepika, Case 1)

> My father died of cancer immediately after my divorce. I am taking care of my mother and my two children. I have deposited my money in the bank on interest of ₹ 4,000 per month. My mother stitches clothes and earns approximately ₹ 5,000 per month. (Preeti, Case 17)

After being left high and dry by their respective husbands both Preeti and Deepika had to lead a troublesome life. Preeti's father died of cancer and she had to support herself with the interest money and the money her mother earned by stitching clothes.

The devastated wives who had married these NRI men were left to struggle alone in the society. Neetu, Rupinder and Manpreet had to fight for their right to survive after their marriages with their respective husbands which was nothing but a fiasco.

> I made all efforts to get maintenance from my husband, but it was of no use. (Neetu, Case 5)

> I have taken up stitching work and earn ₹ 1,500 per month which is not sufficient for me and my children. I am not able to provide good education to my children and I do not want to be dependent on my parents. (Manpreet, Case 10)

> People, from whom we had borrowed money, come calling, saying, 'Where is our money and why is your daughter still here?' Our family's 1.5-hectare land is up for sale to pay off the wedding debts. (Rupinder, Case 11)

In the above narratives, all the women mentioned that they were leading their lives without getting any financial support from their husbands. It was observed that in the above cases, the husbands of the respondents did not even bother to know about their responsibilities towards their wives.

Suman had to go through numerous hardships to fulfil their responsibilities without having any financial assistance from her partner. This is explained below.

> Moreover, I now have many responsibilities. My father is old and so cannot work any longer. My brother keeps drinking the whole day and is a good-for-nothing fellow. My entire family is dependent on me. I cannot even think of getting married again. (Suman, Case 3)

Suman had to take additional responsibility of her parents when her sibling (brother) became reluctant to look after his parents during a difficult time when she herself was deserted by her husband. Eventually, the whole family became dependent entirely on Suman for every possible support. Such a situation had made Suman think more about the future of her family than over her own.

Physical Violence

Violence from the in-laws against victims started verbally in the form of blames and criticism and went on to reach a point where physical force was also used upon them to make them comply with the dowry demands. All the respondents had experienced a certain degree of physical torture in various forms. They were physically harassed, denied food and were treated like servants at their matrimonial home. Physical abuse started with criticism, followed by familiar but unseemly scenes of insults, abuse and demand for more money. They were thrown out of their matrimonial homes when their parents showed their inability to yield to fulfil the dowry demands any more. The victims blamed not only their in-laws but also their husbands for physical torture. Violence against these brides started with verbal criticism, ending up with physical violence by husbands and their parents. Earlier studies have also highlighted the physical abuse faced by the left behind wives of NRIs. Dasgupta (2010) reported that many of these deserted wives are forced to live with their in-laws as virtual servants.

In most of the cases, the victims were thrown out of their matrimonial homes and the reasons are mentioned below.

> My mother in-law forced me to leave the house. When I argued, she threw me out of the house ... (Deepika, Case 1)

> After one month when my father could not fulfil their demands, my mother in-law threw my husband and me out of the house. (Inderjit, Case 2)

> I was given an ultimatum that if I did not procure ₹ 1 lakh and one gold set, I would not be allowed to stay in their home. (Neetu, Case 5)

> My father in-law coldly asked my father to take his daughter back to his house till the money was arranged. My father's pleadings were of no use. (Radhika, Case 6)

It was observed that in all the cases mentioned above, the respondents stated that when their parents could not fulfil the demands of their in-laws they were forced to leave their house and were given an ultimatum if they would not come back with the asked money, they would not be allowed to enter their house. The motive of their in-laws was always one and that was dowry. Deepika and Inderjit were made to leave their respective houses when they raised voice against the demand of dowry made by in-laws. Neetu and Radhika suffered the same fate for a similar reason.

Marriage with these NRI men had taken a toll on these victims both mentally and physically. An example of the same is described below:

> My sister-in-law abused me and even physically assaulted me. One day, my cousin visited our place (in April 2009) and was amazed to see blisters on my hands and disgusted with the way my in-laws treated me. They would beat me and abuse me even in the presence of other people. (Shruti, Case 8)

> *'Oh mainu sardiyan de dina vich thandi zameen te suwande si, te paira te paan layi juraba vi nahin dende si. Ik waar tan mere pati ne mainu aina mareya ke uss ne meri bah hi todh ditti'* (They made me sleep on the cold floor during winters. I was not even given socks to wear. Once, my husband beat me so much that he broke my arm). (Virpal, Case 19)

The above narratives describe the situation of women who had to keep their mouths shut for the sake of their physical well-being because otherwise their respective husbands assaulted them. In both the cases, the men had displayed their sadistic nature to their wives.

No sympathy was shown to the respondents as they were made to slog like servants. Not only the NRI men and their families made them work beyond a reasonable level but they were also physically abused by them. This is explained below:

> *'Mein savere chaar waje uth jandi si te saare ghar da kam, kapde ton toh le ke poche safai takk, sabb mein kardi si. Sab layi roti bana ke, sab nu khilaa ke akhir wich aap khandi si. Meri jindagi kissi naukaraani toh ghatt nahin si'* (I would wake up at four o'clock in the morning and do all the household chores from washing and cleaning to cooking. I would serve food to everyone and eat in the end. My life was no better than that of a servant). (Preeti, Case 17)

> My mother in-law used to keep me busy in household tasks and would say, *'Jadd takk pura ghar da kam nahin karengi tainu roti nahin milegi'* (You will not get food till you finish all the housework) … . She would also beat me up … . (Rajni, Case 4)

After paying a huge amount as dowry, Rajni and Preeti were treated like servants at their husbands' place. They had to start the day with the chores and end the day with it. Both of them were not given food and were still expected to do household chores beyond a person's usual capability.

The torture by the in-laws knew no bounds, as the victims were not the only ones to suffer but babies in the womb also suffered along with the mothers.

> My mother in-law told her maid servant, *'Kal toh tainu aan di lorh nahin, hun saade ghar nawi naukaraani aa gayi hai jo ajj toh iss ghar da saara kamm karegi'* (You need not come from tomorrow. We have got a new maid for our household who will perform the entire household chores). (Manpreet, Case 10)

> I was not spared even though I was pregnant … . She would not let me have enough food even when I was pregnant. (Shweta, Case 12)

It is a shame to learn that a woman is capable of treating another woman in such a shabby manner. Despite experiencing the troubles attached with the maternity, the mothers-to-be were deprived even of food by their mother in-laws. It is shocking that no mercy was shown to Manpreet and Shweta when they were pregnant.

From the above cases, we can understand that most of the victims were harassed by their in-laws and were treated in an inhuman manner. The predominant reason to inflict such torture was dowry. The respective in-laws and husbands had adopted such behaviour towards the victims believing that such actions would prompt the respondents to bring in the money from their parents. They were tolerated in their matrimonial homes till they conceded to their demands. When they resisted, problems arose and aggravated as well. Their husbands/in-laws subjected them to mental torture followed by physical abuse. No mercy was shown to them even when they were pregnant. They were denied food and were treated as servants.

Emotional Violence

This category includes threats of any kind, verbal abuse, and harassment such as insults, filthy language and taunts, harassment for dowry and such humiliating actions as trying to prove that she was insane, treating her like a servant, and embarrassing her in front of others, not permitting her to meet her parents and husband, etc. Studies of Vij (2005) and NCW (2011) had highlighted that it was devastating for a young woman to arrive at her new home in a completely foreign land, only to realize that the person she had married was already married and had children or that the life she was promised was sadly missing. Ramanam (2003) argues that at times the emotional set back that a girl undergoes cannot be compensated with any amount of money or with counselling.

The girls are taunted endlessly usually on issues relating to dowry. This affects them mentally as they are not able to share this with anyone and are rendered vulnerable which makes them susceptible to further deterioration of mental health. The narratives given below throw light on this:

> My mother in-law blamed my family for substandard arrangements in the wedding. (Deepika, Case 1)

> My mother in-law blamed me, saying, *'Tussi tan saadhi beradari wich beizzati karwa ditti hai, assi socheya si ke sada munda foreign kam karda hai ta wiah te tere ghar wale jyada kharach karange'* (You have ruined our reputation in our extended family. We had expected your family to spend more on the wedding because our son works abroad!) (Inderjit, Case 2)

In all the above cases, it can be observed that the only reason to taunt and blame the girls was dowry. It was not realized by the in-laws that their foolish and seemingly strange behaviour would have impact on the girls' psychological health. It was observed that in the cases of Deepika and Inderjit, they were verbally harassed for not bringing a satisfactory dowry (in cash or kind).

A miscarriage or abortion has a deep and sometimes irreversible impact on a girl's physical and psychological health. Their in-laws further augment this by harassing her about her character. If these girls have to deal with this single handedly, it takes a toll on their mental well-being. This can be clarified through an example given below:

> ... my mother in-law told my husband that he was not the father of this child ... added, *'Eh bacha mere munde da nahin hai, jis da hai tu uss kol hi jaa'* (He

is not my son's child and you better go and live with the person to whom this child belongs). (Deepika, Case 1)

She (mother in-law) alleged that I had illicit relations with my brother-in-law and had even aborted his child as it was an unwanted pregnancy. The actual reason for abortion was that they used to torture me physically and gave me only one meal a day. That affected my pregnancy and I had a miscarriage. (Shweta, Case 12)

The above excerpts show that the respondents were accused of adultery when they could not fulfil their in-laws demands for money. A common element in the cases is when the girl conceived, her child was disowned. Deepika was even forced to leave the house while she was pregnant. Shweta was accused of having illicit relations with her brother in-law and was blamed for the abortion of her child whereas the real reason behind the miscarriage was malnutrition and physical torture by the in-laws. It clearly shows that the avaricious in-laws and husbands did anything they could to get rid of the girls even if it meant killing/disowning their own blood.

The girls are forced to stay in such abusive relationships because they and their families invest too much money and put in a lot of effort in the relationship. The narratives below shall explain this in a better manner.

My husband kept harassing me on phone, saying, 'If you fulfil my father's demand, I will call you abroad else rot at your parents' place ... he claimed that he was living in Spain and earning ₹ 1 lakh per month. He also said that he could solemnize his marriage with a daughter of any rich family in India. (Inderjit, Case 2)

I told my husband that my family was not in a position to fulfil their demands this time ... he scolded me and stressed '*Je tu Germany aanaa chahandi hain tan tainu mainu 6 lakh dene hi pangey*' (If you want to come to Germany then you will have to give me ₹ 6 lakh). (Shruti, Case 8)

Inderjit's husband threatened her of desertion if she did not fulfil his parents demand for more money. He explained to her that he could have married into any rich family and could have got his demands met just because he was living in Spain and earning good money. However, in Shruti's case, it was more of a business proposition when she was told by her husband to bring ₹ 6 lakh with her if she wanted to stay with him in Germany.

Usually when the girls are tortured by their husbands/in-laws they become mentally disturbed but never open up about their problems. The narrative given below explains this more adequately.

My husband threatens me on phone and says that he would kill me and my daughter if I do not withdraw the case. (Manpreet, Case 10)

Manpreet's worries did not stop even after getting separated from her husband. When she filed a case against her husband and in-laws she was threatened frequently by her husband on telephone. Her husband continues to threaten her if she does not take the case back, he would kill her and her daughter. For the same reason she was under constant fear.

Suicidal thoughts become common when a person has no hope of living happily or peacefully. The girls became mentally disoriented to the extent that they thought of killing themselves in order to escape their miseries.

> My husband did not even give me emotional support. I was beaten up so much that I often thought of ending my life. (Preeti, Case 17)

Preeti was extremely disturbed by the inhumane treatment meted out to her by her in-laws for being unable to bring more dowry. Preeti confessed that she was not given the emotional support that she deserved from her partner, instead she was frequently beaten up which annihilated her longing to live.

Sometimes the strange revelations can put a person into a shocking state. In these cases, the respondents were in a state of shock on learning about their husbands' particulars which were hidden from them before marriage.

> One of my husband's distant cousins asked me, *'Bhabhi ji tussi veere naal viah karan lai haan kiwein kar ditti, ohh tan sirf duss vi tak padeya hoyeya hai te tussi tan B.com ho'* (Dear sister in-law, how did you accept brother's proposal? He has only studied up to 10th and you are a commerce graduate). Neither was he well-educated, nor he had a PR of England ... he was serving as a waiter at some restaurant. As if this was not enough, Rajni had to bear another shock. Her in-laws had a business of *'afeem'* (opium). (Rajni, Case 4)

> ... he was 32 years old. He did not give me any reason for concealing his age. Thereafter, it was more like a compromise for me to go on staying with him. (Rupinder, Case 11)

Rajni was shocked to learn about her husband's qualification and his family business. Similarly, Rupinder had to compromise and live with her husband after having learnt about his real age.

Most of the major mental illnesses start with a triggering agent. Neetu, Shruti and Simran had experienced such triggering news regarding their respective husbands, which put them in severe trauma.

> One day, I came to know from my distant neighbour's daughter that Sanjay had an affair with a foreigner and wanted to marry her. His parents did not permit him. Instead, they forced him to marry an Indian girl. Under pressure, he married me. (Neetu, Case 5)

> It was just after this meeting that we came to know that Rajat wanted a divorce from me because he wanted to marry a woman who was already staying with him in Germany. (Shruti, Case 8)

> First, he did not utter a word but later on he confessed that he could not arrange the papers to take me to the USA as he was already involved with someone else there. (Simran, Case 9)

Neetu learnt that her marriage was nothing more than a compromise for her husband. Just because his parents did not allow him to marry the woman he was courting, he chose to marry Neetu while still continuing to be involved with the other woman. Her husband's immaturity took a toll on

Neetu's psychological health. While Shruti was being pestered for divorce because Rajat was already seeing another woman; his sister had already started looking for other prospective brides for him. This entirely shattered her hopes and broke her heart. Ironically, Simran was told that if she continued living with her in-laws she would get maintenance funds from her husband who was having an affair with a girl in the country he resided in. She was pregnant at the time of this disgusting revelation and it had a severe impact on her mental health.

If a man is already having love interest elsewhere, he would not pay any heed to what others think or say. The parents of such boys do not realize that it would wreak havoc in the life of the woman who is totally unaware of the entire situation. Such cases are discussed below:

> Earlier, I thought it must be some important call. Then once, I got chance to read all the messages that he had exchanged with that girl and I was shocked! I picked up a quarrel with him … (Neetu Dhanjal, Case 15)

> Aggressively, Jaswinder replied, *'Jo karna hai kar lo mainu kuch nahin pata waise vi eh wiah meri marji naal nahin hoya si'* (Do what you want to! I do not know anything! Anyhow, I had not married your daughter out of my own sweet will). (Navjit, Case 14)

He said, *'Mera lifestyle, jeen da tareeka, sab usde nal milda hai. Saadi understanding vi changi hai'* (My lifestyle is similar to hers. We share a good understanding). (Preeti, Case 17)

The victims in the above excerpts were shocked to learn about their husbands' extra-marital affairs. Neetu and Preeti expressed that their husbands had affairs even before the marriage and stated that it was the predominant reason for leaving their respective husbands. In Navjit's case, her husband had married her out of compulsion and later it was found that he was also having an affair outside his marriage. These revelations had not only ruined the marriages of these women but also adversely affected their mental state.

When a family problem occurs, it also affects the children of the family concerned. However, in the following cases, the situation of the mothers is described in relation to their concern for their children, their expectations from their in-laws for their grandchildren.

> I do not want to go back to my in-laws' house as I believe it is useless to live with people who have not even come to see their grandson. (Deepika, Case 1)

> One day, I called him and said, *'Ke je tu mainu ni le ke ja sakeya, tan vi at least aa k apne bacheyan da haal chaal puchh ja!'* (Even if you could not take me along at least come and enquire about your children's well-being!). (Karam, Case 13)

Deepika and Karam were left in a situation to raise their children without their husbands. Deepika explained that it was not ideal to meet her in-laws who had not even come to visit their grandson. Karam's husband had dodged every request made by her, for meeting his children. She was more concerned and worried for her children who had not met their father for a long time and neither their father had shown any interest in meeting them. It was observed that in both the cases, the strange attitude of husbands and in-laws towards the respondents had put them in an emotional and psychological turmoil.

The NRI men who were driven to marry innocent Indian women just for their greed never realized the permanent mental harm they had done to them. Usually, the women are never able to get out of it and live as outcastes in this highly judgemental society. The following cases throw light on this issue:

> She continues to live with the question that torments most of these women Deepika added, 'Why did he marry me if he planned to leave me in lurch? (Deepika, Case 1)

> Somewhere I knew that Suresh had ruined my life and now he would never come back to India but consciously I refused to accept it as a truth. I would tell myself, *Shayad Suresh wapis aajawe* (Suresh might return). (Suman, Case 3)

> How has my life changed! How can I even forgive them! Though I am getting full moral support from my parents, but it's not easy to forget everything. (Radhika, Case 6)

The above excerpts show the dejected and tormented mental state of the respondents after they were left with persistent questions that nagged their minds. Analysis of narratives of respondents shows that physical abuse was occasional, while verbal and emotional abuse were their everyday experience, which made it impossible for them to continue with their marriage. In almost all cases, the victims had gone through various emotional problems. In majority of cases, victims had been tortured and humiliated for dowry. The ill treatment towards them had started in the very initial months of their marriage. It started with sarcasm with regard to the substandard arrangement in the wedding, later it was linked with the demands for more dowry.

Moreover, based on the observations of the researcher during the interviews, it was evident that the women presented signs of depression due to their economic condition and the feelings of abandonment and separation. Their physical appearance, for instance, showed the signs of enduring physical and emotional pain, as they looked much older than they actually were. They often cried and expressed their feelings of insecurity during the interview. All of them also expressed a desire to go and ask their husbands as to why they had treated them this way.

Legal Problems

The complexity in the legal structure in India has given an advantage to the NRI men who exploit the innocent Indian women using marriage as a medium. Along with this, there is a constant negligence shown by the police department to file the First Investigation Report (FIR) on the complaints by the respondents. According to NCW Report (2011), a woman is denied maintenance in India on the pretext that the marriage had already been dissolved by the court in another country. Gurnani (2005) reported that it can be very difficult to locate the absconding spouse, who may have relocated, quite possibly to a different state. If the residence of the spouse is unknown, courts cannot enforce a support order making it impossible for a woman to receive child or spousal support.

There were a few cases where the victims spoke about their experience with the legal proceedings and the hassles involved in it. The following narratives throw light on the same issue.

> I asked the head of Women's Cell to pressurize my in-laws to compel my husband to come back to India. Instead, I was told that. I should better provide my in-laws with ₹ 10 lakh and get the case resolved. Since that day I have stopped going to the Women Cell for any assistance. I do not want to bother my father who is already suffering from cardiac problems. (Deepika, Case 1)

> When the police officials heard the whole case, they started blaming my family, saying, 'Registration *tah karwa lende, tuhanu wiah di jaldi pai rehandi hai, pata nahin NRI mundiyan wich tuhanu ki nazar aaunda hai*' (You should have got the marriage registered. Your folks are in such a hurry to get your daughters married to NRIs). She says, '*Ethe amiraan di chaldi hai te gharib di kudi nu koi nahin puchda*' (No one hears the woes of a poor man's daughter). (Suman, Case 3)

Deepika was told by officials of Women's Cell that if she wanted to resolve the matter then it would be better for her to provide her in-laws the demanded amount and get rid of the problem. This had sabotaged her faith in the efficacy of the Women's Cell. Given her father's health condition, Deepika and her family had to bear the injustice committed to them by her in-laws and the police personnel. While Suman explained that her parents' ignorance towards the registration of her marriage had left them speechless in front of the police officials, when they had asked for reason of being unaware about their procedure. She stated that instead of listening to their problems, the police officials started blaming them.

Shweta was one such victim who was restrained by the legal authorities. Her experience is described below.

> Instead of listening to us the officials told me, '*Je tu apna ghar basana chahandi hain tan aaram naal apne sasural reh te ohna di respect kar warna allag ho ja*' (If you want to have a peaceful family life, stay with your in-laws and respect them or else get separated). Shweta said, 'Nobody was sensitive to me'. (Shweta, Case 12)

The officials had threatened Shweta's family stating that they better comply with the demand of their in-laws to have a peaceful family life. She was also ordered to respect her in-laws or get separated otherwise.

Also, there were instances where the police officials refused to file an FIR against the NRI grooms and their families.

> Earlier the police officials were not filing our case; it took us atleast two weeks to file a complaint against my in-laws. Through some sources, we came to know that my in-laws had given them bribe … . But somehow by complaining to the higher authorities … our case was registered. (Shruti, Case 8)

In Shruti's case, the police authorities concerned did not show any interest in registering the FIR (First Investigation Report) and it was later learnt that the policemen were being bribed by Shruti's in-laws in order to ignore her complaint against them. Parents of Shruti did not lose hope and took the matter to the higher authorities and got their case registered.

Ineffectiveness on the lawyer's part had also been a contributing factor towards the advantage of such fraudulent NRI men. The following narratives explain the scenario better:

> I have changed two lawyers up to now. The first one would always be quiet in the court and would ever be asking for fees and the second one enhanced his fees later on and would ask me to come to his place alone. (Manpreet, Case 10)

> I have been to the Women's Cell many times and do not want to pursue my case in the court. I have already spent ₹ 70,000 as lawyer's fee and do not have any more money to spend. (Deepika, Case 1)

The extract cited above highlights the depressed feelings of the respondents whose lawyers had exploited them financially in the name of representing her case. Manpreet's lawyer had exploited her financially in the name of pursuing her case. She stated that she had already changed two lawyers who failed to get her relief in the shape of maintenance. Deepika was one of the respondents who could neither spend on her husband's demands nor pay for her lawyer's fee. Thus, victims were in no position to carry on with the legal proceedings due to ineffectiveness of their lawyers and the exorbitant fees they were charging for a mere appearance in the court. This had made them feel that it would be better for them to drop the cases against their NRI husbands who had mentally, physically and financially exhausted and ruined them.

On a whole, a large number of women stated that when they went to lodge a complaint against their husbands/in-laws, the attitude of the police officials harassed them and held them responsible for their situation. A few among them reported that instead of being empathetic; the officials of Women's Cell too were insensitive towards them and did not take any action against their in-laws/husbands. Instead, they were advised by the officials to provide the expected money to their in-laws if they wanted to save their married life.

Socio-Cultural Problems

Society plays a major part in the reconstruction of every victim's life. It has the responsibility to provide them with support and assistance in order to get on with their lives but it does not happen everywhere. The victims are further embarrassed by the indifferent attitude of people around. The major socio-cultural problems the victims faced was primarily related to those who had children to support. The husbands or their families never contacted majority of the affected women in these cases after sending them out of their homes. This had left these victims in doldrums over their respective futures and lives. Following cases throw light on the issue.

> *'Kadi aake mere in-laws ne na mere pati ne apne bache da haal chaal nahin pucheya'* (My in-laws and husband did not even ask about my son's well-being). (Inderjit, Case 2)

> *'Faida ki hoyeya iss wiah da, bache tan mere ajj vi anaath hain, koi nahin ehna nu puchan wala'* (What have I gained from this marriage? My children are orphans even today. There is no one to take care of them). (Manpreet, Case 10)

Inderjit was more disturbed with this than the fact that her husband and in-laws had neither tried to contact them nor asked about their well-being. It appears as if for her, the main upsetting fact was the neglect of the child on part of her husband and in-laws. Manpreet had a second marriage. Before her second marriage, she was staying with her parents along with her child. She gave approval for the second marriage so that she may not get dependent on her parents. She never thought that her second marriage would also make her dependent on her parents when she was left behind by her NRI husband. The thought that troubles her is that even today her children have no support of their father and are still dependent on her parents.

Failure of their marriages with the NRI men had left these women mentally traumatized. This can be clearly seen from the case given below:

> *'Agar mein ik wiah wich khush nai reh saki tan duja wiah kiwe kar sakdi ha'* (If I could not stay happy in one marriage, how can I expect happiness from another marriage). (Suman, Case 3)

> *'Mera tan viah ton vishwaas hi uth gaya hai! Mere nasseb wich hi viah da sukh nahin si'* (I have lost all faith in marriage! I was never destined to enjoy a happy married life). (Navjit, Case 14)

Suman had expressed her loss of faith in marriage by stating the facts from her failed marriage. Navjit's second marriage could not give her the happiness that she and her family expected from this marriage. Navjit did not know how to overcome her troubles. She was not in a position to move away from her past as people constantly questioned her and for the same reason she was not removing her bangles. With a shattered heart, she had accepted her fate, in which she believed, that the existence of happy married life is next to impossible.

Coping with the new life was a daunting challenge faced by victims. Their confidence was already touching the rock bottom and the people they met would always have a question or two about their failures. One such victim, Radhika had talked about her stressful life in the narrative given below.

> I have been staying in Chennai for the last nine months, earning ₹ 30,000 per month. I feel isolated and lonely at my place of work. It's a strange place. The culture is so different. I miss my family a lot. (Radhika, Case 6)

Radhika explained that her life had totally changed ever after her marriage failed. Despite having moved on from the incident, she mentioned about the difficulty in adapting to her new environment, as the society in which she was located was completely different than that of where she earlier belonged.

Respondents are made to live with a heavy feeling of burdensome guilt. As mentioned earlier, it is difficult for these women to answer every question posed by the people around. The miserable plight of these women would not improve unless the society becomes more tolerant and supportive. Deepika's tale of an unsettled life is described below:

> I have stopped attending ceremonial occasions and family functions as people always ask me the same question, *'Hor fir ki baneya tere case da. Munde da kuch pataa laga, aya waapis ke nahin'* (What about your case? Have you come to know about the whereabouts of the boy? Has he come back or not?) (Deepika, Case 1)

Deepika had stopped socializing, as she was not able to face the social stigma of having been abandoned. She would be reminded of her traumatic past whenever she was asked about her husband by the people and to escape that most of the time she preferred to stay inside her house. She also mentioned about the practical problems associated with bringing up a child without his/her father.

There were two cases where the respondents were not even getting their parental support. This further worsens their situations. The narratives of Suman and Baljeet describe the same:

> My father is old and cannot work any longer. My brother keeps drinking the whole day and is a good for nothing fellow. My entire family is dependent on me. I cannot even think of getting married again. (Suman, Case 3)

> Baljeet's parents do not want their daughter with them as they cannot afford. Moreover, they believe that her return to their house will mar the marriage prospects of her siblings. Baljeet continues to live like a servant at her in-laws' home. (Baljeet, Case 7)

For Suman and Baljeet, life became more tough when they realized that their parents could not support them both emotionally and financially. Suman being a sole earning member did not want to get married as she felt that the whole family was dependent on her. While in Baljeet's case, parents were no longer ready to look after her and her child. For the same reason she chose to stay in her matrimonial home despite the problems.

In most of the cases, respondents' faith in marriage was irreparably lost and they did not want to get married again lest they should stumble against the same stone twice. The respondents who had children were left with the tedious task of raising them without any support of their husbands and in-laws. They were more worried and depressed for their children because their husbands and in-laws had neither tried to contact them nor asked about their well-being.

Conclusion

In the present chapter, it has been found that in all the cases, respondents were abandoned immediately after the wedding, even before being taken by their husbands abroad. It was observed that in all the cases, the respondents had faced numerous forms of violence varying from financial to physical and emotional abuse. Majority of them were tortured, ill treated and humiliated for not bringing sufficient dowry. Violence had started even before the wedding when the grooms' families started putting forward dowry demands in cash or kind. It was observed that in such cases parents had fulfilled their demands in every way but they never realized that their demands, would increase with time and the non-fulfillment of the same would convert their daughters' life into hell. Their daughters were tortured and at times threatened also that if they did not comply with their in-laws' demands they would never be taken abroad by their husbands. It was shocking that not only the in-laws of the respondents abused them but their husbands also joined them. It was observed that most of the respondents chose to stay at their matrimonial homes despite the suffering, hoping that once they got sponsored by their husbands their miseries would get over. When the victims opposed their in-laws for dowry, they were beaten up and at times were thrown out of their matrimonial homes even when they were pregnant. The violence against them did not stop there, it continued even when they got separated. They were threatened to withdraw the case and at times were forced to fulfil their demands. Respondents were constantly in the grip of anxiety which ended up leading to their deteriorating health condition. They were never taken care of and were ignored by their husbands and stigmatized by society.

Various theoretical perspectives to explain the issue of gender violence were presented in this paper. Each of these lays stress on specific variable/s, viz., biological factors; psychological make-up; socio-cultural factors; patriarchy; feminism; socio-cultural construction of gender, etc. However, an analysis of various case studies in the present work indicates the tremendous role of cultural norms/group mind/social environment/social system in determining the choices and behaviour of people. In the present study, for instance, the high social premium associated with an NRI status overshadowed all other considerations, including individual choices in context of matrimonial matters, irrespective of gender, class and rural/urban residence. What remains intriguing is a total absence of 'agency' either among the girls as brides or their parents. In all cases, the parents as well as the girls in question got swayed by the strong social currents to which their kinsmen and acquaintances comprising the social environment were a strong party. It was by and large a decision of the parents, asking for the compliance of daughters, who themselves were enslaved to the social prestige attached to these NRI marriage proposals. In some cases, parents of the girls went beyond their financial capacity, and took huge loans and exhausted all their savings, just to match the NRI status in marriage. Was it for the future of the daughter or was it to earn social reputation and prestige? Our findings once again bring Parsonian approach into centre stage wherein the 'agency' or the individual is completely overpowered by the structure, actually determining individual choices. It is another fact that the outcome of the process pushes women into distress and social stigma, making it a gender issue where young women are violated, abandoned, abused and traumatized for life, mainly because decisions about their lives are ruled by cultural norms and status symbols for which 'they' have to pay the price.

References

Bandura, A. and Walters, R.H. 1963. *Social Learning and Personality Development*. New York: Holt, Rinehart and Winston.

Beauvior, D.S. 1974. *The Second Sex*. New York: Vintage Books.

Brownmiller, S. 1976. *Against Our Will: Men, Women and Rape*. Harmondsworth: Penguin.

Chaba, A.A. 2012. 'Harsher Law to Crack Down on Fraud by NRI Grooms: Sukhbir'. *The Indian Express*, 31 May. Retrieved from http://archive.indianexpress.com/news/harsher-law-to-crack-down-on-fraud-by-nri-groomssukhbir/955785/

Chodorow, N.J. 1978. *The Reproduction of Mothering: Psychoanalysis and the Sociology of Gender*. Berkeley, CA: University of California Press.

Chohka, R.K. 2006. 'NRI Marriages: Problems, Causes and Remedial Measures'. *People's Democracy (Weekly Organ of the Communist Party, Marxist)*, 30(31), 30 July. http://archives.peoplesdemocracy.in/2006/0730/07302006_problem%20relating%20to%20nri%20marriage.htm

Daly, K. and Chesney-Lind, M. 1988. 'Feminism and Criminology'. *Justice Quarterly*, 5, 497–538.

Dasgupta, S.D. 2010. 'Abandoned and Divorced: The NRI Pattern'. *Infochange News and Features*. Retrieved from http://infochangeindia.org/women/features/abandoned-and-divorced-the-nri-pattern

de Beauvoir, S. 1981. *The Second Sex* (Translated and edited by H.M. Parshley). Harmondsworth: Penguin Books.

Dekeseredy, W.S. and Macleod, L. 1997. *Women Abuse: A Sociological Story*. Toronto: Harcourt Brace.

Dheer, G. 2012. 'Helpline for Dumped NRI Wives in Punjab'. *Deccan Herald News*, 30 May. Retrieved from http://www.deccanherald.com/content/253410/helpline-dumped-nri-wives-punjab.html.

Engels, F. 1884. *The Origin of the Family, Private Property and the State*. New York: International Publishers.

Firestone, S. 1970. *The Dialectic of Sex*. New York: Bantam Books.

Gosh, R.A. 2012. 'For Brides Married to NRIs, There's No Happily Ever After'. *DNA*, 1 September. Retrieved from http://vinayak.wordpress.com/2012/09/02/for-brides-married-to-nris-theres-no-happily-ever-after/

Gurnani, A. 2005. 'July's Women: The Untold Story of Transnationally Abandoned Women'. *Newsletter*, XXVI (I). Retrieved from http://www.manavi.org/documents/manavinewsletter2005.pdf

Hartmann, H. 1979. 'The Unhappy Marriage of Marxism and Feminism: Towards a More Progressive Union'. *Capital and Class*, 3(2), 1–33.

Hines, D. and Malley-Morrison, K. 2005. *Family Violence in the United States: Defining, Understanding, and Combating Abuse*. Thousand Oaks, CA: Sage Publications.

Lamb, S. 2000. *White Saris and Sweet Mangoes: Aging, Gender and Body in the North India*. Los Angels and London: University of California Press.

Levinson, D. 1989. *Family Violence in Cross-Cultural Perspective*. Newbury Park, CA: Sage Publications.

Lynn, D.B. 1969. *Parental and Sex Role Identification: A Theoretical Formulation*. Berkeley, CA: McCutchan.

Mead, G.H. 1934. *Mind, Self, and Society*. Chicago, IL: University of Chicago Press.

Melwani, L. 2005. 'Dishonor and Abandon'. *Little India*, 28 February. Retrieved from http://www.littleindia.com/news/134/article/1475/2005-02-05.html

Mischel, W. 1966. 'A Social Learning View of Sex Difference in Behaviour', in E.E. Maccoby (ed.), *The Development of Sex Difference*. Stanford, CA: Stanford University Press, pp. 93–106.

Mitchell, J. 1971. *Woman's Estate*. Harmondsworth: Penguin.

Millett, K. 1970. *Sexual Politics*. New York: Avon Books.

Ministry of Overseas Indian Affairs (MOIA). 2006. Report on the Workshop Regarding 'Problems Relating to NRI Marriages and Suggested Measures'. Chandigarh, 20–21 June. Retrieved from http://www.moia.gov.in/pdf/report_on_regional_semina_%20in%20_chandigarh.pdf

Monteiro, J.B. 2012. 'Hit It Out! (15): Why Rescue NRI-Chasing Brides?'. *Udupi Today Media Network*, Chandigarh, 2 June. Retrieved from http://www.udupitoday.com/udtoday/news_hit-it-out-15-why-rescue-nri-chasing-brides_635.html

Murdock, C.P. 1949. *Social Structure*. New York: Macmillan.

National Commission for Women (NCW). 2007. *The 'Nowhere' Brides: Report on Problem Relating to NRI Marriages*. New Delhi: NCW.

——. 2011. *Background Note on Seminar: Issues Relating to NRI Marriages*. New Delhi: NCW. Retrieved from http://ncw.nic.in

Oakley, A. 1981. *Subject Women*. Oxford: Martin Robertson and Company Ltd.

Ortner, S.B. 1996. *Making Gender: The Politics and Erotics of Culture*. Boston: Beacon Press.

Pothen, S. 1986. *Divorce: Its Causes and Consequences in Hindu Society*. New Delhi: Shakti Books.

Ramanan, R. 2003. 'Caught in the Vortex'. *The Hindu (Online Edition)*, 16 July. Retrieved from http://www.thehindu.com/thehindu/mp/2003/07/16/stories/2003071600410100.html

Robert, M. 2005. 'Victims of Betrayal: Deserted, She Dreamed of a New Life in Canada: Now She Weeps for Shame'. *Vancouver Province*, 16 October. Retrieved from http://www.angelfire.com/space2/light11/women/aband-brides1.html

Stoller, R. 1968. Sex *and Gender: On the Development of Masculinity and Femininity*. New York: Science House.

Vij, N. 2005. 'Promises and Lies'. *SciencesPO*, 10 June. Retrieved from http://www.sciencespo.fr/formation/master_scpo/mentions/journalisme/texte_vij.pdf.

Walby, S. 1986. *Patriarchy at Work*. Cambridge: Polity Press and Oxford: Basil Blackwell.

Wood, J.T. 1994. *Who Cares? Women, Care, and Culture*. Carbondale, IL: Southern Illinois University Press.

Wollstonecraft, M. 1792. *A Vindication of the Rights of Women* (Reprinted by bartleby.com in 1999). Boston: Peter Edes.

14

Culture and Honour

Reflections from the Field

Puneet Kaur Grewal

In all societies there exist clear patterns of women's and men's work reflecting close linkages between gender and culture, the latter significantly shaping gender. As indicated in the UNDP sponsored Human Development Report (1995), women's work is greatly undervalued in economic terms and there are cultural explanations for these patterns of undervaluation. Hofstede's (1991) model of cultural dimension of masculinity versus femininity explains that the gender roles are divided wherein men are expected to be assertive, tough and focused on material success whereas women are expected to be modest, soft and concerned with the quality of life. The cultural patterns that segregate women's and men's work by and large deny women's rights and make mockery of the legal provisions. These cultural patterns in turn generate violence in the name of honour, resulting in subordinate and marginalized status of women. The present paper defines culture focusing upon gender concerns of the region like child sex ratio, son preference, dowry practices, etc. by examining the folk songs, proverbs and religious norms. The paper also describes the nature of violence against women through NCRB data and first hand narratives collected from the field. Finally, the paper concludes by suggesting some specific strategies to combat gender violence.

Objectives and Method

This paper aims at tracing the gender bias in Punjab and Haryana, reflected through the skewed sex ratio and persistent gender violence, in the age old cultural practices and language, prioritizing sons over daughters. Thus, an extensive use has been made of the components of popular culture of Punjab (Haryana too has originated out of Punjab), i.e. proverbs, folk songs, common sayings and so on. In addition to these, statistical data generated by National Crime Records Bureau on violence against women in these two states, has also been used to build up an argument that the persistence of the culture of gender bias has been responsible for continued gender violence here. The paper is, therefore, by and large based upon the secondary data.

Depiction of Culture

Culture is the way of life of people: the sum of their learned behaviour patterns, attitudes and material things (Hall 1959). Members of a certain society internalize the cultural components of that society and then act within the limits as set out by what is culturally acceptable to them (Hall 1983: 230). The focus in this paper is on the culture of Punjab and Haryana (the two states share much in common), its religious beliefs, rituals, customs, folk songs, etc. to understand the position of women in these states in different spheres of life. The depiction of cultural patterns is attempted through common phrases, *raginis* of Haryanvi culture, *bolian* (sung by an individual, each verse at increasing pace, a boli's culminating line repeated collectively by a group) and *tappe* (couplet) of Punjabi *giddha*, other traditional norms, values, beliefs and rituals practiced in the states of Punjab and Haryana.

The rationale for choosing these two states is that these are the two progressive states of India whose GDP is constantly on the rise. Figures 1 and 2 show the rising GDP of these two states over the years. However, these states have also earned a notorious status for being 'daughter killer states' due to the lowest sex and child sex ratio in the country.

Gender and Culture

'Gender is not what culture created out of my body's sex; rather; sex is what culture makes when it genders my body' (Wilchins 2006: 30). Gender becomes an issue because of the fundamental differences and inequalities between women and men. It is true that gender discrimination can be better judged from the child sex ratio, which has remained low and has further declined in Punjab and Haryana as per Census Report 2011 as shown in Figure 3. Particularly in Punjab, every fifth girl goes missing because she is a born/to be born as a girl. Gender bias and son preference in these states gets reflected not only through the statistics but even through the language used in common parlance. For example, the family in which a girl is born is often consoled thus:

> Never mind, maybe next time.

Socialization practices are quite different for boys and girls in the region under study. While blessings are sought for would-be mother for son/s, daughters are generally not welcome. In these two states, where poverty, lack of educational and health facilities cannot be cited as factors leading to the devaluing of girls, reasons for gender bias has to be traced in the popular culture which prioritizes men over women, treating men as superior to women. Women are considered as a liability, expected to be passive, submissive, weak and incapable of standing on their own. The roots of gender discrimination are undoubtedly deeply engrained in the cultural practices of the region. For instance, son preference is sufficiently reflected in the following phrases and proverbs used in the region of Haryana.

> *Jitne ladke utna latta, jitne latta utna kabja.*

Which means the more one bears sons, the more hands one has and more hands means more power and control.

Ladka ghar ka chirag sai, ladki ghar ka bhoj.
(Son is the lamp of the house and daughter is a burden for the house).

And we are all familiar with this saying in both Punjabi and Haryanvi culture:

Beti ka baap sada heena.
(The father of a daughter always remains inferior).

Particularly the father of an unmarried daughter is almost considered a curse. According to another popular saying in Punjab:

Babul keo niviaan, dharma kyo niviaan, is babul di kanya kuwari, babul dharma taan niveean.
(Why is the father lower, why is Dharmi lower? This father's daughter is unmarried that is why father Dharmi is lower).

In patriarchal states like Punjab and Haryana, no matter howsoever rich the father of a daughter is, he has to bow before the groom and his family. This is the very reason why in such cultures the birth of a girl and a boy are seen differently. It is almost a sin to be a daughter's father because he has to go through enormous ridicule and humiliation from the side of the groom. The objectification of women and their devaluation is reflected through the derogatory sayings as under:

Jar joru aur zameen, role ki jadd hoya kare.
'Beti ke janam par baaje theekrai (earthen pot),
beta ke pe thali, budha rove, budia rove, rove halli palli'.
(Everyone cries at the birth of a girl).

This means that an earthen pot is smashed at the birth of a girl child and everyone cries during the birth of a girl child. Hence, the birth of a girl and son is traditionally celebrated very differently.

Gender bias is reflected in the blessings showered on the bride during wedding:

Ashta Putra Sowbhagyavati Bhave
(May you be blessed with eight sons)

It is also written in Mahabharata, *Adi Parva*, Section LXXIV:

'She is a true wife who has borne a son'.

Another common Punjabi proverb says:

'Raising a daughter is like watering your neighbour's garden'.

Certain names are given to women showing that they are not wanted. For instance, bathheri, bharpai, sitarah, bharto, etc. There is, thus, ample evidence of gender discrimination in the region of Punjab and Haryana reflected in the traditional names given to girls, also reflected in the folks and proverbs of the region. Thus, gender bias is deeply entrenched in the popular culture, common language, proverbs and stereotypes, comprising the culture of this region.

Gender Constructs: Religion, Culture and Honour

As per the Pew Research Centre Religion & Public Life (2012), 84 per cent of the world population has religious faith and in India, over 93 per cent of the people associate themselves with religion. In an essay 'Religious Discrimination Against Women', G.M. Woerlee (2008) has explained gender discrimination by two major religions of the world, Christianity and Islam. The essay highlighted the text from the Bible as well as from Quran that refers to women being lower than men. The texts give women a second class status. Although the Indian Constitution claims to treat everyone equal, discriminations still exist in the name of religion. Woerlee said that Jews, Christians, and Muslims all scold women for rooting humanity to be driven out of paradise. As a result of the so-called original sin of the first woman, people lost the gift of immortality. They had to work hard to find food and were no longer able to interact directly with God (Torah and Bible, Genesis, Chapter 3). The onus of this original sin rests heavily upon the shoulders of woman. Many passages in the Bible direct that women are not only inferior, but they must also obey men, because God tells us that men are their masters. 'Wives, submit yourselves unto your own husbands, as unto the Lord'.

> 'For the husband is the head of the wife, even as Christ is the head of the church: and he is the saviour of the body.
> Therefore as the church is subject unto Christ, so let the wives be to their own husbands in everything'.
> (Bible, Ephesians 5: 22–24)

The holy book of Islam, Quran too rebukes women. As Woerlee elaborated in his essay that Quran tells its followers that women are inferior to men, and require punishment for even a slight suspected disobedience.

> 'So good women are obedient, guarding in secret that which Allah hath guarded.
> As for those from whom ye fear rebellion, admonish them and banish them to beds apart, and scourge them.
> Then if they obey you, seek not a way against them'.
> (Quran, 4: 34)

Such verses of these holy books can be seen to be directing women to be submissive, accepting their subordinate status with patience and grace. Buddhism has also failed to see women as equal. Many Buddhists throughout the world are taught that women are incapable of awakening or of becoming a Buddha, at least without first being reborn as men. There are reflections of gender bias in the epics like Mahabharata and Ramayana displaying gender discrimination and systems like *sati* and dowry. The sacrifice of Sita to prove her loyalty towards Ram in Ramayana and the epical losing of Draupadi in a bet by her husband are few examples. The status of a Hindu woman in a family, though is getting better at a slow pace, the traditional second class treatment still exists. Thus, religion plays a key role in the persistence of son preference and women's derogatory status in the private as well as public.

Moral policing is done in *gurudwaras* as depicted in picture (Figure 4) taken from inside a gurudwara. In it is written the following phrase:

> *'Aurat sammain te pehchani jandi hai, Aurat bhara nu bhara da dushman bana dindi hai*
> *Aurat nu parde vich rakho, Aurat ton bach ke raho'.*
> A woman is judged at the time of need, a woman turns brothers into enemies, a woman must be kept in veil, one should be wary of a woman.

Such policing is done inside the Sikh gurudwaras. Although the first Sikh guru, Guru Nanak, challenged the prevalence of gender discrimination by declaring that there was equality between men and women. His teachings were against rituals or customs that discriminated against women. He did not consider women impure in any way; rather He wrote in praise of women:

> Of woman are we born, of woman conceived;
> to woman engaged, to woman married.
> Women are befriended, by woman is the civilization continued.
> When woman dies, woman is sought for.
> It is by woman that the entire social order is maintained.
> Then why call her evil of whom great men are born?
> (Guru Nank, Raag Aasaa Mehal 1: 473)

Guru Gobind Singh, the tenth Sikh Guru also forbade female infanticide in the code of conduct for Sikhs, prohibiting Sikhs from having any contact or relationship with those who indulged in this practice. He wrote:

> With the slayers of daughters, whosoever has social contact; him do I curse.
> (Guru Gobind Singh, Rehat Nameh 385)

He also wrote:

> 'Whosoever takes food from the slayers of daughters shall die un absolved'.
> (Guru Gobind Singh, Rehat Nameh 385)

However, female foeticide has persisted unabated in Punjab and even Haryana, reflected through the low child sex ratio, thus indicating a low and subordinate status of women. Arnold et al. (1998) writes that amongst the followers of the Hindu religion, sons are given importance by parents since it is opined that a person's soul can reach heaven only if a son and in his absence a grandson or another male member of the family lights the funeral pyre and sons are also believed to be able to enable the souls of the deceased parents to achieve salvation by performing various rites such as distributing alms and food to the poor and to the priests. Sikhism also favoured widow re-marriage as reflected in the following verses:

> A virtuous wife is not one who burns herself alive with her dead husband.
> She, indeed, would be a sati who dies through shock of separation.
> But, says Nanak, a True Sati is she who bears the shock of separation with courage and lives her natural span of life in a disciplined, dignified and virtuous manner.
> (Guru Granth Sahib 787)

However, despite such religious prescriptions, the present day culture and tradition of the two states reflect the sorry state of the women of the region. Following are some reflections from the field:

> *'Dewar tanne keere paane chahiyen, tanne apne bhai ka ujar ker apna bsaya hai'.*
> (May you rot forever, brother-in-law; you have brought devastation to your brother's life in order to set up your own).

P.J. Fagan (1908) observed that it is not uncommon among the Jats and lower castes for a woman to be shared in common by several brothers though she is recognized as the wife of only the eldest of them.

Other references from folklore of the region:

> *'Rand ke ghar me dewar maula'.*
> (The dewar is ecstatic in a widow's house).
> *'Maar koot ke main papan geri*
> *dewar kar liya ghar ka*
> *mam to mari ho gai he Ram*
> *dhandha ker ke is ghar ka'.*
> (Beaten and forced to live with my brother-in-law in sin,
> Unending house work has emaciated me, oh God!).
> *'Kamzor ki lugai sabh ki bhabhi'.*
> (A weak man's wife is everyone's bhabhi).
> (Brother-in-law to have sexual access to the sister-in-law).
> [Even the father-in-law, given a chance, was not above the sexual exploitation of his daughter-in-law (*Matarbhoomi* movie 2003)].

Reflections in Folk Culture

Folk songs of the region also show gender bias in the culture of Punjab and Haryana.

This following phrase shows selling of daughters:

> *'Dhian vechan kuwarian fad ke, raaj chugatian da'.*
> (They kidnap and sell virgin daughters, such is the rule of the evil).

This phrase shows that preference is given to fair skinned women:

> *'Roop kuwari da din charde di lali'.*
> (The beauty of an unmarried young daughter is like the redness of the raising dawn).

This phrase shows that preference is given to a large number of brothers:

> *'Ve peepal aap vada parivar nada*
> *Tere patina ne chebar laai*
> *Taniyan ton baaj peepla tera vee sarda nahi*
> *Je babul app vada, parivaar vada*
> *Bhaiaan to baaj vee sarda nahi'.*
> (Oh, peepal, you yourself are great, your family is great

Your leaves shed down
Peepal can't grow without branches
If your father is great, family is great.
You can't be great and do without number of brothers).

This phrase shows that preference is given to slim bride:

'Jan ve chad ja has ke veera,
Vohti leaain muteaar, ang di hove patli'.
(Join the marriage procession brother,
And bring a young virgin bride. She ought to be slim).

Father of daughters has to shoulder the responsibility to marry them off at an appropriate time and age:

'Dhiaan hundiaan ne daultaan beganiaan,
Has has tor babula'.
(Daughters are another's wealth; send them off happily, father).

The father of a daughter can't sleep till he marries off his daughter as the following common phrase of the region reflects:

'Uchi madi babul sutean, tenu main rahi haan jaga,
aisi neend kyo sutra, ve ghar dhee hoyi muteaar'.
(Sleeping father, high are your mansions
I'm waking you up
How can you sleep so deeply?
You have unmarried young daughter at home).

Ample evidence has been found of giving dowry in the folk songs of the region. Following are few of the examples:

'Dade dian potian chaar,
chare ladliaan, chohan nu ditte daaj,
ghore te palkiyaan'.
The grandmother has four grand daughters, all four loving, all were given dowry, horses and carriages.

A saying at the time of birth of a girl child:

'Sona mukhra tera ve,
main dekh dekh jivan, sohna mukhra preet ve main dekh dekh jeenva.
Hoya ki je dhee jamm payi par kukh taan sulakhni hoyi.
Jithon kudi hoyi aa, otho munda vee hoyega'.
I live by seeing your beautiful face, I live by seeing your beautiful face, Preet. What if a daughter is born, the womb become perfect. From where daughter is born, son will also be born.

Such cultural preferences for the male child reflected in the folks give birth to loads of gender discrepancies and violence of various types is inflicted upon women. For instance, direct and indirect demand for dowry results in torture inflicted upon bride and her family, rape, honour killings and molestation cases are also a frequent reality.

Violence against Women

The Beijing Platform for Action (1995) defined violence against women as 'any act that results in, or is likely to result in physical, sexual or psychological harm or suffering to women, including threats of such acts, coercion or arbitrary deprivation of liberty, whether occurring in public or private life.' Women are safe neither within the household, nor in the outside world. It is often said:

'Kudiaan nu ghar de andar chuhe kha jande ne
Bahar kaan kha jande'.
(Inside the house, the girls are molested by rats and outside by crows).

Various laws have been made to protect women against violence, yet ample instances of domestic violence, sexual harassment, molestation, rape, honour killings, dowry deaths, cruelty by husband, etc. are registered in the State of Punjab and Haryana. The statistics are evident that violence against women occurs at a high rate in the region of Punjab and Haryana. As per the National Crime Records Bureau (NCRB) 2013, 110 cases have been registered in the year 2013 in Ludhiana as shown in Figure 5. Maximum cases of dowry deaths (NCRB 2013) have also been registered in Ludhiana (Figure 6). Cultural norms and customs can give rise to highly gender-specific forms of violence. One example is dowry death as a result of failure of a wife and her family to meet the dowry demands of the husband and his family. Twenty-one sexual harassment cases (NCRB 2013) have been registered in Ludhiana (Figure 7). Rape cases (NCRB 2013) have again been registered maximum in Ludhiana (Figure 8) and the offenders were known to the victims. The International Violence Against Women Study found that an average of 35 per cent of the female population aged 16 and above had experienced violence, with between 20 and 60 per cent of this population reporting at least one incident of physical or sexual violence since the age of 16 (Johnson et al. 2008). Rates of intimate partner violence ranged from 9 to 40 per cent and were in general much higher than violence perpetrated by strangers. Furthermore, as True (2012) explains across all countries, the trends of violence committed by known partners to the victims were astonishingly high. Molestation cases (NCRB 2013) have been registered maximum in SAS Nagar (Figure 9). Cases of Cruelty by husband or his relatives (NCRB 2013) have been registered maximum again in SAS Nagar (Figure 10). Similarly Haryana statistics show maximum kidnapping cases (NCRB 2013) in Karnal (Figure 11). Molestation cases again have been highest in Karnal (NCRB 2013) (Figure 12). Dowry deaths (NCRB 2013) in Kurukshetra (Figure 13), sexual harassment cases (NCRB 2013) in Faridabad and Rewari (Figure 14), cases of cruelty by husband (NCRB 2013) in Hisar (Figure 15) and rape cases in Gurgaon (NCRB 2013) (Figure 16).

It is to be noted that these statistics include only the registered cases where as many cases go unreported especially from the rural hinterlands of the states of Punjab and Haryana. It is clearly reflected in the responses given below, gathered from the states of Punjab and Haryana. These responses show that much of the violence against women goes unreported and women continue to suffer in silence. Violence has, in fact, become a part of the lives of women.

A women respondent from the State of Punjab said:

'Jananiyaan da taan vichariaan da koi jeen ni,
maar de kuttde ne pee poo ke, kamm ni karna,
burriaan hun kina k kari jaan, jehre karde ne,
apne joga, kha chad de, goliaan kanhade sharaban peende.'

This shows the economic dependence and exploitation of women.

'Hun jadon aa kamm hunde ne taahiion taan kudian
mundean ch farak aa, nai taan
kudiaan sagon jayada kardiyaan maa peo da.
Par munde taan zaroori ne parivaar turea rehnda.
Put nishaan jagg te'.

Now when such things happen, that is the reason there are differences between men and women, otherwise the women love their parents more. But boys are essential to protect the lineage; boys leave a mark in the world.

There is no harm to the reputation of men who run away but when girls run away, their honour is tarnished.

'Je nai mada veejyaa na vadiya 9 kudian ton baad ik munda menu rabb ne deta c,.
'Ladki to chali ja gi apne gharan, ladka vansh bhdata hai'.
'Tuhanu pata hee a, beta taan zaroori hunda,
Je mere pehla munda na hunda,
fer taan main koshish karni hee c. Bete de naal hee tan vansh chalda'

Because I didn't sow anything sour, after giving bith to nine daughters, I was blessed with a son by God's grace.

This means that the lineage continues only with the sons and, therefore, sons are essential to be born in a family.

'Jiddan marzi a, ladkiyaan di marriage karde haan,
mudke oh sahuriaan di ho jandi aa, oh apni marzi ni kar sakdi,
us nu ohna de mutabik chalna paina,
mann lo apapa ghar vee rakhaange,
taan vee apne husband di hee manegi oh.
Munda appa nu nahi puchega taan vee apne bacheaa nu,
apni ghar wali nu taan puchega, vansh taan chalda rahega.
Naam te reh janda naa bach, ladki te agle ghar chali jandi a.'

Howsoever it is, we marry our daughter and then she becomes a part of the in-laws, she cannot do anything on her own, she has to go by the decision of her in-laws, even if we assume that we keep her at home, even then she will listen to her husband. If the son does not take care of us, he will take care of his children, wife; the lineage goes on, the name of lineage continues, the woman goes to the other house.

Sons are preferred over daughters. Daughters are considered a liability. It is considered that there are no economic returns by raising a girl.

'Safai karwa dete hain, das hazar takk ka kharcha ajata hai.
Dactrni le hain paise aur sara kaam ho jata hai.

> *Ladka hain ya ladki batawain sai sari baat.'*
> *'Shadi main Ghana paisa laag ja hai,*
> *fir gani ho to girvani pade hain.*
> *Fir chora na ho to chod de hai aadmi,*
> *tension main aake koi kime kare hai, koi kime kare.'*
> *'Ladki ke jewar ton hum kahi saalon se banan laag liye dhe.*
> *Dari chadar, chota mota lag jate hain karane shuru main hee,*
> *Ladki paida kari to shadi to karni hai,*
> *toom banwayee dhi teeno chorrioo ke sasural tayi.'*
>
> The foetus is removed at an expenditure of ₹ 10,000, the doctor takes the money and the job is completed, the sex of the child is disclosed. At the time of marriage, a lot of money is spent, if the number of girls is more, one has to get them aborted, if son is born, then the husband might leave the wife and under stress, different women adopt different methods. We have been earing and jewellery for our daughter for the last several years, we started to make carpets and cover sheets quite early, if we have given birth to a girl, then we'll also marry her, we gave gold rings for her in-laws during the marriage of my three daughters.

This shows as to why women undergo female foeticide. Dowry and onus of honour on women are the main reasons why daughters are unwanted. A woman is considered an object which can be brought and sent to her parental home at any time. This plight of women is due to the patriarchal nature of the society where women are submissive and their silence is considered honourable by other community men and women.

Thus, the low status of women, on the one hand, perpetuates violence, thus legitimized through the folk culture of Punjab and Haryana, and on the other hand, violence has the impact of keeping women in a subordinated state. This all ends up in a vicious circle which is very difficult to break. Wife-beating is justified on the ground that the wife was not faithful and to control her and preserve the honour of the family, beating her is considered essential. Further, the very privacy of such crimes leads to their under-reporting and, thus, generation of inaccurate statistics. Violence is under-reported also due to feelings of shame or fear of male or family honour and also sometimes because woman herself does not view it as violence. This kind of violence reflected in the cultural practices is sanctioned in the State of Punjab and Haryana. Honour killing is an example of such violence rooted in patriarchal cultural norms that tie family honour to female virtue. As a consequence, such killings carry the cultural sanction.

According to Michael Kurkiala (2003), 'If a woman refused to comply with the rules set down by her cultural community, her immoral behaviour contaminated the whole family. If other strategies to make the women comply failed, the only remedy for her male relatives was to kill her in order to protect the family honour. Thus, the murders were culturally sanctioned and designed to uphold a specific moral order.'

As per United Nations Population Fund (2000), 5,000 women and girls were killed each year in the name of honour. Women are greatly connected with the honour of men of the region of Punjab and Haryana. Hassan (1999) elaborates that honour killings are the 'unlawful killing of a woman for her actual or perceived morally or mentally unclean and impure behaviour'. Also, as defined by Farlex (2007), honour killing is an act in which a male member of the family kills a female relative for tarnishing the family image. Therefore, it is generally the men who control the movements and behaviour of women whether he is a father, brother, husband or uncle. Stories of honour killings are often flooded in the newspapers. This paper includes the responses from the perpetrators of the so-called honour killing. The paper captures their reactions after such acts of vengeance and pen against these inhuman and violent practices that exist in the name of honour, religion, customs and traditions. Here are some of the narratives from the perpetrators of honour killings:

> *'Os kudi ne taan sanu kite da ni chadea'.*
> *'Mooh kala karwa lea c apda, hor asin kee karde'.*
> *'Matlab hee ni banda, maar daan ge,*
> *sathon bahar ni jangiaan sadiaan kudiaan'.*
> *(Uncle of a deceased daughter about honour and choice of marriage)*
> That girl disgraced us, not leaving us to show our face, she got her face blackened, what could be done, there is no excuse, we will kill, our daughters don't go beyond our control.
>
> *'Hor kee Karde?'*
> *'Sanu aa din dekhna pea us kanjri karke'.*
> *'Asin kee ni keeta ohde layi, vadia padhay likhaya, te ohne aa din dikhaya.*
> *Miti ch rol ti meri sari izzat. Hor gareeban kol kee hunda'.*
> What else could be done? We had to face this day because of that whore? What did we not do for her, we gave her the best of education, and she made us see such a day. My whole honour was lost, what else the poor have except honour?

Thus, the perpetrators indulge in violence and injustice in the name of culture and honour on the pretext of preserving tradition and culture (Kumar 2007). The perpetrator is usually a brother or father whose cultural role is actually to protect the victim from any harm. The perpetrators in such killings are motivated to kill by the assumption that they can bring back the so-called lost honour of the family, by eliminating the family member who brought the so-called dishonour to the family and the community. This perceived dishonour is normally a result of the loss of control felt by the male members of the family on the sexual behaviour of a female member of the family as reflected in almost all the responses. As Radhika Coomaraswamy also explains that in such societies the value of education is lower than that of family status and the ideal of masculinity is underpinned by a notion of honour of an individual man, or a family or a community and is fundamentally connected to policing female behaviour and sexuality (2005: 42–63).

Most, if not all, victims of honour killings tend to be women, often young women. The vast majority of perpetrators are men, generally family members, most often the victim's brother, father, uncle or husband. But women, particularly older women, to maintain the social order and so-called family honour, may be indirectly involved, instigating violence through gossip or pressure on male members or colluding in arranging the murder.

Young respondents from the region of Punjab and Haryana, who were related to the victims of honour killings gave statements contradicting the perpetrators.

> 'Killing is never just'.
> 'There is no right to kill'.
> 'No one should be killed'.
> 'All killing I am against'.
> 'of course they are not fair'.
> 'They are like terrorism'.
> 'There are other ways to deal with it'.

There were sharp contrasts in the way young respondents viewed honour killings. They had certain empathy towards the victims while the perpetrators showed no mercy. There also seems to be conflict between traditionalism and modernism, individuality and concept of collective decision-making, where cases of honour killings are concerned. The bottom line is that there is a wide generation gap. To add to it, there is a dangerous mix of tradition and modernity, individualism and collectivism. Especially in a rural set-up, both in Punjab and Haryana, gender coupled with caste at times plays havoc with the lives of young boys and girls, all constitutional provisions notwithstanding. An upper caste boy can marry a lower caste girl but an upper caste girl cannot dare and is not allowed to marry a lower caste boy.

Conclusion

Punjab and Haryana, thus, continue to be two highly patriarchal states perpetuating the suppression and subordination of women. Women continue to be regarded as symbols of family/caste/village honour and, thus, become the targets of violence. The reasons for this sorry state of affairs can be traced to the cultural preferences of Punjab and Haryana legitimizing son preference, by devaluing the girl child. The collection, analysis and dissemination of gender specific data on education, employment, crime and health could be the first step to draft gender sensitive government policies. Change has to be brought at the grassroots, i.e. in the age old beliefs, proverbs and folk culture. Clear son preference prevails, with a cultural fixation reflected through the folk songs and common vocabulary of men and women, especially in the rural milieu. So long as honour continues to be attached with women only, they will have to carry the burden even at the risk of their lives and, therefore, gender equality at the level of mindset has to be effected. Finally, societies must develop zero tolerance for gender violence in any form, both in private and public spaces. Statistics in the paper show that violence against women persists through large cities and towns and is not merely a rural phenomenon. Thus, aggressive campaigns must accompany the legal provisions so that gender violence is recognized as a serious offence by the people in general, thus shunning it.

Appendix

Figure 1
GDP of Haryana

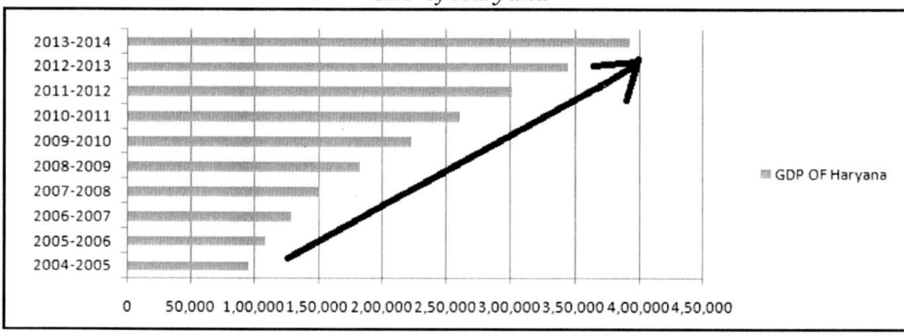

Source: Census of India 2004–2014.

Figure 2
GDP of Punjab

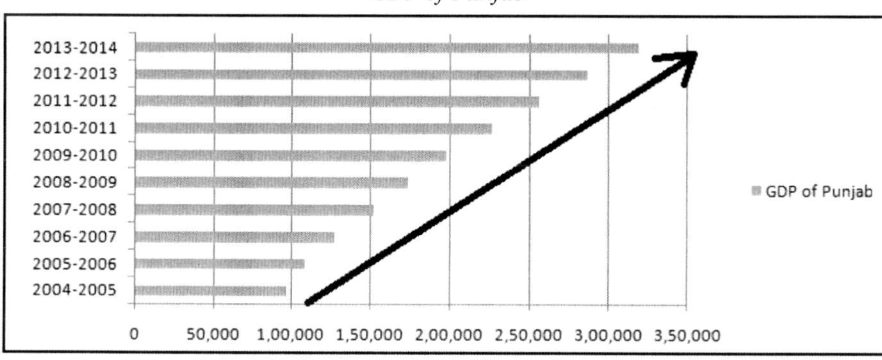

Source: Census of India 2004–2014.

Figure 3
Gender Concerns

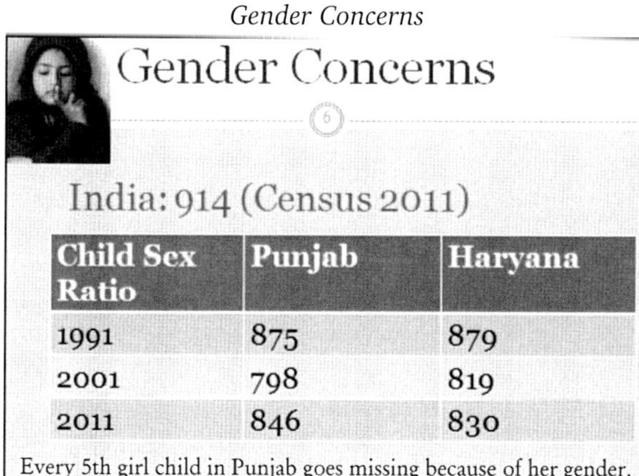

Child Sex Ratio	Punjab	Haryana
1991	875	879
2001	798	819
2011	846	830

Source: Census of India 1991–2011.

Figure 4

How Religion is Biased?

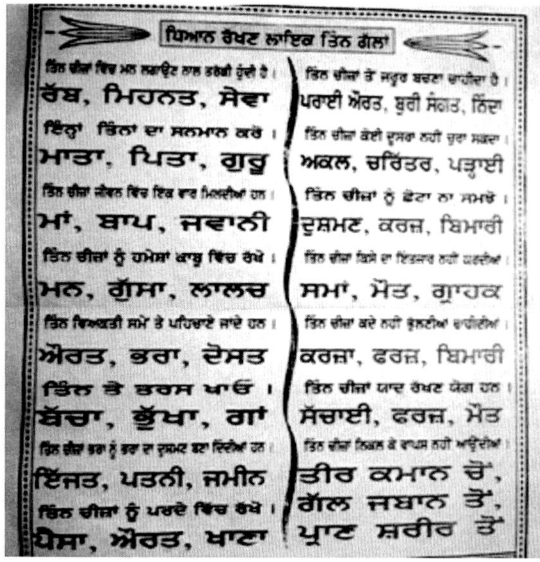

Source: Field Survey 2014.

Figure 5

Punjab Crime Records (Maximum cases in Ludhiana)

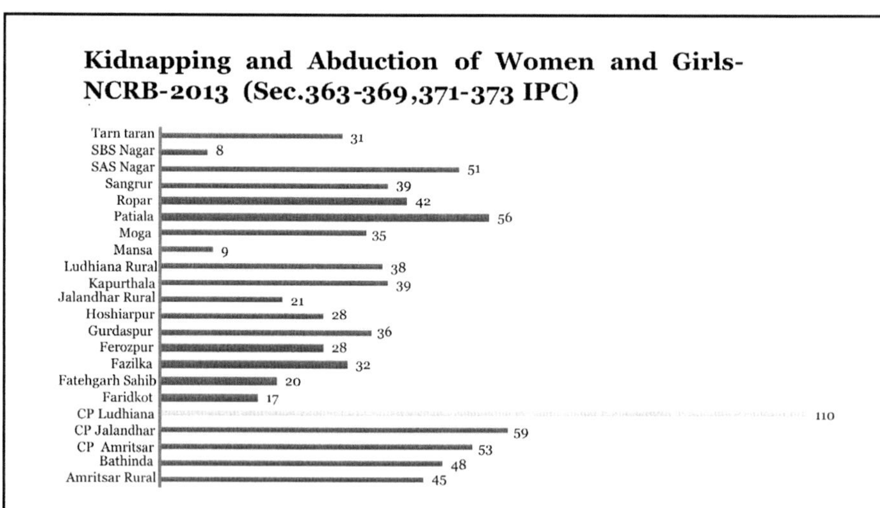

Source: National Crime Records Bureau 2013.

Figure 6

Dowry Deaths in Punjab

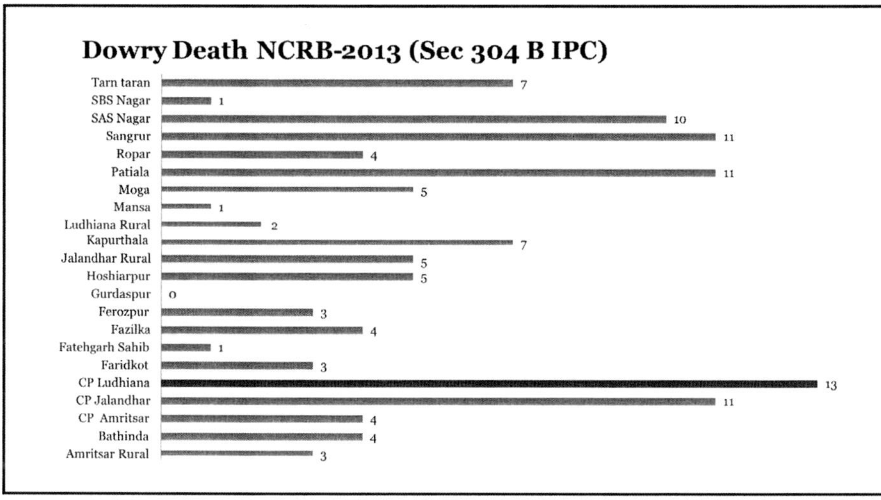

Source: National Crime Records Bureau 2013.

Figure 7

Punjab Crime Records (Maximum cases again in Ludhiana)

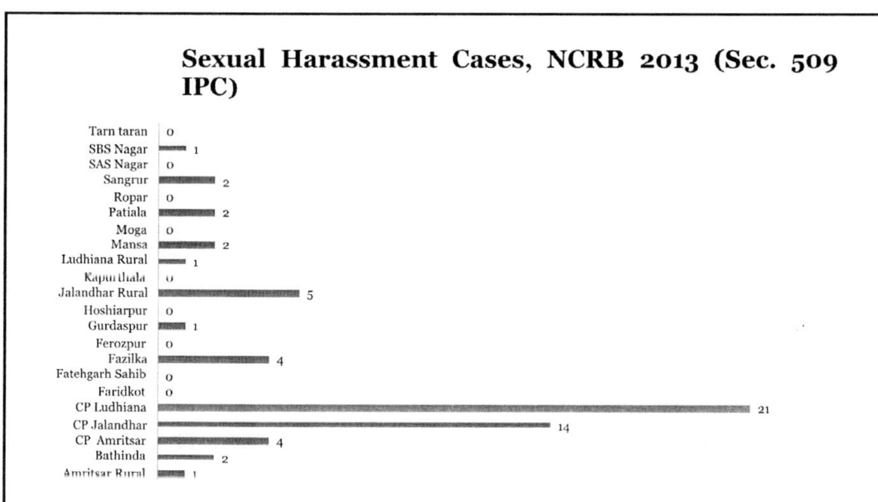

Source: National Crime Records Bureau 2013.

Figure 8

Punjab Crime Records (Maximum cases again in Ludhiana)

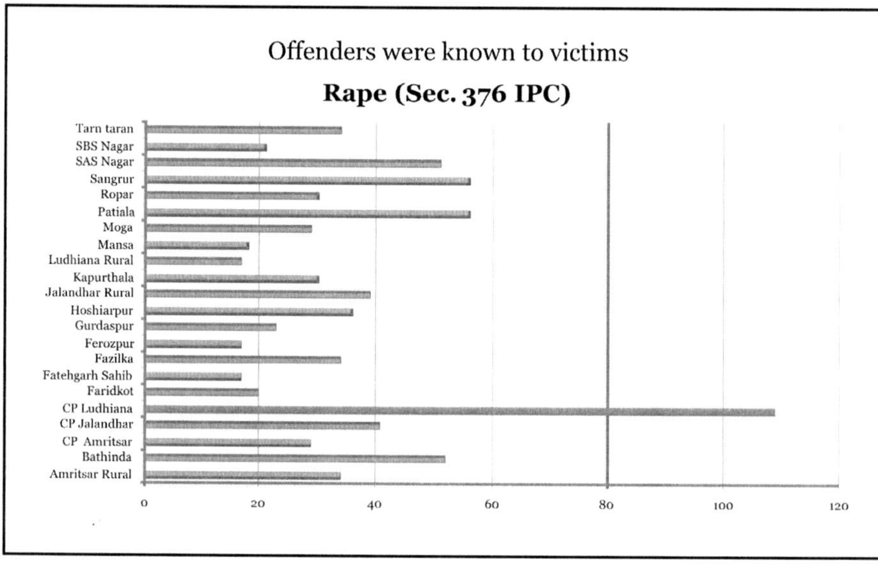

Source: National Crime Records Bureau 2013.

Figure 9

Punjab Crime Records (Maximum cases in SAS Nagar)

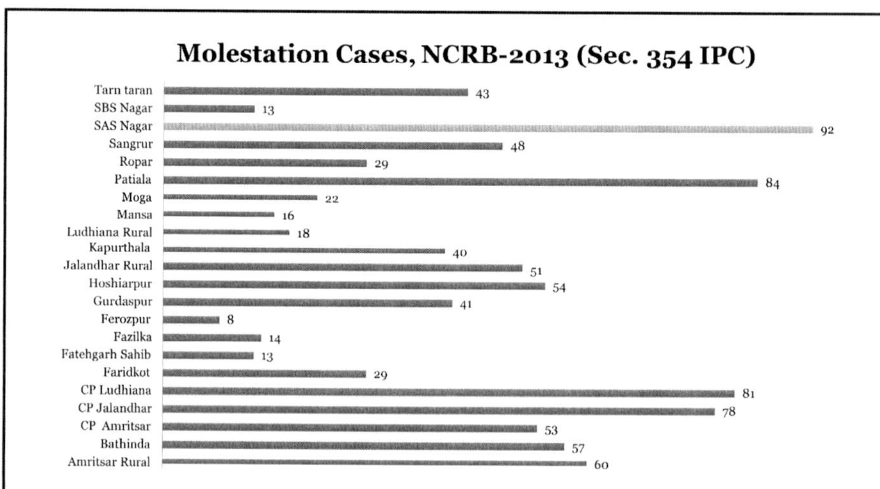

Source: National Crime Records Bureau 2013.

Figure 10

Punjab Crime Records (Maximum cases again in SAS Nagar)

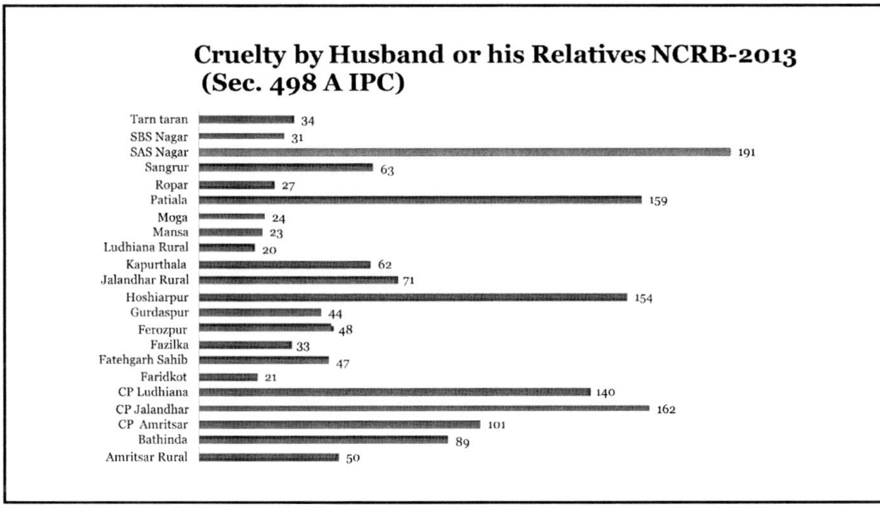

Source: National Crime Records Bureau 2013.

Figure 11

Haryana Crime Records (Maximum cases in District Karnal)

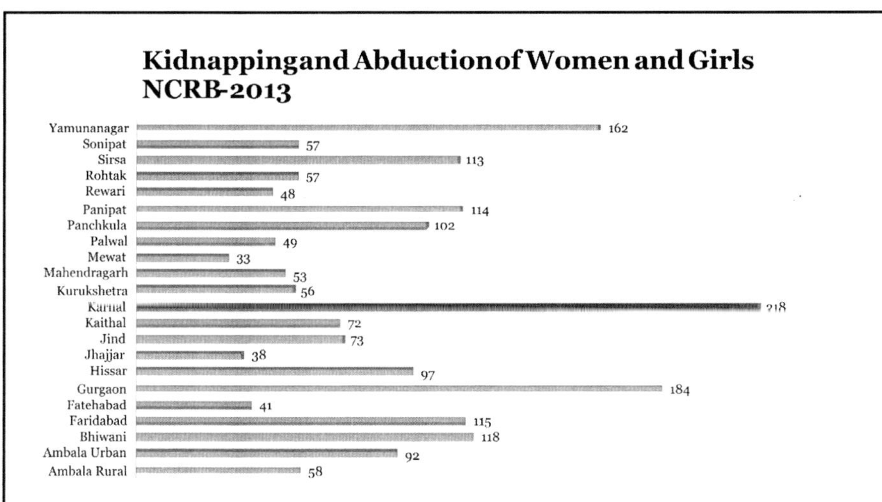

Source: National Crime Records Bureau 2013.

Figure 12

Haryana Crime Records (Maximum cases again in District Karnal)

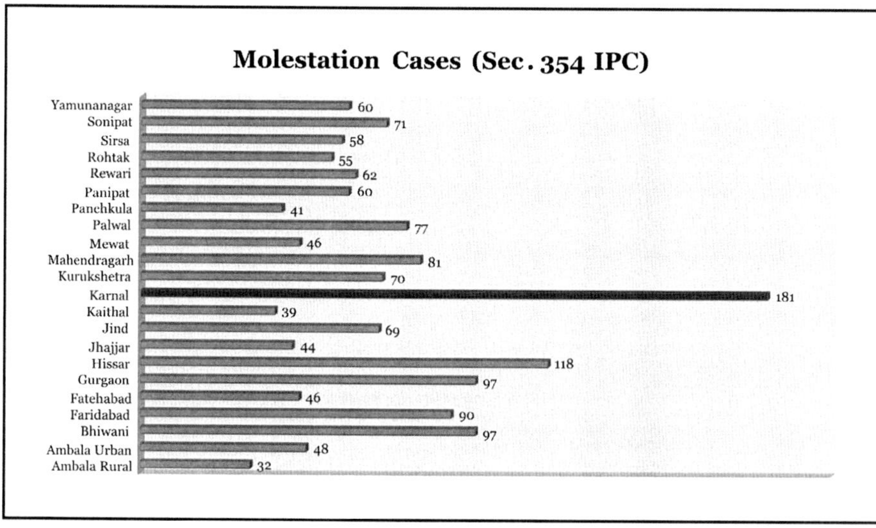

Source: National Crime Records Bureau 2013.

Figure 13

Haryana Crime Records (Maximum cases in District Kurukshetra)

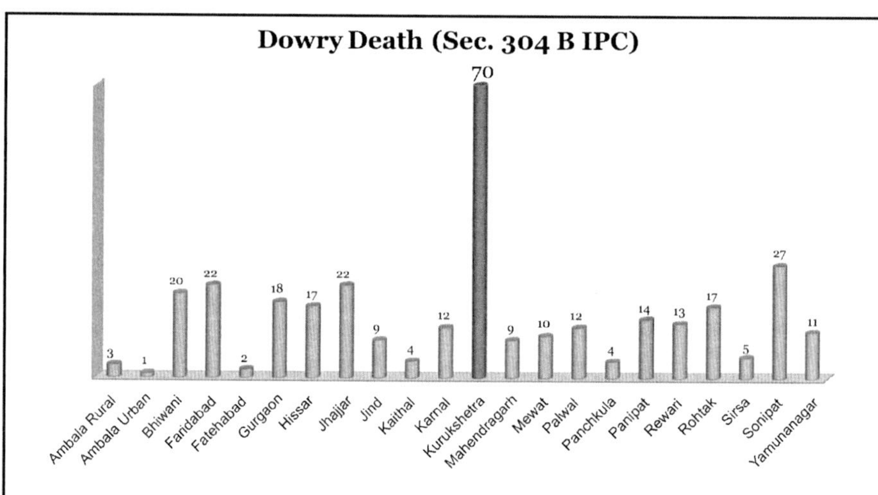

Source: National Crime Records Bureau 2013.

Figure 14

Haryana Crime Records (Maximum cases in District Faridabad and Rewari)

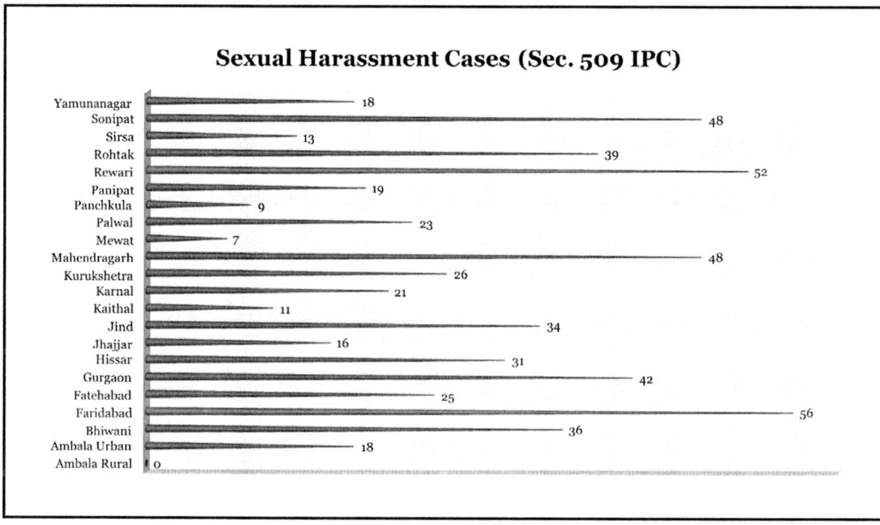

Source: National Crime Records Bureau 2013.

Figure 15

Haryana Crime Records (Maximum cases in District Hisar)

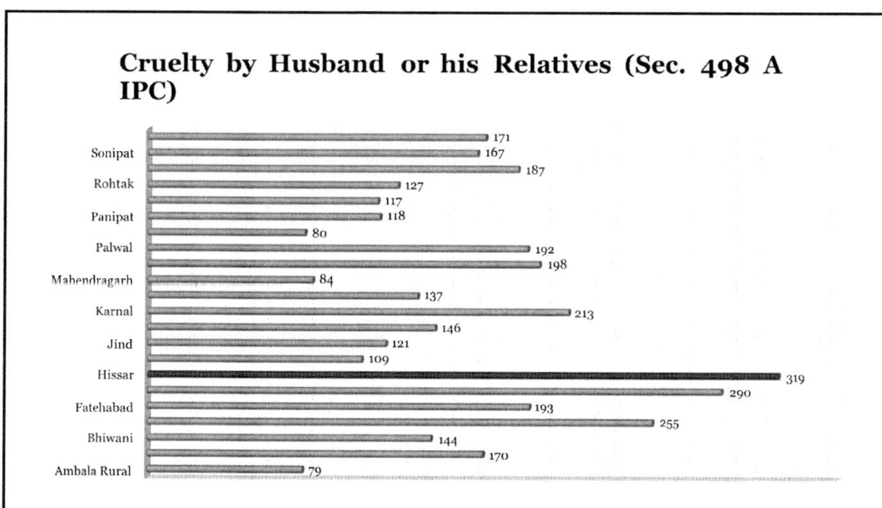

Source: National Crime Records Bureau 2013.

Figure 16

Haryana Crime Records (Maximum cases in District Gurgaon)

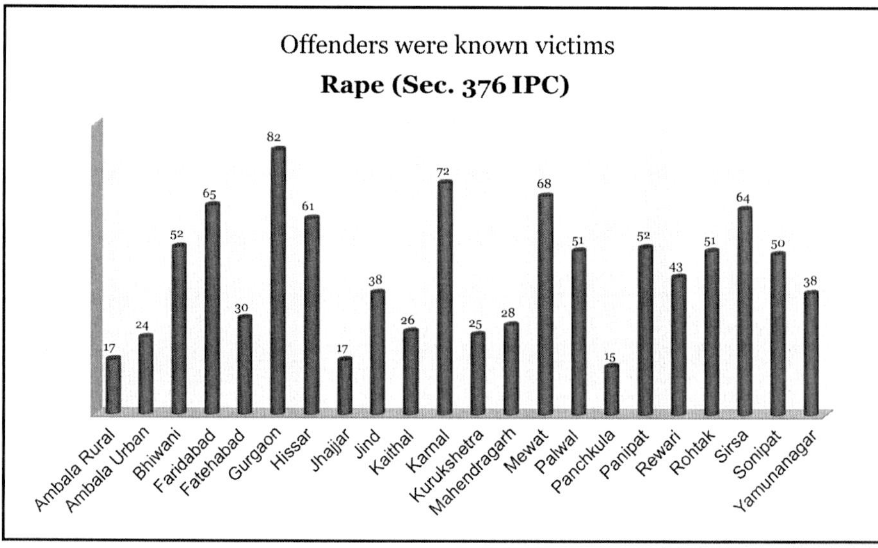

Source: National Crime Records Bureau 2013.

References

Arnold. F., Choe, M.K. and Roy, T.K. 1998. 'Son Preference, the Family Building Process and Child Mortality in India'. *Population Studies*. Vol. 52, No. 3. pp. 301–315.

Census of India. 1991–2011. New Delhi: Office of the Registrar General of India.

Census of India. 2004–2014. New Delhi: Office of the Registrar General of India.

Chowdhry, Prem. 1990. 'An Alternative to the Sati Model: Perceptions of a Social Reality in Folklore'. *Asian Folklore Studies*, 49(2), 259–274.

Coomaraswamy, Radhika. 2005. 'Violence Against Women and Crimes of Honour', in Lynn Welchman and Sara Hossain (eds), *Honour: Crimes, Paradigms and Violence Against Women*. London: Zed Books, pp. 42–63.

Fagan, P.J. 1908. *Hissar District Gazetteer, 1904*. Lahore: Government of Punjab.

Fourth World Conference on Women. Beijing, China. September 1995. Action for Equality Development and Peace: Platform for Action. United Nations.

Government of India. 1974. *Towards Equality: Report of the Committee on the Status of Women in India*. Department of Social Welfare, Ministry of Education and Social Welfare, New Delhi.

Hall, E. 1959. *The Silent Language*. New York: Doubleday.

——. 1983. *The Dance of Life: The Other Dimension of Time*. New York: Doubleday.

Haq, Mahbub ul. 2000. *Human Development in South Asia*. Human Development Centre, Karachi: OUP.

Hariyanavi, Madan. 1962. *Hariyana Lokgeet Sandarbh (The Folk Songs of Haryana)*. Delhi: Dehati Pustak Bhandar.

Hassan, Yasmeen. 1999. 'The Fate of Pakistani Women'. *International Herald Tribune*, 25 May.

Hofstede, G. 1991. *Cultures and Organizations: Software of the Mind*. New York: McGraw-Hill.

'Honour Killing'. 2007 in Forlex: The Dictionary.com, viewed on 12 January 2017 at http://www.thefreedictionary.com/honour+killing.

Johnson, H., Ollus, N. and Nevala, S. 2008. *Violence Against Women: An International Perspective*. New York: Springer Press.

Kumar, D. 2007. *Caste Panchayats: Law Should Prevail Over Tradition*. http://www.merinews.com/article/caste-panchayatslaw-should-prevail-overtradition/126277.html (accessed on 25 November 2014).

Kurkiala, Mikael. 2003. 'Interpreting Honour Killings: The Story of Fadime Shindal (1975–2002) in the Swedish Press'. *Anthropology Today*. Vol. 19, No. 1. pp. 6–7.

Monro, S. 2005. *Gender Politics: Citizenship, Activism and Sexual Diversity*. London: Pluto Press.

National Crime Records Buecass. 2013. viewed at ncrb.gov.in

Pew Research Centre. 2012. 'The Global Religions Landscape'. Washington DC (18 December).

Puri, D. 1999. *Gift of a Daughter: Change and Continuity in Marriage Patterns Among Two Generations of North Indians in Toronto and Delhi*. Unpublished doctoral dissertation, University of Toronto.

Sangari, Kumkum and Vaid, Sudesh. 1989. *Customs in a Peasant Economy: Women in Colonial Haryana*. New Delhi: Kali for Women.

Singh, Nahar and Gill, R.S. 2004. 'Folk Songs of Punjab'. *Journal of Punjab Studies*, 11(2), 171.

Stein, D. 1988. 'Burning Widows, Burning Brides: The Perils of Daughterhood in India'. *Pacific Affairs*, 61: 465–485.

True, J. 2012. *The Political Economy of Violence Against Women*. Oxford: Oxford University Press.

United Nations Development Programme (UNDP). 1995. *Human Development Report 1995*. New York: Oxford University Press.

United Nations Population Fund. 2000. *Ending Violence Against Women and Girls: State of the World Population 2000*; New York: United Nations Population Fund.

Wilchins, R. quoted in Monro, Surya. 2006. *Gender Politics: Citizenship, Activism and Sexual Diversity*. London: Pluto Press. p. 30.

Websites

ncrb.gov.in

www.thefreedictionary.com

www.un.org

www.unfpa.org.in

www.who.org

15

Menstruation and its Cultural Connotations in Rural Haryana

Richa Walia

Physiological changes during adolescence comprise a normal biological process. With the onset of puberty, the girl gets spontaneously transformed into a woman. The process entails a number of drastic changes of a physiological and cultural nature for the girl experiencing the change, especially in a conventional rural set-up. Although, in physiological terminology, menstruation is a normal physiological phenomenon indicating the capability of the young woman for procreation, yet this normal phenomenon is accompanied by a whole lot of superstitions, sanctions and restrictions. The onset of menstruation is generally followed by the expressions such as the following,

'Ladki badi/sayani ho gayi hai'
and *'ub isku idhar udhar jaana band karo.'*

Review of Literature

A study conducted by Dasgupta and Sarkar (2008) on menstrual hygiene among adolescent girls indicated that menstruation and menstrual practices were still clouded by taboos and socio-cultural restrictions resulting in adolescent girls remaining ignorant of the scientific facts and hygienic health practices, which sometimes resulted into adverse health outcomes. Another descriptive, cross-sectional study was conducted on 160 adolescent girls of a secondary school situated in the field practice area of Rural Health Unit and Training Centre, Singur, West Bengal, with the help of a pre-designed and pre-tested questionnaire. Results show that out of 160 respondents, 108 (67.5%) girls were aware about menstruation prior to attainment of menarche. Mother was the first informant regarding menstruation in case of only 60 (37.5%) girls. Regarding practices, only 18 (11.25%) girls used sanitary napkins during menstruation. For cleaning purpose, 156 (97.5%) girls used both soap and water. So far as various cultural restrictions are concerned, as many as 136 (85%) girls observed several restrictions during menstruation.

Kirk and Sommer (2006), in a study, found the lack of sanitary protection during menstruation as a barrier to girl's regular attendance in school. In many poor families providing adequate clothing for the whole family can be a challenge. Insufficient or inadequate sanitary protection can be very embarrassing for a girl attending school during her monthly period. Kamble (2001), in a similar study entitled 'A Study to Assess the Knowledge and Practice of Menstruation and Menstrual Hygiene Among Girls' studying in high schools in Belgam city, found that 61.66 per cent of the girls had an average knowledge regarding menstrual hygiene, while 87.66 per cent of the girls followed correct practices.

Another study was conducted to examine the psycho-social behaviour of urban Indian adolescent girls during menstruation (Goel and Kundan 2011). A total of 478 adolescent girls in the age group of 15–19 years from three educational institutes of Rohtak city were contacted. Feeling of sickness was the most common (in more than two-third of subjects) behavioural symptom followed by irritability and emotional disturbances. More than three-fourth of the subjects did not offer prayers at the place of worship during menstruation, 45 per cent were not allowed in kitchen and nearly one-fourth followed dietary restrictions. More than 16 per cent subjects thought menstruation to be a sign of onset of a disease and a little more than 7 per cent thought it to be a curse. More than half of the girls discussed their menstruation related problems with their mothers and one-third preferred to discuss these with friends. Six girls said that they discussed their menstrual related problems with their father. The results of the study revealed that there was a lack of awareness regarding menstruation among adolescent girls.

The Present Study and Methodology Used

The present study is descriptive in nature and is based upon both quantitative and qualitative research techniques. The study was conducted on two villages, namely Kharvan and Khizrabad, situated in District Yamunanagar, Haryana. Kharvan and Khizrabad are the most populated villages with 7839 and 5704 persons, respectively in the state of Haryana as per Census 2011. The study was focused upon adolescent girls in these two villages. A list of unmarried girls in the age group of 12–18 years was prepared in the two sample villages separately (a) for those enrolled in school and (b) those out of school, and information was obtained from them with the help of an interview schedule constructed for the purpose.

Both quantitative and qualitative data were collected from adolescent girls and their mothers by using separate interview schedules. Apart from personal interviews, group discussions were also conducted to procure relevant data.

Objectives

An effort has been made to:

1. Find out the major problems faced by adolescent girls during mensuration.
2. Elicit the beliefs, perceptions and sources of information regarding menstruation among the adolescent girls.
3. Assess the status of menstrual hygiene among adolescent girls.

Discussion on Menstruation: A Taboo

Menstruation is considered as a polluting physiological phenomenon in the Indian society. Various restrictions are imposed upon the girls during menstruation period as it is considered to be polluting in religious texts. The practice and meaning of menstruation can be grouped into three types of taboos: concealment, communication and activity. Concealment refers to the belief that menstruation must be kept a secret. In India girls are told by mothers, peers and even teachers that menstruation cannot be talked about in public. Communication taboo means that menstruation should be concealed verbally and physically. Activity taboos are the restrictions imposed on women/girls during menstruation (Williams 1983).

Figure 1 shows that out of 200 girls, 175 were experiencing menstruation. Figure 2 reveals that among 175 girls who started menstruating only 34.85 per cent were aware about menstruation before they achieved the menarche, while the remaining 65.15 per cent girls had no knowledge about it. Adolescent girls understood that menstrual cycle was an important process in a woman's life in absence of which one could not become a mother. Most of the girls who participated in FGDs stated that it was an impure blood and hence the waste got excreted out of the body every month. Village-wise data

Figure 1

Menstruation among Girls

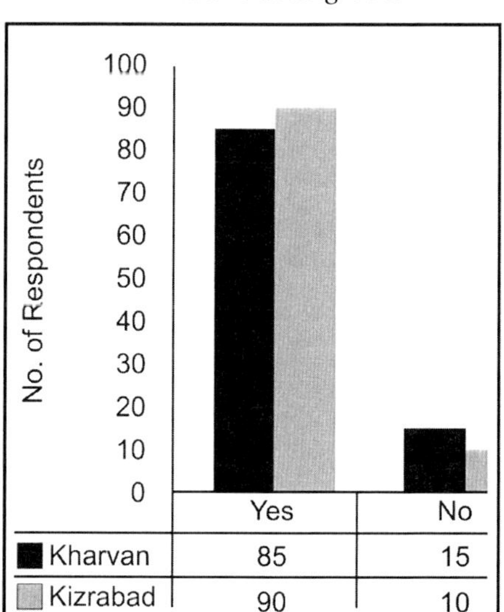

Figure 2

Knowledge about Menstruation

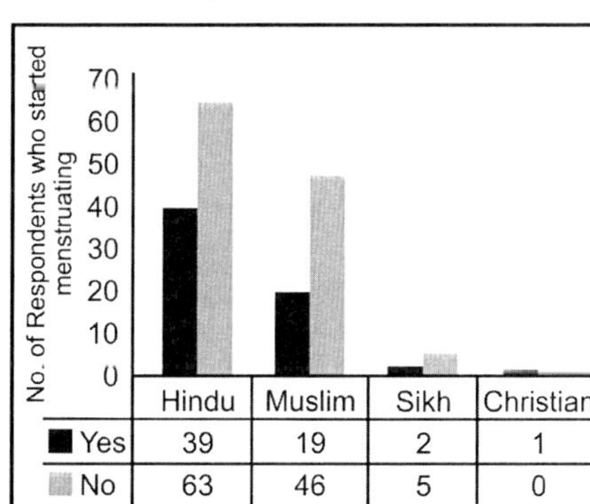

show that the degree of awareness was found to be maximum among respondents from joint families as they gathered information from elder sisters/cousins or sisters-in-law.

Majority of the adolescent girls did not have any prior knowledge about menstruation, irrespective of religious affiliation, and the proportion of such girls was the highest among Muslims. The one Christian girl experiencing menstruation admitted having prior knowledge about it. It was observed that girls did not know what would happen when they began to menstruate, because it was never discussed in their families. Respondent girls revealed that they did not know about menstruation because their religion considered it bad to talk about it. Among all the four religious communities, i.e. Hindus, Sikhs, Muslims and Christians, Muslim girls were made to suffer during menstruation the most, due to cultural norms and stigma attached to it. Several Muslim girls opined that they were not expected to openly talk about menstruation. They further said:

> It is considered as dirty and filthy in religious text.
>
> Following statements were made by girls during discussion:
>
> *'Date ke bare mein hum kisi ko na batawe, chhupa ke rakhe jab aawa'.*
> It is normally kept secret; you would not allow other people to know this. (Standard 9th, Hindu girl)
>
> *'Dusro ko iske bare mein nahi pata lagne dete kyuki date ki baat karne ko ganda mana'.*
>
> Others should not know about menses as it is considered dirty to talk about these issues. (Non-school going Muslim girl)
>
> *'Agar hum apni seheliyo ko batate hai iske bare mein tou wo mazaak karti hai'*
>
> If we discuss with our friends about menses they ridicule us. (Standard 8th Hindu Girl)

None of the girls was able to explain as to what caused menstruation or how it works in their body. The primary reason for such an ignorance about an important fact was that it was a taboo, to be kept secret and not to be discussed in public. The mothers of these girls were also completely ignorant about the physiological process underlying menstruation.

Restrictions on Adolescent Girls at the Time of Menstruation

Menstruation was considered to be polluting by all religious communities. Among Hindus, women and girls are not allowed to visit a temple, pray or cook during menstruation. They are not allowed to touch a religious scripture and have to stay away from kitchen because they are seen as impure. Among Muslims, menstruating women are prohibited from touching the Quran.

Figure 3 indicates that there was negligible inter village variation in terms of restrictions on girls during menstruation. Almost 98.8 per cent respondents admitted that they had to obey restrictions. Although such restrictions were found in all religious communities, yet these were the highest among Hindus (especially among Brahmins). Girls revealed that they did not have the same freedom as they had enjoyed before they began menstruating. The girls used the word *unclean* or *dirty* while talking about the restrictions associated with menstruation. Girls from all religions, castes and income groups have to following restrictions during menstruation. During discussions, one of the Muslim girls from Khizrabad said:

Figure 3

Restrictions during Menstruation

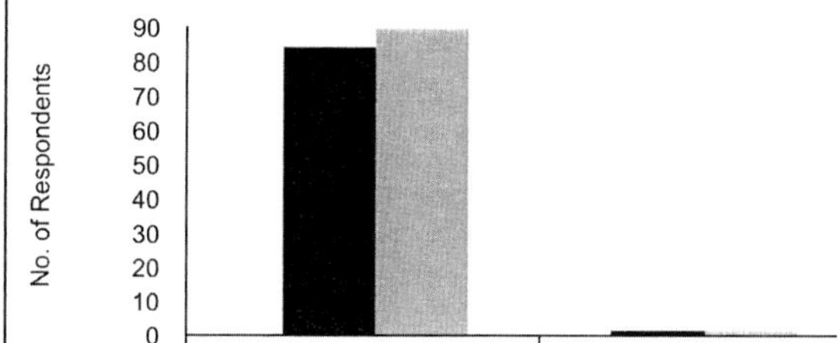

	Yes	No
Kharvan	84	1
Khizrabad	89	1

> *Mere Ma ji ne bola hai ki jab mahina aaye tou apne sath pyaz ya lasun rakhna chaiye or choraha nahi tapna chaiye.*
>
> My Mother told me that when I menstruate I need to keep a garlic or onion and should not cross the carfax (*chorasta*). (13-year-old Muslim girl)

When probed further she said that garlic and onion fight the odour of impure blood during menstruation and during menses a girl was prone to evil spirits. Myth, mystery and superstitions have long enveloped the fact of menstruation. Friends emerged as the major source of information on menstruation which is in consonance with the findings of other studies (Ghattargi and Deo 2005: 30). In a study conducted in Kolkata by Dasgupta and Sarkar, mothers were found to be the main source of information on this subject followed by mass media (2008: 33). In the present study, however, mothers were the main source of information for only 44 (5.5%) of the girls. This could be due to lack of communication between mothers and daughters since following the traditional taboos, discussion on this issue was found to be awkward and embarrassing.

Figure 4

Superstitions Observed during Menstruation

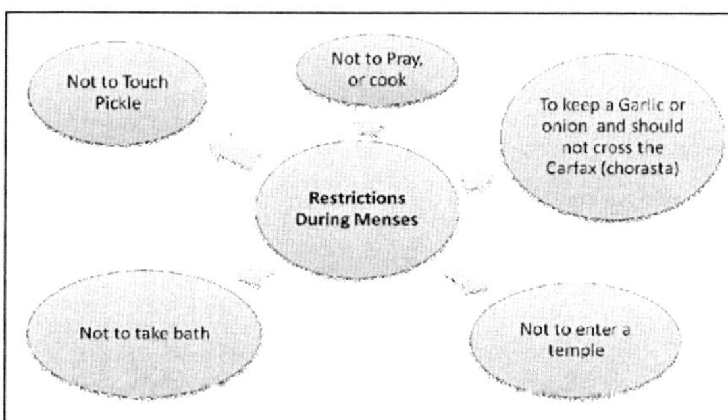

Rationalization Lies in Religion

Researcher interviewed mothers, priests and Muslim priests to learn about the concept of impurity related to menstruation. Mothers believed that menstruation was an impure thing because it was mentioned in the religious text. However, mothers were not able to give an exhaustive explanation about concept of impurity related with menstruation. Therefore, in order to gain an insight, the Hindu and Muslim priests were contacted. In Hinduism, menstruating women are not supposed to enter the temple because they are 'unclean', and menstruating women are supposed to keep away from sacred spaces and objects even within their homes. In Islam, menstruating women are not supposed to touch the Quran, enter the mosque and recite the *salat* (the ritual prayer). A *maulvi* also added that all restrictions are mentioned in various Hadiths, which are tools for understanding the Quran.

The Hindu priest mentioned during interview, that in Indian philosophy there are three *gunas* (or qualities), these are:

- *Tamas* (black)
- *Rajas* (red)
- *Sattva* (white)

Anything that is emitted from the body, i.e. sweat, blood, tears, etc. is toxic and hence is classified under *tamas*. Menstruating blood excreted from body, being impure, is therefore considered as *tamas*.

However, there is another explanation in Hindu mythology brought out in a study by Bhartiya (2013) which has revealed that women got 'rajaswala dosha' (menstruation) when Lord Indra (the King of Gods and God of lightning and thunder) severed the head of Vishwaroopacharya (the second teacher of the gods). Since Lord Indra killed a Brahmin he got *brahmahatya dosha*. He got rid of it by distributing it amongst the *prithvi* (land), *samudra* (water), *vriksha* (tree) and *stree* (woman). The women from that day started menstruating every 28–30 days and got the ability to give birth. Hence it is believed that menstruation is a *dosha* (defect) and hence it is considered impure.

Leslie (1992) described in her study that a menstruating woman was considered as impure and polluted and the main causes for the restrictions had been quoted in sacred Vedic ritual are Varuna's noose and Indra's curse. Indra's curse is said to be the mythic catalyst that led to restrictive rituals that must be adhered to when a woman is participating in religious sacrifice. The Taittariya Samhita reveals that when Indra killed Visvarupa, he transferred one-third of the 'stain' of murdering a Brahmin to women. The 'stain' that was transferred to women comes in the form of menstrual blood, and is seen as dangerous and impure. It is regarded in this way because the menstrual blood is literally Indra's curse. Therefore, when a woman is menstruating she is not able to perform her religious duty; a ritual must be postponed or a substitution is made in her place. Varuna's noose is the other mythic tale that has given authority to the types of restrictions that women must endure. Although the notion of Varuna's noose is to restrain the power of women, it also represents the many aspects of femininity that are crucial for worship and religious sacrifices. The wife of the sacrificer is bound with a species of grass called *munja*, which occurs once the wife enters the sacrificial area. She is bound while sitting because it is said that she becomes virile while in this type of position. The binding of the waist is a symbolic representation of Varuna's noose, which he uses to ensure that the propagation of the created world occurs within the bounds of a properly conceived cosmic order (Leslie 1989: 25).

Figure 4
Material used during Menstruation

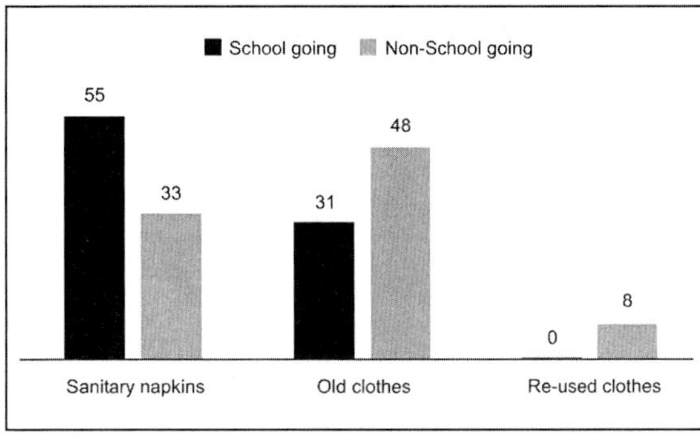

Figure 4 indicates that about 50.2 per cent of girls were using sanitary napkins, while 45.4 per cent were using old cloth and only 4.4 per cent reused cloth during menses. The proportion of girls using old and reused cloth was the highest among Muslims. There was difference across religions in the proportion of girls using sanitary napkins. It was found that as compared to other religions, a larger proportion among Muslim girls were using re-used cloth during menses. Sanitary napkins were used primarily by girls belonging to financially well placed families. Poverty was one of the reasons to use cloth during menstruation.

Reasons Given for Not Using Sanitary Napkins

The type of absorbent material used during menstruation is of primary concern since reusable material could be a source of infection if improperly cleaned. Figure 5 indicates that out of 200 girls 88 girls were not using sanitary napkins. It was found that 53.3 per cent of girls from Khizrabad were not aware about sanitary pads, while 46.7 per cent of girls from Kharvan had never heard about sanitary napkins. There were variations between school going and non-school going girls. While there was only one school going girl from Kharvan who did not know about sanitary pads, the proportion of such girls was much higher in Khizrabad as 27 of non-school going girls were not aware about sanitary pads.

Figure 5
Awareness of Sanitary Napkins among Girls using Cloth during Menses

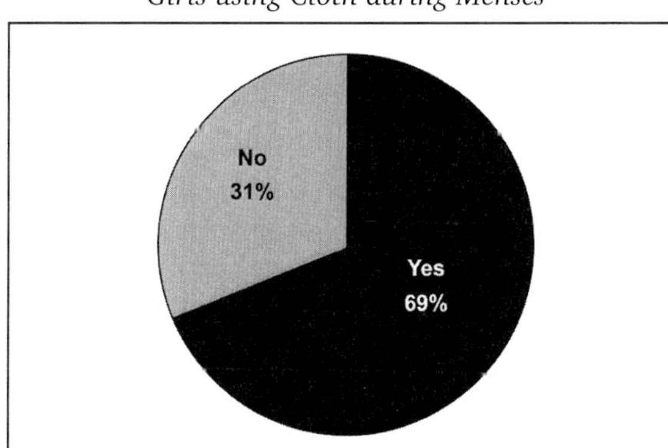

FGDs with girls revealed that they did not use sanitary napkins because they could not afford cloth/pads every month. So they washed the cloth and re-used it twice or thrice before destroying it. School going girls added that they were using sanitary napkins because it was difficult for them to carry cloth. Many adolescent girls added that they felt more comfortable using cloth than sanitary napkin. A majority of school going girls were reluctant to use cloth during menstruation. They said that if they had an option to choose between sanitary pad and cloth they would prefer sanitary napkins.

However, a number of Muslim adolescent girls stated that they do not use pad because of shyness.

> *Hum pad paise ki waja se nahi sharam ki waja se nahi lete.*
> We do not ask for pad because of shyness.
> (14-year-old Hindu girl)

> One of them stated:

> *Madam ji hamko sharam aati hai ye sab bolte hue,*
> *Upar se pad lene kon jaega*
> *Kon dukandar jo ki aadmi hota hai*
> *Usko kahega ki hamko pad chaiye*
> Madam we feel shy to talk about these issues. Secondly who will ask for a pad from male shopkeeper. (13-year-old, a Muslim girl)

Source of Knowledge about Menstruation

Figure 6
Method of Disposal

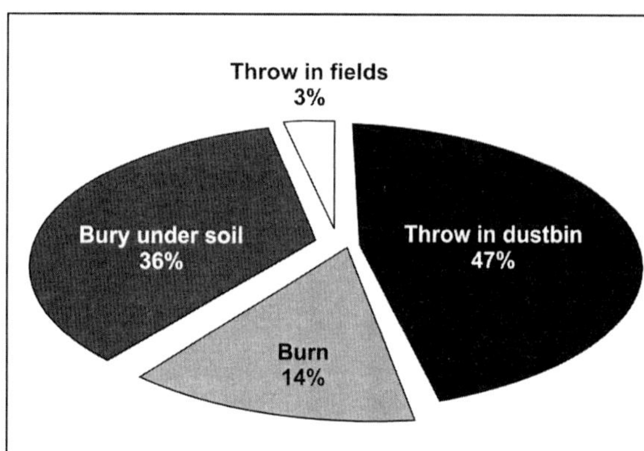

A large proportion of girls were partially aware about menstruation before they experienced it. It was found that the most important source of information about menstruation in Khizrabad comprised mother (5), sister (5) and sister-in-law (4). Teacher is considered as the main source of information on menstruation but data revealed that only one girl from Khizrabad came to know about menstruation from her teacher. While in the other village, i.e. Kharvan, 12 girls came to know about menstruation from their mothers while 10 girls came to know about menstruation from sister and 11 from their friends. Most of the girls during FGDs said that they felt comfortable with mother and sister, while talking on such issues. They further said that they were told to change pads/cloths twice a day. They did not even know from where blood comes. While responding, they would cover their face with *dupatta* and smiled without answering. The researcher persuaded them to respond but with little success and they said, *Madam aise batein humko nahi pata* (We don't know about these issues). Some female teachers from Kharvan revealed that mothers and teachers also felt uncomfortable while discussing menstruation.

One of the teachers said:

> 'If the parents or neighbours heard her talking
> about menses what would they think of me'.
> (32 years, female teacher, Karvan)

She said that village was a small community where people knew each other. She said, 'If she discusses issues regarding sex/menses with young girls it could create a problem for her. Therefore, they remained silent on these issues for the fear of being blamed'.

Myths Associated with the Disposal of Menstrual Waste

Figure 6 shows variation in the practices for disposal of menstrual waste, i.e. 47 per cent of the girls disposed their menstrual waste in dustbin. However, a large number of girls, i.e. 36 per cent disposed their menstrual waste by burying these in nearby fields. It was found that most of the Muslim girls preferred to burn and dig their menstrual waste. Different reasons were provided by adolescent girls about the method of disposal of pads, i.e. to burn and dig them. Most of the girls said that they did not know the reason but one of the girls explained that they buried their menstrual cloth to prevent witchcraft that could lead to infertility. The concept of magic is strong in rural India. The piece of cloth/pad used for menstrual bleeding is considered impure of a different order by the people. Therefore, its disposal held special importance in the daily lives of Indian women/girls. During focus group discussion girls said:

> *Hum daba de ya kurdi mein fek de.*
> We throw it away on the garbage heap or bury it under the earth.
> (15-year-old, Muslim Girl)

A few of the girls from Khizrabad said, 'We bury stained cloth out of shame, what if somebody sees our stained pads/cloth'.

One of the adolescent girls from Khizrabad added, 'If we throw it away in the open it may scatter around in the whole village that is why bury it so that nobody can see it'. They also believed that if the menstrual waste was not buried it could lead to infertility.

Researcher was curious to know how menstrual cloth if not buried leads to infertility? Adolescent girls did not elaborate and just moved their heads by saying:

> *Humko nahi pata.*
> We don't know.

Further, the mothers of some of the adolescent respondents were approached and one of them explained, 'Among Muslim religion it is said that jinn is attracted to blood which leads to infertility, that is why girls are supposed to burn or dig menstrual waste'. Westermarck (1926) also gave a similar explanation in his study. He elaborated that the *jinn* were attracted to urine, foul odour, semen and blood. Thus, cleanliness was crucial for managing vulnerability to malevolent *jinn*. *Jinn* were especially drawn to genital blood from menstruation, childbirth, miscarriage, or circumcision. They further indicated that they believed that if a *jinn* attacked a woman during her menstrual period, she may become infertile, argue with her husband or have severe headache. Therefore, if a menstruating woman got subjected to infertility, irritability, headache, or illness she would interpret this as a result of an attack by *jinn* who drawn to her menstrual blood. *Jinn* could enter a woman through her menstrual blood, possess her, and cause her great harm (Westermarck 1926, I: IV). So this might be the reason why girls had been trained to bury menstrual waste instead of throwing it in a dustbin.

Menstrual Experiences and Coping Strategies Adopted by Adolescent Girls

Figure 7 reveals that 39 per cent of girls got scared when they had menstruation for the first time. However, 35 per cent of non-school going girls cried when they saw blood for first time. A few of the girls said that they had to face an embarrassing situation as they did not have any previous knowledge about menstruation.

Figure 7
Menstrual Experience

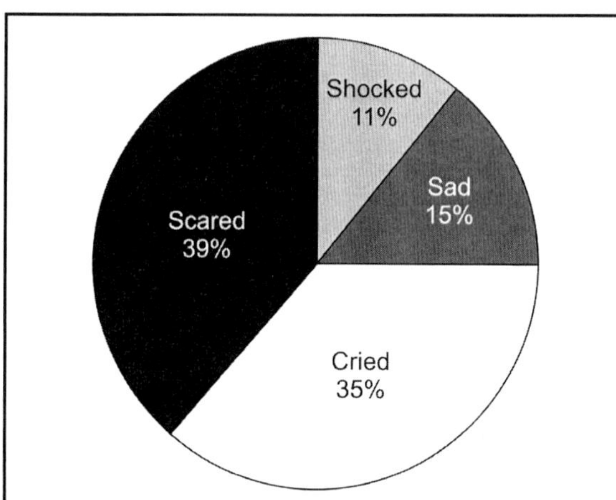

Village-wise data do not reflect much variation between the two villages regarding menstruation problems. It was found that during menstruation, abdominal pain, Leukorrhea and backache were the most common problems faced by respondents. A few girls were also found to be suffering from UTI (Unitary Tract Infection). The Focused Group Discussions (FGDs) revealed that participants sought both modern medical and conventional interventions to recover from these ailments. Medical interventions included taking pain-killers and visiting Registered Medical Practitioners. Respondents were also found to be visiting traditional healers and tried various alternative medicines, including Ayurveda. During the FGDs, many girls shared that due to these physical symptoms they felt mentally stressed during menstruation. They also became very cautious about their mobility. An 18-year-old girl studying in class 9th shared her menstrual problems with the researcher. She had attained menarche at 15 years of age. Her body weight was much lower than the average body weight and she was suffering from anaemia. During her last menstruation, she suffered heavy bleeding for continuous six days and this has been constant for the last two years. She said that menstruation was a disease and has affected her life enormously.

School going girls confided that they always had to take two to three days off during menstruation. One of the girls who was suffering from leukorrhea said:

> *Jab safed pani padta hai tab badi dikkat aati hai.*
> (14-year-old school going Muslim girl)

The girl further said that she had to wear two shorts to manage the discharge. She was not taking any treatment for this as she felt ashamed to share the problem with her mother. Many girls do not talk about menstrual problems with anyone. During FGDs, adolescent girls said, that it was a sensitive topic, very private, leading to shame and embarrassment.

Majority of the adolescent girls during focus group discussions said that they were scared/shocked and they cried when they had menstruation for the first time. They were of the opinion that girls should be explained everything about menstruation before its onset, as a lot of problems, for instance knowing whom to turn to when the bleeding is first noticed, would probably be avoided if mothers or other family members talk more openly about it. Various coping strategies were adopted by girls to deal with the problems faced at the time of menstruation. Majority of the girls said that they felt scared on the onset of menstruation cycle. One of the girls stated that when she saw blood first time the first thought which came to her mind was that she was having some incurable disease. She further added that she did not share this incidence with anyone and used cotton to cope with the situation. When the blood stopped she took a sign of relief. When it came again the next month she told her mother about it and she explained that it was not a disease.

Menstrual Experience: An Embarrassing Situation

A 16-year-old Hindu girl said:

> *'Mein saatvi mein thi or khel rahi thi.*
> *Muje daag lag gaya tou ladke mera mazak banane lage.*
> *Mujhe itni sharam aai ki mein hafte tak school ni aa ke badi*
> *Fir mere mummy ne samjaya ki ye sab ladkiyo nu howe'*
> I was in 7th grade, I was playing in the ground when I got a blood stain, and boys of my, class ridiculed me. Because of that embarrassment, I did not go to school for many weeks. After that my mother told me that it was menstruation and a normal phenomenon.

Although adolescent girls showed their discomfort because of menstruation, yet they felt proud that they were menstruating and had turned into complete women. Few of them ridiculed the girls who were not menstruating and added with a mischievous smile:

> *Itni badi ho gai hai, madam ji ye, fir bhi inko tou periods aate nahi hai.*
> She has grown up yet she is not mensurating.
> (A 16 years, non-school going girl)

One of the respondents from Kharvan said that when she had menses for the first time, she was in school and had got a stain. Boys ridiculed her. She went home and told her mother about the whole thing. She said even today she feels embarrassed about that incidence. Majority of the girls who did not know about menstruation before its onset told their friends about it when they had menses for the first time. It was observed that majority of the girls took help of an elder sister and friends to cope with the situation. Majority of girls agreed that a lack of a private place for girls to wash and change at school caused menstrual related absenteeism from school. The second-most prevalent reason was the fear of staining clothes followed by the discomfort and pain they had during this period.

Figure 8

Knowledge of Girls on Hygiene Required during Menses

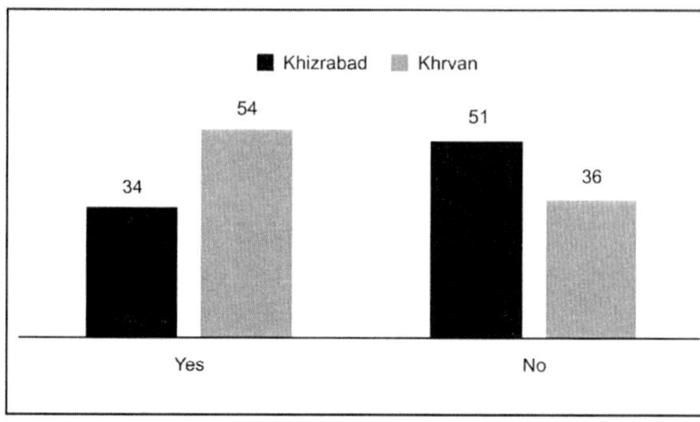

Menstrual Hygiene: A Matter of Concern

The hygiene related practices of girls during menstruation are important, as they affect their health by increasing their susceptibility to infections, especially infections of the urinary tract. Figure 8 indicates that the proportion of girls having knowledge about the hygiene required during menses was higher in Khizrabad, i.e. 61.4 per cent, than in Khavan (38.6%).

It was observed that girls who were aware about hygiene required during menses were fewer. School curriculum especially in rural areas did not include any information on menstruation; even at family level no such information was given to girls. It was found that only 10 girls from Kharvan cleaned their genitalia. The reason for not cleaning the external genitalia was lack of knowledge about menstrual hygiene and privacy. Non-availability of water was also one of the main reasons. It was noticed during field work that the proportion of girls having knowledge about hygiene required during menses was higher among Hindus. Only a few of Muslim girls were aware about menstrual hygiene. Muslim girls added that they did not share these issues with anyone except their sisters. The information they were provided in family related only to the use of cloth, practices of rituals and various restrictions during periods. Very little information was shared regarding the physiological process involved. The field experience shows that young girls grow up with limited knowledge of menstruation because their mothers and other women feel shy on discussing these issues with girls. School going girls reported that they did not change pads/cloths in school as it was difficult to manage their periods in school due to lack of water and proper wash rooms. Many of the girls said that they had to go home during lunch break to change the pad. Girls during focused group discussions added that there was no proper facility of toilets in their schools. Sometimes they had to miss their school because of periods.

One of the girls added:

> *Ma'am paani tou hota nahi bathroom mein.*
> There is no water in the washroom.
> (14-year-old girl from Khizrabad)

Some girls during FGDs from Kharvan added:

> Mam, there is no place in school where we can change and dispose menstrual waste. So we go back home to change cloth/pad.

Corroborating our findings, another study in West Bengal by Dasgupta and Sarkar (2006) had also revealed that menstrual hygiene was far from satisfactory among large proportion of adolescents while ignorance, false perceptions, unsafe practices regarding menstruation and reluctance of the mother to educate her child were quite common among them. Similar findings were reported in a study among female adolescents of Tehran suburbs; where only one-third of the study participants practised personal hygiene, such as taking a bath, and used hygienic materials during menstruation (Poureslami and Osati-Ashtiani 2002).

Recommendations

Menstruation is a very important natural phenomenon experienced by adolescent girls, which often becomes a nightmare for them for want of awareness as well as the difficulty in handling it. The whole experience gets aggravated due to the cultural restrictions and taboos resulting into various kinds of disabilities among the menstruating girls and women both within and outside home. Being a tabooed topic, one is not supposed to discuss the issue with anyone and the adolescent girls in rural set-up hesitate talking even to their own mothers. All these circumstances lead to serious issues relating to health and well-being of adolescent girls and women. Lack of toilets in schools, lack of access to sanitary napkins, coupled with numerous myths and superstitions surrounding menstruation leave the adolescent girls in a pathetic condition. Therefore, there is a need to create an environment where timely information is imparted to adolescent girls and adequate infrastructure is provided to them in schools so that they do not drop out and the period of menstruation does not prove to be a nightmarish experience for them. On the basis of our findings, the following recommendations are proposed:

- Girl students before the age of puberty be educated about the onset of menstruation, its significance and ways to cope with it.

- Provision may be made in the schools to create awareness among adolescent girls regarding menstrual hygiene and its significance by using participatory methods.
- Some basic sex education must be provided to children, both male and female, in schools by trained teachers.
- Provision of sanitary napkins in schools must be implemented with the broader objective of reproductive health.
- It should be mandatory for every school to have adequate toilet facilities, with the provision of water, dustbins, etc. to ensure the health, well-being and attendance of girls;

References

Bhartiya, Aru. 2013. 'Menstruation, Religion and Society'. *International Journal of Social Science and Humanity*, 3(6), 523–527.

Dasgupta, A. and Sarkar, M. 2008. 'Menstrual Hygiene: How Hygienic is the Adolescent Girl?'. *Indian Journal of Community* Medicine, 33(2), 77–80.

Ghattargi, C.H. and Deo, D.S. 2005. 'Perceptions and Practices Regarding Menstruation: A Comparative Study in Urban and Rural Adolescent Girls'. *Indian Journal of Community Medicine*, 30(1), January–March.

Goel and Kundan. 2001. 'Psycho-Social Behaviour of Urban Indian Adolescent Girls during Menstruation'. *Australian Medical Journal*, Vol. 4 (1).

Kamble, Rajashree R. 2001. *A Study to Assess the Knowledge and Practice of Menstruation and Menstrual Hygiene Among Girls Studying in Selected High Schools of Belgam City*. Dissertation, Rajiv Gandhi University of Health Sciences, Bangalore, Karnataka.

Kirk, J. and Sommer, M. 2006. *Menstruation and Body Awareness: Linking Girls' Health with Girls' Education*. Amsterdam: Royal Tropical Institute. http://www.schools.watsan.net/content/download/323/2726/(accessed on 1 September 2010).

Leslie, Julia. 1989. *The Perfect Wife*. Delhi: Oxford University Press.

Leslie, Julia. 1992. *Roles and Rituals for Hindu Women*. Rutherford: Dickinson University Press.

Mittal, L.N. 1992. 'Gender Bias in Nutrition'. *Social Welfare*, 39(2), 30–31 May.

Parwej, S., Kumar, R., Walia, I. and Aggarwal, A.K. 2005. 'Reproductive Health Education Intervention Trial'. *Journal of Pediatrics India*, 72(4), 287–291.

Poureslami, M. and Osati-Ashtiani, F. 2002. 'Attitudes of Female Adolescents About Dysmenorrhea and Menstrual Hygiene in Tehran Suburbs'. *Arch Iranian Med*, 5(4), 219–224.

Westermarck, Edward. 1926. *Ritual and Belief in Morocco*. Vols 1 and 2. London: Macmillan and Company Limited.

Williams, L.R. 1983. 'Beliefs and Attitudes of Young Girls Regarding Menstruation', in S. Golub (ed.), *Menarche: The Transition from Girl to Woman*. Lexington, MA: Lexington Books, pp. 139–147.

Section III

Handling Gender Violence: Policies and Statutes

16

Gender Implications of Interface between Personal and Customary Laws

The Meos of Mewat in Haryana

Abha Chauhan

The interface between personal and customary laws has acquired a new meaning in the changing context of the communities that are placed in the intermediary or fuzzy situation. The Meos of Mewat region in Haryana, constitute one such community. Known to be the believers of Islam for centuries now, they still practise the non-Islamic customary laws prevalent among their neighbouring Hindus. The Meos consider themselves to have been originated mainly from Rajput castes and are placed quite high in the local social hierarchy. Through different historical periods, the Meo identity defined by caste and religion remained intact with no contradiction perceived between the two despite several upheavals that the community faced. Meos continued to follow many customary practices regarding their marriage and kinship, quite different from those prescribed by Islam.

The events of communal violence at the wider level in the 1990s and the persistent role of organizations like the Tablighi Jama'at in the region created wedge between the Hindus and the Muslims to a certain extent. These organizations insisted upon the Meos to leave the customary practices totally and be true Muslim following their personal law. Such changes also strengthened the patriarchal forces that began to undermine Meo women's status in society. Today, customs and religion have coalesced to produce new configurations in Meo society having significant gender implications. On the one hand, the Meo's rules of inheritance follow customary law that deprives daughters of their share in their fathers' property, and on the other hand, efforts are made to impose personal laws that may deprive women of some of their traditional customary rights related to marriage and divorce without adequately making them gender just. The role of caste, community and religion becomes important as many decisions are taken by the traditional panchayats in consonance with the customary practices violating basic human and constitutional rights.

This paper is an attempt to understand the gender implications of the interface between customary and personal laws in Mewat district of Haryana to bring out gender injustice either in the name of custom or religion and suggest measures to work towards gender-just society. It is based on the secondary sources as well as on the primary methods of data collection. The census, gazetteers, monographs and reports were consulted to understand the historical and socio-economic background of the Meos. The primary data for this paper are drawn from the field-work done in the two villages of Mewat – Nagina of Nagina block and Ghata of Firozepur Jhirka block in different time periods from 2003–2005. From these villages, the cases of inter-regional marriages were also identified. Insights are also drawn from informal interviews and discussions with Meos, mainly women from different villages of Mewat district.

Mewat is the 20th district of the state of Haryana formed in April 2005 consisting of six blocks and 431 villages and 297 panchayats with a population of 10,89,406. As per 2011 Census, Mewat has a sex ratio of 907 females for every 1000 males, and a literacy rate of 54.08 per cent. The male literacy rate is 69.94 per cent and female literacy rate is 36.60 per cent (Mewat District: Census 2011 Data). This suggests a huge difference between male and female literacy rates. For the Meo women, it is much less going to as low as 2–5 per cent in different villages of Mewat.

Ninety-five per cent of the population of Mewat is rural and agriculture is the main occupation of the people along with allied and agro-based activities (Vohra et al. 2001). Earlier, a large number of them lived at the subsistence level remaining at the mercy of local *sahukars* (money-lenders) for a long time (Rathee 1971: 42–43). Today, nearly 80 per cent of the total land is cultivated and the agricultural and irrigation facilities as well as agricultural technology have improved considerably over the years. Sixty per cent of the families own land, most of them belonging to the category of 'small and middle peasants' (5–10 *bigha*) (Vohra et al. 2001).

Women, though not owners of land, do work for nearly 14–16 hours per day in agriculture and animal husbandry related activities as well as in household chores which also include arranging for water, fuel and fodder. Muslims form only 4.57 per cent of the total population of Haryana, while in the Mewat region, they are 20 per cent (Chowdhry 2007: 164). The bulk of Muslims here are the Meos.

Muslim Personal Law and Customary Laws with Special Reference to Meo Women

The Muslim tribes of Punjab and Haryana by virtue of Section 5, Punjab Law Act, 1872, were governed by customary law in regard to succession, special property of females, betrothal, marriage, divorce, adoption, guardianship, family relations, Wills and legacies, gifts, partitions or any other religious usages and institutions. The Meo, designated as a tribe during British rule, was governed by customary law, particularly in matters of heirs and adoption (Aggarawala 1989). The Punjab Law Act has been repealed by the Muslim

Personal Law (Shariat) Application Act of 1937 under which all the Muslims are to be governed by the Muslim law, except in those areas where customary law is still specifically or by necessary implication retained.

The Meos are ordinarily governed by the recognized principles of Hanafi Law in theory, but in practice they follow the principles of uncodified Hindu law of succession. In this law, women are largely excluded from property, which is transmitted only agnatically or in a male line. Records of customs, such as *Riwaz-i-am, Wajih-ul-urz,* manuals, gazetteers and text books are used for proving the claims of the alleged custom. In the absence of such proof, the courts take a judicial notice that the parties will ordinarily be governed by the Hanafi law.

The Meo widows, according to the custom and entries made in the settlement of *Wajih-ul-urz* and *Riwaz-i-am,* have a life interest and are entitled to succeed and to inherit the entire movable and immovable property left by the deceased husband. However, they are not allowed to inherit as sharers, but take a life estate in the whole property instead of the specific portion which they would inherit absolutely according to the Islamic Law. Thus, the Meo widows according to the custom inherit agricultural land and movable property from their husbands only as a life interest without power of alienation, except for necessity. Daughters do not have any claim to their fathers' immovable property although they have the right to maintenance in their families both before and after marriage. A daughter is excluded by the sons or by the widow or by the male kindred of the deceased, related through males, of any degree. She is entitled to receive *dahej* (dowry) at the time of her marriage, but beyond this she is not entitled to any share in her father's property (Shams 1983: 158–159).

Since the Meos follow customary law in matters of descent and succession as well as in other issues like residence, maintenance and adoption, women do not own immoveable property or have any ownership rights in it, though they have right to maintenance in their families, both natal and marital. Being a dominant agricultural community where possession of land has been an essential asset, its ownership has been restricted to the male line. This was facilitated by the feature of Meo social structure of village exogamy, which made it necessary for the daughters of the village to move out. Having a son or sons, therefore, so that the property could be passed to the next generation in a male line was considered to be almost essential.

In case of an absence of a son, the most preferred step was to adopt one and usually the adoption was made from patrilineal joint family or the same clan. However, usufruct rights have existed for women who play a very important role in Meo economy and maintenance rights are granted to women, which become more important in case they were widowed (Shams 152–156). Therefore, even though women do not have similar rights to property that are granted to them under the Muslim law, they have the right to maintenance even after divorce. The Meos have right to adoption unlike the Islamic law and like it also the provision of divorce, polygyny and remarriage which provide some rights to women as well.

Marriage and Divorce among Muslims and the Meos

Marriage among Meos is a civil contract based on *ijab-o-kabul* (offer and acceptance). The contract is not made by the bride and groom directly but in most cases indirectly by the parents and guardians depending upon the situation (Shams 1983: 69). It is a voidable contract which may be repudiated at the instance of the aggrieved party and whose consent is not freely obtained.

Marriage among Meos follows the rule of caste endogamy apart from clan and village exogamy. The bride's father or brother usually takes the initiative. The principal elements of marriage include the engagement or *sagai* accompanied by gift giving from the bride's side to the groom's side, the marriage proper which includes the ritual preparation of the bridal couple, the ritual service by the paternal aunt, the gift of the ceremonial presentation or *bhat* by the maternal uncle and other ceremonies in which the groom comes forward to take on *dan*, his future wife and the dowry. *Mehr* (amount given or promised to be given by the bridegroom to his bride) is usually given at the time of *nikah*.

The *nikah* takes place at the mosque in bride's village after the *barat* (marriage party) reaches the bride's house. The bride's father along with a *moulvi* and two or three local witnesses go to the mosque situated near the place where the *barat* (marriage party) is staying and the proceedings start. The marriage contracted without witnesses is regarded irregular though not void. Among the Meos generally no written record of the marriage is made and the presence of *baratis* at the time of *nikah* is sufficient proof of marriage having taken place. The male relatives usually communicate the consent of the girl (*ijab-o-kabul*) to the *kazi* in presence of the boy and other *baratis* who are also considered witness to the marriage. The *nikah* is considered to be the most important event and its performance even without any rituals and ceremonies is considered sufficient to validate the marriage and confer all the rights of a valid marriage (Shams 1983: 70). In actual practice, however, marriage among Meos is usually performed largely with customary practices and rituals.

The *milni* (meeting of relatives from both the sides) ceremony, the *salam* (official seeing and blessing of the bridegroom by the bride's female relatives) and the *bidai* (send off of the bride to her husband's house after marriage) are the other ceremonies that take place at bride's house. Some ceremonies take place at the groom's home once the *barat* reaches there like *muh dikhai* (seeing of bride's face by female relatives at the bridegroom's house) and *valema* (a feast once the marriage is understood to have been consummated). *Gauna* (final departure of bride) is subsequently performed. The ceremonies like *salam* and *valema* are Islamic while others are customary.

There are many rituals practiced by the Meos which are closer to the neighbouring Hindus. Some of these are secular in character while others are religious and still others can be placed in between the two. Those that are religious, like the ritual of *kuan pujan* (worshipping of well) have been given up, while the more secular ones like the *bhat* (gift given by maternal uncle to niece or nephew at the time of marriage) ceremony are still continuing. *Challa* or *gauna* is an important event in Meo woman's life which takes place when the bride leaves for her husband's house to stay there more or less permanently when she is mature enough to take up household responsibilities. This usually happens after the gap of first, third, fifth, seventh or ninth year of marriage depending upon the age of the girl at marriage. The data from the field show that even if the age of a girl at marriage is low, she starts her married life at the right age when she moves to her conjugal household. These days as the age at marriage of girls has increased, the *gauna* is performed immediately and is called *pher-patta*.

Some of those rituals which are in between have either been adopted partially or given up totally. For instance, *burqa* signifies Islamic element, but women do not observe it (though customarily they maintain *purdah* in their conjugal homes) as they have always learnt to treat men in their families, clans and villages as their consanguine relations whom they should not marry. They are either like sons, brothers or fathers to the girls of the same village. Here we see that structural principles of clan and village exogamy not only define the relationships and interactions among people, but also determine various cultural aspects. Therefore, any change in these cultural elements, which is not detrimental to their social structure, is tolerated and accepted, but whatever goes against it, is opposed quite staunchly.

The fact that many of these structural principles are not in contradiction to the Islamic injunctions, the Meos find no justification, not even the religious ones to change them. On the contrary, they have reasons to stick to their customary rules, which have been followed by their ancestors since generations. For instance, Islam has very few marriage prohibitions and prescriptions and allows marriage between close as well as the wider circle of blood and kin relations. But it does not say that one should not marry outside one's clan or village. It is also important to keep in mind that though several of the customary practices of the Meos were closer to neighbouring Hindu castes, many of these were not identical to the high castes, or more particularly to the Brahmanical ideology. The occurrence and acceptance of divorce or widow remarriage, particularly in the form of levirate among Meos also suggest their differences with Brahmanical ideology and practice.

Consequently, as the economic conditions of the Meos improved with better irrigation facilities in the region, they started leaving many of the features which were identified with the middle or lower groups and started adopting those of the higher castes like giving up of bride price or *ther* marriage and taking on the dowry form of marriage. Bride price in this region, like in many parts of India, has a negative connotation. It is understood to be a marriage transaction in which an amount is given by the bridegroom's side to the bride's side at marriage. Among the Meos, it is usually associated with the poor economic condition of the families and only those who cannot give dowry or cannot enter into exchange marriage go in for such kind of *ther* marriage. In recent years, due to the less number of girls because of skewed sex ratio, Meo men who are poor, aged, divorced, widower or not married for some reason get wives from outside Mewat by paying money. Though this is justified as *mehr,* people do not have a high esteem for such marriages and locally term these as *paise dekar ladki lana* (to get a bride by paying money).

Unlike bride price, dowry is transferred along with the bride to the bridegroom's house. It customarily refers to those gifts that are given by the parents and relatives of bride to be taken by her to her conjugal household at marriage. Though dowry existed among Meos earlier, but it increased significantly since the 1980s as the economic condition of the people improved. Dowry giving and taking incidents incurring exorbitant expenses with a lot of pomp and show have increased over the years, though one does not come across many cases of dowry harassment or dowry deaths. However, some people feel that they are not in tune with Islamic tenets and must be abandoned. Some people have indeed stopped taking *barat*, displaying dowry and avoiding any pomp and show. They call this *ladki ko ghar kar ke anna* (leaving the daughter at her husband's place). On the whole, however, the impact is little as marriage with dowry has status and taking a *barat* is a display of that, while it also gives social recognition and is an age-old custom.

What is significant is that incidence of cases in which people approach court to claim dowry in cases of divorce or separation has risen, increasing intra familial conflicts having significant implications for women. Cases are being filed under Section 498A Indian Penal Code (IPC) of Dowry Prohibition Act 1961, related to dowry harassment and cruelty. In a discussion during the fieldwork, an advocate of Ferozepur Jhirka tehsil of Mewat revealed that 40 per cent of the cases which come to the Judicial Court of the tehsil annually fall in the category of Section 498A. He said that most of the dowry related cases were made up either for extracting money or taking revenge by the girls' parents, some of which are false ones. Earlier, parents got money through bride price and since that is not prevalent anymore they see in the dowry laws an alternative for receiving money from the boy's parents. The advocate said that on the basis of his experience in talking to the couples it can be said that in half of the cases they were willing to compromise and stay together, but their parents were very adamant in ensuring that the divorce came through.

Mehr is an important and essential component of Muslim marriage. However, the concept of 'prompt' and 'deferred' *mehr* is not followed in Mewat and Meos follow customary dower or *mehr* (Shams 1983: 92). The customary dower of a woman is fixed with reference to the social position of her father's family and her own personal qualifications. Meos consider a marriage incomplete, imperfect and un-Islamic without fixing the amount of dower in the marriage. The usual practice among Meos is to give silver or gold ornaments as *mehr* to the bride at the time of *nikah* though earlier some coins were given. The amount which is generally preferred is 32-and-a-half *tola* of silver, corresponding to approximately 325 grams. However, it is reported that in the majority of the cases, the Meo women forgo their claim to dower either at the time of marriage or at the time of husband's death (Shams 1983: 94).

According to *Riwaz-i-am* of the Meos, there is no regular custom of dower, and the instances in which it is paid are very rare. They do not even know the exact amount of the legal dower and say it is 10 *dirham* which is ₹ 32 and some *annas*. In most cases, the woman remits the whole or any portion of the dower in favour of her husband or his heirs. The remission of dower is customary. It is made either at the time of first meeting or at the time of husband's death. In the former case the persuasion by the husband on account of one reason or the other; mainly the domestic circumstances forces the wife to withdraw. While in the latter, it is deemed by her as a moral, religious and spiritual duty towards her husband to forego the claim of her *mehr*. Also, as widow, a Meo woman is not allowed to retain property of her husband in lieu of her unpaid dower (Shams 1983: 94–95).

Nowadays, a gold *hansali* (necklace) is usually given as *mehr* during the ceremony of *nikah*. The giving of gold ornament as *mehr* is relatively a recent phenomenon. There has been a shift from the silver to the gold ornament showing the signs of prosperity and growth among the Meos. Besides this change, it is noticed that a much larger number of people, nearly 80 per cent now pay *mehr* at the time of marriage, and much smaller number either forgive or delay the payment. This was revealed by women in both villages, Nagina and Ghata, where nearly all young and middle-aged married women were seen wearing gold *hansali* which they said they got as *mehr* at the time of their marriage. Many times, *mehr* is paid late or at the time of divorce while in certain cases, the woman remits the whole or any portion of *mehr* in favour of her husband or his heirs. In Mewat, *mehr* is not seen exclusively as a woman's property, but of the whole family, especially at the time of crisis, divorce or death. Thus, in the real sense of the term, *mehr* is arbitrarily given, not contributing to woman's substantial property limiting her rights in the family and society.

It is further observed that in Mewat region during *nikah* (marriage) the consent of the girl is not taken directly but through her father in the village mosque. The marriages are not registered and, therefore, divorce becomes easy. Marriages are usually monogamous and divorce is not common, but there are some cases of polygamous marriages as well as divorce and remarriage. Remarriages also take place in the form of levirate and are usually taxing on women. The status of women who come from outside Mewat through marriage is not the same. Due to skewed sex ratio in Haryana and the indispensability of women in agricultural economy, getting brides from different states is not an unusual feature since the 1980s. It has only increased subsequently. As seen during the field visits, usually the older men, the divorcees, widowers or those who are poor, go in for such marriages.

Despite the precept of the Prophet that 'with Allah, the most detestable of all permitted things is divorce', in Muslim law of modern India, divorce is recognized and practiced in its uninhibited form. Divorce among Meos is a rare phenomenon but is increasing in the present times. The Meos belong to Hanafi School and, therefore, follow the method of *talaq-ul-biddat* in divorce cases. A Meo man can pronounce *talaq* either in the presence of the wife or in her absence. In the former case he can do so without giving any reason and by simply pronouncing *talaq* three times addressing his wife. In the latter case, *talaq* must be given in writing (*fargati*) in the presence of at least two male witnesses or a Meo Panchayat assembled for the purpose. Even according to the local custom, women cannot divorce their husbands, but when a married woman elopes with another man, the matter can be settled amicably on the payment of an amount called *jhagra* by the second husband to the first, decided by the panchayat. A marriage can also be dissolved by mutual consent of the parties before a council of village chiefs (Shams 1983: 100–104).

Therefore, some of the Meo men divorce their wives without assigning any reasonable justification, attributing their acts to be in consonance to the Muslim law. By making use of religion, divorce can be manipulated and is arbitrary in many cases. Men either do not give divorce or harass their wives by not freeing them to remarry or divorce them instantaneously if they see any harm coming to them. Sometimes the man denies that he was ever married, primarily in order to avoid paying maintenance to her, or just refuses to give divorce to the wife who desperately seeks it, and provides no maintenance to her.

In these circumstances, the application of Section 125 Criminal Procedure Code (Cr. P.C.), which entitles a divorced woman the right to maintenance becomes meaningless. Thus, even though divorced Muslim women do have right to maintenance in view of the Muslim (Protection of Rights on Divorced) Bill 1986, yet whatever rights are granted are hardly claimed. According to the Muslim Personal Law, after the divorce, the wife is free to contract a new marriage once the period of *iddat* is over and is entitled for maintenance for this period from her husband. But in reality, no maintenance is given either for this period or for other times if the divorce has not taken place. It is clear that the Meo follow a mix of customary and personal law in matters of divorce and in neither of the two systems, women have equal rights as men.

Caste and Kinship Principles among the Meos and their Gender Implications

The Meo is a patrilineal and patrilocal community where name, descent, succession and inheritance pass in the line of males. A person is a member of his agnatic group, while succession to office and inheritance of property follow the rule of patriliny, and residence is patrilocal. Meo is a caste category that follows the rule of caste endogamy. The Meos claim themselves to have originated from the Rajputs, currently placed in the category of Other Backward Classes (OBC).

According to *Riwaz-i-am* of the Meos, a man could not marry a woman of his own *gotra* or *pal*, a woman of the village his mother belonged to, a woman of the village his father belonged to, and a woman whose relation can be traced through consanguine kin. Besides this, a Meo could also not marry a woman from an inferior caste, a woman undergoing *iddat* and a woman of a different religion (Wilson 1882: 151). Caste endogamy is recognized as an important feature of Meo community like other Muslim castes of the region – the *Lohar, Nai, Mirasi* and the *Sakka.*

The first or primary marriage fixed and performed at the right age and within the caste and community between two never-married Meo woman and Meo man is the most preferred one and is usually arranged on the basis of the kinship rules of the Meos. There are, however, cases where Meo men, especially those divorced, old, disabled, poor and widowers marry non-Meo

Muslim women from outside Mewat, mainly for their labour and reproductive functions. For most of them it is the second or third marriage, though for some it may be the first, but it certainly happens due to their vulnerability being in extreme poverty. The women are brought from states like Andhra Pradesh, Orissa, West Bengal, Assam, Bihar and even Bangladesh. It was noticed during visits to the villages in Mewat that some of them were brought through *nikah* by paying *mehr* while others were either purchased or exchanged from alien places through different hands promoting trafficking in women as a form of violence against young girls. It is said that 'these women are not necessarily *wives* in the strict sense of the term and occupy unrecognized and indefinable status in contemporary Haryana' (Chowdhry 2007: 298).

Only Meo men have the right to perform such marriages which are acceptable and legitimized even when not given the same social status. The uncertainty of the caste and class backgrounds of the bought-in women always keeps their alliance under suspicion. Considering the shortage of girls in Haryana and adverse sex-ratio, the customary and essential rule of 'caste endogamy' is diluted for them. As these women are from very different regions and culture, and do not understand the local language as well as the customs with ease they face the stigma of secondary marriage which is not performed through proper procedures. They and their children find difficult to be incorporated in the Meo society. However, with time some strong women, like Goshia of Firozpur Namak in Nuh block are able to find place and have their say in the local setting.

The prevalence of this form of marriage stands recognized among the Meos, though it gained momentum during late nineteen eighties. During the fieldwork in 2005 in village Nagina, 20 cases of marriage of Meo men marrying non-Meo Muslim women were identified. Of these, 18 Meo men were from poor background and were illiterate or barely literate. Similarly in village Ghata, there were 14 such cases and all Meo men were illiterate and from poor labourer families.

Besides this, in recent years there is another change in the rule of 'caste endogamy' whereby educated male Meos have started marrying non-Meo educated Muslim women from outside Mewat. Such marriages are given good status and these women received respect. Village Ghasera in Nuh block had a Kashmiri Muslim girl, wife of ex-Sarpanch who was a post-graduate and commanded significant respect. Though there was very little influence of Islam on such unions, the fact that Islam does not oppose such marriages had worked as a catalyst in this area. Such alliances were justified in the name of religion, readily accepted by the people. Education and employment have particularly enhanced women's status, but one does not generally come across Meo educated women marrying outside Mewat and to non-Meo Muslim men. The Meos still think it is fine to get a Muslim woman from outside Mewat, but they do not give their girls as brides to the outside non-Meo men. Marriage outside the religion is unthinkable.

The Meos follow the rule of clan and sub-clan exogamy most rigidly. Earlier they followed the four-*gotra* rule (Meo man could not marry in his own *gotra*, and in that of his mother, paternal-grandmother and maternal grand-mother), but lately they restrict to one *gotra* rule, i.e. to their own *gotra* as reported by Pratap Aggarwal in his study of Meo village in Rajasthan (1971: 119). This was also found during the field work (2003–2005) among the Meos in the villages of Mewat district in Haryana.

The Meos are divided into a number of clans and the mythical founder ancestor of each clan is considered to be the descendant of Hindu divinity (Chauhan 2003: 75–79). This is evident from their oral tradition, which becomes visible during occasions like marriage. The details regarding the ancestors are kept updated by a Brahmin genealogist or the *Jagga* while the *Mirasi* performers sing in praise or *jas* of the clan ancestor during marriage and other ceremonies. There are several myths and rituals that appear in the oral tradition, which depict the theme of the descent of the Meo clans from Hindu Gods (Mayaram 1997).

The rule of '*gotra* exogamy', if transgressed, is met with the severest of punishment. In the early 1960s, the *maulvis* of Uttavar, Ruparka and Ghasera villages sponsored three cases of such marriages that were patrilineal parallel-cousin marriages or marriages between children of two brothers. The Meos not only boycotted these marriages, but also attacked the *maulvi* and butchered one of them (Sharma 1969: 183). During the visit to the town of Firozepur Jhirka in 2003–2004, it was told to the researcher by the local people that in 1998, a boy and a girl of two brothers were done to death in a village in Firozepur Jhirka block for the same reason. The incident had the support of the people in general and also of the Meo Panchayat. None of them openly opposed the decision as they considered the act on the part of the two young people as violation of the rule of *gotra* and village exogamy.

The rule of village exogamy is strictly followed in the context of *gotra* exogamy as usually every village has a dominant *gotra* and therefore *gotra* exogamy becomes village exogamy. The rule that a village is a wife-taker or a wife-giver village vis-à-vis another village is also always maintained. The 'wife-givers cannot be wife-takers' rule is applied both to the *gotra* as well as village making the relationship asymmetrical (Chauhan 2003: 78–79). Thus, the rules that compel women to leave their natal places and spend their lives in a totally different patriarchal setting with several restrictions curtail women's freedom to a considerable extent. Also, women are required to do lot of strenuous work in the agrarian economy of Mewat, both within and outside the households, in the fields and the forests. As told by many women, they are also called by their natal family members to work in the fields during peak harvesting season.

In Mewat, as much as in the whole of Haryana, the non-statutory traditional caste or *khap* panchayats act to maintain the customs and cultural practices of the people based upon concepts of *izzat* (honour), *bhaichara* (brotherhood), *biradari* (community), and village *aika* (unity). They continue to wield dictatorial power like an extra-judicial body (Chowdhry 2007: 13–14). This is seen today in Haryana, particularly in the case of young people who are defying the prescribed marriage and kinship principles, caste restrictions, sexual codes of conduct and taboos, and clan or *gotra* and village exogamy rules to get married. Their actions are taken as a direct attack on the honour of the family, caste and community and are met with much opposition and also violence leading to killing for saving honour on the basis of panchayat decisions (Chowdhry 2007: 10–11).

Among the Meos who follow *gotra* exogamy, the parallel-cousin marriage, i.e. between a man and woman of two brothers, is not possible. So for the Meos, *gotra* exogamy is not the only taboo but prohibitions extend to marriages between cousins. The Meos, unlike Muslims, as a rule, do not marry among cousins, either from the father's or the mother's side, i.e. patrilateral and matrilateral parallel cousin marriages as well as patrilateral and matrilateral cross-cousin marriages. All these four types of cousin marriage prohibitions have been prevalent among the Meos of Mewat till the late 1970s (Aggarwal 1976: 278) and the eighties (Jamous 1996: 189; 2003: 110). It can, therefore, be said that the rule among the Meos in forming marriage alliance is – no marriage between cousins-cross or parallel, even if they belong to different 'gotras'.

However, since the late 1980s and the early 1990s, a change has come about in the structural rule of the Meos, which is extremely significant. Meos have now accepted and started practicing what in anthropological parlance is referred to as matrilateral cross-cousin marriage, i.e. the marriage between a man and a daughter of his mother's brother. There are cases all over Mewat where a woman's own *fufi* (father's sister) is her mother-in-law. However, such cases are still very few. All these marriages took place in 1990s and in the beginning of the present century. Though people have accepted and started arranging such alliances, they are not a common feature. The patrilateral cross-cousin marriage, i.e. between a man and his paternal aunt's daughter, is not allowed as it would violate another kinship rule, i.e. the rule of the wife-givers and wife-takers as completely different sets of people. The kinship rule that wife-givers are not the wife-takers is still prevalent in Mewat among the Meos. It is said in local parlance *bhanji ko got bachayo, fufi gail bhatiji jaye* (i.e. maternal uncle's *gotra* is avoided [in marriage] and the girl goes with her paternal aunt).

The Meos vehemently oppose patrilateral parallel-cousin marriage, i.e. between the children of two brothers, even today, as it would violate the *gotra* exogamy rule. This is supported by the popular maxim among Meos, *goti so bhai baki ke sab asnai* (person of the same *gotra* is a brother, all others are potential lovers). Not a single case of intra-*gotra* marriage was witnessed in the field, nor does one hear of it in the normal situation. Some people do narrate stray incidents of this kind but in such cases either the people concerned met with severe punishment or had to leave the village and the area. The matrilateral parallel cousin marriage (marriage between children of two sisters), usually does not take place as other kinship rules come in the way.

Besides kinship, village is an important unit that determines marriage alliances among the Meos. Though Muslims, the Meos strictly follow the rule of village exogamy, which extends beyond family and lineage to the entire village cutting across caste and community lines. Till as late as 1960s, it was noticed (Aggarwal 1971: 118; Sharma 1969: 183) that among the Meos in Mewat, the father and son did not marry in the same village. Some later studies also supported this (Jamous 1996: 189; 2003: 115). Today, these rules have undergone change and there are no restrictions on a man from getting a wife from the same village from where his mother or grandmother came. The only restriction being that he cannot take wife from the same village as his own. Ninety per cent of the people in Mewat follow the rule of village exogamy strictly (Chauhan 2005: 539–553).

The kinship and village exogamy rules compel women to move out of their natal home and go further away from their natal kin. These rules are a reflection of caste and community characteristics wherein wife-givers and wife-takers rules apply and place women in an asymmetrical relationship, keeping them in a subordinate position. Nevertheless, given these structural constraints, women are able to articulate their agency and create new linkages and networks that situate them in a better state. Thus, it is not caste alone, but kinship rules and residence, that is, women's natal home (*pihar*) and a place of conjugal residence (*sasural*) from which women draw their identity. However, violations of these rules are not tolerated in rural Mewat region of Haryana and are enforced through community and village panchayats. The dimensions of village, caste, kinship rules and religion have to be maintained at any cost. Some changes are witnessed due to education and employment or even Islamization, but men's transgression of these rules is tolerated or co-opted to a larger extent and met with lesser degree of violence than those by women.

Islamization Process and Other Factors of Change in the Customary Laws of the Meos

Since the mid-1920s, the Meos began coming under the influence of Tablighi Jama'at (T.J.), though efforts were earlier made by several Sufis and *Ulemas* to Islamize them (Sikand 1999: 184–185). T.J. was a Muslim religious revival movement started in Mewat by Maulana Muhammad Ilyas of Nizamuddin, Delhi. Muhammad Ilyas developed a set of techniques of missionary or Tabligh work consisting of 'six points' – the *kalima* (the Islamic creed of confession that there is no God but Allah and Muhammad is his prophet); *namaz* (ritual prayer); *ilm* (knowledge of the basis of Islam); *zikr* (remembrance of God); *ikam-i-Muslim* (respect for other Muslims); *tashih-i-niyyat* (the purification of intention); and lastly *tafrigh-waqt* (devoting time for *Tabligh* work) (Sikand 2000: 342).

It was, however, observed that by the time of Ilyas death in 1944, a 'veritable new revolution' had taken place among the Meos, with several Islamic schools and mosques being set up in the region (Sikand 2000: 343). The movement became active after 1947 and the Meos were urged to abandon their Hindu customs and adopt Muslim practices. Under its influence, the Meos gave up many of the Hindu rituals, ceremonies and festivals. The activities of Tabligh increased day by day as large number of people opted for Jama'at. Besides the distant travels undertaken by males, the neighbourhood meetings for women were also held which served occasions for those committed to assemble and for others to be drawn. In this way Tabligh offered opportunity for women to congregate.

Incidents and happenings like efforts of Muslim leaders at the times of crisis to provide relief to the Meos and get their lands back, the bitter experience when many Meos were forced to flee to Pakistan, the ruthlessness at the hands of the rulers of Alwar and Bharapur States in Rajputana, forceful conversion of Meos to Hinduism through '*shuddhi* movement', strengthened the process of Islamization. The development in economic conditions whereby the land of Meos was given to the 'lower' castes and the Hindu and Sikh refugees from Pakistan gave further impetus to Islamic identity.

According to Aggarwal, this 'low' caste assertion irked the Meos immensely and they realized that 'it is futile to try to regain their high rank in the Hindu caste hierarchy'. Meos, therefore, thought that it was better for them to become complete Muslims (Aggarwal 1969). Besides this, the other external factors further provided added incentives to the Islamization, i.e. improved means of communication and spread of education through Mewat schools. Today, as noted by some scholars (Maheshwari 2003: 87–90), the best building in any village is the mosque for which money is coming from outside sources.

The changes are most visible in the recent years with an increase in the number of Madrassas and the number of children, particularly girls attending them. A large number of mosques have come up in the area as well. The people have become more religious in offering *namaz* (prayer), keeping *roza* (fast) and going for *haj* (pilgrimage). A large number of people now participate in Jama'at after going through some training. The T.J. adopted peaceful methods and preached people the tenets of Islam and asked them not to follow those that are un-Islamic. As Meos are rural and rustic people following several customary practices, the educated and more refined Meos ask them to leave the present social life of *jehalat* (backwardness) and become true Muslims (observation and personal communication).

Thus, one can discern certain reasons for Islamic revival in Mewat. These are – experiences of Meos during 1947 (Aggarwal 1984: 520), active role of T.J., decline of caste system and of Meos' position, improvement in communication and other developments (Aggarwal 1984: 520), forging links with the Muslim community outside Mewat and the growing animosity between the Hindu and Muslim communities (Jamous 1996: 194–195).

The dilemma for Meos today is to what extent they should adopt Islamic tenets and values within Meo social life and structure. Despite several changes, the co-existence of the customary and the personal laws has, indeed, been a challenge for the Meos in their everyday lives. Several contradictions crop up in day-to-day handling of affairs. For instance, on the one hand, the Meo women do not have inheritance rights in their parental property in Mewat even though the same is enshrined in the Muslim Personal law. On the other hand, personal law is used against women in cases of divorce or maintenance. In fact, whatever little freedom women have been granted in the customary law like divorce at women's initiation, is being taken away without adequately making provisions for gender-just laws.

However, many traditional rituals are still observed, the *barat* is taken with a large number of people, and dowry is given and displayed in many cases. Very few marriages in Mewat are registered and verbal contract is still the usual practice. In such situations, marriage may be proved directly by means of the oral testimony of the *baratis* and *maulvi* present at the marriage.

Since Meo is an agricultural community and women have to work in the fields, they do not wear *burqa,* and observe *purdah* only in their husband's house and village (village exogamy and also *gotra* exogamy make this possible). Also, people go for adoption and settlement of various problems through community or village panchayat. It was observed that the Meos organize their panchayat meetings which are huge congregations, occasionally, to take decisions regarding the adoption of Islamic features and leaving those of their customary life. For example, in a community panchayat held on 23 April 1999 at Firozepur Jhirka attended by a large number of Meos, 12 things were considered important and the Meos were asked to strictly adhere to them. Among these, some of the important ones included: the *nikah* should be simple and duly registered, dowry should not be displayed and the things given for the mosque should be given directly to the Imam, instead of taking *barat* with pomp and show only a few people should go and bring the bride after *rukhsat* (final departure), and the customary rituals must be given up and instead the Islamic ones must be adopted.

However, many of the initiatives taken by the Meo panchayat, which comprises only male members, are detrimental to the status youth and women. The panchayat calls for maintaining restrictions regarding choice in mate selection, meeting of the proposed couple before marriage and restricting the movement of girls to fairs and markets. The impact of Islamization is also reflected through the declining of a few customs like levirate and bride price. The Meos are no longer reluctant in giving up these traditional customs, observed for ages. Besides Islam, the impact of modern education, employment, development and empowerment through statutory panchayats is also visible. But the Meos still feel that the rules of kinship and marriage constitute the foundation of their social structure, providing safety and stability to them, and therefore changes in them are vehemently opposed. Any transgression to the age-old marriage and kinship rules are met with violence, even killings, for the sake of preserving honour as is happening all over Haryana.

As the Meos have established their Islamic identity, the need to follow Islamic laws more closely is felt even more. However, this is not possible yet since the personal law is used arbitrarily, particularly in the cases of divorce as mentioned earlier. There are many such areas of concern that call for an analysis as well as intervention in the sphere of civil laws or more accurately personal laws of the Muslims where initiatives are needed to be taken.

The development efforts are, however, required most urgently. The general attitude of neglect and antipathy by the government is not new in this area since the area is not politically very significant. The people of Mewat comprise a mere 3 per cent of the population of Haryana and do not count much in terms of votes. Absenteeism among employees is endemic and most of the employees consider working in Mewat as a punishment posting (*kalapani*) and their residences are outside the area (Maheshwari 2003: 86). Some people come to Mewat to make money, while some others start social work to earn money through development funds that flow to Mewat in huge amounts. Till the image of Mewat as 'backward area' and of the Meos as *jahil* or 'backwards' does not change, there is little hope for improvement. The government, the people and various non-governmental organizations have to play a strong and concrete role in at grassroots.

Conclusion and Policy Implications of the Study

This paper explores the interface between customary and the personal laws of a dominant Muslim community in Mewat district of Haryana, the Meos. By implication, the inferences drawn from its analysis and the conclusion reached are applied to the other Muslim communities in the region. From the field data and other sources, it may be inferred that both forms of laws and practices, the customary and the personal, have often produced dilemma for the Meos. Though they have not been able to reconcile with the two, the Meos have become conscious of their identity as Muslims and are making all efforts to strengthen it. The internal and external factors, identified in the study, have played an important role towards this.

Though Meos are proud Muslims and follow the basic tenets of Islam, in some of the areas, especially in matters of marriage, residence, inheritance and succession they still follow the customary rules. The Meo social structure with traditional caste and community panchayats and rural agrarian based economy is akin to the neighbouring Hindu communities. Women do not own immovable property like land and have limited inheritance rights. They largely marry within their caste and outside their village and *gotra*. Though to a lesser extent, but they still practice levirate form of marriage, divorce and remarriage. *Mehr* is an essential part of their marriage and dowry is widely prevalent. Like other Muslims, they do not marry their cousins and generally follow the rule of asymmetrical marriage alliance in reference to wife-givers and wife-takers.

Some significant changes have occurred due to Islamization process as noted above, and also due to the process of development and modernization. The Muslim women from outside Mewat are accepted and also sought after; matrilateral cross-cousin marriage is now followed, even though to a lesser extent and many Hindu rituals are being abandoned. The skewed sex ratio and increasing education and occupational diversification in Mewat have introduced new criteria of mate selection which have led to changes in the traditional criteria. Education, employment, dowry, besides family background and the personal characteristics of groom and the bride are being given increased importance. Both Islamization and modernization processes have thus resulted into a weakening of traditional and customary practices.

However, the adoption of personal law is partial and arbitrary. Attempts to impose the personal law on the Meos have created uncertainty and further confusion for the Meos. The unsatisfactory adoption of the Muslim personal law with continuance of customary law by the Meos has pushed them into a conundrum of newer forms of patriarchal inequality and social injustice. Problems are at the various levels: First, the Muslim women do not have inheritance rights like men, especially in land. Second, although the choices in marriage for both women and men are largely limited, yet it applies more to women as it is accepted that the Meo man can marry Muslim woman from outside Mewat, but the reverse is not permissible. Third, the Muslim personal law which itself is not codified deprives women of several rights, including the right to divorce. Fourth, no effort has been made by women's organizations, Non-Governmental Organization (NGOs) or leaders to bring about gender-sensitive changes in the cultural and social fabric in this region.

Fifth, the dominance of Meo panchayat reinforces patriarchy of both community and religion and works as an extra-judicial body and at times in undemocratic manner imposing even greater restrictions on women. Sixth, in Mewat, Muslims, women in particular, are making very little use of the Constitutional and other Statutory provisions in their favour. A few Sections like 498A of the Indian Penal Code are rather being misused due to lack of education and awareness as narrated by the Advocate in Ferozepur Jhirka court of Mewat district. It is important that proper and significant use of criminal laws is made to improve Muslim women's legal position. Thus, from one form of inequality, women in Mewat seem to have moved to another one.

The efforts made by Muslim women in the country have not reached Mewat and they must either be extended to Mewat or some such similar efforts are required by the people in this region. The 'All India Muslim Women's Law Board' (AIMWLB) was formed in January 2005 to adopt strategies for the protection and continued applicability of Muslim Personal Law in India, with a particular focus on women's issues like marriage, divorce, and other legal rights. As recent as in July 2013, Mumbai's first Sharia Court was set up to settle civil and marital disputes in the Muslim community. This is to be followed by setting up of similar courts in other cities. Started by Bharatiya Muslim Mahila Andolan (BMMA), the first all-women Sharia Court deals with various family issues, including marital discord, divorce as well as property related disputes (PTI, *The Hindu*, 5 October 2013).

The Bharatiya Muslim Mahila Andolan (BMMA) was inaugurated in January 2007 as a mass organization of Muslim women from across the country to become an alternative progressive voice of the community to raise their socio-political and economic concerns. It is an alternative progressive voice of the community fighting for the citizenship rights of the Muslims emanating from the Constitution. It continues to facilitate an organized initiative to bring about gender-just reforms in Muslim family law by moving towards the codification of Muslim law.

Both the AIMWPLB and BMMA worked to create a new model *nikahnama,* providing more egalitarian provisions concerning women's rights. The BMMA released a draft on 23 June 2014, 'Muslim Marriage and Divorce Act' recommending that polygamy be made illegal in Muslim Personal Law of India. NGOs such as *Awaaz-e-Niswan* in Mumbai are engaged in the advocacy of women's rights and the spread of legal awareness through Islamic scriptures and reinterpretations of the *Sharia*. Women like Bader Sayeed, D. Sharifa Khanam and Jaibunisha from Tamil Nadu are waging an unusual war within faith to free women from the practice of arbitrary triple *talaq* (divorce) and the vexatious issue of derisory alimony (De 2013).

Though most of the provisions of the Criminal Laws work for all people irrespective of community or religion, in certain cases as in Shah Bano case that saw the passing of *Muslim Women (Protection of Rights on Divorce) Act, 1986*, rights of divorced Muslim women for maintenance are severely curtailed. However, over the last two decades, resolute Muslim women and sympathizing judges have interpreted the 1986 law to hold that 'reasonable and fair' provision during the *iddat* had to be sufficient to maintain the divorced women for the rest of their lives.

Since 1980s, courts have continued to rule on questions of Islamic law and pick interpretations that have favoured women, with little opposition from Muslim leaders. This is a positive sign, but it is important that judiciary works independently and its decisions are not bogged down by the executive government functionary. More legal initiatives towards codification of Muslim personal laws like *Dissolution of Muslim Marriages Act, 1939* that provides Muslim women a statutory right to divorce within their religious boundaries are required. Gender-based crimes are a violation of human and constitutional rights of women irrespective of religion to which they belong, and must be seen and tackled in a similar manner.

Policy Implications

An important policy implication of this study is drawn from the relationship between the customary and the personal laws followed by the Meos of Mewat region in Haryana and elsewhere. This is relevant for many Muslim communities placed in a similar situation all over the country. K.S. Singh, in his well known and widely acclaimed project *People of India* (1992), identified 415 such communities that still follow customary laws of the region but are of different faiths. As these communities placed in fuzzy or intermediary situations are trying to establish their Islamic identity, the personal law amongst them, like among the Meos, is used arbitrarily.

It is important for the policy makers to take initiative towards codification of personal laws, in this case of Muslims (if it is not possible to take steps towards uniform civil code) so that they are not misused, particularly against Muslim women. In this direction, the effort made is miniscule as only a few Acts have been passed. Some initiatives as seen by AIMWPLB and BMMA are required to be taken by women's groups and other organizations to work towards making Muslim personal law gender just in Mewat region of Haryana.

Besides this, the application of criminal laws needs to be uniform without succumbing to the pressures of religious groups and people. They are important to protect women from violence and against violation of their fundamental rights, the most recent one being – The Protection of Women from Domestic Violence Act, 2005; and The Protection of Women against Sexual Harassment at Workplace (Prevention, Prohibition and Redressal) Act, 2013.

Law against crime of honour killings which is in the pipeline needs to be framed and implemented to curb the menace perpetrated by the diktats of panchayats or any such informal hierarchical organization that impinges upon individual democratic rights. Research studies and activism are required to see that this is materialized. It is important to put pressure on the government to amend IPC or initiate new law on 'Honour Killings'. Such incidence of such cases happens to be highest in Haryana including in the Mewat region.

The other policy implication deals with the process of development. Haryana is not identified as one of the priority states and many government projects and non-governmental efforts are not directed towards it. The state is not considered to be a backward state on the parameters of development though the sex ratio is adverse and the violence against women is rampant. Besides this, 'Mewat district' is the most backward districts of all.

It is, therefore, recommended that rather than the whole 'state', the development parameter must be of the 'district' level and the regions like Mewat with Muslim dominant population, must receive special attention. In light of the Sachar Committee Report, education of Muslim women should be on high priority. Greater involvement of NGOs is required for achieving this.

References

Aggarwal, P.C. 1969. 'Islamic Revivalism in Modern India: The Case of the Meos'. *Economic and Political Weekly*, IV(42), 18 October, 1677–1681.

——. 1971. *Caste, Religion and Power*. New Delhi: Shri Ram Centre for Industrial Relations.

——. 1973. 'Caste Hierarchy in a Meo Village of Rajasthan', in Imtiaz Ahmad (ed.), *Social Stratification Among Muslims in India*. Columbia: South Asia Books.

——. 1976. 'Kinship and Marriage Among the Meos of Rajasthan', in Imtiaz Ahmad (ed.), *Kinship and Marriage Among the Meos of Rajasthan*. Delhi: Manohar.

——. 1984. 'Meos', in Richard V. Weekes (ed.), *Muslim Peoples: A World Ethnography Survey*. Westport, Conn.: Greenwood, pp. 518–521.

Aggarawala, O.P. 1989. *A Digest of Customary Law*. Allahabad: The University Book Agency.

Ali, Hashim Amir. 1970. *The Meos of Mewat: Old Neighbours of New Delhi*. Delhi: Oxford and IBH.

Chauhan, Abha. 2003. 'Kinship Principles and the Pattern of Marriage Alliance: The Meos of Mewat'. *Sociological Bulletin*, 52(1), March, 71–90.

——. 2005. 'Village Exogamy and Kinship Rules Among the Meo of North India: A Gender Perspective'. *The Eastern Anthropologist*, 58(3–4), July–December, 539–553.

Chowdhry, Prem. 2007. *Contentious Marriages, Eloping Couples: Gender, Caste, and Patriarchy*. New Delhi: Oxford University Press.

De, Rohit. 2013. 'Personal Laws: A Reality Cheque'. *Frontline*, 6 September. http://www.frontline.in.

Diwan, Paras. 1978. *Customary Law of Punjab and Haryana*. Chandigarh: Publication Bureau, Panjab University.

Jamous, Raymond. 1996. 'The Meo as a Rajput Caste and a Muslim Community', in F.J. Fuller (ed.), *Caste Today*. New Delhi: Oxford University Press.

——. 2003. *Kinship and Rituals Among the Meo of Northern India: Locating Sibling Relationship*. New Delhi: Oxford University Press.

Maheshwari, Belu. 2003. 'The Meos of Mewat: Perspective on Ethnicity and Nation Building'. *Social Change*, 33(1), 81–91.

Mayaram, Shail. 1997. *Resisting Regimes: Myths, Memory and Shaping of a Muslim Identity*. Delhi: Oxford University Press.

Mewat District: Census 2011 Data. *Population Census 2011*. Haryana State.

PTI. 2013. 'All-Women Sharia Court Starts Functioning in Pune'. *The Hindu: Business Line*, 5 October. www.thehindubusinessline.com

Rathee, C.R. 1971. 'Meos of Mewat: An Economic Analysis'. *Mainstream Annual*, 10(1), 42–45.

Report of a Baseline Survey to Examine the Socio-economic Status of People in Mewat. Haryana Institute of Public Administration (HIPA), 2015, Gurgaon.

Shams, Shamsuddin. 1983. *Meos of Mewat: Their Customs and Law*. New Delhi: Deep and Deep Publications.

Sharma, S.L. 1969. 'Structural Continuity in the Face of Cultural Change'. *Eastern Anthropologist*, 2, May–August, 177–186.

Sikand, Yoginder. 1999. 'The Emergence of the Tablighi Jamaat Among the Meos of Mewat', in Noor Muhammad (ed.), *Indian Muslims: Precepts and Practices*. Jaipur: Rawat Publications.

——. 2000. 'The Tabliqhi Jamaat in Post-1947 Mewat'. *The Eastern Anthropologist*, 53(3–4), 341–350.

Singh, K.S. 1992. *People of India: Introduction*. Vol. I, National Series, New Delhi: Oxford University Press.

Vohra, M.B.L., Kaur, M. and Gulati, R. 2001. *A Report of a Baseline Survey to Examine the Socio-Economic Status of People in Mewat*. Gurgaon: HIPA.

Wilson, J. 1883. *Codes of Tribal Customs of Twenty-One Tribes*. Lahore. Superintendent of Government Printing Press.

17

Gendercide in the Womb!

Law Alone Won't Do

Geeta Joshi

Son Preference: An Eternal Wish

An epitome of courage, boldness, love, affection, and sacrifice, woman, in John Milton's words, is the best of all God's work. In old times her position was no less than a goddess. Addressed as Mother goddess in her various forms, she was known as the *ardhangini* (one half of her husband's body). No religious ceremony by the husband could bear fruit without her participation. Her honour was described as entwining and weaving heavenly roses in our earthly life (Frederich Schiller's poem: 'Honor to Woman'). She was seen as a source of salvation (as mentioned in Mahabharatha). But sadly, this same woman became the 'woe' of man. She was subjected to dishonour, disgrace, discrimination and degradation. During the course of history, she lost her honoured position from a relatively high status and nobility of the Vedic times. Evil customs and practices like *sati, purdah* system, child marriage, forced widowhood, dowry system, crept in the society, leading gradually to the decline in women's status inside and outside the home. Today, this fall in status has led to a socio-economic and religious-cultural deprivation of women. From the womb to tomb woman has become a victim of violence and deprivations and crime against her continues to rise and has, today undoubtedly, risen to alarming proportions. Indian women have suffered and are suffering discrimination in silence. Self-sacrifice and self-denial are their nobility and fortitude and yet they have been subjected to all inequities, indignities, inequality and discrimination (*Madhu Kishwar v. State of Bihar*, 1996). Women in India have been the victims of the patriarchal ideology that oppresses them. The birth of a son has been regarded very significant to satisfy worldly, religious and spiritual aspirations. Desirability of male child is accentuated by ritual considerations and reinforced by repressive Hindu religious diktats prejudicially embarked upon by staunch patriarchs against the women. The nebulous labyrinth of the remnants of repressive orthodox patriarchal values assign a devalued life and status to women laden with multifarious deprivations. This vicious circle of deprivations begins even prior to life of a female owing to pre-conception sex selection techniques that makes it possible not even to conceive a particular sex. In case conception does take place, she can be further denied and deprived of her right to be born through selective elimination of the female foetus. This cruel deprivation leads to the discrimination, harassment and exploitation of woman, irrespective of the country to which she belongs, unmindful of the religion which she professes and oblivious of the time frame in which she lives. Female foeticide is, perhaps, one of the worst forms of violence against women where a woman is denied her most basic and fundamental right, 'Right to Life'.

Female foeticide is the act of aborting a foetus because it is female. It is no exaggeration to call this gendercide. Women are missing in their millions – aborted, killed, neglected to death (*The Economist* 2010). All involved in female foeticide deliberately forget to realize that when the foetus of a girl child is destroyed, a woman of future is crucified. To put it differently, the present generation invites the sufferings on its own and also sows the seeds of suffering for the future generations, as in the ultimate, the sex ratio gets affected and leads to manifold social problems. Most people know China and northern India have unnaturally large number of boys. But few appreciate how bad the problem is, or that it is rising. The frequency of female foeticide is indirectly estimated from the observed high birth sex ratio that is the ratio of boys to girls at birth. The natural ratio is assumed to be between 103 and 107 and any number above it is considered as suggestive of female foeticide. In China the imbalance between the sexes was 108 boys to 100 girls for the generation born in the late 1980s; for the generation of the early 2000s, it was 124 to 100. In some Chinese provinces the ratio is an unprecedented 130 to 100. The destruction is worst in China but has spread far beyond. Other East Asian countries, including Taiwan and Singapore, former communist states in the western Balkans and the Caucasus, and even sections of America's population (Chinese and Japanese-Americans, for example): all these have distorted sex ratios. Gendercide exists in almost every continent. It affects rich and poor; educated and illiterate; Hindu, Muslim, Confucian and Christian alike (*The Economist* 2010).

According to the decennial Indian census, the sex ratio in the 0 to 6 age group in India has risen from 102.4 males per 100 females in 1961 to 104.1 in 1981, to 107.8 in 2001, to 108.8 in 2011 Census 2011). India is one of the several countries where higher human sex ratio is observed. This ratio is believed to be caused by female foeticide, an assumption that is the subject of considerable scholarly debate and continuing scientific studies.

The natural human sex ratio at birth was estimated, in a 2002 study, to be close to 106 boys to 100 girls. Human sex ratio at birth that is significantly different from 106 is generally considered to be correlated to the prevalence and scale of sex-selective abortion (http://en.wikipedia.org/wiki/Female_foeticide_in_India). India's child sex ratio was 108 according to its 2001 Census, and 109 according to its 2011 Census (Census 2011).

Table 1 presents the child sex ratio data for India's states and union territories, according to 2011 Census of India for population count in the 0–1 age group (Census 2011).

Table 1

State wise Sex Ratio (0–1 Age) 2011

State/UT	*Boys (0–1 age) 2011 Census*	*Girls (0–1 age) 2011 Census*	*Sex ratio (Boys per 100 girls)*
Andaman & Nicobar Islands	2,727	2,651	102.9
Andhra Pradesh	6,26,538	5,88,309	106.5
Arunachal Pradesh	11,799	11,430	103.2
Assam	2,80,888	2,67,962	104.8
Bihar	10,57,050	9,57,907	110.3
Chandigarh	8,283	7,449	111.2
Chhattisgarh	2,53,745	2,44,497	103.8
Dadra & Nagar Haveli	3,181	3,013	105.6
Daman & Diu	1,675	1,508	111.1
Delhi	1,35,801	1,18,896	114.2
Goa	9,868	9,171	107.6
Gujarat	5,10,124	4,50,743	113.2
Haryana	2,54,326	2,12,408	119.7
Himachal Pradesh	53,261	48,574	109.6
India	1,06,33,298	96,77,936	109.9
Jammu & Kashmir	1,54,761	1,20,551	128.4
Jharkhand	3,23,923	3,01,266	107.5
Karnataka	4,78,346	4,55,299	105.1
Kerala	2,43,852	2,38,489	102.2
Lakshadweep	593	522	114.0
Madhya Pradesh	7,33,148	6,77,139	108.3
Maharashtra	9,46,095	8,29,465	114.1
Manipur	22,852	21,326	107.2
Meghalaya	41,353	39,940	103.5
Mizoram	12,017	11,882	101.1
Nagaland	17,103	16,361	104.5
Odisha	3,45,960	3,24,949	106.5
Puducherry	9,089	8,900	102.1
Punjab	2,26,929	1,93,021	117.6
Rajasthan	7,22,108	6,35,198	113.7
Sikkim	3,905	3,744	104.3
Tamil Nadu	5,18,251	4,86,720	106.5
Tripura	28,650	27,625	103.7
Uttar Pradesh	18,44,947	16,55,612	111.4
Uttarakhand	92,117	80,649	114.2
West Bengal	6,58,033	6,24,760	105.0

The data suggest that 18 states/UTs had birth sex ratio higher than 107 implying excess males at birth and/or excess female mortalities after birth but before she reaches the age of one, 13 states/UT had normal child sex ratios in the 0–1 age group, and four states/UT had birth sex ratio less than 103 implying excess females at birth and/or excess male mortalities after birth but before he reaches the age of one. Discrimination between males and females got pronounced in the census of India 2011, depicting the evident deficit of females in zindian population. As per 2011 Census, in the age group of 0–6 years there are only 914 females for 1000 males where as the overall sex ratio is 940 females for 1000 males. The trend is worrisome as there is an increase in overall sex ratio on the one hand but a perceptible decrease in the child sex ratio on the other.

In India, female foeticide is taking place for various factors, viz., economic, socio-ritual, and technological.

Economic Factors

The female foeticide in the 21st century has a great deal to do with capitalist modernity. There are aspects of it lying behind these phenomena.

For rural households with landed property there is a clear inverse correlation between the income level and child sex ratio. It is especially evident in south India. Again there is gender-based wage level. For the same work, females are paid less remuneration. In most cases, women enter in the domestic non-paid services, which a patriarchal society gives, little or no value at all, so they are regarded as liability than assets.

Cultural politics of dowry in the Indian society are a major cause for this pernicious phenomenon. Since the turn of century the recorded dowry deaths are increasing. Nearly 7,000–8,000 brides are put to death per year due to the demand of dowry. Thousands of brides are committing suicides for dowry. Brides are thought as commodities and the pre-marriage and marriage has been described as 'consumption oriented reproductive journey'. For these economic reasons females are not desired. An old folk song from Uttar Pradesh may be quoted here in this context:

> '*Oh, God, I beg of you,*
> I touch your feet time and again,
> Next birth don't give me a daughter,
> Give me Hell instead ...'

Socio-Ritual Factors

Female foeticide has its roots in the social thinking which is fundamentally based on certain erroneous notions, ego-centric traditions, pervert perception of societal norms, and obsession with ideas which are totally individualistic sans the collective good (*Voluntary Health Association of Punjab v. Union of India 2013*). Women continue to remain vulnerable to the brutalities of the men in the form of physical, mental and sexual assaults and traumas in the patriarchal societal structure of India. Females are subjugated, condemned, and deprived in every sphere of life. Every parents of a girl child is at risk for their daughter in this patriarchal society for the mentioned causes. Again for the funeral ceremonies of the parents, presence of a son is a must. According to Manu, man cannot attain *moksha* (redemption) unless he has a son to light his funeral pyre. In old age the sons will care for them believably. These socio-rituals factors including illiteracy and orthodox society norms lead to crave for a male baby, discarding the females one after another.

Technological Factors

Female foeticide is the latest trend of long established gender bias. We are civilized with time and our killing female babies have also been civilized. The presence of low-cost technologies like ultrasound, have led to sex-based abortion of female foetuses, and an increasingly smaller percentage of girls born each year (Khatun and Islam 2011).

Population Policy

Indian family planning policies promote a two-child family and health workers say this often leads to abortion of female foetuses in efforts to have a 'complete family' with at least one son. Female foeticide or 'death before birth' has become a social hazard in the era of ultrasound technology and capitalist modernity.

Historically, in the absence of genetic testing, infanticide was the only inhumane option for discarding the female child. This heinous practice continues today in the southern parts of India where families cannot afford an illegal ultrasound test. People in Punjab, Haryana and other Western states can afford illegal test to determine the sex of the baby and discard it (*The Tribune* 2003).

It is unfortunate that for one reason or the other, the practice of female infanticide still prevails despite the fact that the gentle touch of a daughter and her voice has soothing effect on the parents [*CEHAT, MASUM and Sabu George (Petitioners) v/s Union of India & Others (Respondents) 2001*]. The situation remains grim even today. The traditional system of female infanticide whereby female baby was done away with after birth by poisoning or letting her choke on husk continues in a different form by taking advantage of advance medical techniques. However, the traditional system of killing the girl child after her birth has now given way to the more modern techniques of sex selection and female feticide. Knowing full well that it is immoral and unethical as well as it may amount to an offence foetus of a girl child is aborted by qualified and unqualified doctors or compounders.

Magnitude of the Problem

A study of the Census reports of 1991 and 2001 shows, that the situation has worsened in most parts of India. The Census 2001further reveals that the situation is far worse in respect of girl child population in the age group of 0–6, particularly in the affluent areas of Punjab (793 girls to 1000 boys), Haryana (820), Chandigarh (845), Himachal Pradesh (897) and Delhi (865).

Notorious for female foeticide, Haryana ranks a poor 31 among Indian States and Union Territories on sex ratio with just 877 women per 1,000 men. Though no concrete figures are available on the exact number of female foeticide cases, an estimated 37,000 girls are killed every year in the state before they are born. The fact that Haryana, with just 2.2 per cent of the total children in India, accounts for 4 per cent of the female foeticide cases speaks volumes about the extent of problem. Though the law prohibits sex-determination and illegal termination of pregnancy, social workers argue that the situation on the ground has not changed much over the years. 'Despite all the laws, the implementation is poor. It is only in certain cases where the senior officials take keen interest in checking the menace that the situation has shown some improvement. Like in Jhajjar, the Deputy Commissioner concerned was strict on illegal sex-determination and took action against even some politically well-connected doctors engaged in the malpractice. But it is rare,' said 42-year-old Vinod Bala, the woman president of Sarvkhap Panchayat (*The Hindu* 2014).

The Anti-Foeticide Law

Realizing the grave implications arising out of the misuse of the prenatal diagnostic techniques, the Parliament intended to regulate its use only for certain medical purposes. The government understood that abuse of techniques for determination of sex of the foetus leading to female feticide is discriminatory against the female sex and also affects the dignity and status of women. With the above objectives, the Parliament in its wisdom passed the Pre-Natal Diagnostic Techniques (Regulation and Prevention of Misuse) Act 1994; which came into force from 01.01.1996).

Pre-Natal Diagnostic Techniques (Regulation and Prevention of Misuse) Act, 1994

Hi-tech Sexism (Sen 2001) with the advent of the sophisticated technology of sex-determination in India in 1974 (All India Institute of Medical Sciences, New Delhi introduced amniocentesis to detect foetal abnormalities) has reverberated the patriarchal values.

This Act provides for the regulation of the use of pre-natal diagnostic techniques for the purpose of detecting genetic or metabolic disorders or chromosomal abnormalities or certain congenital malformations or sex-linked disorders and for the prevention of the misuse of such techniques for the purpose of pre-natal sex determination leading to female feticide. The legislation seeks to achieve the following objectives:

- Prohibition of the misuse of pre-natal diagnostic techniques for determination of sex foetus, leading to female foeticide.
- Prohibition of advertisement of the techniques for detection or determination of sex.
- Regulation of the use of techniques only for the specific purpose of detecting genetic abnormalities or disorders.
- Permission to use such techniques only under certain conditions by the registered institution.
- Punishment for violation of the provisions of the Act.
- To provide deterrent punishment to stop such inhuman acts of female foeticide.

An Infringement of Our Fundamental Right: Right to Life

Our Constitution provides for the Right to Equality under Article 14 and Right to Live with dignity under Article 21. Sex – detection tests violate both these rights. Right to life is a well-established right and is recognized by various international instruments. Globally, constitutions recognize the sanctity of life, yet have failed to adequately protect the life of foetus. Judicial pronouncements are also not conclusive and vary in different jurisdictions. In India the right to life is guaranteed to every person under the Constitution of India. The concept of personhood complicates the position of legal status of foetus. As complex issues arise regarding the personhood of the foetus, our courts have often avoided to answer this baffling question relating to it. There is a desperate need for the courts to come clear on this vital issue and recognize the rights of the foetus (Prasanth 2005). Article 21 of the Constitution guarantees the life and liberty of every person (Article 21 of Indian Constitution). But it is doubtful if this would include the life of foetus as the meaning is restricted by the use of the word person. The Indian Constitution has recognized the right to life under Article 21 as also recognized in several cases (*Meneka Gandhi v. Union of India*, AIR 1978 SC 597). But this is hardly available to the unwanted girl child.

Role of Judiciary

The Supreme Court of India, as early as in 2001 (*Centre for Enquiry into Health and Allied Themes v. Union of India*), had noticed the misuse of the Act and gave various directions for its proper implementation. In 2003, on noticing the non-compliance of its earlier directions (*Centre for Enquiry into Health and Allied Themes v. Union of India 2003*) this Court gave various other directions. Having noticed that those directions as well as the provisions of the Act are not being properly implemented by the various states and Union Territories, the apex Court passed an order on 8.1.2013 directing personal appearance of the Health Secretaries of the States of Punjab, Haryana, NCT Delhi, Rajasthan, Uttar Pradesh, Bihar and Maharashtra. This was with the purpose to examine the steps taken by them for the proper and effective implementation of the provisions of the Act as well as the various directions issued by this Court.

It was noticed by the court that even though the Union of India had constituted the Central Supervisory Board and most of the states and Union Territories had constituted State Supervisory Boards, Appropriate Authorities, Advisory Committees, etc. under the Act, their functioning was far from satisfactory. The court observed that there was no effective supervision or any follow-up action so as to achieve the object and purpose of the Act. More alarming was the mushrooming of various sonography centres, genetic clinics, genetic counselling centres, genetic laboratories, ultrasonic clinics, and imaging centres in almost all parts of the country. The court called for more vigil and attention by the authorities under the Act. But, unfortunately, the Act is lacking in the proper monitoring and supervision of the functioning by the authorities. There is no way by which any misusing of the pre-natal diagnostic techniques (for determination of sex of foetus) leading to foeticide could be detected. Seldom, the ultrasound machines used for such sex determination in violation of the provisions of the Act are seized and, even if seized, they are being released to the violators of the law only to repeat the crime. Hardly few cases end in conviction. Cases booked under the Act are pending disposal for several years in many Courts in the country and nobody takes any interest in their disposal. Rarely, those cases end in conviction and sentences, a fact well known to the violators of law. Many of the ultra-sonography clinics seldom maintain any record as per rules and, in respect of the pregnant women, no records are kept for their treatment and the provisions of the Act and the Rules are being violated with impunity.

Enforcement of PNDT Act in Haryana and Punjab

As per statistics available, there are 1,347 registered ultrasound centres available in Punjab and 42 in Haryana which are supposedly inspected by so-called sensitised appropriate authorities. The level of lukewarm commitments is visible through the 654 suspensions and 123 court cases registered since the inception of Act in Punjab and 49 court cases filed in Haryana for violations.

There is a landmark case of *Voluntary Health Association of Punjab v. Union of India and Others* [Writ Petition (Civil) No. 349 of 2006] in which Justice J. Radhakrishanan had given detailed instructions to the supervisory boards for implementation of the PNDT Act 1994 to get effective results but there is a lot which is yet to see the light of day effectively in its earnestness. The court had given an advisory regarding awareness campaigning in this order: 'A cosmetic awareness campaign would never subserve the purpose. The authorities of the Government, the Non-Governmental Organisations and other volunteers are required to remember that there has to be awareness camps which are really effective. The people involved with the same must take it up as a service, a crusade. It must engulf the concept of social vigilance with an analytical mind and radiate into the marrows of the society' (*Voluntary Health Association of Punjab v. Union of India and Others 2006*). There is no doubt that the states have been paying lip service and the declining ratio of girl child is the proof enough of their lackadaisical approach. There is an urgent requirement of proactive coordination between the government machinery judiciary, media, civil society and political bodies to take measures for periodical stock taking of progress made and mid-course corrections to steer the campaign with accountability at all levels.

There is a need to strengthen the provisions of the Act and make the sex selection practices, a high-risk business, instead of a low-risk business. Under the Act, violation of the provisions is punishable with imprisonment and fine, whereas under Rule 11(2), if the appropriate authority seizes any ultrasound machine or other equipment capable of detecting sex of foetus, which is used by an organization not registered under the Act, the machine of the organization is released only on payment of penalty equal to five times the registration fee. The Rule takes away the rigour of the punishment provisions under the Act. This rule is required to be deleted; otherwise, it will be misused by those who are indulging in heinous practice of sex determination of foetus.

Concluding Remarks

Female foeticide is a malaise and law alone cannot deal with it single handedly. The solution lies in soul searching and self-regulation. The PC and PNDT Act can, however, be an enabling tool for achieving social transformation. The nation needs to raise the value of girls. Female education must be encouraged; laws and customs that prevent daughters inheriting property must be abolished; examples of hospitals and clinics with impossible sex ratios should be set; more women should be engaged in public life – using everything from television newsreaders to women traffic police. Mao Zedong said 'women hold up half the sky.' The world needs to be awakened. Gendercide has to be prevented at all costs. Otherwise this murder in the womb will have the sky crashing down!

References

CEHAT, MASUM and Sabu George (Petitioners) v/s Union of India and Others (Respondents). In the Supreme Court of India, Civil Original Jurisdiction, Writ Petition (Civil) No. 301 of 2000 (4 May 2001), 5 SCC.

Centre for Enquiry into Health and Allied Themes v. Union of India (2001) 5 SCC 577.

Centre for Enquiry into Health and Allied Themes v. Union of India (2003) 8 SCC 398.

Deepak Mishra, J. 2006. Voluntary Health Association of Punjab v. Union of India and Others [Writ Petition (Civil) No. 349 of 2006].

http://en.wikipedia.org/wiki/female_foeticide_in_india.

http://www.censusindia.gov.in/ad_campaign/press/datahighlights.pdf.

India at Glance: Population Census. 2011. http://www.census2011.co.in/p/ glance.php

Khatun, Samsunnessa and Islam, Aznarul. 2011. 'Death Before Birth: A Study on Female Foeticide in India'. *MS ACADEMIC*, 1(3), 94–99.

Madhu Kishwar v. State of Bihar, AIR 1996 5 SCC 125.

Maneka Gandhi v. Union of India, AIR 1978 SC 597.

'No Relief from Female Foeticide in Haryana'. *The Hindu*, 9 March 2014.

Population Enumeration Data (Final Population). 2011. Census of India. Ministry of Home Affairs, Government of India. http://www. censusindia.gov.in/(wantn13cutkqwlvryp3dmi45)/2011census/population_enumeration.aspx

Prasanth, S.J. 2005. 'Right to Life of Foetus'. *AIR*, 92(1098), June.

Sen, Amartya. 2001. 'The Many Faces of Gender Inequality'. *Frontline*, 18(22), October 27–November 9, 4–14.

The Tribune. Chandigarh, September 2003.

'The War on Baby Girls: Gendercide'. *The Economist*, 4 March 2010. http://www.economist.com/node/15606229.

Voluntary Health Association of Punjab v. Union of India (2013) 4 SCC 1.

18

Assessing Land Acquisition Law from Gender Perspective

Sukhwant S. Sidhu

This paper attempts to highlight the gender concerns in the acquisition of land. The social impacts of these acquisitions are gendered, i.e. different on men and women. The enactment of Right to Fair Compensation and Transparency in Land Acquisition Rehabilitation and Resettlement Act, 2013 (RFCTLAR & R. Act 2013) has made it mandatory to carry out Social Impact Assessment (SIA) of every developmental project. SIA is a process of monitoring, evaluating and managing the intended and unintended consequences of planned interventions on the stakeholders. An endeavour has been made to offer some suggestions that are based on the social impacts experienced by the Project Affected Population (PAP) keeping in mind the gender perspectives and emphasizing the role of the women and their coping mechanisms in such planned interventions.

The paper is divided into three sections. The first section is related with the history of Land Acquisition Laws in India. The earlier regulations did not take into account the Social Impacts on PAP's. The concern for gender was out of question. In the second part an attempt has been made to understand the gender concerns in the RFCTLAR & R. Act, 2013 and the subsequent role of Social Impact Assessment as a technique to minimize the unintended consequences of land acquisitions on stakeholders and the third segment highlights social impacts of land acquisition especially on women of village Jheur Heri, district SAS Nagar, Punjab.

The idea of development has guided the policies of many countries of the world. As a major ideology, development has shaped the purpose and efforts of states and of public as well as organizers (Sutton 1989, quoted by Guha). It is a multi-coloured phenomenon painted by various forces such as socio-economic, political and cultural. The economic force is the most powerful one which influences the other and is influenced by them (Sahoo 2004). Development requires spatial and social mobility of population both of which provide contexts for racial, social and cultural discriminations across and within nations. It produces stress upon human beings, the subjects of development (Oommen 1992). An infrastructural development is generally followed by displacement of population. The rural is to be displaced by the urban, agriculture by industry, low, simple or traditional technology by high, complex or modern technology. The estimates regarding displacement vary vastly. According to one such estimate every year, over five lakh people are displaced by infrastructure construction, including hydro-electric projects, mines, industrial complexes, housing colonies and thermal and nuclear power plants (Kothari 1997, quoted by Mehta). Let us now see the Laws relating to Acquisition of Land in post-Independence India.

Land Acquisition Laws in India

The acquisition of land by the government agencies is carried out throughout the world and India is no exception. Land acquisition can be defined as the action of the government whereby it acquires land from its owners in order to pursue certain public purpose or for any company. This acquisition may be against the will of the owners but compensation is, however, paid to the owners or persons interested in the land. This can be distinguished from an outright purchase of land from the market. Land acquisitions by the government generally are compulsory in nature, not paying heed to the owner's unwillingness to part with the land (George 2009).

The trail of the acquisition of land goes back to the early 19th century when the British enacted various Acts in the then Presidency towns and later expanding across the country to facilitate the land acquisition process for the construction of roads, canals and other 'public purposes' with compensation to be determined by specifically appointed arbitrators (Tenth Report 1958). The Land Acquisition Act of 1894 was supposed to bring some sort of uniformity in the acquisition process. It meant to amend the law for acquisition of private land for public purpose and private enterprises and to determine the amount of compensation to be made to the Project Affected Population (PAP).

The Tenth Report of the Law Commission mentions that in order to justify the land acquisitions the administration quote these two maxims, i.e. *salus populi est suprema lex* (regard for public welfare is the highest law) and *necessitas publica major est quam private* public necessity is greater than private necessity (*Tenth Report* 1958). After Independence in 1947 the Government of India adopted the 1894 Land Acquisition Act and it was rendered a concurrent list subject and hence both the Centre and the states were empowered to make laws on requisition and acquisition of property. Under Jawaharlal Nehru's model of modernization, new cities of Jamshedpur, Chandigarh, etc. were constructed and acquisition of land took place. India pursued the policy of development along with the maintenance of social equity. A number of laws and amendments after Independence such as abolition of Zamindari system, town planning, land reforms, slum clearance, resettlement of refugees, etc. have been enacted (Wahi 2013).

It was repeatedly felt by the government that the Right to Property was a roadblock in land acquisition as it was a fundamental right. In 1978, the government through the 44th Amendment to the Constitution abolished the right to property as a fundamental right but it declared that it would remain a legal right. This Act was amended by Act 68 of 1984, which came into force with effect from 24 September 1984. The effect of this amendment is that in case of breach of this Right, an aggrieved person may approach the High Court (under Article 226) and not the Supreme Court (under Article 32), an option that was available earlier that ensured speedy remedy (Singhal 1995).

There has been increase in the public outrage regarding the land acquisitions especially for the reward of fair compensation, valuation of land, definition of 'public purpose' and other issues since Independence. There has been massive displacement of traditional communities, tribal people and environmental damage that has resulted in lot of conflicts throughout India. The Land Acquisition Act, 1894, in spite of amendments, has been draconian because the government does not account for the emotions, sentiments of the displaced (George 2009).

The government has amended the Act in 1984 and notified the National Rehabilitation and Resettlement Policy 2007 (in October 2007), and followed that up with the Rehabilitation and Resettlement Bill 2007 and the Land Acquisition (Amendment) Bill 2007. It was amended and represented in the Union Cabinet which cleared it in December 2012 (Iyer 2009). The Bill after being discussed in both the houses got the assent of the President and The Right to Fair Compensation in Land Acquisition, Rehabilitation and Resettlement Act came into force on 1 January 2014.

The Right to Fair Compensation in Land Acquisition, Rehabilitation and Resettlement Act, 2013 (RFCTLAR & R. Act, 2013) and Social Impact Assessment

The Government of India, succumbing to the pressure and outrage of the citizens and complying with the guidelines of the international funding agencies, made it mandatory to carry out Social Impact Assessment (SIA) of every developmental project involving land acquisition.

Social Impact Assessment originated in USA as a part of the 1969 National Environment Policy Act (NEPA). The Environmental Impact Assessment (EIA) became an imperative component of environmental planning and decision-making and has enjoyed a remarkable rise to the prominence in academic and applied social science literature. SIA has been evolving from its modest beginnings in the early 1970s when few guidelines were available, and a Social Impact Assessment was generally carried out as an afterthought to Environmental Impact Assessment (Barrow 2000).

The planners, decision-makers and the government across the globe have recognized a need for better understanding of the social consequences of projects, programmes and policies. In response to this need, a group of social scientists formed the Inter-Organizational Committee on Guidelines and Principles for Social Impact Assessment (ICGPSIA), with the purpose of outlining a set of guidelines and principles that will assist state agencies, private parties and the stakeholders in fulfilling their obligations under NEPA. The term 'Social Impact Assessment' was first used when the Department of the Interior of the United States was preparing the report on Environmental Impact Assessment for the Trans-Alaska pipeline in the early 1970s (ICGPSIA 2003).

The International Association for Impact Assessment (IAIA) defines Social Impact Assessment as 'a process of analyzing, monitoring and managing the intended and unintended social consequences, both positive and negative, of planned interventions (Policies, Programs, Plans, Projects) and any social change processes invoked by those interventions. Its primary purpose is to bring about a more sustainable and equitable biophysical and human environment' (ICGPSIA 1994).

This definition of IAIA not only incorporates the concept of a priori assessment of social impacts, but also includes post facto components. The terms monitoring and managing are crucial in dealing with the social effects of development. There is a lot of difference between preparing a technical report regarding the future social impacts on one side and initiating a process to manage and minimize the social impacts of a developmental project.

The 'International Guidelines and Principles for Social Impact Assessment' prepared by the IAIA will act as a guiding source in this study. The important features of Social Impact Assessment are as follows:

1. Social impact assessment should be carried out to bring about a more socio-culturally and economically sustainable and equitable environment. It promotes community development and empowerment, enhances capacity building and develops social capital.
2. The major concern of SIA is a proactive stance to development and better outcomes of development and not just the amelioration of negative and unintended outcomes.
3. SIA contributes directly to the process of adaptive management of policies, programmes and projects.
4. SIA utilizes participatory processes and builds on local knowledge to analyse the concerns of all the stakeholders. The stakeholders are involved in the assessment of social impacts, analysis of all the available alternatives, and monitoring the development of planned intervention.
5. SIA recognizes that social, economic and biophysical impacts are complex in nature and are intrinsically interconnected. Any alteration in one domain may lead to subsequent change in the other domains.
6. The analysis of the impacts of past activities should be done for the growth of the discipline of SIA. It must be reflexive and evaluative of its theoretical bases and of its practice.
7. SIA is typically applied to planned interventions; the techniques of SIA can also be used to consider the social impacts that derive from other types of events, such as disasters, demographic change and epidemics (ICGPSIA 1994).

SIA is best understood as an umbrella or overarching framework that embodies the evaluation of all impacts on humans and on all the ways in which people and communities interact with their socio-cultural, economic and biophysical surroundings. The social impacts of the developmental projects should be the most important consideration of any government. Adverse social impacts can decrease the intended benefits of a proposal, and can even threaten its viability. In such cases, a social impact assessment is carried out along with EIA. This approach is used to analyse the impacts of a proposal on individuals and communities, and to lessen the adverse effects and enhance the positive effects. It also provides a framework to manage social change.

Social impacts are the consequences faced by people of any proposed action that changes the way they live, work, relate to one another, organize themselves and function as individuals and members of society. It includes social-psychological changes, for example to people's values, attitudes and perceptions of themselves and their community and environment. Indeed, some SIA practitioners consider social impacts to be only 'as experienced' (e.g. stress, disruption, hunger) and differentiate these from the causal processes, e.g. over-crowding, infrastructure pressure, poverty, etc. (ICGPSIA 2003).

F. Vanclay (2002) opines that social impacts include all human impacts – 'aesthetic, archaeological and heritage, community, cultural, demographic, development, economic and fiscal, gender, health, indigenous rights, infrastructure, institutional, political (human rights, governance, democratization, etc.) poverty-related, psychological, resource issues (access and ownership of resources), the impacts of tourism and other impacts on societies'. The social impacts may be positive or negative or both. These bring about changes in income, standard of living, employment patterns, sources of livelihood, place of residence, environment, political systems, health and well-being, perception, attitude and aspirations.

With the increase in the number of developmental projects in the developing countries more and more people are being displaced affecting their social milieu in more than one ways. Social impacts are impacts of developmental interventions on human settlements. Such impacts not only need to be identified and measured but also need to be managed in such a way that the positive effects are magnified and negative ones minimized.

Types of Social Impact

The assessment of impacts can be carried out effectively only if one has proper understanding of the type of social impacts. These are multi-dimensional in nature and type, duration and intensity of these impacts depend upon the different phases of the project. These impacts are gendered, i.e. the men and women are differently affected during the course and after the completion of the project. The different types of them can be listed as under:

1. temporal impact
2. direct and indirect impact
3. differential impact
4. cumulative impact

Temporal Impact

As the name suggests these impacts are related with the time and life cycle of the project. ICGPSIA (2003) has delineated four major stages through which an infrastructural development project passes. Each phase has its own relevance and requires different types of consideration for the impact assessment. These are the pre-construction phase, construction phase, post-construction phase, and de-commissioning phase.

Pre-Construction or Planning Phase

This phase begins with the proposal of private party or government to pursue a particular project. There are all sorts of speculations enhanced by the media coverage. The social, economic, political, cultural systems are affected immediately after the announcement of a project (Walker et al. 2000).

The initial impacts are felt by the common people that are psychological and are related with the perception. People are eager to gather information about the nature and magnitude of the project. The speculations run very high and people try to gain financially by spreading rumours related to the location of the project. The politicians of the region generally become active and try to lobby with the project developers and even the government to meet their political ends (Burdge and Johnson 1994). The women especially in the rural areas are kept in dark during this period because of the patriarchal and patrilineal nature of the society.

These are future oriented impacts generally related with the perception, displacement, compensation, rehabilitation in the anticipation of development and change (Walker et al. 2000).

Construction Phase

This phase involves the dislocation of the people. There may be reluctant and protesting residents who are not willing to part with their land. The land is cleared and the construction work is initiated. There is a large influx of vehicles and migrant construction workforce at the site. There may be health concerns for the people living in proximity to the construction site (Burdge and Johnson 1994). The commuters may also face the problem of traffic jams. There may be pollution caused by the machines or the mixers used for mixing sand, gravel, cement. The contractors have to deal with onlookers who are curious to gather information about the development. The impacts of this stage may have far-reaching consequences from displacement, change in occupation, loss of traditional source of livelihood, change of neighbourhood and geographically severing of old social ties. The movement of local women is restricted as there is influx of construction workers.

Post-Construction Phase or Operation Phase

It is also called the operation phase or the phase of development during which the positives are realized. The community stabilizes, there are benefits of new infrastructure, wealth generation, employment opportunities and new patterns of social organization emerge (ICGPSIA 2003).

De-Commissioning Phase

The de-commissioning takes place once the project becomes operational. These impacts can be felt depending on the region or the situation of the community. There may be loss of employment for local labourers, environmental degradation, community composition may change, and local industry and business may need to adapt to the new socio-economic set-up.

Direct and Indirect Impact

Direct impacts are those impacts that are directly experienced by the members of the affected families. The population may be displaced, there may be loss of livelihood, there may be rehabilitation, health and environmental issues, the people might face problems related to transport and communication and stress or tensions. These are gendered impacts.

Indirect impacts may include those impacts that may be experienced by those individuals who are not directly affected by the acquisition of land or dislocation. These may be marginal landless labourers who may not be the owners of the land but depend on that land for their livelihood. The population of nearby areas may be affected by construction of roads, transmission lines, and increased vehicular traffic and by other associated works. There may be impact on the business of the local community because of the project.

Differential Impact

These are the impacts on the most vulnerable groups of society like women, elderly, differently abled and ailing residents. The psychological impacts (stress, perception, attitudinal changes) on these sections of society may have far reaching consequences on their personality. These impacts may be identified through Gender Impact Assessment, Vulnerability and Resilience Mapping, etc.

Cumulative Impact

The planned interventions do not take place in isolation from the surrounding region and communities. There may be a number of different Projects, Plans and programmes (PPP) being undertaken in that region and the impact of these disparate actions will interact with each other in unexpected ways (Barrow 1997).

The intensity of impacts may increase as the life of the project is extended, as the time passes more external factors such as new projects, plans and policies could be undertaken and these would interact with the existing ones in an unprecedented way (Geisler 1993).

Cumulative effects may last for a long time, affecting the social milieu directly and increasing the exposure to foreign culture. It may further lead to the erosion of traditional beliefs and values.

The assessment of the cumulative impacts is very difficult and a complex process. The Cumulative Effects Assessment Working Group (CEAWG) observes that the Cumulative Effects Assessment (CEA) involves the identification and active involvement of all the stakeholders that are the valued components of the project. The valued components are based on societal beliefs and local knowledge of the life world.

There is no single factor responsible for cumulative impacts so these are complicating in nature. These impacts may not only be felt on the local population but may spread to the entire region. In order to deal with these impacts the cooperation of all proponents, regulators and government is required.

Role of SIA in Developmental Projects

Increasing importance is being attached to facilitate dialogue among stakeholders involved in development projects, to development interventions, and to increasing the voice of the poor in policy-making at all levels. In this context, the stakeholders are active social actors with three key characteristics:

1. Practical consciousness derived from life experience
2. Their own theories about social relationships and power
3. Systems of reflective monitoring on how things work (Giddens 1984).

One of the essential aspects of any impact assessment is the proper identification of all stakeholders. It is imperative to consider the full range of potentially involved and affected population. The success or failure of Impact Assessment depends on a judicious identification of all stakeholders. In the present study, an attempt has been made to identify all possible stakeholders in accordance with the in the guidelines prepared by the International Agency of Impact Assessment (IAIA).

Some of the potential stakeholders for most projects are listed below:

- The population ought to be displaced.
- The population whose land (agricultural, residential or commercial) will be acquired.
- The most vulnerable groups like socially and economically weaker sections of society, women, elderly and ailing residents.
- The people those are directly or indirectly dependent on the land that will be acquired.
- The residents of the locality where the displaced persons will be relocated.
- Neighbouring communities, villages (including local people) whose livelihoods may be affected or threatened as a result of the project.
- The population that ought to be affected by construction of roads, transmission lines, increased vehicular traffic and by other associated works.
- The workers at the site and their families.
- The people of villages or colonies where construction workers will be located.
- The people who may have religious/spiritual attachment to the land or native title to land near the project.
- Local, national and international environmentalists who may be interested in the ecological conditions that may be threatened by the project.

In addition to these stakeholders that might probably face negative consequences of development, there are on the other side the beneficiaries of the project. These may be the developer himself/herself, associate contractors, workers, funding agencies, local, state governments and other people who may benefit from the project (Vanclay 1999).

Selection of the SIA Team

The state SIA unit shall be responsible for selecting the SIA team for each project from the individuals and institutions registered or empanelled in the State Database of qualified SIA Resource Partners and Practitioners. The Requiring Body shall not be involved in any way in the appointment of the SIA team being appointed to carry out the SIA.

The SIA team may be constituted by appointing individuals or an organization with experience in conducting SIAs or related field-based assessments and the team may include:

(a) A combination of independent practitioners, qualified social activists, academics, technical experts, who are not directly connected with the requiring body.

(b) At least one woman member (gender expert).

The SIA team shall collect and analyse a range of quantitative and qualitative data, undertake detailed site visits, use participatory methods such as focused group discussions, participatory rural appraisal techniques and informant interviews in preparing the Social Impact Assessment report. The SIA team shall prepare a draft report in local language which should be distributed among the stakeholders before the acquisition of land.

Social Impact of Land Acquisition on the Residents (Especially Women) of Village Jheurheri

The government has acquired 306 acres, and 18 marlas of land from the village Jheur Heri. The land has been acquired to upgrade the existing domestic airport to the international airport. The land was acquired by the Punjab Government at a rate of ₹ 1.5 crore per acre. The social impacts experienced by men and women belonging to the Project Affected Population were different. These impacts were gendered in nature and are as follows:

Impact on Demographic Structure

There have been profound effects on the demographic structure of the village and the women have experienced adverse impact. The comparative analysis of the demography of the village according to Census 2001 and Census 2011 has been described in Table 1. There is an addition of 40 households and an increase of 10.58 per cent to the population from Census 2001 to Census 2011. There is 0.68 per cent increase in both male and female population and a negative growth of 1.87 per cent in the population below six (6) years. There is a negative growth 12.2 per cent in female population below 6 years indicating the possibility of the practice of female foeticide.

The decrease in the 0–6 female population can be attributed to the fact that after the acquisition of land in 2008 the residents got the monetary sources, which they were earlier lacking, to go for Pre-Natal Diagnostic Technique (PNDT) for the determination of the sex of the foetus and even go for preconception gender selection methods.

Table 1

Comparative Demographic Profile of Jheur Heri (Census 2001 and 2011)

	Census		
	2001	*2011*	*Change (+)*
No of Households	145	185	+40
Total Population	894	991	+97 (+10.85%)*
Male Population	472 (52.8%)	530 (53.48%)	+58 (+0.68%)
Female Population	422 (47.20%)	461 (46.52%)	+39 (+0.68%)
Population below 06 yrs.	125 (13.98%)	120 (12.11%)	–05 (+1.87%)
Population below 06 Male	66 (52.8%)	78 (65%)	+12 (+12.2%)
Population below 06 Female	59 (47.2%)	42 (35%)	–17 (–12.2%)
Total SC Population	295 (33%)	365 (36.8%)	+70 (+ 3.8%)
SC Population Male	158 (53.56%)	198 (54.25%)	+40 (+0.69%)
SC Population Female	137 (46.44 %)	167 (45.75%)	–30 (–0.69%)
Number of ST	0	0	0

Source: Census 2001 and 2011.

* Decadal Growth percentage has been calculated by using the following formula–

$$PR = \frac{(V.present - V.past)}{V.past} x\ 100$$

Where – PR = Per cent Rate; V. present= Present Value; V. past= Past Value

Source: http://pages.uoregon.edu.

The comparison of Census 2001 figures with that of Census 2011 figures with regards to the female population below 6 years (with the backdrop of acquisition of land in 2008) indicates that some of the residents may have gone for the Pre-Natal Diagnostic Techniques. The residents though deny of carrying out any unethical act and they contribute the increase in the ratio of male children first to the grace of god and secondly to the fact that they are now more health conscious and there is less tension or burden of work on both males and females.

Impact on Education and Literacy Rate

The acquisition of land had a positive effect on the girls and women of the land owning villagers whose land has been acquired. The parents who were now willing to send their girls to the schools and colleges in the neighbouring cities of Mohali and Chandigarh were providing them higher education. The villagers realized the importance of educating the girl child especially in case they want to marry her in a good urban family. They are now aspiring to get an educated, well qualified and a wealthy groom for their daughters.

Table 2 shows a comparison between literate and illiterate population according to Census 2001 and 2011.

On the other hand, the male members after completing their school have either set up an enterprise or are acting as absentee landlords. The landless, marginal sections and the land owners whose land has not been acquired are sending their wards to the primary school at the village. There is not much change in attitude of these people towards the educational system of the country. They are of the view that being a matriculate or a graduate would not guarantee them any job especially in the government sector.

Table 2

Comparison of Literate and Illiterate Population of Jheur Heri

	Census		*Change +*
	2001	*2011*	
Literate Population	611 (79.45%)	726 (83.35%)	+3.90%
Male Literate	349 (57.12%)	402 (55.37%)	–1.74%
Female Literate	262 (42.88%)	324 (44.63%)	+1.75%
Illiterate Population	283 (31.66%)	265 (26.74%)	18 (–4.92%)
Male Illiterate Population	123 (43.46%)	128 (48.30%)	05 (+4.84%)
Female Illiterate Population	160 (56.54%)	137 (51.70%)	23 (–4.84%)

Source: Census 2001 and 2011.

The total literate population over 6 years was 79.45 per cent in Census 2001 and it has increased up to 83.35 per cent in Census 2011. The proportion of literate population of the village has increased by 4.92 per cent in Census 2011. The female literate population has increased from 42.88 per cent in 2001 Census to 44.63 per cent in 2011 Census. The female illiteracy has decreased from 56.54 per cent in Census 2001 to 51.70 per cent in Census 2011. The increase in female literacy and the simultaneous decrease in the illiteracy of women highlight the fact that after getting huge sums of compensatory money post-land acquisition, the residents want to educate the girl child.

Impact on Socio-Political Relations

The socio-political relations amongst the Project Affected Population (PAP) were adversely affected. There was around 54 acres of land belonged to panchayat, i.e. common village land (Deh Sham-Laat). The amount of compensation for this land turns out to be ₹ 81 crore. A respondent from the lower section stated that they demanded 25 per cent of the compensation of the Deh Sham-Laat but the members of land owning castes (mainly Jat Sikhs) refused to part with the amount (which they will get as compensation of Deh Sham-Laat). Some of the residents have even filed a case claiming their right over common village land (Deh-Sham-laat) and the matter is now sub-judicious.

The members of the landless castes (Nai, Dhobi, Jehur and the Balmiki) of this village, who did not get any compensation, joined hands and elected the Sarpanch of their community to safeguard their interests. In 2008, the seat was reserved for scheduled caste women. Two panches belonged to OBC and the other two belong to general category.

The residents regretfully say that the lady Sarpanch is just a rubber stamp and it is her husband who calls the shots. When one of the respondents (belonging to upper caste), was asked about the village Sarpanch, he/she did not even know the name of the woman Sarpanch, but recalled the name of her husband. The women especially from the backward section were happy as someone especially a female from their community was the head of the village.

Impact on Occupational Structure

Most of the villagers were earlier selling milk in the nearby towns/cities, have now stopped selling milk. The number of the milching animals (cows and buffaloes) has also gone down. The women belonging to the families whose land has been acquired are now free, earlier they used to assist their husbands in milching animals. The women go for morning and evening walks as categorically mentioned by a resident of neighbouring village of Kandala.

Many families have bought agricultural lands in other villages. They are now acting as absentee landlords and renting out their lands to the other cultivators. The women of these families were neither consulted nor informed about the spending of compensatory money.

The landless labourers now go to other villages, towns and cities in search of work. Some of them unload the material from trucks that bring raw material (cement, bricks, sand, gravel etc) to the construction site. One of the villagers said that they keep on waiting for the trucks to come and they get ₹ 400 for unloading material from the truck.

The women of these labourers work as a domestic help in the houses of the land owning community. One of the women remarks that earlier we use to get some agricultural land on lease and used work independently and out of our own volition. Now the things have been changed and they have work as servants. They are distressed at their husbands after unloading material from the truck they get drunk or take drugs.

The social milieu of the village has been disturbed and village is divided into factions. The plight of the landless community of the village is deplorable. One of the landless labourer remorsefully stated that they are now bereft of any open space, even to make cow dung cakes. The women of the community have no option but to work as domestic help in the houses of the land owning community.

Conclusion

The acquisition of land results in changes at the structural and institutional level of the Project Affected Population (PAP). The impacts are though gendered but the women's perspective is not taken into account. The Land Acquisition Acts concentrated on 'Public Purpose' and 'Public Consent' without involving all the stakeholders involved in the project.

The Right to Fair Compensation in Land Acquisition, Rehabilitation and Resettlement Act, 2013 (RFCTLAR & R. Act 2013) is an initiative taken by government to ensure inclusive development. The fact that there is a women member in the SIA team is a welcome step towards ensuring the participation of women in the developmental process.

It is evident that the PAPs of the Jheur Heri village has witnessed a lot of changes at the structural and institutional level. The men and women have been affected differently. Some of the villagers have come to terms with these changes but others, especially the elderly and women, are facing a lot of problems.

The women belonging to the families whose land has been acquired lament that both father and son have started drinking even during day time. The instances of domestic violence and wife abuse have increased since they received the compensatory money. All major decisions in the family are taken by the males. There is some respite to the women in their chores as they are being assisted by appliances or a domestic helper. The in-laws of their daughters (that were married prior to land acquisition) have started demanding dowry in terms of the share of their daughter in the land. The elderly widows that owned some land have been asked to give their thumb impression on the papers and have been kept in dark regarding the compensatory money.

The women belonging to the marginal sections have been adversely affected. Prior to the acquisition of land, they used to help their husbands in the field and were acting as marginal workers. They are now working as domestic helpers in the homes of the land owners.

The major gainers from the land acquisitions are the people who already have control over the resources, i.e. those owned the land. The marginal sections, landless agricultural workers and women are adversely affected by the land acquisitions. The Land Acquisition Laws in India should involve all the stakeholders in the process of acquisition of land especially the special provisions should be made to assess the impacts or negative consequences of any planned intervention on the women.

References

Barrow C.J. 1997. *Environmental and Social Impact Assessment*. London: Arnold.

——. 2000. *Social Impact Assessment: An Introduction*. London: Arnold.

Burdge, R.J. and Johnson, S. 1994. 'Socio-Cultural Aspects of the Effects of Resource Development', in Rabel J. Burdge (ed.), *A Conceptual Approach to Social Impact Assessment*. Middleton, WI: Social Ecology Press, pp. 25–40.

Geisler, C.C. 1993. 'Rethinking SIA: Why Ex Ante Research Isn't Enough?'. *Society and Natural Resources*, 6, 327–338.

George, Robin. 2009. *Constitutional Validity and Land Acquisition Act, 1984*. Available at http://www.legalserviceindia.com/article/l295-land-acquisition-act.html (Retrieved on 31 May 2014).

Giddens, Anthony. 1984. *The Constitution of Society*. Berkeley and Los Angeles: University of California Press.

ICGPSIA. 1994. *Guidelines and Principles for Social Impact Assessment*. US Department of Commerce, National Oceanic and Atmospheric Administration, available from IAIA. www.iaia.org/publicdocuments/.../iaia-sia-international-principles.pdf (Retrieved on 5 March 2010).

——. 2003. *Principles and Guidelines for Social Impact Assessment in USA*. Impact Assessment and Project Appraisal, 21(3), September, 231–250. Available at http://www.nmfs.noaa.gov/sfa/reg_svcs/social%20guid&pri. pdf (Retrieved on 15 March 2013).

Iyer, Ramaswamy R. 2009. 'Land Acquisition (Amendment) Bill: A Slow But Sure Step Forward'. *The Hindu*, 7 August.

Kothari, S. 1997. 'Whose Independence? The Social Impact of Economic Reform in India'. *Journal of International Affairs*, 51(1), 85–116 as quoted by Lyla Mehta (ed.), *Displaced by Development*. New Delhi: Sage Publications, pp. 166–194.

Oommen, T.K. 1992. 'Reconciling Pluralism and Equality: The Dilemma of "Advanced" Societies'. *International Review of Sociology* (new series), 3(1), 141–172.

Sahoo, Basudeb. 2004. 'Understanding Development in the Context of Social Change'. *Vision*, XXIII(3–4), January–June, 2–9.

Singhal, M.L. 1995. 'Right to Property and Compensation Under the Indian Constitution'. *J.T.R.I. Journal* (First Year), Issue 2, April–June (Retrieved on 25 November 2014).

Sutton, F.X. 1989. 'Development Ideology: Its Emergence and Decline'. *Daedalus*, 118(1), Winter, as quoted by Ramchandra Guha in *Sociology and the Dilemmas of Development*. New Delhi: ICSSR, p. 31.

Tenth Report of the Law Commission of India. 1958. Available at http://lawcommissionofindia.nic.in/1-50/report10.pdf (Retrieved on 31 May 2014).

Vanclay, F. 1999. 'Social Impact Assessment', in J. Petts (ed.), *International Handbook of Environmental Impact Assessment*. Vol. 1, Oxford: Blackwell Science, pp. 301–326.

——. 2002. 'Conceptualising Social Impacts'. *Environmental Impact Assessment Review*, 22(3), 183–211.

Wahi, Namita. 2013. *Land Acquisition, Development and the Constitution*. Available at http://india-seminar.com.../namita_wahi.html (Retrieved on 31 May 2014).

Walker, Jennifer L., Mitchell, Bruce and Wismer, Susan. 2000. 'Impacts During Project Anticipation in Molas, Indonesia, Implications for Social Impact Assessment'. *Environmental Impact Assessment Review*, 20, 513–535.

19

Legal Protection for Women against Sexual Harassment at Workplace in India

An Assessment

Reena Chaudhary

One of the most revolutionary consequences of the feminist movement across the world has been the massive entry of women into the workforce. Though they entered first in the so-called feminine occupations, mostly at the lowest rung of the economy, of late they have successfully walked into almost all professions and occupations, breaking the gender boundaries. There are of course substantial differences in the level of female workforce participation between the developed and the developing countries. India, for that matter, has all through had a very low level of female workforce participation, mainly due to the patriarchal mindset, although women have always been working outside their homes among the lowest income groups, for household survival. In general, when women work, they tend to be engaged in low-paid and low productivity jobs (ILO and ADB 2011). Thus, the widespread entry of women into the labour market has not always been out of choice, as it may be distress driven and may not reflect an increased access to decent jobs. It is widely recognized that women's work in the developing world is overlooked, under-valued and underreported because women are often home based, largely contributing to non-market activities, such as care giving (Beneria 1982; Boserup 1970; Donahoe 1999). According to 2011 Census, the proportion of women workforce in India is only 29 per cent. A low rate of female labour force participation is indeed a major factor that keeps India's overall rate of labour force participation low. It is stated in the ILO's *Global Employment Trends Report 2013*, that out of 131 countries with available data, India ranks 11th from the bottom in terms of female labour force participation (ILO 2013). It is another fact that a huge majority of these gainfully employed women are concentrated in the unorganized sector, with no job security and facing discrimination of all kinds.

From times immemorial, women in India have been working as family labour supporting the agricultural Indian economy, though they were never designated as paid workers. Though most women in India work and contribute to the economy in one form or another, much of their work is not documented or accounted for in official statistics. Women's role in reproduction and in a range of activities within households, such as caring for the young and old, cooking and other household chores, does not get recognition in the system of national accounts or other economic statistics (Mazumdar and Neetha 2011). It is only when Indian women started working in formal sector that they were counted as workers. Initially women were mostly engaged in unskilled or semi-skilled occupations. Anker (1998) found the concentration of women in India in professions like nursing, teaching, house-keeping and related services. Even though the concentration of women in formal sector continues to be in the lower rank occupations, women are also showing their presence in all occupations. They are gradually entering into occupations, formerly falling exclusively in the male domain. However, women's entry into the public spaces has been accompanied by numerous problems and challenges, perpetuating due to the persistent social norms ruling masculinity and femininity. Despite equal right to employment, equal wages and work, women continue to be discriminated against in matters of wages, working conditions, job security and decision-making positions. It is fairly well accepted that women, whether urban or rural, are not a homogeneous category and, therefore, their problems at work place vary across categories. Socially and economically marginalized women enter the labour market out of compulsion and the level at which they work is often vulnerable, unprotected and inadequately remunerated.

To undo the aforesaid discrimination and exploitation, several provisions were made in the Constitution of India for the protection and security of women workers. These provisions besides the Preamble, are contained in Articles 14, 15, 16, 23, 39, 43 and 46 of the Constitution. Different protective legislations like The Payment of Gratuity Act, 1972, The Minimum Wages Act, 1948, The Payment of Wages Act, 1936 and The Equal Remuneration Act, 1976, The Sexual Harassment of Women at Work Place (Prevention, Protection and Redressal) Act, 2013 are there. Theseare provided by Constitution of India for the protection and security to women workers. It was the ruling of the Supreme Court (1997) in the famous Vishaka case that brought the issue of sexual harassment of women at workplace to the public forum.

Concept of Sexual Harassment

It is interesting to note that the term 'sexual harassment' was only coined in the 1970s. Since then the issue has been recognized throughout the world, though in different cultural and occupational contexts. According to the ILO, sexual harassment is a clear form of gender discrimination based on sex, a manifestation of unequal power relations between men and women. The problem relates not so much to the actual biological differences between men and women; rather, it relates to the gender or social roles attributed to men and women in social and economic life, and perceptions about male and female sexuality in society that can lead to unbalanced male-female power relationships (Haspels et al. 2001).

The UN Convention on the Elimination of All Forms of Discrimination Against Women (CEDAW) has also noted the seriousness of the issue, describing sexual harassment in the workplace as gender discrimination and a form of gender-based violence. The CEDAW Committee has called on state parties to the Convention to take steps to address the problem – 'State parties should include in their reports information on sexual harassment, and on measures to protect women from sexual harassment and other forms of violence or coercion in the workplace' (1992).

A large number of countries worldwide have adopted some form of legislation on sexual harassment, either by addressing it under another broader statute such as human rights, or equal opportunity and treatment like in non-discrimination, labour, contract, personal injury and criminal laws.

According to guidelines and norms laid down by the Hon'ble Supreme Court in *Vishaka and others v. State of Rajasthan and others* [JT 1997(7) SC 384], sexual harassment has been defined as unwelcomed sexually determined behaviour (whether directly or by implication) as:

(a) Physical contact and advances
(b) A demand or request for sexual favours
(c) Sexually coloured remarks
(d) Showing pornography
(e) Any other unwelcomed physical, verbal or non-verbal conduct of sexual nature

The definition of sexual harassment in the Act is in line with the Supreme Court's definition in the Vishaka judgement. Conduct of a sexual nature includes a range of behaviours or actions, since there is a wide range of activities which are expressions of sexuality or have sexual connotations in our society. Therefore, behaviour which may appear relatively innocent (such as joking, innuendoes, flirting and asking someone for a date) to behaviour which is blatantly illegal (such as forced fondling, attempted or actual rape and sexual assault) can all constitute conduct of a sexual nature, making it a very comprehensive definition.

Extent of the Problem of Sexual Harassment

The available research indicates that a vast majority of workers subjected to sexual harassment are women (Livingstone 1982; Maypole and Skaine 1983; Rudman et al. 1995). A CII study (2005) underlined gender bias apart from gender inequality and sexual harassment at work place in recruitment as a major issue affecting women and influencing attrition rates of women in larger companies where the ratio of women has dwindled further in managerial positions. Gruber and Morgan (2005) have argued that the experience of sexual harassment is universal.

Amongst the 22 countries covered by the IPSOS, Reuters survey (2010), India recorded the highest incidence of sexual harassment. Similarly, Centre for Transforming India Survey (2010) revealed that nearly 88 per cent of women witnessed some form of workplace related sexual harassment during the course of their work. Additionally, the survey found that there were poor awareness levels among female employees on sexual harassment at workplace and, therefore, a majority of them continued with their ordeal of suffering due to fear of professional victimization. Though sexual harassment is rampant in corporate India, as stated by Shukla (2002), it is the most under reported form of gender discrimination.

Panda (2006) stated that sexual harassment at work place was an extension of violence in everyday life, discriminatory and exploitative, thriving in an atmosphere of threat, terror and reprisal. Working women most commonly face many problems, especially sexual harassment. Chaudhary (2011) revealed that 71 per cent women faced one or the other form of sexual harassment at workplace. According to news report 17 per cent of working women in Bangalore have admitted having faced some kind of sexual harassment at their workplace (*The Times of India* 2012). Another survey conducted in various metropolitan cities in India reported that about 37 per cent women had been the victims of sexual harassment at work place (Oxfam India and Social and Rural Research Institute 2011–12).

Aggarwal (2012) reported that since a majority of women in unorganized sector are the sole bread winners of their families continue to face harassment and do not raise objections because they fear of losing the job. Other factors, such as absence of any compliant mechanism at the workplace, fear of getting stigmatized, and unawareness of existing redress mechanisms, etc. have been reported as reasons for not filing any complaint. Doss et al. (2014) reported similar findings and stated that women working in the unorganized sector are more susceptible to sexual harassment due to lack of awareness of legislation and being the sole earning member of their families, indicating that economic vulnerability further makes women more vulnerable to harassment at the workplace.

Background of the Act

Sexual harassment at the workplace has remained one of the central concerns of the women's movement in India since the early 1980s. Before 1997, women experiencing sexual harassment at the workplace had to lodge a complaint under Section 354 of the Indian Penal Code that deals with the 'Criminal Assault of women to outrage women's modesty, and Section 509 that punishes an individual for using a 'word', gesture or act intended to insult the modesty of a woman'. These sections of the IPC left the interpretation of outraging women's modesty to the discretion of the police officer.

In 1997, the Supreme Court passed a landmark judgement in the Vishaka case laying down guidelines to be followed by establishments in dealing with complaints about sexual harassment at workplace. The Apex Court stated that these guidelines were to be implemented until legislation was enacted to deal with the issue. Visakha's judgement was delivered in 1997 and for 16 years after that no efforts were made in the direction of enacting a law. So the guidelines continued to be the law required to be followed across the country. But the guidelines were followed more in their breach. Very few complaints committees were set up, service rules were not amended and the judgment was widely disregarded both by public and private employers. But one of the fallouts of the judgement was that many civil society organizations became aware of it and started to publicize it and pushed for its implementation. Around the same time many women who were being sexually harassed started breaking their silence and started demanding action from the employers. In fact, a number of these cases arose from university and college campuses. The response of the employers by and large was to sweep such cases under the carpet and at times even to victimize the women. But one could still see an increasing fervour of protest. The media also started giving important space and time to this issue.

On pursuance of Government of India, the National Commission for Women (NCW) along with several women's organizations and women lawyers drafted the legislation. The Bill introduced in Parliament came to be known as the Sexual Harassment of Women at the Workplace (Prevention and Redressal) Bill, 2004. It was only after the Delhi Rape case in December 2012 that the Government got serious about bringing about this enactment. The Indian Parliament passed the Sexual Harassment of Women at Workplace (Prevention, Prohibition and Redressal) Bill in the Lok Sabha on 3 September 2012 and Rajya Sabha on 26 February 2013 and it was made effective on 23 April 2013 by way of publication in the Gazette of India and the Act finally came into force with effect from 9 December 2013.

The Act went one step ahead and included various issues which had so far remained unaddressed in the past such as extension of the definition of workplace to include almost all types of establishments including private sector organization, dwelling places or houses, inclusion of the term domestic worker and unorganized sector in order to address the issue of sexual harassment of women. It gave a very comprehensive definition of sexual harassment, apart from chalking out a detailed system for the prevention, prohibition and redressal of sexual harassment of women at workplace.

The Act has been enacted with the objective of providing women with protection against sexual harassment at the workplace and for the prevention and redressal of complaints of sexual harassment. Sexual harassment is considered as a violation of the fundamental right of a woman to equality as guaranteed under Articles 14 and 15 of the Constitution of India and her right to life and to live with dignity as per Article 21 of the Constitution. It has also been considered as a violation of a right to practice or to carry out any occupation, trade or business under Article 19(1)(g) of the Constitution, which includes a right to a safe environment free from harassment. Thus, the Act is an attempt to provide working women a mechanism to counter the menace of sexual harassment at workplace. It has streamlined the guidelines given in Vishaka judgement and has also mandated a Statutory obligation on employers to follow its provisions.

Cases of Sexual Harassment at Workplace

There have been some cases resulting is landmark judgements on sexual harassment of women at workplace which occurred much before the Act was enacted. Some of the cases are discussed below:

Vishaka and Others v. State of Rajasthan and Others (1997)

Bhanwari Devi was a village-level social worker or a *saathin* of a development programme run by the state government of Rajasthan, fighting against child and multiple marriages in villages. As part of this work, Bhanwari, with assistance from the local administration, tried to stop the marriage of Ramkaran Gujjar's infant daughter who was less than one-year-old. The marriage took place nevertheless, and Bhanwari earned the ire of the Gujjar family. She was subjected to social boycott, and in September 1992 five men including Ramkaran Gujjar, gang raped Bhanwari in front of her husband, while they were working in their fields. The days that followed were filled with hostility and humiliation for Bhanwari and her husband. The only male doctor in the Primary Health Centre refused to examine Bhanwari and the doctor at Jaipur only confirmed her age without making any reference to rape in his medical report. At the police station, the women constables taunted Bhanwari throughout the night. It was past mid-night when the policemen asked Bhanwari to leave her lehenga behind as evidence and return to her village. She was left with only her husband's bloodstained dhoti to wear. Their pleas to let them sleep in the police station at night were turned down.

The trial court acquitted the accused, but Bhanwari was determined to fight further and get justice. She said that she had nothing to be ashamed of and that the men should be ashamed due to what they had done. Her fighting spirit inspired fellow *saathins* and women's groups countrywide. In the months that followed they launched a concerted campaign for justice for Bhanwari. In December 1993, the High Court said, 'It is a case of gang rape which was committed out of vengeance'. As part of this campaign, the groups had filed a petition in the Supreme Court of India, under the name 'Vishaka', asking the Court to give certain directions regarding the sexual harassment that women faced at the workplace. The court was moved greatly after this brutal gang rape of a lady who was working for such a significant cause in the country.

The facts of the case made judges to think and feel for the pitiable and miserable conditions of women in the country and this situation accompanied by the legislative absence compelled the Court to take such an unexpected decision. The result is the Supreme Court judgment, which came on 13 August 1997, and gave the Vishaka Guidelines.

Radha Bai v. D. Ramchandran Union Territory of Pondichery (1995)

Radha Bai was working as Assistant Director of Social Welfare Department, Government of Pondicherry. In 1978, she made a written complaint before the Governor of the Pondicherry wherein it was alleged that Home Minister of Pondicherry, Ramchandran, and other ministers named therein were misusing the shelter home for women for illegal and immoral purposes. An attempt to molest her was also alleged. The Governor, in his capacity as the administrator of Pondicherry, directed for an enquiry into the allegations which was followed by her dismissal. She suffered agony in the long battle, had lost her reputation and honour. But there were materials available in the records to show that the appellant was a highly competent, hard-working, sincere and devoted official. She had been referred to as an asset to the department which worked in her favour. But for the period of 17 years no redress or remedy was rendered to the victim. It was only in 1995 that the Supreme Court passed the judgment in her favour, and she was given salary and perks with effect from the date of her dismissal.

Rupan Deol Bajaj v. Kanwar Pal Singh Gill (1996)

Rupan Deol Bajaj, an officer of the Indian Administrative Service (IAS) belonging to the Punjab Cadre and then working as the Special Secretary, Finance, lodged a complaint in 1988 with the Inspector General of Police alleging commission of offences under sections 341, 342, 352, 354 and 509 of the Indian Penal Code (IPC) by K.P.S. Gill, the Director General of Police, Punjab. In this case, the victim and the offender (both government officers) were present at a dinner party at another government officer's residence. Ladies and gentlemen were sitting in separate semicircles in the lawns. The accused crossed over to the ladies' circle and called the victim, saying he wanted to talk to her over some matter. She went to him and when she was about to sit on a chair the accused drew that chair close to touch his chair, which happened twice. Realizing that something was wrong, the victim moved away and sat at her original place. To this, the accused commanded the victim in an obnoxious manner, to get up and accompany him and also blocked her way in such a manner that she could not get up from the chair without touching him. She immediately drew her chair back, got up and tried to leave the place. On this, the accused slapped her on her posterior in full view of all the ladies and gentlemen present. Rupan Deol Bajaj filed a suit against him, despite the public opinion that she was blowing it out of proportion, along with the attempts by all the senior officials of the state to suppress the matter. The High Court announced three months' Rigorous Imprisonment to K.P.S. Gill under Sections 294 and 509 of the Indian Penal Code. Further, the case was taken up to the Supreme Court, where K.P.S. Gill was fined ₹ 2.5 lakh in lieu of three months' imprisonment.

Apparel Export Promotion Council v. A.K. Chopra (1999)

A.K. Chopra was working as a Private Secretary to the Chairman of the Apparel Export Promotion Council. In 1988, it was alleged that he tried to molest a junior woman employee of the Council, who was at the relevant period working as a clerk-cum-typist. The accused pressurized her to come with him to a hotel to take dictation from the Chairman and type out the matter. Under pressure she went to take the dictation from the Chairman. While she was waiting for the Director in the room, the respondent tried to sit too close to her and despite her objection did not give up his objectionable behaviour. Taking advantage of his position, he continued with the acts of unwelcomed sexual advances and created hostile work environment for her. In this case, the departmental inquiry was conducted on the basis of which the offender was dismissed in June 1989. Then his appeal to the High Court gave him relief. Then, the council appealed in the Supreme Court which upheld and restored the orders of departmental inquiry.

Medha Kotwal Lele v. Union of India and Others (2013)

Actually it was the case of Medha Kotwal Lele which led to the making of the Act. In this judgement, the Hon'ble Supreme Court highlighted the non-compliance and non-adherence to the Vishaka Guidelines in workplaces in India and urged the need for legislative enactment in this direction. This case arose when Medha Kotwal Lele, coordinator of Aalochana, a centre for documentation and research on women and other women's rights groups, together with others in 2012, petitioned the court highlighting a number of individual cases of sexual harassment and arguing that the Vishaka Guidelines were not being effectively implemented. In particular, the petitioners argued that, despite the guidelines, women continued to be harassed in the workplace because the Vishaka Guidelines were being breached in both substance and spirit by state functionaries who harass women workers via legal and extra legal means, making them suffer and by insulting their dignity. The matter disposed of in 2013, with the direction that aggrieved parties could approach the respective High Courts, in case of non-compliance with directions issued in Vishaka case.

Women complainants in these cases, who dared to complain against their harassers at work (irrespective of perpetrator's powerful position), proved that sexual harassment was not to be taken lightly and should not be ignored. In all above cases, victims were determined to fight for their rights and were aware of their rights. They dared to challenge the highly influential perpetrators. Though victims were given compensation and justice was delivered by our legal system, but all this happened after a wait of a long period. Of course, the battle was not easy for them to fight, it aggravated their problems. All these cases also depict that these women had strong support system to fight against the perpetrators. The judgments in these cases have identified sexual harassment as a question of power exerted by the perpetrator on the victim. Therefore, sexual harassment in addition to being a violation of the right to safe working conditions is also a violation of the right to bodily integrity of the woman.

The landmark decision of *Vishaka and Others v. State of Rajasthan and Others* (1997) proved to be a milestone in a long drawn struggle for justice. It makes a significant rupture of the boundaries between the political sphere and society, between the home and the world, between the workplace and street, between the classes and the castes. In this judgement, for the first time in India, guidelines were laid down for prevention and punishment of sexual harassment at the workplace. The Supreme Court held that each incident of sexual harassment results in a violation of the fundamental rights of gender equality and the right to life and liberty under the Indian Constitution.

Challenges: Legislation Alone Not Sufficient

Sexual harassment is all about expressions of male power over women that sustain patriarchal relations. It is used to remind women of their vulnerability and subjugated status. In a society where violence against women, both subtle and direct, is legitimized by the patriarchal values operating in society, women's conformity to gendered roles gets ensured. In stark contrast to the global efforts, the handling of sexual harassment cases in India at workplace is still at its initial stages. The Prevention of Workplace Sexual Harassment (Prevention, Prohibition and Redressal) Act, 2013 applies to both the organized and unorganized sectors. However, there is a spurt in these cases in the organized sector. A series of high-profile complaints of sexual harassment have hit the headlines recently e.g. cases against R.K. Pachauri, former chair of the Intergovernmental Panel on Climate Change and ex-director of The Energy and Resources Institute (Teri); Tarun Tejpal, editor of the investigative journalism magazine *Tehelka*, who has been accused of attempting to rape a young female colleague; Justice Swatanter Kumar, a retired Supreme Court Judge, has been accused by women lawyer of sexual harassment, etc. reflect sordid reality of workplace harassment.

Studies indicate that sexual harassment is still endemic, often hidden, but present in all kinds of organizations. It does not mean that women in unorganized sector do not face any problem. The issue is that they remain silent and are unwilling to come forward. They do not want to be stigmatized or labelled (for example, as 'frigid' or 'easy', or having 'asked for it'). They may also be afraid of losing their income, or reluctant to confront the harasser who may be a superior or someone of prominent social standing, who may be able to negatively influence their career movement. There is a large section of women who lack awareness of what sexual harassment actually is, or lack awareness about what to do about it, or they may feel that nothing can be done unless it involves rape or sexual assault.

With such a scenario, there is a need to start a rigorous awareness campaign about legislation and its redressal mechanism since the number of cases of sexual harassment has seen a spurt in the very year in which a law to prevent such harassment at the workplace was enacted. This also indicates that law has accorded to women the power to come out in the open and protest against any attacks on their dignity and honour. Most sexual crimes against women in India, however, still go unreported. This is primarily because the structures of patriarchy, power and control over women allow such crimes to happen, making it all that more difficult for women to report them for fear of stigma and further victimization. Sexual harassment of women at workplace is aided by skewed gender equations in the organizational hierarchy. The law in India now makes a clear link between sexual harassment and the violation of women's fundamental right to equality. It is also clear that for the law to be effective, each organization and institution must work for its proper implementation and any violation should be checked with strict penalty. But will law alone eradicate this scourge? No. Harassment at the workplace is often about abuse of power by a 'superior', and change in mindset of the oppressor and the victim coupled with a strict application of the law and commensurate punishment for offenders, might help victims to report such crimes with greater confidence. There is, therefore, a pressing need to devise a more comprehensive mechanism that compliments and acts in conjunction with the existing legal regime to tackle sexual harassment at the workplace.

This Act no doubt is a big step towards enhancing gender equality at workplaces in India. There is need to make people aware about this legislation because people (the perpetrators, the victims) themselves are not aware that what sexual harassment actually implies. Even the educated people are not aware of this Act then how we can expect that illiterate women, working in unorganized sector, will know about it. Further, mostly, it is the act of physical contact, that is considered as sexual harassment but workplace harassment has a broad spectrum. Jesudasan (2008) argued that most people think of violence as physical assault or using guns and bombs. But, workplace violence has a broad spectrum, i.e. from prejudice, discrimination, bullying, oppression, to acts in which a person is abused, threatened, intimidated or assaulted and to rumour mongering, gossiping and bitching behind someone's back. Workplace violence also includes threatening behaviours such as shaking fists, slamming doors, destroying property or throwing objects; verbal or written threats, harassment, behaviour that demeans, embarrasses or humiliates person; swearing, insulting or using condescending language and of course physical attacks.

Further, a woman who is aware of this Act and dares to complain, often finds nobody to support her and is treated as an accused, troublemaker, facing social disgrace. Piotrkowski (2002) quotes Mackinnon who stated in 1978 that historically sexual harassment of women employees was ignored, denied, made to seem trivial, even implicitly supported. Women were blamed for it too. Women subjected to sexual harassment have also been found to experience a wide range of physical and psychological ailments. They keep quiet to avoid the stigma attached and retaliation from the harasser. They keep mum because of the fear of loss of job. Women are afraid that they will be accused of provoking it, of being called liars and made the subject of gossip, which actually leads to the under-reporting of this crime. In India, social stigma is attached to a woman who is sexually harassed, especially if she lodges a complaint, in such a case her character comes under question and this can jeopardize her other social relationships, for instance in her family, leading to 'neglect, hatred, domestic violence, divorce'. Gilbert et al. (1998) suggested that the true extent of sexual harassment is often hidden, disguised by the conspiracy of silence which shrouds the issue. Chaudhuri (2006) mentioned that most women workers do not complain to supervisors or the management about their experiences of sexual harassment at work and deal with it on their own. They do not report due to fear of further harassment, apprehension of adverse effect on their employment, lack of confidence in the complaint mechanism, possible defamation or threats from the perpetrators and other such reasons. A number of studies have shown that although the number of reported cases of sexual harassment has risen, yet women employees are most reluctant to report the matter to the authorities concerned mainly due to lack of confidence in the redressal system. Indeed, a woman suffers silently and avoids lodging report.

Critical Appraisal of the Act

To deal with the incidents of sexual harassment of women at workplace, the Act was enacted and undoubtedly, the guidelines of Supreme Court in Vishaka Judgement are the fountainhead of the Act. However, India's long awaited legislation took 16 long years since the Vishaka judgement to view the light of the day, which actually raises more questions than it answers. Are our law-makers really giving the immune system and making efforts sincerely to strengthen the legal framework for betterment of women? Enactment of law has to be accompanied by an effective system of implementation. The newly enacted Act includes many provisions, viz., the ambit of the Sexual Harassment Act is very wide; it is applicable to the organized sector as well as the unorganized sector, provision of Internal Complaints Committee, Interim Relief, time-bound inquiry process, prescribed procedures for making complaint and inquiry, monetary compensation for the victim, punishment for false and malicious complaints, etc. Still, strong implementation of this legislation is required as women face this violence in silence. An effective implementation of the Act will contribute to the realization of women's right to gender equality, life and liberty, and right to work. The sense of security at the workplace will improve women's participation and performance in work, resulting in their economic empowerment and inclusive growth. In the above mentioned cases, women reported illegal and unwelcomed behaviour with significant victories but achieved after a long wait of a decade or so. It is a known fact that there is long pendency of sexual harassment cases in courts and conviction rate is very low indicating the sorry state of affairs. The Supreme Court of India expressed concern over poor implementation of the Vishakha Guidelines in the case of *Medha Kotwal Lele v. Union of India and Others* (2013). This case brought to the fore the blatant non-compliance with the Vishaka Guidelines. The recent cases of sexual harassment against big shots like the Editor of *Tehalka* magazine (Tarun Tejpal) and a retired judge of Supreme Court (A.K. Ganguly) have blown the lid off the hypocrisies and the issue of sexual harassment and gender rights at the workplace. These cases have underlined the difficulties in implementing this law especially when the offenders are very well connected and powerful.

Although the Supreme Court came out with the guidelines in Vishaka case in 1997, yet compliance to these has been far from satisfactory. A majority of the employers still do not have Complaints Committees in place. Apart from a few public sector bodies, universities, and some large private companies, Complaints Committees are either not set up on a large scale, or these are often hurriedly formed on receipt of a complaint of sexual harassment. Even when constituted, these remain largely non-functional. Moreover, when allegations are against the boss, he manipulates the situation by constituting Complaints Committees of his personal and favourite individuals, resulting in patriarchal and biased decisions, which aggravates the victim's problems. Further, treating the complainant as an accused, and the accused as a complainant has become a regular practice to victimize the women complainants.

Though law provides the much needed grievance redressal system that working women so badly require at their workplace, yet it has failed to give confidence among the working women facing victimization. The problem of sexual harassment at workplace continues due to the conventional mindsets governed by male chauvinism. The patriarchal attitudes and values constitute the biggest challenge in implementation of any law concerning women in our society. They are first treated as women at workplace and then as employees. Sadly, our legal system does not provide any solution to these age-old cultural norms that actually govern our lives. These continue to regulate the systems of governance irrespective of what laws prescribe.

Discussion

Sexual harassment is a serious manifestation of gender discrimination at the workplace and a violation of fundamental rights enshrined in the Constitution of India. It is yet another form of violence against women reflecting patriarchal mindset and gender based discrimination that women experience at work. It is also a manifestation of power relations, as women are much more likely to be the victims of sexual harassment because of their already existing vulnerability, insecurity, and social conditioning to accept discrimination in silence. Legal recourse, however, comes with risks and limitations. Its outreach and enforcement in the context of poverty, illiteracy and unorganized labour in many parts of India is a challenge for legal systems that are distant and inaccessible to the poor generally, and women in particular. It is difficult for uneducated, poor women to carry on the struggle for a long time without any support system and resources. In the case of women's issues, the law more often than not, reproduces and reinforces dominant gender stereotypes of the 'good' and 'bad' woman, shifting scrutiny upon the victim, her behaviour, morality, dress, and so on, rather than the harasser, the workplace code of conduct, and employer responsibility.

These contested issues and barriers highlight the limited nature of relief that law provides. The drafting of a comprehensive law in and of itself offers a normative respite but one must remain mindful of public education and training inputs that would help challenge the gendered interpretation and implementation of the law. It serves to emphasize that law cannot play a central role in addressing women's discrimination issues and that other interventions through policy, programmes and public education at the family, community, and institutional levels are equally important, as is the participation of all these sectors in such initiatives. The Act on Sexual Harassment which came into force after a long wait, in order to be effective, requires significant transformation in the cultural norms and stereotypes glorifying masculinity and femininity. The Constitutional spirit of gender equality has to be incorporated right from the beginning in the educational curriculum. Both men as well as women need to develop a gender sensitive approach. Women need to be bold enough to come out openly and raise their voice against exploitation at workplace. They need to know that this Act has been enacted with the objective of creating safe and secure workplace not out of benevolence but as their legal right and no one can take away their right to work with dignity at workplace. Hopefully, unlike some of the other laws, this particular statute is implemented well, which in itself would go a long way in protecting the women who have been granted the Fundamental Right to Work.

Conclusion

Sexual Harassment of Women at Workplace (Prevention, Prohibition and Redressal) Act, 2013 which came after a long wait, can definitely create safe work environment for working women, if implemented in true spirit. Keeping in view the low levels of literacy and indifference, aggressive campaigns towards sensitizing the general public about this legal protection are required. Besides legislation, there is a need for attitudinal change towards women workers. Different stakeholders involved in the implementation of this Act, e.g. lawyers, members of complaints committees, judiciary, employers, etc. apart from women victims, need to be gender sensitized to get optimum results.

References

Aggarwal, A.P. 2012. *Sexual Harassment: A Guide for Understanding and Prevention*. Toronto: Butterworths.

Anker, R. 1998. *Gender and Jobs: Sex Segregation of Occupations in the World*. Geneva: International Labour Office.

Apparel Export Promotion Council v. A.K. Chopra. AIR 1999 SC 625 (India).

Beneria, L. 1982. 'Accounting for Women's Work', in Lourdes Beneria (ed.), *Women and Development: The Sexual Division of Labor in Rural Societies*. New York: Praeger, pp. 119–147.

Boserup, E. 1970. *Women's Role in Economic Development*. New York: St Martin's Press, p. 283.

CEDAW Committee. 1992. General Recommendation No. 19. http://www.un.org/womenwatch/daw/cedaw/recommendations/recomm.htm#recom1

Centre for Transforming India. 2010. *The Workplace Sexual Harassment Survey Reveals Startling Revelations*. New Delhi. available at: https://cftingo.wordpress.com/page/5/

Chaudhary, R. 2011. *Sexual Harassment: Threat to Working Women*. New Delhi: Deep & Deep Publications.

Chaudhuri, S.N. 2006. *Human Rights and Poverty in India*. New Delhi: Concept Publishing Company.

Confederation of Indian Industries (CII). 2005. *Understanding the Levels of Women Empowerment in the Workplace*. New Delhi. available at: www.fes_india.org/media/GBV-SH/Paper-Anagha Sarpotdar.pdf

Donahoe, D.A. 1999. 'Measuring Women's Work in Developing Countries'. *Population and Development Review*, 25(3), 543–576.

Doss, E.N., Mukherjee, P.K. and Kumar, A. 2014. 'A Study on Sexual Harassment Among Women Workers at Work Place in Vellore City'. *Indian Journal of Applied Research*, 4(12), 287–308.

Gilbert, D., Guerrier, Y. and Guy, J. 1998. 'Sexual Harassment Issues in the Hospitality Industry'. *International Journal of Contemporary Hospitality Management*, 10(2), 48–53.

Gruber, J.E. and Morgan, P. 2005. *In the Company of Men: Male Dominance and Sexual Harassment*. Boston: Northeastern University Press.

Haspels, N., Kasim, Z., Thomas, C. and McCann, D. 2001. Action Against Sexual Harassment at Work in Asia and the Pacific. International Labour Organization. Available at www.ilo.org/wcmsp5/groups/.../-asia/-ro.../wcms_bk_pb_159_en.pdf

International Labour Organization (ILO) and Asian Development Bank (ADB). 2011. *Women and Labour Markets in Asia: Rebalancing for Gender Equality*. Bangkok. Available at www.ilo.org/wcmsp5/groups/.../-asia/-ro-bangkok/.../wcms_154846...

International Labour Organization (ILO). 2013. *Global Employment Trends 2013: Recovering from a Second Jobs Dip*. Geneva. Available at www.ilo. org/wcmsp5/groups /public/-.../wcms_202326.pdf

IPSOS Reuters. 2010. *The Reuters/Ipsos Poll on Assault and Harassment in the Workplace*. IPSOS Global Advisory. Available at http://ipsosmarkinor.co.za/news/the-reuters-ipsos-assault-poll.

Jesudasan, Usha. 2008. 'Rights, Violence'. *The Hindu*, 22 June, 8.

Livingstone, J.A. 1982. 'Responses to Sexual Harassment on the Job: Legal, Organizational, and Individual Actions'. *Journal of Social Issues*, 38(4), 5–22.

Maypole, D.E. and Skaine, R. 1983. 'Sexual Harassment in the Workplace'. *Social Work*, 28(5), 385–390.

Mazumdar, I. and Neetha, N. 2011. 'Gender Dimensions: Employment Trends in India, 1993–94 to 2009–10'. *Economic and Political Weekly*, 46(43), 118–126.

Medha Kotwal Lele v. Union of India and Others. AIR 2013 1 SCC 297.

Oxfam India and Social and Rural Research Institute. 2011–2012. *Sexual Harassment at Workplaces in India*. Available at http://www.talkitover.in/consultation/preventing-sexual-harassment/how- secure-are-women-working-in-the-unorganized-sectors/

Panda, P.K. 2006. 'Poverty and Young Women's Employment: Linkages in Kerala'. Working Paper, Centre for Development Studies, Thiruvananthapuram.

Piotrkowski, C.S. 2002. 'Gender Harassment, Job Satisfaction, and Distress Among Employed White and Minority Women'. *Journal of Occupational Health Psychology*, 3(1), 33–43.

Radha Bai v. Union Territory of Pondicherry. AIR 1995 SC 1476.

Rudman, L.A., Borgida, E. and Robertson, B.A. 1995. 'Suffering in Silence: Procedural Justice Versus Gender Socialization Issues in University Sexual Harassment Grievance Procedures'. *Basic and Applied Social Psychology*, 17(4), 519–541.

Rupan Deol Bajaj v K.P.S. Gill. AIR 1996 SC 309 (India).

Shukla, S. 2002. 'Indecent Proposal'. *Business Today*, Cover Story. Retrieved from http://archives.digitaltoday.in/businesstoday/20020901/cover1.html

The Times of India. 2012. 'Sexual Harassment at Work Can't Be Taken Lightly'. 6 October. Available at http://timesofindia.indiatimes.com/news/india/sexual-harassment-at-work-cant-be-takenlightly-hc/articleshow/5092168.cms.

Vishaka and Others v. State of Rajasthan and Others. AIR 1997 6 SCC 241.

20

Women in Short Stay Homes

A Study at Amritsar, Punjab

Satinder Kaur

Women in distress since long have attracted the policy-makers with a special area of concern to incorporate provisions to provide them relief through appropriate governmental policies. A number of support services for women in destitution and victims of violence have also been set up by the State from time to time. These include helplines for women in distress, awareness generation programmes, family counseling centres, short stay homes, etc. The Scheme of Short Stay Homes (SSH) for women and girls was launched in 1969 by the Department of Women and Child Development, Government of India. The scheme was later revised in the year 1999 to make it more effective and financially feasible and was handed over to Central Social Welfare Board (CSWB) for its implementation.

A brief description of the scheme is reproduced below. The scheme of SSHs has to be implemented through NGOs, which are provided grants-in-aid for the purpose. The scheme was specifically launched for the purpose of providing temporary shelter to women and girls in difficult circumstances. The women/girls in difficult circumstances under the scheme have been defined as those being forced into prostitution, as a result of family tension or being discarded, those forced to leave their homes without any means of subsistence, women who have no social protection from exploitation and are facing litigation on account of marital disputes, who have been sexually assaulted and are facing problems of re-adjustment in the family or society, victims of mental maladjustment, emotional disturbances and social ostracism, who escape from their homes due to family problems, mental/physical torture and need shelter. The inmates are either sent under court orders or themselves seek admission at the SSH.

Existing Studies on the Subject

Before going into the basic objectives and the research methodology, it would be pertinent to review some studies on the subject. SSHs are a highly neglected area of study. In the past 47 years or so since the scheme first came into existence, there have been only a handful of studies on the subject. At the same time, a number of studies have focused on government policies and programmes for women's welfare. However, these only marginally deal with the basic issue of SSHs.

The history of Shelter Homes in India was studied by the Planning Commission of India, entitled, *Social Welfare in India* (1955). The study reveals that Arya Samaj in 1875 took the initiative to help women in helpless conditions and this resulted into Rescue Homes. Bombay and Calcutta (1908) have been quoted in the work as first cities to establish such 'women homes'. The study looks upon women as victims of circumstances and the need for respectable Homes for what it calls 'social outcasts'.

Sudha Karkhanis and Rinki Bhattacharya (1998) in their study 'Women and Shelter' have emphasized the need for Shelter Homes in the context of the discriminated situation of women in Indian society. Such Shelter Homes become a priority area when both the father's and the husband's homes are closed for them. The study also stresses on the need to generate employment for destitute women.

Another aspect of proactive approach, necessitating the need for shelter was taken up by Shilpa Phadke (2005) in her article entitled 'You Can Be Lonely in a Crowd: The Production of Safety in Mumbai'. The researcher raises a question on the safety of working women and highlights their insecurity at public places. The article also focuses on the sexual control of women by the State and community. It further stresses upon the need for the State to evolve better public policies offering improved infrastructure and relief for destitute women.

Emphasizing the need for such provisions by the State, Razeena (2003) views provision for shelter as a basic necessity for destitute women. As the number of destitute women is constantly increasing, provision of Shelter Homes becomes an imperative. In a similar vein, Debjani Pal Choudhri (2007) regards Shelter Homes as a refuge for battered women, a physical space where a woman can temporarily escape from violence and find safety as well as overcome a sense of isolation.

Shelter is also identified by Neera Desai (c.f. Iyer 1999) as the primary need of a woman wanting to opt out of an oppressive situation and rebuild her life. She views right to shelter as one of the most basic human rights. It is the lack of shelter or alternative arrangements which keep women within violent or oppressive relations. Within this category, it is the economically weaker sections that are in dire need of shelter. On the same lines, a study by Shirwadkar (2009) focuses on the oppressive situation of women due to family violence. Krishna (2008) has highlighted the adverse effect of development process on women and the necessity to provide adequate safety shelter to women by the State. A similar study by Enarson, Chakrabatti and Dhar (2010) clearly explains the need of shelter for destitute women in the times of disaster.

As a part of a larger study on Destitute Women and Children in Orissa, Hagman and Karlsson (1992) have also studied three SSHs in the state of Orissa. These Homes are run under the auspices of Orissa Branch of the

Association for Social Health in India. The authors trace the causes pushing women into these Homes as desertion, marital violence, dowry, alcoholism or even marital problems due to inter-religion marriages. The major problems noticed by them include shortage of funds and separation of children from their mothers as the child is sent away to an orphanage. However, on the whole, they opine that these Homes are actually successful in empowering the women inmates.

The only holistic evaluation study of SSHs was conducted in the mid-1990s by the *Programme Evaluation Organisation* (GOI 1999), which sought to study the overall performance of the Scheme and the impact on the target group. This study found differing patterns in the various SSHs. For instance, some had a large number of accompanying children, while others did not allow any child. Moreover, some of the Homes did not follow the guidelines for admission; others had very few inmates, while still others were functioning as vocational training institutes. The inmates were devoid of various services including medical examination, vaccination and inoculation, nor were the buildings found to be satisfactory. The study also took into consideration the views of the ex-beneficiaries, all of whom found the SSHs to have an extremely significant role, but also emphasized the need to improve their functioning.

Rationale of the Study

As mentioned earlier, the Scheme of SSHs for women and girls was launched in 1969 by the Government of India to provide temporary shelter as well as empowerment to destitute women through social as well as financial support systems. Nevertheless, there were just 225 SSHs in India in the year 2012–13 (GOI 2012–13) with a population of 5,86,46,9174 women (Census of India 2011). Further, out of the total crimes committed in the year 2013, crimes against women in India was 52.24 per cent. In Punjab this percentage was lower at 38.16 of the total crimes committed in the year 2013 (NCRB 2013) with just two SSHs. It is worth noting that in Amritsar, 45.88 per cent of the total crimes targeted women while the district had only one SSH. This also depicts the growing unsafe environment for women. Besides this, it is significant to mention that no extensive study has yet been conducted on SSH in Amritsar. In this backdrop, there is a need to evaluate the Scheme of SSHs for women and girls.

Objectives of the Study

The overall objective of the study was to critically assess the effectiveness of the Scheme of SSH for destitute women in Amritsar. Other specific objectives are as follows:

- To study the reasons which make women take shelter in these homes
- To capture women's narratives on their experiences as beneficiaries
- To understand the versions of functionaries in the Short Stay Home, Amritsar.
- To suggest recommendations for policy change.

Research Methodology

This study is based upon an evaluation of SSH situated at Amritsar with respect to its effectiveness from the perspectives of beneficiaries and officials by employing a combination of qualitative and quantitative methods. Multiple methods were triangulated for procuring authentic data and capturing reality. Primary data were obtained with the help of personal interviews with the beneficiaries, functionaries and NGOs, apart from observation. At the time of study, there were 11 inmates in the Home. In-depth interviews of five inmates were taken. Other than these, six functionaries were also interviewed. Secondary data included books, articles, journals, etc. The data collected from primary and secondary sources were analysed to arrive at inferences.

Short Stay Home at Amritsar

The Short Stay Home at Amritsar is managed by the All India Women's Conference (AIWC). AIWC was formed in 1927 with an objective of upliftment and well-being of women and children. The SSH in Amritsar was established on 21 September 1984. Located on a busy road, a gatekeeper is deputed to guard the compound. The premises of the Home were all of concrete with no provision of garden or lawn. The office was operated from the same building. Staircase from the ground floor takes one to the inmates' rooms which are located on the first floor. There were four rooms for the inmates with six beds in each room. The inmates shared common bathrooms which were clean. The kitchen-cum-dining room was neat and clean and well organized. Though there was provision of a cook at the Home, inmates too cooked food sometimes. It also had the provision of a television. There was no provision of any indoor or outdoor games or activities for the inmates. It is important because such facilities/activities have been mandated in the Scheme. The Home also did not have any facility to arrange outings for the inmates. However, it had provision of a dispensary inside the campus. There was no provision of superintendent's residence within the campus. The Home had an efficient counsellor. It also had provision to teach vocational courses such as beauty care and computer literacy for the inmates. During the study, it was revealed that one young inmate at the Home was working as a domestic help at the residence of one of the members of the executive committee of the NGO managing the Home. Besides this, though the Home was protected by high walls, safety and security of the inmates was questionable as one male peon and a driver had been staying within the campus.

Analysis

The socio-economic profile of the respondents shows that 11 inmates were residing at this Home during the time of survey. Two inmates were below 18 years of age, seven of them were between 18–25 years of age, one inmate was between 26–40 years and one was above 60 years of age. Looking at the age pattern, it can be argued that destitution has no age and woman of any age can be a destitute. One of the inmates lodged at the SSH in Amritsar was above 60 years of age.

Out of 11 inmates, three were Hindus and the remaining eight belonged to Sikh religion. Eight inmates belonged to General Category, two came from SC families and one inmate was an OBC. Further, seven inmates came from urban areas while four belonged to rural areas. It shows that more women from urban areas took shelter at Home as a result of destitution.

Marital status of the inmates shows that women are prone to incidences of violence at all the stages. Eight out of 11 inmates were never married, one was deserted and two of them were widows. The findings reveal that single women are more vulnerable and insecure, facing different kinds of atrocities both within and outside home. The widowed women inmates had not been accepted by their in-laws and lacking any other support, they had landed up at the Short Stay Home. They were not able to return back to their maternal home for want of any support. During interaction seven of the inmates revealed that they came from nuclear families, three lived in joint families while one lived in extended family structure. None of the married women had their children living with them at the Home.

So far as the educational status of these inmates is concerned, eight of them had not even completed matriculation, and one each had completed matriculation, senior secondary level of school and graduation. By and large therefore these women inmates were found to be without proper education or the skills to support themselves. Further, the data indicated that these destitute women belonged to lower middle socio-economic strata, with a family income below 20,000 per month. They did not hold any vocational degrees or skills making it very difficult to survive on their own.

That these women had been forced to leave their homes, considered to be the most secure space, for the following reasons: The first major reason was extreme poverty. Two inmates had left their homes due to extreme poverty/economic reasons, while their families had never tried to stop them or later take them back. Seven of the inmates had faced domestic violence and two of them were deserted by their families. The most common cause of domestic violence was the extra marital affair of the husband coupled with alcoholism and drug addiction of the husband. These inmates failed to garner any support from their families and hence had sought shelter at the Home. Nobody had ever tried to take them back and this greatly hurt them emotionally.

Facilities provided to the inmates were also examined in the backdrop of the provisions mandated in the Short Stay Home Scheme. Only three inmates were aware about this Scheme, while eight of them were totally unaware. Among those who were aware, two had learnt about it from their friends while one inmate had come to know about the SSH through an NGO. The Scheme in its mandate states that a woman shall not be allowed to stay for more than three years at the SSH. This time frame is based upon the presumption that this time span is sufficient for them to get out of trauma, be counseled and simultaneously learn a vocational skill which shall secure and empower them to earn a respectable livelihood and live an independent life. The SSH at Amritsar was found adhering to the norms given in the mandate as none of the inmates lived for more than the stipulated time. Further, providing minimum basic facilities to the inmates is ensured in the mandate of the Scheme. One inmate revealed that the Home provided them with facilities like television and education while ten inmates also mentioned provision of clothes in addition to education and television.

The women inmates were not found to be satisfied with the food served at the Home. Ten inmates complained that special food was served only to the sick inmates while one of them contradicted by saying that there was no such provision. Besides this, some inmates also assisted in the kitchen in various activities like cooking, washing utensils, cleaning, etc. When asked if they wanted to give any suggestion, they responded by suggesting that there must be inclusion of fruits and milk in daily diet and emphasized that the quality and variety of food should be improved.

The Scheme also mandates medical facilities for the inmates. When asked whether doctors visited SSH for medical check-up of the inmates, all of them said 'yes'. Reporting further, some argued that women and girls suffered from various infections and problems relating to menstrual cycle which many times resulted into excessive bleeding. They complained that they remained unattended during that period and resultantly became weak as they did not receive any necessary supplements like iron or calcium tablets and antibiotics on time. One of them told that in absence of medical advice, inmates had to remain dependent on the SSH staff and take medicines without any medical prescription, especially for infections like common cold, fever, body pain, etc. However, all the inmates informed that the SSH provided medicines to them. However, they also told that no gynaecologist had ever visited the Home. They also said that the Home had a separate room for medical checkup for the inmates. The inmates also reported that in case a male doctor visited the Home for medical checkup, a woman attendant – either an inmate or a counselor, was always present with the sick inmate. However, during interaction, it was found that none of the inmates was aware of the health facilities mandated in the Scheme. Only two inmates knew that serious cases were supposed to be referred to specialist doctors.

Mandate of the Scheme states that: Home should have properly ventilated rooms with provision of clean toilets and washrooms. Along with the availability of such sanitation facilities, toiletries being provided to the inmates is also equally pertinent. Regular supply and availability of toiletries is a significant factor in promoting health and sanitation conditions. When asked about the source of toiletries, all the inmates told that SSH issued them toiletries on monthly basis. Similarly, ten inmates informed that they received clothes through donations while one inmate told that she always got her clothes from her home. None of the inmates was found to be aware about the provision of sanitation facilities available to them under the Scheme. None of them was able to suggest any measures to improve the condition of sanitation at the Home.

As per the mandate, after granting admission at the Home, when the interview and diagnosis are completed, women are to be given counselling services, according to individual requirements. Interestingly, while all the inmates said that counselling services were available at the Home, yet none of them had admitted having ever undergone a counselling session. All of them opined that it was useful. They further told that there was provision of a separate room for counselling. None of them, however, was aware about the mandatory provision of counselling facility under SSH Scheme.

The mandate states that vocational skills and training shall also be provided to every inmate according to her requirements. Although all the inmates said that there was provision for vocational training at the Home, yet only eight inmates were learning vocational skills. Three of them were not learning any of the skills being taught at the Home though all of them felt that vocational skills were very useful. None of them had any knowledge regarding the mandatory provision of vocational training for inmates in the Scheme. When asked about suggestions to improve the vocational skills at Home, three inmates suggested that the Home should outsource more work so that the inmates can earn more. One of them said that the SSH should leave old technology and must train inmates is contemporary technology.

The Scheme also states that inmates should be involved in recreational activities. There should be facilities for organized recreation and group activities. Indoor and outdoor games should be provided. Girls should be taken out for cultural shows, outings, movies, exhibitions, etc. at least once a month. Besides this, festival pertaining to all religions should be celebrated besides Republic Day, Independence Day and the birthdays of the inmates. When asked about means of recreation available for the inmates, they admitted having a television at the Home. They also informed that all important festivals were celebrated with full fervour. Some of the inmates suggested that the Home should have a CD/DVD player at Home.

The Scheme mandates that the inmates must be facilitated for outings at least once in a month. It also states that the women and girls whose parents or close relatives are alive should be granted a 15-day leave once in a year, in case they so desire. During interaction, all of them reported that there was no provision of local or outstation outings at Home and the functionaries had never taken them out. One of the inmates expressed that the staff was scared of losing an inmate during the outing, which could put their job in jeopardy. When asked about their opinion about outings, seven inmates told that there should be a provision of outings but the young girls should be accompanied by Home officials during the visits and must not be sent alone. Besides this, the residents should be allowed to meet visitors, i.e. parents/guardians/close relatives. They also suggested that the list of the visitors should be scrutinized by the Superintendent/Case Worker. Visitors should be allowed only on Sundays from 4 p.m. to 6 p.m. All inmates except one said that their family members/relatives visited them. In case of one inmate, nobody had ever come to visit her at Home.

When asked about availability of the Superintendent, all the inmates told that the Superintendent was never available at the time of need. They further told that they never shared their complaints with the Superintendent. None of them was satisfied with the working of the Superintendent. Inmates complained that there was no provision of a Case Worker at Home. However, none of them was facing a court trial. Similarly, feedback of NGO Member is crucial for smooth functioning of the SSH. Seven inmates informed that the NGO members do visit the Home while four rejected the claim.

Overall, it was noticed that none of the inmates was aware about the provisions mentioned in the mandate regarding various facilities. A large number of them did not give any suggestion as they believed that nothing was going to change at the SSH. It was, however, observed that the inmates were not much satisfied with the quality and variety of food, health facilities and sanitary conditions available at the Home. Changes in the vocational courses were also suggested by many. It was observed that a lot still needs to be done to improve the living conditions and functioning of the SSH at Amritsar. Finally, there was hardly any coordination between the inmates on the one hand and the officials on the other. Most of the guidelines of the Scheme were not being followed, thus highlighting the lacunas in the implementation of the Short Stay Home Scheme. Linking the available provisions at the Home with the suggested mandate of the Scheme the situation was further critically analysed. This helped to identify the existing gaps in the 'provisions available' and 'actual availability' under various categories.

The Scheme was critically analysed in relation to the mandate, particularly the mandate regarding the maximum period of stay of any inmate in a Home, not to exceed three years. Although the SSH at Amritsar was found to be following the criteria, it had no provision for job placement. The mandate states that counselling shall not be limited only for those who are undergoing trials, rather it should be made a daily practice and inmates must be counselling. The Amritsar Home had provision of a counsellor. Regarding approaching the Home, the mandate states that the women who are in moral danger, may come on their own or referred by other people or authorities. The above mentioned norm was adhered to by the SSH at Amritsar as inmates either came on their own or were referred by other people or authorities. The mandate strictly prescribes maintenance of case history/register with a documentation of each case. These records are important for the counsellor and other authorities at the time of need. However, Amritsar Home did not maintain complete case history of the inmates. There was no registration of some of the inmates in the register and the registers were not maintained properly. According to the mandate, there should be a mandatory medical check-up of every new inmate at the time of her admission. It is important especially for those who have been victims of violence or those suffering from serious or chronic illness. It was observed that this was partly adhered to by the Home. The mandate mentions that the Home should take custody of belongings/valuables owned by the inmates and issue a receipt in return bearing proper signatures and date. The above mentioned provision was not being implemented. Regarding number of inmates to be accommodated the mandate states that the Home should have an average of 30 residents at a time with facilities for a minimum of 20 and a maximum of 40 residents. The Short Stay Home at Amritsar was found to be ill equipped to accommodate even a minimum of 20 inmates.

It is further stated in the mandate that women facing court proceedings are to be provided help and there must be a provision of Case Worker in all the

Homes. However, it was noticed that there was no provision of a Case Worker in the Short Stay Home at Amritsar. The mandate also states that for proper functioning of Home, staffing pattern has to be strictly followed. However, Amritsar Home was not fulfilling the staff pattern. It did not have a Case Worker. Mandate for the Short Stay Homes states that an Advisory Committee is to be constituted for giving directions to the staff for day-to-day management of the Home. In accordance to the mandate, an advisory committee was constituted at Amritsar Home. The mandate states that a protected, caring and compassionate environment is to be provided to the inmates for helping them rebuild their devastated life. The desired environment suitable for the inmates was maintained by the Short Stay Home at Amritsar. However, there was a lack of coordination between the inmates and the Superintendent. According to the mandate, nutritious food, rest and congenial company should be provided to the inmates so that they can forget their past and start life afresh. However, Amritsar Home did not fulfil the desired criteria. Necessary supplements and nutrients were not being supplied to the inmates. There was also no diet plan or diet scale at Amritsar Home. This situation is really alarming as health and nutritional concerns should be taken care of by the Home on priority basis. The Home provided free medical facility to the inmates for their physical and mental health. According to the mandate the inmates should be provided with vocational training enabling them to earn their living. The SSH at Amritsar had provision of vocational skills for the inmates but not all of them were pursuing these.

It is mentioned in the mandate that each inmate must have a bank or post office account where she can deposit her earnings. However, no inmate had a bank account at Amritsar Home. The mandate makes sure that office of the Superintendent and her residence is to be located in the same building/premises. It was observed that offices of the Superintendent and the staff were located in the same building but the Superintendent was not residential. It is mentioned in the mandate that an open space for movement or exercise and facilities for indoor and outdoor games or gardening are to be provided to the inmates. During the fieldwork, it was found that the Short Stay Home at Amritsar was partially adhering to the stipulated norms. It is mandated that the organizations running these Homes should expand networking with various departments and avail common public services for the benefit of inmates. The above suggested mandate was not fulfilled. A strong networking means more ways to seek justice and develop a chain of service providers. Therefore, most of the provisions as mandated in the Scheme were lacking at this Home.

Conclusion and Recommendations

The above study reveals that the Home had most of the facilities for inmates but did not have the provision of Case Worker nor was the building found to be satisfactory. Although it provides vocational skills to its inmates, yet these were found not of much benefit to them mainly because of the redundant skills being imparted, without any market value. Vocational skills should be according to the contemporary demand of networking with employment agencies. The Home should also employ a Case Worker. The Board should ensure that every inmate has a bank/post office account in order to enable them to have some funds of their own when they are discharged from the Home. The Board should also ensure timely disbursement of funds to the Homes in order to help them, ultimately helping in meeting the required objectives of the Home. Without funds the whole objective of providing a meaningful shelter remains illogical. The Home should promote the concept of community marriage or mass weddings. This will help the helpless women and girls settling down in their life. The Short Stay Home should come forward to ask for help and should liaison with existing community resources like training centres, public resources, employment exchanges, recreation clubs, civil hospitals, dispensaries, free legal aid cells, etc. to ensure maximum utilization of public resources rather than depending on grant-in-aid from the government every time. Outings should be promoted as it freshens up the mind. The Home should avoid keeping the staff on ad hoc basis and gender sensitive staff should be employed. The Home should pay special attention on the health of the inmates. There is a need to improve the quality as well as quantity of food, nutrients, vitamins, etc. The Central Social Welfare Board should also prepare a consolidated data of inmates who are staying and had stayed in the Short Stay Home at an all India level to further enhance research and advocacy on the same. It was observed that the Short Stay Home at Amritsar was partially adhering to the mandate of the Scheme. This state of Home has to improve so that it doesn't defeat the purpose of its existence. Rehabilitation of the inmates was found to remain the weakest point of the Scheme. Actually, these Homes are supposed to be only transitory accommodation for destitute women and their main purpose is to support them in difficult time, and train them and rehabilitate them in life. However, most of the inmates were without any bank accounts or savings of their own, signifying their dependent status. Further, they had little support coming from their families, who had almost discarded them due to social stigma carried by them. Therefore, communities also need to be sensitized in an effort to erase this stigma from society, which makes life hell for these destitute women and does not allow them to resume normal life.

References

Bande, Usha and Kaushal, Anshu (eds) 2011. *Violence in Media and Society*. Jaipur: Rawat Publications.

Census of India. 2011. Government of India, New Delhi: New Delhi: Office of the Registrar General of India.

Central Social Welfare Board. *Annual Report 2012–13*. Department of Women and Child Development, Ministry of Human Resource Development, Government of India, New Delhi

Chawla, Romila. 2012. *Reader on Women Trafficking*. Life Span Publications and Distribution. New Delhi.

Choudhri, Debjani Pal. 2007. *Community Planning for Intervention for Victims of Domestic Violence: Adaptation of the Model from Kassel, Germany for Disadvantaged Urban Neighbourhoods in Pune City, India*. Kassel: Kassel University Press.

Desai, Neera quoted in Iyer, Saroj. 1999. *The Struggle to be Human: Women's Human Rights*. Bangalore: Books for Change.

Dobash, R.E. and Dobash, R. 1979. *Violence Against Wives: A Case Against Patriarchy*. New York: Free Press,

Enarson, Elaine and Chakrabarti, P.G. Dhar. 2010. *Women, Gender and Disaster: Global Issues and Initiatives*. New Delhi: Sage Publications.

Ghadially, R. 2007. *Urban Women in Contemporary India*. New Delhi: Sage Publications.

Government of India. 1969. *Scheme of Short Stay Homes for Women and Girls*. Central Social Welfare Board, Ministry of Women and Child Development, New Delhi.

——. 1999. *PEO Evaluation Study of Short Stay Homes for Women and Girls*. Planning Commission of India, New Delhi.

Hagman, K. and Karlsson, N. 1992. *A Study on Indian Destitutes: Aspects of the Lives of Destitute Children and Women in Orissa, India*. Malmo, Sweden: School of Education, No. 759.

Karkhanis, Sudha and Bhattacharya, Rinki. 1998. 'Women and Shelter', in Shirin Kudchedkar and Sabiha Al-Issa (eds), *Violence Against Women: Women Against Violence*. Delhi: Pencraft International.

Krishna, Sumi. 2008. *Women's Livelihood Rights: Recasting Citizenship for Development*. New Delhi: Sage Publications.

National Crime Records Bureau (NCRB). 2013. *Crime in India*. Ministry of Home Affairs, Government of India, New Delhi.

Padmam, M.S. Razeena. 2003. *Destitute Women in Kerala: Psychological Resources and Psycho-Social Needs*. Discussion Paper No. 51, Kerala Research Programme on Local Level Development, Centre for Development Studies, Thiruvananthapuram.

Phadke, Shilpa. 2005. 'You Can Be Lonely in a Crowd: The Production of Safety in Mumbai'. *Indian Journal of Gender Studies*, 12(1), 41–62.

Planning Commission of India. 1955. *Social Welfare in India*. Publications Division, Ministry of Information and Broadcasting, Government of India, New Delhi.

Shirwadkar, Swati. 2009. *Family Violence in India: Human Rights, Issues, Actions and International Comparisons*. Jaipur: Rawat Publications.

Tapan, Neeta. 2000. *Need for Women Empowerment*. Jaipur: Rawat Publications.

Section IV

Conclusions and Inferences

21

Gender Question in Punjab and Haryana

Cultural Fixation

Rajesh Gill

The process of development across the countries has been accompanied by a spurt in violence against women of all strata; as a result of which strong State interventions have been made in all realms – Constitutional, legal, political, economic, educational and social, in order to fulfil the global agenda of gender equality and gender justice. This has become mandatory for the States all over the globe, in view of great pressure of international organizations, particularly the United Nations, especially its Women's Forums that have mustered sufficient data to place different countries all over the globe on Gender Development Index and the like. At least three of the Millennium Development Goals formulated in 2000 at the UN Millennium Summit relate to gender equality and these were targeted to be achieved by 2015. No State today can afford to remain a silent spectator to the issue of gender discrimination and violence. In this context, Indian State too has taken various measures towards gender equality. Persistence of patriarchy manifested through the continued violation of women's human rights notwithstanding, the State interventions along with the emergence of women's movement at the grassroots have placed the contemporary Indian woman in an extremely advantageous position as compared to her mother and grandmother, irrespective of religion, caste and region. While the Constitution of India, much prior to the so-called developed countries, formally granted her equal rights with men in arenas of employment, education, freedom of speech, personal liberty and so on, later Constitutional Amendments have further promoted her rights and representation to various governing bodies. While issues of imperfect and half hearted implementation, along with politicization of gender issues in a populist democracy have frequently been highlighted in academic and political discourses, the fact remains that women in this country have already made their visibility felt in local, regional and national political bodies, sports, bureaucracy, academics, art and literature, science and technology, defense services, corporate sector and so on.

The gender question in the states of Punjab and Haryana deserves special attention in view of the fact that these states have presented to the nation a model wherein economic and agricultural development has carried along the age-old patriarchal culture and practices keeping the conventional gender equations intact, of course with some changes here and there, indicating a greater visibility of women in public life. While huge gaps continue to exist between cities and villages, even the metropolitan cities constitute spaces which are highly gendered, with 'safe' and 'unsafe' spaces marked for women. While the economic growth model has collapsed given its failure to percolate to grassroots as also to translate the economic development to gender development and empowerment, the State interventions too have not been able to make a dent in the strong cultural ethos characterized by the supremacy of masculinity; gendered division of labour at home and outside; violation of women as a norm; a highly gendered language to the extent of dehumanizing women, used both within homes and in public; and treating women as carriers of family/caste/community 'honour' which is extremely fragile, to be protected by men.

This volume has brought out the cultural fixation in the states of Punjab and Haryana in the context of gender, especially the experience of being a woman. Of course there have been enormous changes in that female literacy rates have gone up; more women have joined the workforce; more girls are going in for professional and higher education; women have a greater political participation at the grassroots level; women have become more mobile and independent, and so on. However, all this has made women more vulnerable too and they are facing greater violence of all kinds being exposed to public spaces, not always out of volition. National Crime Record Bureau Reports indicate a rise in reported crimes against women; a fact which can be interpreted in terms of greater awareness resulting in greater reporting, but it is also a fact that still a large number of cases go unreported. In order to make sense out of this volume, the following inferences can be drawn.

First, gender in the context of Punjab and Haryana can only be understood in the context of caste and religion. This is especially true for rural population which continues to be governed by communitarian norms, even if in contravention to the Constitutional provisions. Women continue to be the custodians of honour – of the caste, religion and the community; and they dare not risk this honour. Not only men but women are even more aggressive in following the traditional norms which are severely tilted against women. Most of the folk songs projecting women as appendages of their men are sung by women themselves on different occasions. Similarly, it is women who are the first to celebrate the birth of a son, treating it as a status enhancement. It is again the women who join men in eliminating young girls in case they challenge the communitarian norms. The resilience of caste in recent times reinforcing gender discrimination is very aptly brought out by Justice Kannan in his paper. Citing casteism as the culprit, he has shown how a series of legislations providing for gender equality and freedom of choice have been rendered ineffective. Constitutional rights to Indian citizens providing for marriage across caste or religion have little meaning amidst the persisting and reinforced boundaries between castes and religions. Laws have little meaning also in view of the rigid mindsets of the judges who are supposed to translate these laws while adjudicating. While the Indian Constitution symbolizes the values of secularism, democracy, equality, liberty and freedom, these have no meaning in real life situations in the society drenched in the idioms of caste, religion and gender. Hence it is futile to understand gender out of the context of caste and religion.

Such is the complexity of social transformation that on the one hand, women among the upper echelons of society have moved up in educational ladder, having gained a niche in the professional field. But on the other hand, it is the women among the upper castes, mainly in rural pockets, who face the severest restrictions on movement, marital choices and reproductive rights. The caste/*khap* panchayats, running parallel to constitutionally elected village panchayats regulate the sexuality and freedom of choice of young girls with a very strong collective conscience (to use Durkheimian term), rendering individual conscience meaningless.

Secondly, neither economic development nor education has been able to break the patriarchal structures, mainly responsible for subjugating women in private and public spheres. Communities continue to be governed by personal and customary laws, in complete violation of Constitutional provisions. Legal prohibition of dowry notwithstanding, the magnitude and form of dowry have expanded manifold, having percolated to the bottom of the society. Daughters, as a consequence of this, are now a greater liability than ever before, thanks to the commercialization of the rituals of marriage across religions. Situation in rural areas is pathetic for young girls who find it extremely difficult to pursue their school education in absence of even the most basic amenities like clean toilets and water in schools. Under the circumstances, menstruation becomes a handicap for them, eventually leading to their dropping out of the school. The State objective of female education cannot be realized unless these basic requirements are met so that attending school turns out to be a comfortable and emancipating experience for young adolescent girls. Cultural taboos and superstitions tend to overshadow the scientific knowledge supposed to be imparted in schools to these children, courtesy the cultural fixation not only among the parents, but the teachers too, who reinforce the conventional beliefs and convictions.

Thirdly, while women are more visible today, particularly in public life, in various occupations and educational institutions, yet the fact remains that they are persistently being targeted in cases of sexual violence of various kinds both in rural and urban areas in the states of Punjab and Haryana. Despite the Law providing protection to women against sexual harassment at workplace, women continue to face violence of all sorts amidst an utter insensitivity as a result of the persistent notion of aggressive masculinity. Using abusive language against women continues to be a symbol of masculinity; passing lewd comments to young girls also implies masculinity; and such kinds of behaviour and acts are legitimized not only by men but more by women as an integral part of culture and heritage. The PCPNDT Act has not been very successful too, courtesy the strong desire to have son/s and an easy access to technology for sex determination tests, even at doorsteps. Nexuses have developed among doctors, radiologists and health workers, who are on constant look-out for customers. Interested parties have started moving across borders to soft areas, for getting these tests done. Law alone is just not sufficient to change attitudes, especially when these are drawn from age-old belief systems.

Similar is the case with The Sexual Harassment of Women at Workplace (Prevention, Prohibition and Redressal) Act, 2013. Though after the Delhi Rape case, there has been a constant pressure to put in place the redressal systems to counter sexual harassment of women at workplace, yet the fact remains that women have failed to develop confidence in these systems, resulting into great reluctance in filing formal complaints and pursuing these. Once a woman files such a complaint, which normally is against her male superior, she has to undergo tremendous harassment as if she is the accused. The Complaints Committees are rarely gender sensitive and there is no attempt to ensure that these are so. Lawyers and even judiciary are yet to develop a gender sensitive approach to such cases and understand the law in its true spirit, which is quasi-judicial in nature. Once a complaint is registered, every effort is made to suppress it, get it withdrawn by none other than the Committee members. Hence, the implementation of law is extremely ineffective, again due to the absence of a conducive mind set among the implementers.

Fourthly, the cultural fixation reflected through folklore, literature and common parlance, has refused to die. The mechanisms forming masculinity and femininity continue to persist within homes and outside. The journey from *quissa-kavya*, viz. Heer-Ranjha, Sassi-Punnu and Sohni-Mahiwal till date, has kept the masculine and feminine identities intact, the changing gender roles notwithstanding. While a man is free to satisfy his sexual urges outside marriage, with multiple partners, with little regard to any norms, a woman just cannot afford to cross the boundaries of caste, religion or community. The whole onus of honour lies on her, which she has to save with her blood and life. It is the woman who has to bear the moral policing, complying with the strict restrictions on dress, language, movement and behaviour.

Finally, the discussions in this volume reveal the fact that the process of democratization of political system and modernization in terms of higher use of technology has itself been mediated through the idioms of caste, religion and gender, often leading to a shameless abuse of values of gender equality, legal rights, etc. especially at the grassroots and in the agrarian context. The *khap* panchayats for that matter in theory have now granted space to women, youth and lower castes, but continue to remain masculine spaces dominated by upper castes. Whether it is a question of wives abandoned by NRI husbands or purchased brides or young girls, the centres of power continue to evade them, keeping them at margins even if they occupy the membership of panchayats (ceremoniously). *Lok biradari* and collective conscience continue to exercise greater control than constitutional provisions of democracy, secularism and equality.

To sum up, structured and institutionalized norms at grassroots have yet not been touched by the more secular and democratic principles especially in context of gender. It is very apt here to conceptualize gender as proposed by Connell as *'Gender if the structure of social relations that centres on the reproductive arena, and the set of practices that bring reproductive distinctions between bodies into social processes'* (2004: 10). Women continue to be on the margins so far as control over resources is concerned. Women do two-third of the world's work for one-tenth of the world's income and own less than one per cent of the world's property and women make up two-third of the world's illiterate. Variations within the feminist theories notwithstanding, it is well established today that gender is a matter of social and political regulations rather than a law of nature.

We would rather go with the anti-essentialist critique of the feminist theories, proposing that within the structured institutions and norms, women's real life experiences involving multiple identities and 'agency' make the whole process of 'gendering' very complex, making it almost impossible to arrive at any generalizations. For instance, women in cities are more mobile, have better access to resources but continue to suffer varying degrees of vulnerability depending upon their economic, educational, occupational and family status. Gill in her paper speaks about the 'gendered spaces' within a city, which makes women continuously negotiate with their movement between 'safe' and 'unsafe' spaces. Similarly, in Sidhu's paper, women's vulnerability has increased with a sudden windfall caused by huge compensation received by their men in turn of land acquisition, resulting into alcoholism and drug addiction. The NCRB data point at a higher incidence of violence against women but is it a positive or a negative indicator of gender equality?

I find it appropriate to summarize this volume with the conceptualization offered by Walby in which she defines patriarchy as 'a system of social structures and practices in which men dominate, oppress and exploit women' (Walby 1990: 20). According to her, the patriarchal system of social relations comprises of six structures as under:

(a) Patriarchal mode of production, household, wherein 'housewives are the producing class, while husbands are the expropriating class (Walby 1990: 21).
(b) Patriarchal relations within paid work, i.e. segregating women in low paid work.
(c) State's systematic bias, i.e. policies benefiting men and condoning violence against women.
(d) Violence against women, i.e. rape, domestic violence, sexual harassment arousing FEAR.
(e) Patriarchal relations in sexuality, i.e. compulsory heterosexuality.
(f) Patriarchal relations in cultural institutions, i.e. religion, education and media, portraying women within a patriarchal gaze.

Walby, thus, argues that patriarchy has moved from private structures to the public ones, and there is no woman who can escape these constraints. However, every woman keeps on negotiating the patriarchal constraints with the help of her 'agency' in her everyday life. Such a negotiation using her agency within the structures of patriarchy are brought out by Rakesh Thakur and Kanwalpreet Kaur in their articles in this volume and it makes sense. Even the 'Heer', 'Sassi' and 'Sohni' as narrated by Madhurima struggle in the patriarchal norms with their agency; and similarly, the women in agrarian Punjab, undergoing a transformation in their reproductive behaviour, as brought out by Kumool Abbi, keep compromising within the patriarchal structures.

The gender canvas, therefore, especially in the context of Punjab and Haryana has to be understood within the context of a heterogeneously situated women in terms of age, caste, religion, etc. through the processes of negotiations and compromises made by them using their agency, and thus constructing multiple realities instead of a single one.

References

Archer, Margaret. 1982. 'Morphostasis versus Structuration: On Combining Structure and Action'. *British Journal of Sociology*, 33.

——. 1996. *Culture and Agency: The Place of Culture in Social Theory* (revised edition). Cambridge: Cambridge University Press.

Butler, Judith. 1990. *Gender Trouble*. London: Routledge.

Connell, R.W. 2004. *Gender*. Cambridge: Polity Press.

Jones, Pip, Bradbury, Liz and LeBoutillier, Shaun. 2011. *Introducing Social Theory*. Cambridge: Polity Press.

Walby, Sylvia. 1990. *Theorizing Patriarchy*. Oxford: Blackwell.

Index